QUALITY AND EDUCATION IN THE 21ST CENTURY

QUALITY AND EDUCATION IN THE 21ST CENTURY

BY

D. H. STAMATIS, Ph.D., CQE, CMfgE, MSSBB

Professor at Anhui University of Finance and Economics, Bengbu, China
President of Contemporary Consultants Co., Southgate, MI, USA

www.bookstandpublishing.com

Published by
Bookstand Publishing
Morgan Hill, CA 95037
3396_3

ISBN 978-1-58909-985-2

IABLS, Inc.
14890 Southview Dr.
Southgate, MI 48195
Tel: 734-281-9182
Fax: 734-281-4023
E-mail: ccc@iabls.com

TABLE OF CONTENTS

FIGURES

TABLES

ACKNOWLEDGEMENTS

To write a book is a cumulative effort of many years and a collaboration of many colleagues, and friends. This book is no exception. I have thought about it for a very long time and at the insistence of many friends, I decided to tackle the issue of education. Of course, everything in this book is my responsibility. After reviewing the academic, the general literature on education and training, as well as evaluating my own experiences in teaching at a university level and being involved with adult training for the last 30 years, I came to a conclusion that if I were to write a book on education, I must include all tiers of education. That is K-12, and post secondary institution.

The goal was herculean but with the help and encouragement of many, I believe I have, at least, scratched the surface of some of the issues of education and its improvement. I hope that the discussion will continue by others in the name of *continual improvement*. I cannot acknowledge everyone who has helped due to space limitations. However, I thank all of them. Several individuals stand out and have to be recognized for their unique contributions.

First and foremost on the list is Dr. D. Witthey, a retired superintendent of Southgate School District. His countless hours of coaching and recommendations about issues and concerns of K-12, I believe have made this book more interesting.

Mr. C. Candella, a retired Principal of the Southgate School District provided a tremendous input on the involvement of parents and the discussion of student discipline.

Mr. G. Pallicaris, a faculty at Lawrence University and Macomb Community College who provided me the opportunity to discuss issues of administrations and reform measures.

Dr. C. Brown, Prof. of Educational Leadership at Wayne State University, who kept challenging me on issues of responsibilities and reform.

Dr. R. Richey, Prof. of Instructional Technology at Wayne State University, who taught me not only what it means to be excellent in teaching but also how to involve the learners in the process of learning.

Dr. J. Childs, Prof. of Instructional Technology at Wayne State University, who spent many hours with me discussing issues and concerns about improving education and introducing reforms in our institutions.

Dr. C. Marcotte, Prof. of Education Evaluation and Research at Wayne State University, who was willing to spend time with me discussing issues of reform and evaluating educational outcomes.

Dr. R. Kapur, President of Six Sigma Solutions, who discussed with me the many options of including a variety of tools for the monitoring and improvement of any educational institution.

Ms. N. Simons, President of Simons-White, for discussing the issues of education and providing many suggestions for improving the flow of the book.

The editors of the book who through their excellent suggestions have made this into a final product.

Finally, a big thank you goes as usual to my chief critic, editor, partner in life, for her unwavering belief in me to finish this project. She was my supporter, motivator and always there when I needed her the most. She is of course my wife – Carla. Thank you so much.

DEDICATION

To the newest addition of the Stamatis family
Dean

PREFACE

Quality education is holistic and prerequisite for education for sustainable development (ESD) for our times as well as the future. It upholds and conveys the ideals of a sustainable world. It takes into consideration the social, economic and environmental context. Quality education is locally relevant and culturally appropriate. It is informed by the past and relevant to the present, and prepares individuals for the future. In other words, the education of the future at all levels must not focus purely on the theoretical, but rather blend several theories and practice to respond to the real needs of real people. The question asked in evaluating every possible change is simple: Is it in the best interest of the students?

To be sure, education teaches people to be better individuals, family members, community members and citizens. However, in order for that success to occur, education must offer a balance of relevancy and results. That is where Education for Sustainable Development comes into play with its four major thrusts:

1. *Promote and improve basic education*: Basic education is an issue for developing and developed countries alike. While access to education is more often an issue for the former, the latter are challenged with retention problems. Basic literacy, although an important first step, is only a partial answer to these issues. Education should teach skills, values, and perspectives that can foster grass-roots community participation and decision-making. Basic education empowers and engages communities with skills such as critical thinking, the ability to question arguments, or to break with the status quo. However for all these to occur, educators at all levels must possess the appropriate knowledge, skills, disposition and be committed to a life learning mode. This is shown in Figure P.1

Figure P.1. Key ingredients to improve education

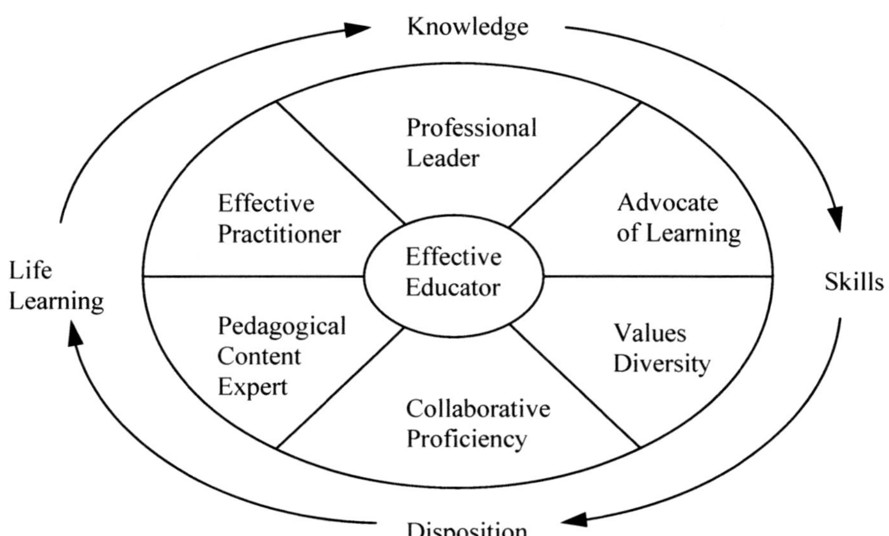

2. *Reorient existing education programs at all levels to address sustainable development*: Questioning, rethinking, and revising education from pre-school through university to include more principles, knowledge, skills, perspectives and values related to sustainability is important to our current and future societies. Reorienting the programs should be undertaken in a holistic and interdisciplinary context, and focus on engaging society at large, while the implementation of programs themselves should remain under the scope of individual regions. This implies a review of existing curricula in terms of their objectives and content to develop trans-disciplinary understandings of the social, cultural, economic and environmental dimensions of sustainability. It also implies that efficiency, accountability and improvement of the process should be reevaluated, adjusted when and if

necessary and improved. Obviously, this implies recognition of diversity in both students and school systems. As such, appropriate and applicable measures should be taken to take advantage of that diversity.

3. *Develop public awareness and understanding of sustainability*: Education for Sustainable Development goes beyond schools and addresses the general public. Progress towards sustainability requires that the growing global awareness of social, economic, cultural and environmental issues is transformed into understanding of root causes and that local, national and global visions of what it means to live and work sustainably are developed.

4. A knowledgeable and involved citizenry can help communities and governments enact sustainability measures and move towards more sustainable societies. A more sustainable society requires widespread community education and a responsible media committed to encouraging an informed and active citizenry.

5. *Provide training*: K-12, community colleges, universities and higher education institutions are encouraged to include sustainable development topics in all university and research programs. Business and industry are key sites for on-going vocational and professional training and can ensure a more sustainable, environmentally friendly work environment.

6. Modern education attitude demands from everyone – including business, industry, higher education, governments, non-governmental organizations – to train their leaders and employees in sustainability issues. That is: methods that improve learning, cost of learning, quality of learning, efficiency of learning, and improvements of the management of learning.

For education to be effective, learning must take place. Learning is a process of synthesizing different types of knowledge, behaviors, skills, values, preferences, understanding and information for either a personal or societal improvement. The ability to learn is inherent in both humans and animals and as of late with artificial intelligence in some machines.

Learning in humans may occur in a variety of ways as part of formal or informal education or personal development over the course of a lifetime. It is indeed, a never ending process. Of course, this may be goal oriented and in fact it may be accelerated by some form of motivation. Scientifically, how learning occurs is part of neuropsychology, educational psychology, learning theory, pedagogy and andragogy. It may also occur consciously or without conscious awareness.

The process of learning has been studied for a very long time. However, it was Benjamin Bloom (1956) who first defined three domains of learning. They are:

1. *Cognitive*: such as learning to recall facts, to analyze, and to solve a problem.
2. *Psychomotor*: such as learning to perform the correct steps in a dance, learning to swim, learning to ride a bicycle, or drive a car; and
3. *Affective*: such as learning how to like someone, "to hate sin," to love one's country (patriotism), to worship God, or to move on after a failed relationship.

These domains are not mutually exclusive. In each of the three domains Bloom's Taxonomy is based on the premise that the categories are ordered in degree of difficulty. An important premise of Bloom's Taxonomy is that each category (or 'level') must be mastered before progressing to the next. As such the categories within each domain are levels of learning development, and these levels increase in difficulty.

The simple matrix structure that he developed enables a checklist or template to be constructed for the design of learning programs, training courses, lesson plans, etc. Effective learning - especially in organizations, where training is to be converted into organizational results - should arguably cover all the levels of each of the domains, where relevant to the situation and the learner.

xviii

For example, in learning to play a violin, the person will have to learn the rules of the music (cognitive domain); but he also has to learn how to hold the violin, the bow and move the fingers properly so that music comes out rather than a screech noise (psychomotor). Furthermore, later in the development the person may even learn to love the playing itself, value its applications in the music field, and appreciate its development (affective domain).

Various people have since built on Bloom's work, notably in the third domain, the 'psychomotor' or skills, which Bloom originally identified in a broad sense, but which he never fully detailed. This was apparently because Bloom and his colleagues felt that the academic environment held insufficient expertise to analyze and create a suitable reliable structure for the physical ability 'Psychomotor' domain. While this might seem strange, such caution is not uncommon among expert and highly specialized academics - they strive for accuracy as well as innovation. In Bloom's case it is as well that he left a few gaps for others to complete the detail; the model seems to have benefited from having several different contributors fill in the detail over the years, such as Anderson, Krathwhol, Masia (2001), Simpson (1972), Harrow (1972) and Dave (1970) (these last three having each developed versions of the third 'Psychomotor' domain).

Certainly, the learner should benefit from development of knowledge and intellect (Cognitive Domain); attitude and beliefs (Affective Domain); and the ability to put physical and bodily skills into effect - to act (Psychomotor Domain). However, as important as learning is, in this book we are going to address Quality in education not only from the learning perspective but also from the business side of education and its effectiveness in the learning process. We are going to talk about the process of improvement in the educational environment. Specifically, we are going to talk about:

Chapter 1: **Essence of education.** This chapter attempts to address why education and how basic improvement may be introduced at all levels of the education process

Chapter 2: **Quality in education.** This chapter discusses the issues of quality in the educational process and attempts to give some ideas of improvement.

Chapter 3: **Leadership.** This chapter addresses the issue of leadership in education and its effect in the educational process from K-12 and college/university levels.

Chapter 4: **Educational methodologies in education**. This chapter addresses the methodologies used to assimilate and infuse knowledge to students.

Chapter 5: **Stakeholders in education: Parents, learners, administration, and society.** This chapter defines and identifies the stakeholders of the educational system from K-12 and post secondary levels.

Chapter 6: **Customer satisfaction and service.** This chapter defines customer satisfaction and service and applies the concept to all educational levels.

Chapter 7: **Tools for improvement**: This chapter identifies and explains some of the most common yet powerful tools of improvement.

Chapter 8: **Six sigma in education**. This chapter explains the six sigma methodology for education. It discusses both DMAIC and DCOV models.

Chapter 9: **Lean approaches to education.** This chapter introduces the concept of lean and how it may be used in the educational system to eliminate waste.

Chapter 10: **Educational reform**. This chapter addresses reforms in the educational system with the intent of making education more effective and efficient. It also identifies the seven deadly sins that stall improvement and or reform.

Epilogue

Appendix A: **Planning guide for developing the school improvement plan**. A very detailed improvement planning guide for K-12 based on Michigan law.

Appendix B: **Six sigma helps - tools and forms used in the six sigma methodology**. A very extensive summary of both tools and forms in the pursuit of six sigma.

Appendix C: **Tools and forms used in the lean methodology**. A very extensive summary of both tools and forms used in the pursuit of lean in education.
Appendix D: **Useful basic statistics**. Formulae of several key statistics that may be used in the educational environment.
Appendix E: **When to use selected quality tools**. A selected quality tool anthology for education. The focus is to identify each tool and provide some guidelines as to their optimum use.
Appendix F: **Training development guide for SMEs**. A short introduction to: analyze the need for training; set training objectives; determine the most effective method(s) of delivering training; and the role of editing; introduction of instructional domains.

References

Anderson, L. W., Krathwohl, D. R., and Bloom, B. S. (2001). *A taxonomy for learning, teaching, and assessing: A revision of Bloom's taxonomy of educational objectives* (Abridged ed.). Longman. NY.

Bloom B. S. (1956). *Taxonomy of Educational Objectives, Handbook I: The Cognitive Domain*. David McKay Co Inc. NY.

Bloom,B., Krathwhol, Masia, (1964). *Taxonomy of educational objectives: The classification of educational goals. Handbook II: The affective domain*. David McKay Co Inc. NY.

Dave, R. H. (1970). *Developing and writing educational objectives* (Psychomotor levels pp. 33-34). In R. J. Armstrong. (1975). Ed. Educational Innovators Press. NY.

Eisner, E. W. (2000). *Benjamin Bloom 1913-99*. UNESCO: International Bureau of Education. NY.

Harrow, A. J. (1972). *A taxonomy of the psychomotor domain: A guide for developing behavioral objectives*. David McKay Co. NY.

Hannah, and Michaelis (1977). *A comprehensive framework for instructional objectives: A guide to systematic planning and evaluation*. Addison Wesley. Upper Saddle River, NJ.

Simpson, E. J. (1972). *The classification of educational objectives in the Psychomotor domain*. Gryphon House. Washington, DC.

Selected Bibliography

Bloom, B. S., D. R. Krathwohl, B. B. Masia and M. D. Emgelhart. (1956). *Taxonomy of educational objectives:The classification of educational goals*. Longmans, Green. NY.

Burr, V. (1995). *An Introduction to Social Constructionism*. Routledge, London.

Dewey, J. (1916). *Democracy and Education. An introduction to the philosophy of education*. New York: Free Press. NY.

Hauenstein, A. D. (1998). *A conceptual framework for educational objectives: A holistic approach to traditional taxonomies*. University Pres of America. Washington, DC.

Krathwohl, D. R., B. S. Bloom, B. S. And B. M. Bertram. (1973). *Taxonomy of Educational Objectives - the Classification of Educational Goals. Handbook II: Affective Domain*. David McKay Co., Inc. NY.

Marzano, R. J. (2001). *Designing a new taxonomy of educational objectives*. Corwin Press. Thousand Oaks, CA.

Shambaugh, N., and S. G. Magliaro (2006). "Student models of instructional design." *Educational Technology Research and Development*. Vol. 54. No. 1, pp. 83-106.

INTRODUCTION

Whereas *education* is a broad concept, referring to all the experiences in which students can learn something, *instruction* refers to the intentional facilitating of learning toward identified goals, delivered either by an instructor or other forms, and *teaching* refers to the actions of a real live instructor designed to impart learning to the student.

On the other hand, *training* refers to learning with a view toward preparing learners with specific knowledge, skills, or abilities that can be applied immediately upon completion. As it was mentioned in the preface, education is a lifelong process in the learning of knowledge, information and skills for some improvement. However, that improvement is never ending.

The right to education has been described as a basic human right: since 1952, Article 2 of the first Protocol to the European Convention on Human Rights obliges all signatory parties to guarantee the right to education. At world level, the United Nation's International Covenant on Economic, Social and Cultural Rights of 1966 guarantees this right under its Article 13. The fulfillment of this right to education is based on the 4As approach which is:

- Availability – education is free and government-funded and there is adequate infrastructure and trained teachers able to support education delivery.
- Accessibility – the system is non-discriminatory and accessible to all, and positive steps are taken to include the most marginalized.
- Acceptability – the content of education is relevant, non-discriminatory and culturally appropriate, and of quality. The school itself is safe and teachers are professional.
- Adaptability – education can evolve with the changing needs of society and contribute to challenging inequalities, such as gender discrimination, and can be adapted locally to suit specific contexts.

Globally education is divided into categories. They are:

- *Pre- Primary* (Preschool: below 5 years old; and Kindergarten: between 5-6 years old).
- *Primary*: Primary (or elementary) education consists of the first years of formal, structured education. In general, primary education consists of six or seven years of schooling starting at the age of 6 or 7, although this varies between, and sometimes within, countries. Globally, around 70% of primary-age children are enrolled in primary education, and this proportion is rising (UNESCO 2008; Kneller 1971). Under the Education for All programs driven by UNESCO, most countries have committed to achieving universal enrollment in primary education by 2015, and in many countries, it is compulsory for children to receive primary education. The major goals of primary education are achieving basic literacy and numeracy amongst all pupils, as well as establishing foundations in science, geography, history and other social sciences. The relative priority of various areas, and the methods used to teach them, are an area of considerable political debate.
- *Middle School* (Junior High School: starting at 12 or 13 years old): Middle School or Junior High School serves as a "bridge" between elementary school and high school. The terms can be used in different ways in different countries, sometimes interchangeably. In some governmental and institutional contexts, "middle school" may be used as no more than an alternative name to "junior high school," or it might imply a pedagogical shift away from primary and secondary school practices.
- *Senior High Schools* (staring at 15 or 16 years old): Secondary education is the stage of education following primary school. Secondary education is generally the final stage of compulsory education.

The next stage of education is usually college or university. Secondary education is characterized by transition from the typically compulsory, comprehensive primary education for minors to the optional, selective tertiary, "post-secondary", or "higher" education (e.g., university, vocational school) for adults. Depending on the system, schools for this period or a part of it may be called secondary schools, high schools, gymnasia, lyceums, middle schools, colleges, vocational schools and preparatory schools and the exact meaning of any of these varies between the systems.

The exact boundary between primary and secondary education varies from country to country and even within them, but is generally around the fifth to the tenth year of education. Secondary education occurs mainly during the teenage years. In the United States primary and secondary education together are sometimes referred to as K-12 education. In Australia it is known as P-12 education. The purpose of secondary education can be to give common knowledge, to prepare for either higher education or vocational education, or to train directly to a profession.

- *Junior Colleges*: Generally speaking a junior college is a two-year post secondary school whose main purpose is to provide academic, vocational and professional education. The highest certificate offered by such schools is usually an associate's degree, although many junior college students continue their education at a university, transferring some or all of the credit earned at the junior college toward the degree requirements of the four-year school.
- *Vocational Schools*: A vocational school (or trade school or career college), providing vocational education, is a school in which students are taught the skills needed to perform a particular job. Traditionally, vocational schools have not existed to further education in the sense of liberal arts, but rather to teach only job-specific skills, and as such have been better considered to be institutions devoted to training, not education. That purely vocational focus began changing in the 1990s "toward a broader preparation that develops the academic" and technical skills of students, as well as the vocational.
- *Universities* (undergraduate and graduate programs): A university is an institution of higher education and research, which grants an academic degree in a variety of subjects. A university provides both undergraduate and postgraduate education. The word university is derived from the Latin *universitas magistrorum et scholarium*, roughly meaning "community of teachers and scholars."

Higher education includes teaching, research and social services activities of universities, and within the realm of teaching, it includes both the undergraduate level (sometimes referred to as tertiary education) and the graduate (or postgraduate) level (sometimes referred to as graduate school). Higher education in a country generally involves work towards a degree-level or foundation degree qualification. In most developed countries a high proportion of the population (up to 50%) now enters higher education at some time in their lives. Higher education is therefore very important to national economies, both as a significant industry in its own right, and as a source of trained and educated personnel for the rest of the economy.

Higher education, also called *tertiary, third stage*, or *post secondary education*, is the non-compulsory educational level that follows the completion of a school providing a secondary education, such as a high school, or secondary school. Tertiary education is normally taken to include undergraduate and post graduate education, as well as vocational education and training. Colleges and Universities are the main institutions that provide tertiary education. Collectively, these are sometimes known as tertiary institutions. Tertiary education generally results in the receipt of a certificate; diploma; or an academic degree.

- *Life learning* (Continuing education): This is education that an individual receives throughout their lives with formal and informal education through a variety of ways primarily through some kind of technology. Technology is an increasingly influential factor in education and an important contributor to the learning process. Computers and mobile phones are being widely used in developed countries both to complement established education practices and develop new ways of learning such as online education (a type of distance education). This gives students the opportunity to choose what they are interested in learning. The proliferation of computers also means the increase of programming and blogging. Technology offers powerful learning tools that demand new skills and understandings of students, including multimedia, and provides new ways to engage students, such as Virtual Learning Environments. Technology is being used more not only in administrative duties in education but also in the instruction of students. The use of technologies such as PowerPoint© and interactive whiteboards are capturing the attention of students in the classroom. Technology is also being used in the assessment of students. One example is the Audience Response System (ARS), which allows immediate feedback of tests and classroom discussions.

In all these categories computers play a very important role. In fact, the term "computer-assisted learning" (CAL) has been increasingly used to describe the use of technology in teaching. Collectively all applications of computers usage in the education process are known as the information and communication technologies (ICTs). In essence, they are a diverse set of tools and resources used to communicate, create, disseminate, store, and manage information in the process of learning. These technologies include computers, the Internet, broadcasting technologies (radio and television), and telephony. There is increasing interest in how computers and the Internet can improve education at all levels, in both formal and non-formal settings (Aghion and Howitt 1998). Older ICT technologies, such as radio and television, have for over forty years been used for open and distance learning, although print remains the cheapest, most accessible and therefore most dominant delivery mechanism in both developed and developing countries (Barro and Sala-i-Martin 2004).

The use of computers and the Internet is still in its infancy in developing countries, if these are used at all, due to limited infrastructure and the attendant high costs of access. Usually, various technologies are used in combination rather than as the sole delivery mechanism. For example, the Kothmale Community Radio Internet uses both radio broadcasts and computer and Internet technologies to facilitate the sharing of information and provide educational opportunities in a rural community in Sri Lanka (Acemoglu, Johnson and Robinson 2001). The Open University of the United Kingdom (UKOU), established in 1969 as the first educational institution in the world wholly dedicated to open and distance learning, still relies heavily on print-based materials supplemented by radio, television and, in recent years, online programming (Anushek and Woessmann 2008). Similarly, the Indira Gandhi National Open University in India combines the use of print, recorded audio and video, broadcast radio and television, and audio conferencing technologies (Mincer 1970).

As the claims for these technologies and improvements in teaching, curricula designs, presentations, and funding so many other changes that have been introduced in the education domain, we find that we still have failures all across the categories that we just mentioned. The failures are so great that politicians, parents, students and educators are all screaming for yet another change.

The Mackinaw Center for Education of Michigan in a recent study identified some of these failures. For example: The failure of U.S. K-12 public schools to perform satisfactorily on academic measures of student progress is substantial. More than a third of Michigan students leave high school without possessing basic skills in reading, writing, and arithmetic. This forces post-secondary schools and employers to teach these individuals basic skills.

Providing post-secondary remedial education is just one expense society must shoulder to make up for the failure of students to learn these minimal competencies. Other costs—the cost of coping with those who never acquire these skills—include everything from lost productivity to more expensive criminal justice and social welfare systems.

The literature for education reform is full of specific failure example. However, here we are not so much interested in the specifics rather than the fact that they exist in all programs and in all regions. Exceptions exist but they are rare.

We believe that quality principles can be applied to schools of any kind and that is the intent of this book. Improvement is a way of attitude and looking at the change as a dynamic way of getting things better than they were. Quality principles allow for that change in a very pragmatic way.

References

Acemoglu, D., S. Johnson, and J. A. Robinson. (December 2001). "The Colonial Origins of Comparative Development: An Empirical Investigation." *American Economic Review* 91,no.5 pp.1369-1401.
Aghion, P. and P. Howitt. (1998). *Endogenous Growth Theory*. MIT Press. Cambridge, MA.
Barro, R. J. and X. Sala-i-Martin. (2004). *Economic Growth*. 2nd ed. The MIT Press. Cambridge, MA.
Hanushek, E. A, and L. Woessmann. (September 2008). "The role of cognitive skills in economic development." *Journal of Economic Literature*. 46, no.3 pp. 607-608.
Kneller, G. F. (1971). *Introduction to the Philosophy of Education*. John Wiley and Sons. NY.
Mincer, J. (March 1970). "The distribution of labor incomes: a survey with special reference to the human capital approach." *Journal of Economic Literature*. 8, no.1 pp. 1-2.
UNESCO. (2008). *Education For All Monitoring Report 2008*. Net Enrollment Rate in primary education. UN. NY.

CHAPTER 1

ESSENCE OF EDUCATION

This chapter opens up the discussion of what education is all about and why it is important to pursue it. It also reexamines the process of education and reaffirms that education is not only for educators - although they play a major role – but for students, parents, government, and society at large. Furthermore it identifies some possible changes that may indeed help in the overall improvement of education.

The term *education* is very convoluted in many ways. However, it is certain that it does not necessarily mean knowledge on a specific subject but as Plato defined it "the effort to develop a healthy mind where logic is maintaining a balance between the desire and anger." In that respect human error may be quantized as to how far away from the balance state a person is. Therefore, after going beyond a limit out of balance, there is a tremendous destructive power of human mind. For example, to build a house it takes a lot of effort of constructive power of human mind including labor, time and human energy, but to destroy such a house it may take a few seconds from just one person. Historically, if an individual, or a group of people are condemned for one reason or another the only way for them to survive is to use the destructive power of their minds. This action either will totally destroy them if the society reacts properly or, they will succeed. If they succeed they will gradually gain political and economic strength using always the destructive power of their minds and they will impose their own rules on the rest of the society.

This is the situation today worldwide including the United States to have more such imposed rules and other countries to a lesser degree. However, educated people are the only hope to help society and its rulers to gradually improve their performance by using more the constructive power of their minds and by convincing, like Aristotle said, that this is the only way to have *quality in life*.

Therefore, education to support its actions (whatever they may be or defined), needs ideals and bases. This is not a small thing. In fact it is a herculean feat, because too many people – even specialists in the field – have many ideas and interpretations as to what an excellent education is let alone what "education" itself is. For example: If you ask five individuals to complete the sentence, "The purpose of education is...?" it is likely that you'll have five different statements. Some will place the focus on knowledge, some on the teacher, and others on the student. Yet people's beliefs in the purpose of education lie at the heart of their teaching behaviors – see appendix F for the instructional domains.

Webster defines *education* as the process of educating or teaching. *Educate* is further defined as "to develop the knowledge, skill, or character of..." So, one may from these definitions, assume that the purpose of education is to develop the knowledge, skill, or character of students. Unfortunately, this definition offers little unless we further define words such as develop, knowledge, and character.

What is meant by knowledge? Is it a body of information that exists "out there" - apart from the human thought processes that developed it? If we look at the standards and benchmarks that have been developed by many states and or countries all over the world - or at Hirsch's (1987) list of information needed for *Cultural Literacy*, we might assume this to be the definition of knowledge. There is also considerable research leading others to believe that knowledge arises in the mind of an individual when that person interacts with an idea or experience.

However, this is hardly a new argument. In ancient Greece, the purpose of education was for making someone a *good citizen*. In fact, Socrates argued that education was about drawing out what was already within the student. (The word education comes from the Latin *e-ducere* meaning "to lead out"). At the same

1

time, the Sophists, a group of itinerant teachers, promised to give students the necessary knowledge and skills to gain positions with the city-state.

There is a dangerous tendency to assume that when people use the same words, they perceive a situation in the same way. This is rarely the case. Once one gets beyond a dictionary definition - meaning that is often of little practical value - meaning we assign to a word is a belief, not an absolute fact. To make the point let us see some examples that demonstrate the diversity of beliefs about the purpose of education from some very well known educators.

- "The only purpose of education is to teach a student how to live his life-by developing his mind and equipping him to deal with reality. The training he needs is theoretical, *i.e.,* conceptual. He has to be taught to think, to understand, to integrate, to prove. He has to be taught the essentials of the knowledge discovered in the past - and he has to be equipped to acquire further knowledge by his own effort," Ayn Rand.
- "The one real object of education is to leave a man in the condition of continually asking questions," Bishop Creighton.
- "The central task of education is to implant a will and facility for learning; it should produce not learned but learning people. The truly human society is a learning society, where grandparents, parents, and children are students together," Eric Hoffer.
- "The aim of education should be to teach us rather how to think, than what to think - rather to improve our minds, so as to enable us to think for ourselves, than to load the memory with the thoughts of other men," Bill Beattie.
- "No one has yet realized the wealth of sympathy, the kindness and generosity hidden in the soul of a child. The effort of every true education should be to unlock that treasure" Emma Goldman.
- "The central job of schools is to maximize the capacity of each student," Carol Ann Tomlinson.

Even though these are a very small sample of definitions, the fact of the matter is that there is no definition of education that is agreed upon by all, or even most, educators, society and politicians. The meanings they attach to the word are complex beliefs arising from their own values and experiences. To the extent that those beliefs differ, the experience of students in today's classrooms can never be the same. Worse, many educators have never been asked to state their beliefs - or even to reflect on what they believe. At the very least, teachers owe it to their students to bring their definitions into consciousness and examine them for validity.

To make matters more complicated, theorists have made a distinction between the *purpose of education* and the *functions of education* (Callaway1979). A *purpose* is the fundamental goal of the process - an end to be achieved. *Functions* are other outcomes that may occur as a natural result of the process - byproducts or consequences of schooling. For example, some teachers believe that the transmission of knowledge is the primary purpose of education, while the transfer of knowledge from school to the real world is something that happens naturally as a consequence of possessing that knowledge - a function of education.

Because a purpose is an expressed goal, more effort is put into attaining it. Functions are assumed to occur without directed effort. For this reason it's valuable to figure out which outcomes you consider a fundamental purpose of education. For example: Which of the following is actually included in the planning of education, makes a difference.

- Acquisition of information about the past and present: includes traditional disciplines such as literature, history, science, mathematics. Or, formation of healthy social and/or formal relationships among and between students, teachers, others.
- Capacity/ability to evaluate information and to predict future outcomes (decision-making). Or, Capacity/ability to seek out alternative solutions and evaluate them (problem solving).
- Development of mental and physical skills: motor, thinking, communication, social, aesthetic. Or, Knowledge of moral practices and ethical standards acceptable by society/culture.
- Capacity/ability to recognize and evaluate different points of view. Or, respect: giving and receiving recognition as human beings.

- Indoctrination into the culture. Or, capacity/ability to live a fulfilling life.
- Capacity/ability to earn a living: career education. Or, sense of well-being: mental and physical health.
- Capacity/ability to be a good citizen. Or, capacity/ability to think creatively.
- Acquisition of cultural appreciation: art, music, humanities. Or, understanding of human relations and motivations.
- Acquisition/clarification of values related to the physical environment. Or, acquisition/clarification of personal values.
- Self-realization/self-reflection: awareness of one's abilities and goals. Or, self-esteem/self-efficacy.

In the field of quality we say that *what gets measured gets done*. Regardless of the high sounding rhetoric about the development of the total child, it is the content of assessments that largely drives education. How are the capacity and or ability to think creatively are assessed in today's schools? To what extent is the typical student recognized and given respect? How often are students given the opportunity to recognize and evaluate different points of view when multiple choice tests require a single 'correct' answer?

Teachers who hold a more *humanistic* view of the purpose of education often experience stress because the meaning they assign to education differs greatly from the meaning assigned by society or their institution. It is clear in listening to the language of education that its primary focus is on knowledge and teaching rather than on the learner. Students are expected to conform to schools rather than schools serving the needs of students.

Stopping to identify and agree upon a fundamental purpose or purposes of education is rare. One sees nebulous statements in school mission statements, but they are often of the trivial variety that offers little substance on which to build a school culture. For example: Many school districts will spend enormous amount of resources on sports, cultural and diversity activities rather than the academic programs of mathematics, science and writing. Creating meaningful and lasting change in education is unlikely without revisiting this basic definition. At the very least, educators must be challenged to identify and reexamine their beliefs in the light of present knowledge.

It is time for the focus of education to shift from what's "out there" - the curriculum, assessments, classroom arrangement, books, and computers - to the fundamental assumptions about and definitions of education held by educators and policymakers.

Furthermore, it is time to reexamine the process of education as well as the funding, alternatives and the allocation of resources. Education is too important to be left only to the educators. Parents, students (learners), educators, government and society at large must get involved to recreate a system that is overdue for realignment and willing to take the challenges of the 21st century.

Currently we know from anecdotal stories, politicians, parents, and society that the education process is not working. We also know from the students themselves that what is offered does not meet their requirements. In one example of redefining education we have the state of Oregon. To find answers, in the state of Oregon they set up a Commission that looked at educational research, classroom practice, public values and professional opinion. Using the data, a model was developed that sets a cost per student at a prototype elementary, middle and high school, then multiplies that cost by the number of students at each level across the state. Each prototype provides a vision of a high-performing school with goals for class size, number of teachers and specialists, help for students having trouble, materials and supplies, technology and more.

By factoring in different elements such as reducing class size or adding more computers for students, school officials can weigh the impact and calculate the cost of each funding decision. This is a breakthrough in the educational process because for the first time we are able to look at funding for k-12 on a line by line item and therefore administrators and school boards have an objective way to evaluate cuts and their impact on students.

The Oregon Model (Quality Education Model – known as QEM) found a profound gap between current funding and the expected outcomes from the students in K-12 programs. However, with the evidence that the research brought forth they were able to show what students need to meet standards and to help the Legislature, Governor, Department of Education, and other groups decide where to allocate dollars.

To be sure, there are two sides to the accountability equation – even for the state of Oregon. On one hand, schools are expected to deliver on the promise of a quality education for every Oregon student. On the other hand, the Legislature is accountable for providing schools with the resources they need to do the job. The QEM provides detailed, reliable standards for measuring the success of both local and state decision-makers. It is of interest however, to point out that the Commission recommended the following:

- A continued focus on reading in the early grades
- Staff professional development. Ongoing training for teachers and principals supports schools in meeting academic goals and helps to attract and retain qualified staff.
- High school restructuring. High school programs need to be restructured to be consistent with new requirements and to equip students for life after graduation.

The Oregonians have successfully trail blazed the issue of reform in education and indeed have provided at least the beginning of a workable model. The model is an available, recognized tool that we can use to evaluate the performance of elected officials and state agencies. It clearly outlines what must be done to meet Oregon's goals for education, but it can also be applied to other states as well.

So, what is education for? Certainly education is not the answer for everything. Take for example the German educational system in the first half of the 20th century. It was the best in the world. It was based on a foundation that produced Kant, Goethe and so many other scientists but it resulted in the Holocaust, a black eye not only for the Germans but for society at large. Why did this happen? The primary reason was because education was sterile. It emphasized theories, concepts, abstraction, answers, ideology and efficiency. It failed miserably in defining values, human beings, consciousness, the opportunity to ask questions and more importantly to focus on conscience. It was a way to prepare the Germans for the natural world.

Does it sound familiar? Our educational system is following the same path. We have failed to recognize that education is no guarantee of decency, prudence, or wisdom. More of the same kind of education will only compound our problems. If we examine the past we can get a glimpse of this misdirection that has caused us the trouble in our educational process. In the literature world, for example, we find the essence of the modern drive to dominate nature and thus our failure:

- Christopher Marlowe's Faust, who trades his soul for knowledge and power;
- Mary Shelley's Dr. Frankenstein, who refuses to take responsibility for his creation;
- Herman Melville's Captain Ahab, who says "All my means are sane, my motive and object mad."

On the other hand, historically,

- Francis Bacon's proposed union between knowledge and power foreshadows the contemporary alliance between government, business, and knowledge that has wrought so much mischief.

- Galileo's separation of the intellect foreshadows the dominance of the analytical mind over that part given to creativity, humor, and wholeness.
- In Descartes' epistemology, one finds the roots of the radical separation of self and object.

These points are not meant as arguments for ignorance, but rather as statements that the worth of education must now be measured against the standards of decency and human survival. Why? Because the issues of our global world that loom about us are so large and significant and will continue for the foreseeable future. It is not education that will save us, but education of a certain kind.

In order for us to understand the proper education for the 21st century we must understand some of the perpetual trouble spots in the process. I have adopted, summarized and editorialized (expended) some of them based on Orr (1991):

- *Ignorance is a solvable problem.* Ignorance is not a solvable problem, but rather an inescapable part of the human condition. All knowledge regardless of its stage, always carries with it some form of ignorance (the unknown). Many examples fit this issue. The DDT, asbestos, chloroform carbon and so many others. All of them were used with the best of intentions but the side effects turned out to be detrimental for humans and environment. In the end, they were all taken out of use.
- *With enough knowledge and technology we can manage "everything" especially planet Earth.* This is the most dangerous statement that we keep on saying. In fact, we have said it for so long that a lot of segments of our society believe it. It sounds good and impressive in a world that technology is moving in an exponential pace, but the fact of the matter is that we as humans cannot manage the planet earth. Too many things remain and will remain unknown for our finite mind. The best we can do is to manage us. Take for example the ecology of the top inch of topsoil which is still largely unknown, as is its relationship to the larger systems of the biosphere. We pretend to understand it where in fact, we should redirect our efforts in understanding our human desires, economies, politics, and communities. By diverting our attention we get caught by those things that avoid the hard choices implied by politics, morality, ethics, and common sense. It makes far better sense to reshape ourselves to fit a finite planet than to attempt to reshape the planet to fit our infinite wants.
- *Knowledge is increasing and by implication human goodness.* This is another dangerous assumption in our educational process. To be sure, there is an information explosion going on, by which I mean a rapid increase of data, words, and paper. In fact, Keng (2007) reports that the doubling of knowledge is occurring every 32 hours. But this explosion should not be taken for an increase in knowledge and wisdom, which cannot so easily by measured. What can be said truthfully is that some knowledge is increasing while other kinds of knowledge are being lost and yet in others we just do not know what happens in a catastrophic decline. Examples of these are plentiful. A classic one is the Savannah River Nuclear Facility in South Carolina, where nuclear weapons and components used to be made, had, in 1963, five operating nuclear reactors and a workforce of 6,000 people. In the early 1980s, there were three reactors left operating and a workforce of somewhere between 7,000 and 12,000 people. The last reactor was shut down in 1988. By 1993, with no reactors working, the workforce was 25,000. By 1996, downsizing had reduced this workforce to 16,000, still 10,000 above the number of workers needed when the facility was functioning at peak capacity.

  In another example, Ehrenfeld (1999) has pointed out that biology departments no longer hire faculty in such areas as systematics, taxonomy, or ornithology. In other words, important knowledge is being lost because of the recent overemphasis on molecular biology and genetic engineering, which are more lucrative, but not more important, areas of inquiry. We still lack the science of land health that Leopold (1995) called for half a century ago.

Again, the problem is not just knowledge in certain areas that we're losing, but vernacular knowledge as well, by which I mean the knowledge that people have of their places. In the words of the famous environmentalist, Lopez (1999): "[I am] forced to the realization that something strange, if not dangerous, is afoot. Year by year the number of people with firsthand experience in the land dwindles. Rural populations continue to shift to the cities.... In the wake of this loss of personal and local knowledge, the knowledge from which a real geography is derived, the knowledge on which a country must ultimately stand, has come something hard to define but I think sinister and unsettling."

The point here is that data with knowledge is a deeper mistake that learning will make us better or ethical people. But learning, as we pointed out in the preface is endless and may be obtained from several sources. Ultimately, however, it may be the knowledge of the good that is most threatened by all of our other advances. All things considered, it is possible that we are becoming more ignorant of the things we must know to live well and sustainably on this earth.

- *Higher education is a place where we restore that which we have dismantled.* In the modern curriculum we have fragmented the world into bits and pieces called disciplines and sub-disciplines. As a result, after 12 or 16 or 20 years of education, most students graduate without any broad *integrated* sense of the unity of things. The consequences for their personhood and for the planet are large. For example, we routinely produce economists who lack the most rudimentary knowledge of ecology. This explains why our national accounting systems do not subtract the costs of biotic impoverishment, soil erosion, poisons in the air or water, and resource depletion from gross national product. We add the price of the sale of a bushel of wheat to GNP while forgetting to subtract the three bushels of topsoil lost in its production. As a result of incomplete education, we've fooled ourselves into thinking that we are much richer than we are.
- *Education is giving you the means for upward mobility and success.* It has been said that Thomas Merton once proclaimed that modern day education is "mass production of people literally unfit for anything except to take part in an elaborate and completely artificial charade." It may sound harsh but the fact is that many uneducated (informally schooled) individuals have made themselves successful in many ways. Here it depends how we define success. Different people find success in different things. By the same token, many PhDs end up driving taxis. The moral here is that there is no guarantee for success or upper mobility with or without education.

Given these assumptions let us look how we can rethink education, so that we can define its purpose. Obviously there are many more but here we will address some of the basic principles for an agenda that is fitting our goals as a modern day society.

The first principle comes from the Greek concept of *paideia*. The goal of education is not mastery of subject matter, but of one's person. Subject matter is simply the tool. Much as one would use a hammer and chisel to carve a block of marble, one uses ideas and knowledge to forge one's own personhood. For the most part we labor under a confusion of ends and means, thinking that the goal of education is to stuff all kinds of facts, techniques, methods, and information into the student's mind, regardless of how and with what effect it will be used. The Greeks knew better. Their goal was a better citizenry. Education then, should improve the character of all citizens.

Second, we must view all education as a holistic process of learning. This implies that all education is environmental in nature. This means that the education must be sensitive to what is included and excluded from learning as part of the curriculum (K-12, or post secondary education). It must be linked with items that are relevant to overall system improvement or understanding. For example: To teach economics with reference to the laws of thermodynamics or those of ecology is to teach a fundamentally important ecological lesson. After all, physics and ecology have plenty to do with the economy. Again, to teach

Political Science with reference to citizenship is a major link in our societal behavior and control. The same is true throughout the curriculum. Education then should be relative and systematic to fulfill the expectations of the learner and society.

Third, education should provide knowledge and responsibility as well as accountability. All knowledge carries with it the responsibility to see that it is well used in the world. However, because of the unknown factor, that knowledge has to be tempered with risk. Education, therefore, should introduce learning in the areas of statistics, risk and economies of scale.

Fourth, it is fundamentally important before we proclaim "eureka" or "success" for something we understand the effects of this knowledge on real people and their communities. Many times science (especially) will come up with something that looks or sounds great but later will have serious effects. Classic point here is the breast implants with silicon. Originally very good idea for therapeutic and cosmetic reasons but later on after several years of being implanted there was leakage and cancer followed. Education should introduce methodologies for analysis, evaluation and decision making for problems and opportunities in relationship to society.

Fifth, education is about *freedom*, *truth* and *integrity*. Yet, in modern education we do just the opposite. We teach one thing but we do another. Students learn, without anyone ever saying it, that they are helpless to overcome the frightening gap between ideals and reality. Examples are too many to mention. Students are being taught about global responsibility while being educated in institutions that often invest their financial weight in the most irresponsible things. They are taught about freedom of speech, yet in most educational systems including higher learning institutions when a speaker of a counter political view or a not politically correct point of view is presented, demonstrations, physical and expulsion threads are common. They are taught about individual performance but the real world needs teamwork. They are practicing tasks that they will never encounter and they do not learn things that they need to survive. They are taught the importance of their own work, but in the real world they see the powerful, the successful and the influential use speeches and write entire books that others write (speech writers and ghost writers) and yet they claim them as their own. What is desperately needed are teachers and administrators who provide role models of integrity, care, thoughtfulness, and institutions that are capable of embodying ideals wholly and completely in all of their operations. Education should provide the way of learning what leading by example is all about.

Finally, we must all recognize and internalize that the way learning occurs is as important as the content of particular subjects. Process is important for learning. Courses taught as lecture courses tend to induce passivity. Indoor classes create the illusion that learning only occurs inside four walls isolated from what students call without apparent irony the "real world." We must be flexible to introduce variety and dynamic methods, processes and exercises that revitalize the intellectual capacity of the learner whenever and as often as possible. In this spirit we must – perhaps - go as far as encourage ideas and processes that diffuse and or eliminate the sterile environment of learning of passivity, monologue, domination, and artificiality with realism, dynamism and effectiveness. A good example to prove this point is Biology. Dissecting frogs in biology classes teaches lessons about nature that no one would verbally profess. The point is simply that students are being taught in various and subtle ways beyond the content of courses.

So, modern day and future education must begin to teach learners knowledge about specific relevant subjects. Furthermore, this new education process must start to teach analytical and critical thinking, so that, the learners know and understand how to analyze resource flows when given the opportunity to participate in the creation of real solutions to real problems.

Critical to this change is the introduction of basic subjects that will help in the understanding of what education is for and how it should be used. We believe that beyond the traditional and classic subjects (Math, reading, writing and so on), the following subjects should be introduced to all learners at critical phases of their learning, such as:

- Thermodynamics
- Principles of ecology
- Energetics
- Cost and benefit analysis
- Limits of technology
- Concept of proportionality - appropriate scale
- Statistics

In addition to these subjects the fundamentals of *steady-state economics* should be understood. The phrase "steady state economy" originated from ecological economics, most notably from the work of Daly (1991), but its roots are in classical economics, most notably the "stationary state" as touted by John Stuart Mill. The steady state economy is often discussed in the context of economic growth and the impacts of economic growth on ecological integrity, environmental protection, and economic sustainability. Therefore, use of the phrase "steady state economy" requires a clear definition of *economic growth*.

Economic growth is an increase in the production and consumption of goods and services. For distinct economic or political units, economic growth is generally indicated by increasing gross domestic product (GDP). Economic growth entails increasing population times per capita consumption, higher throughput of materials and energy, and a growing ecological footprint.

Economic growth is distinguished from "economic development," which refers to qualitative change independent of quantitative growth. For example, economic development may refer to the attainment of a more equitable distribution of wealth, or a sectoral readjustment reflecting the evolution of consumer preference or newer technology.

Environmental ethics is one more fundamental area of knowledge that the new learners must posses for the future. They grew up in response to the work of scientists such as Carson (1962) and events such as the first Earth Day in 1970, when environmentalists started urging philosophers to consider the philosophical aspects of environmental problems. Environmental ethics is the part of environmental philosophy which considers extending the traditional boundaries of ethics from solely including humans to including the non-human world. It exerts influence on a large range of disciplines including law, theology, ecology, sociology, geography and economics. The important issue here is for the environmental knowledge to be scientifically sound and without any bias from political groups.

I suppose at least one reason for education to be viewed as we just discussed it here, is in Leopold's (1995) words, know that "they [learners] are only cogs in an ecological mechanism such that, if they will work with that mechanism, their mental wealth and material wealth can expand indefinitely (and) if they refuse to work with it, it will ultimately grind them to dust." So, Leopold asked: "If education does not teach us these things, then what is education for?"

There has been a great deal of work on learning styles in education over the last two decades. Dunn and Dunn (1978, 1984) focused on identifying relevant stimuli that may influence learning and manipulating the school environment, at about the same time as Renzulli (1985, 1994) recommended varying teaching strategies. Gardner (1993) identified individual talents or aptitudes in his *Multiple Intelligences* theories.

8

Based on the works of Jung, the Myers-Briggs "Type Indicator" and Keirsey's "Temperament Sorter" focused on understanding how people's personality affects the way they interact personally, and how this affects the way individuals respond to each other within the learning environment. The work of Kolb (1984) and Gregorc's (1982) "Type Delineator" follows a similar but more simplified approach. It is currently fashionable to divide education into different learning "modes." The most common learning modalities (Swassing 1979; Barbe 1979) are:

1. Kinesthetic: learning based on hands-on work and engaging in activities.
2. Visual: learning based on observation and seeing what is being learned.
3. Auditory: learning based on listening to instructions/information.

It is claimed that, depending on their preferred learning modality, different teaching techniques have different levels of effectiveness (Barbe (1979). A consequence of this theory is that effective teaching should present a variety of teaching methods which cover all three learning modalities so that different students have equal opportunities to learn in a way that is effective for them. However, Stamatis (1986) found that the method is not that important as much as the intrinsic motivation of the learner.

Teachers need the ability to understand a subject well enough to convey its essence to a new generation of students. The goal is to establish a sound knowledge base on which students will be able to build as they are exposed to different life experiences. The passing of knowledge from generation to generation allows students to grow into useful members of society. Good teachers can translate information, good judgment, experience and wisdom into relevant knowledge that a student can understand, retain and pass to others. Studies from the US suggest that the quality of teachers is the single most important factor affecting student performance, and that countries which score highly on international tests have multiple policies in place to ensure that the teachers they employ are as effective as possible.

Some critics of today's schools, of the concept of learning disabilities, or special education and of response to intervention, take the position that every child has a different learning style and pace and that each child is unique, not only capable of learning but also capable of succeeding.

Sudbury model of democratic education schools assert that there are many ways to study and learn (see note 1). They argue that learning is a process you do, not a process that is done to you. The experience of Sudbury model democratic schools shows that there are many ways to learn without the intervention of teaching, to say, without the intervention of a teacher being imperative. In the case of reading for instance in the Sudbury model democratic schools some children learn from being read to, memorizing the stories and then ultimately reading them. Others learn from cereal boxes, others from games instructions, and others from street signs. Some teach themselves letter sounds, others syllables, others whole words. Sudbury model democratic schools adduce that in their schools no one child has ever been forced, pushed, urged, cajoled, or bribed into learning how to read or write, and they have had no dyslexia. None of their graduates are real or functional illiterates and no one who meets their older students could ever guess the age at which they first learned to read or write. In a similar form students learn all the subjects, techniques and skills in these schools.

Describing current instructional methods as homogenization and lockstep standardization, alternative approaches are proposed, such as the Sudbury model of democratic education schools, an alternative approach in which children, by enjoying personal freedom thus encouraged to exercise personal responsibility for their actions, learn at their own pace and style rather than following a compulsory and chronologically-based curriculum (Potashnik and Capper (2008); Taghioff (2009); Open University of the UK (2009); Indira Gandhi National Open University (2009). Proponents of unschooling (homeschooling) have also claimed that children raised in this method learn at their own pace and style, and do not suffer from learning disabilities.

Where all of us value education and believe it should be a top public priority, the fact is that we can no longer rely on property taxes or a booming economy to pay the bills. The time has come to decide whether we are going to fulfill the promise of a *quality education* for all students.
Fortunately, we have the tools we need to make an informed decision. This is where *Quality methodology* and thinking comes into play. In addition the QEM provides detailed information about the meaning and cost of quality. It also paints a picture of exactly what's at stake in the struggle to provide long-term, stable and adequate funding for schools. Now the question is: will we use it?

It isn't just about adding more money. We need to resolve issues such as the cost of health coverage, energy and insurance to get more dollars into the classroom and certainly be more efficient in the utilization of all the resources that are being used in the system of education.

Furthermore the legislature needs to look at each state's changing demographics, at how we manage the system, at transportation, capital spending, class size and length of school year. All these things impact student outcomes. Finally, colleges and universities must utilize their endowments with efficiency and purpose in mind.

Note 1: The 'Sudbury' name refers to Sudbury Valley School, founded in 1968 in Framingham, Massachusetts. It was the first school of this type and the inspiration for other schools to define themselves as Sudbury schools. These schools are not formally associated in any way, but generally maintain good communication with each other, and recognize a loose camaraderie. In this sense they practice a form of democratic education in which students individually decide what to do with their time, and learn as a by-product of ordinary experience rather than through classes or a standard curriculum. Students are given complete responsibility for their own education and the school is run by a direct democracy in which students and staffs are equals.

Certain facets of the model separate it from other democratic schools and free schools, although there are evident similarities, such as:

1. *De-emphasis of classes*: classes arise only when an individual creates them, and staffs are not expected to offer classes as any sort of curriculum - most democratic schools offer at least some basic curricula. Sudbury schools' attitude on classes, stems from the belief that every individual learns what they need to know through life and that there is no need to try and design a curriculum that will prepare a young person for adult life.
2. *Age mixing*: students are not separated into age-groups of any kind and allowed to mix freely, interacting with those younger and older than themselves; free age-mixing is emphasized as a powerful tool for learning and development in all ages.
3. *Autonomous democracy*: Another prominent difference is the limitation - or total absence - of parental involvement in the administration of Sudbury schools; Sudbury schools are run by a democratic School Meeting where the students and staff participate exclusively and equally. Remarkably, the democratic School Meeting of a Sudbury school is also the sole authority on hiring and firing of staff — a facet that separates these schools from all others.

Summary

In this chapter we have addressed the purpose of education and have given some alternatives for future improvements. In the next chapter we will address the issue of quality in education

References

Barbe, W. B., and R. H. Swassing, with M. N. Milone. (1979). *Teaching through modality strengths: Concepts and practices*. Zaner-Bloser. Columbus, OH.

Callaway, R. (1979) "Teachers' Beliefs Concerning Values and the Functions and Purposes of Schooling." *Eric Document Reproduction Service No. ED 177 110*.

Carson, R. (1962). Silent Spring. Houghton Mifflin. Boston, MA. Reprint (2002) by Mariner Books. Boston, MA. The original book serialized in three parts in the June 16, June 23, and June 30, 1962 in *The New Yorker* magazine

Daly, H. (1991). *Steady-State Economics*. 2nd ed. Island Press. Washington, D.C.

Daly, H. (1994). *For the Common Good: Redirecting the Economy toward Community, the Environment, and a Sustainable Future*. Beacon Press. Boston, MA.

Dunn, R., Dunn, K., and Price, G. E. (1984). *Learning style inventory*. Price Systems. Lawrence, KS.

Dunn, R, and Dunn, K (1978). *Teaching students through their individual learning styles: A practical approach*. Reston Publishing Company. Reston, VA.

Ehrenfeld, D. (January – February 1999). "The Coming Collapse of the Age of Technology." *Tikkun*. pp. 33-38, 71-72.

Gandhi National Open University. Official website. Retrieved 04-8-2009

Gardner, Howard (1983; 1993) *Frames of Mind: The theory of multiple intelligences*. Basic Books. NY.

Gregorc, A. F. (1982). *An Adult's Guide to Style*. Gabriel Systems. Maynard, MA.

Hirsch, E. D. Jr. (1987). *Cultural Literacy*. Houghton Mifflin. NY.

Keng, L. (November 24, 2007). "Human Knowledge Is Doubling Every 32 Hours." Quoting Nido Qubein. *Optimum Performance Technologies*. P. 1.

Kolb, D. A. (1984). *Experiential Learning*. Prentice Hall. Englewood Cliffs, NJ.

Leopold, A. (November-December 1995). "Ecology and Humankind." *International Wildlife*. P. 58.

Lopez, B. (1999). *Journeys on the Threshold of Memory*. Vintage. NY.

Open University of the UK. Official website. Retrieved 04-8-2009

Orr, D. (1991). What is education for?" *In Concert*. Context Institute. P. 52.

Potashnik, M. and Capper, J. "Distance Education: Growth and Diversity." (PDF). http://www.worldbank.org/fandd/english/pdfs/0398/0110398.pdf. Retrieved on 2008-12-06.

Renzulli, J.S. (1994). *Schools for talent development: A practical plan for total school improvement*. Creative Learning Press. Mansfield Center, CT.

Renzulli, J.S., and Reis, S.M. (1985). *The schoolwide enrichment model: A comprehensive plan for educational excellence*. Creative Learning Press. Mansfield Center, CT.

Stamatis, D. H. (1986). *Hierarchical and elaboration in an adult training*. Ph.D. Dissertation. Wayne State University. Detroit, MI.

Swassing, R. H., W. B. Barbe and M. N. Milone. (1979). *The Swassing-Barbe* Modality Index: Zaner-Bloser Modality Kit. Zaner-Bloser. Columbus, OH.

Taghioff, D. "Seeds of Consensus – The Potential Role for Information Technologies in Development." http://web.archive.org/web/20031012140402/http://www.btinternet.com/~daniel.taghioff/index.html. Retrieved on 2009-04-07.

CHAPTER 2

QUALITY IN EDUCATION

In the last chapter we addressed the purpose of education and gave some ideas of future improvement. In this chapter we are focusing on quality. As there are many anecdotal stories in many sectors of our country (including: students, parents, administrators, teachers, employers, government and society at large) that they feel that the educational process is broken, quality comes along and provides at least some hope for improvement of the process. Specifically, in this chapter we will discuss what quality does mean to education.

So what is "Quality in Education?" This is an interesting question, isn't it? It is likely that your definition of quality and mine is different, based on our background, knowledge, context and personal experiences. So when we talk about it, are we talking about the same thing? Probably, we are not.

Webster's definition of quality is "An inherent or distinguishing characteristic; a property." My definition of quality is "value as perceived by the customer." In other words, everyone has more or less "his own" definition of what quality really means. But who is the customer? In education, there is a problem in having an exclusive customer for we have several: Society, government, administrators, teachers, parents, employers and students. Generally, quality in education is defined by school districts (school boards, administrators, classroom logistics or teacher). This point is very important for all of us to understand. This is so, because unless "quality" can be defined, described as well as understood by all stakeholders, it won't be able to accomplish its mission, which of course is improvement.

To me, quality in education means being better tomorrow that we are today; being better next week, next month and next year than we are this week, this month and this year. This is of course the definition of sustainability. In other words, quality in education is a journey, defined by the individual and organization for some future improvement having started at a given point. In other words, success for improvement starts with "you" the individual person – whatever the position you hold is. This is shown in Figure 2.1. Continual improvement initiatives focus on student achievement, but *quality tools* are also extended to support services such as food and nutrition, community relations, transportation, accounting and all other projects and services, which play an integral role in creating a positive learning environment.

Educators need to be able to define quality and continual improvement in order to achieve it. It has been my experience that in education we "talk" quality without a clear understanding of what it really is. We say we're focused on continual improvement, without really being able to define what we mean. Until an organization can define quality and describe what continual improvement looks like, it won't be able to clearly set and communicate direction for future success with quality.

It is the responsibility of leadership to "paint a vivid picture" of what quality and continual improvement look like, sound like and feel like. It is only when stakeholders can define it and personalizes it, that they can achieve it. District leaders need to define it so it can be understood by school leadership teams. School leadership teams need to interpret it so it can be understood by classroom teachers. Society must define it so that objectives may be set to measure the improvement. Teachers need to define it and translate it so it can be understood by their students. Students must understand it so that they can put forth effort to participate and improve their performance in the set objectives that have been set for them and with them for improvement. Ultimately in the schools, students need to define quality and make a personal commitment to continual improvement.

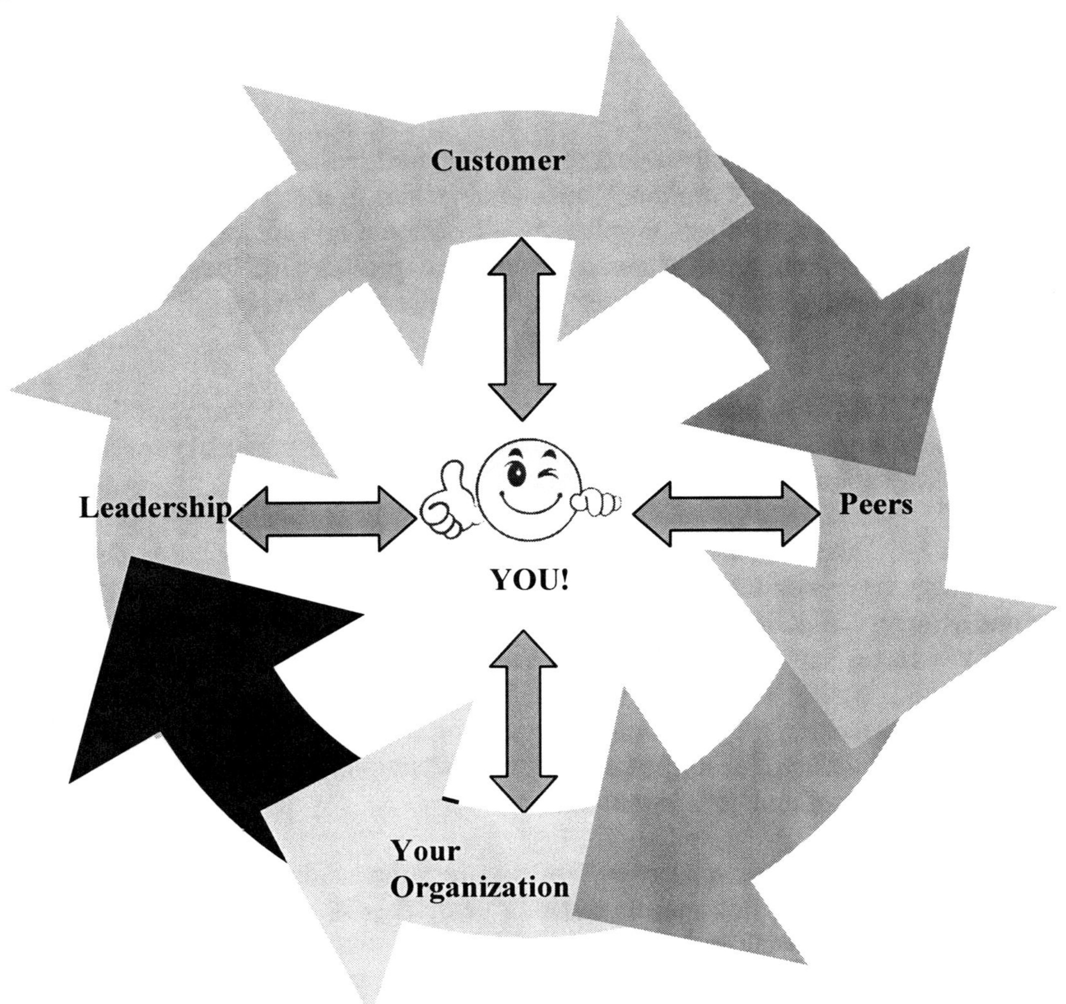

When all stakeholders define quality and continual improvement with consensus and make it theirs, real change occurs. Therefore, educational leaders need to make sure that when implementing continual improvement:

1. Clear expectations are set and communicated with *all* stakeholders.
2. There is a plan to create internal capacity and support for change.
3. There is a way to measure the deployment of continuous improvement.

The first two may be implemented with mission, vision, objectives and the third one with a specific instrument that can measure the improvement. This measurement serves as a way to be accountable for defining what they defined is happening, measuring the progress, and adopting systems of improvement. A typical model to follow for measurement is shown in Figure 2.2. If this measurement does not happen it is very difficult to use quality principles and proper questions to organize the work. In other words, with no measurement, there is a good probability that we would stay with the status quo or we would be doing unrelated planning. A typical measurement instrument is shown in Table 2.1. A more difficult and yet detailed approach to this measurement is the Baldrige (2011-2012) framework which provides a series of important questions, and regardless of the initiative at hand, the criteria's questions drive the process. The Baldrige framework does two things: a) It focuses on the process and b) holds leaders accountable for the decisions they make.

Table 2.1. A typical measurement instrument

Continual Improvement Elements and Components Implementation and Deployment Instrument		1	2	3	4	5
Mission, Vision and Alignment	**District Mission-** The District "Strategic Plan on a Page" is posted in the classroom data center (or work area). **School Mission-** A school mission statement has been created by staff and is displayed in the classroom data center (or work area). **Classroom Mission-** A classroom mission statement has been developed by the students and is displayed in the classroom data center (or work area). **Student Mission-** Individual student mission statements have been created and are included in the student's data folder in the classroom data center (or work area). **Ground Rules -** Classrooms ground rules have been developed by the students and are displayed in the classroom data center (or work area).					
Goal Setting	**Classroom Goals-** Classroom measurable goals have been established, are aligned to school improvement plan (SIP) goals and are displayed in the classroom data center (or work area). **Student Goals-** Individual students set goals for themselves. These goals are monitored, tracked and placed in the student data folder.					
Data and Feedback	**Comparative Data** – The use of comparative data (comparing class results to other classrooms in the school, district, State or Nation) in the classroom. **Classroom Data Center -** A Data Center has been created and is utilized to monitor and track student performance and when new data is available to the teacher, it is used to inform instruction. (Data centers may contain: SIP goals, District Strategic Plan, student-created ground rules, classroom mission statements, classroom goals, data and charts demonstrating progress toward classroom goals, student satisfaction data, etc.) **Classroom Feedback -** Customer feedback is collected from students and/or parents to improve classroom processes (e.g. fast feedback, plus/deltas or surveys). Summary results are displayed in the data center (or work area). **Classroom Data Folders -** Students utilize data folders to track and monitor their own performance in the classroom. (Student data folders may contain: classroom mission and goals, individual mission and goals, charts and graphs for individual student performance.) **Class Meetings -** Classroom meetings are held in the classroom on a regular basis. Students lead the meeting and facilitate the discussion around the progress of the class goals, measures and mission. Student feedback is used to drive the class meetings					
Quality Tools and Action Research	**Classroom Action Research** – The use of Action Research / plan, do, study, act (PDSA) in the classroom is used and it is publicly displayed in the classroom (or work area). **Classroom Tool Usage -** Quality tools are used. Evidence of quality tool usage is evident in the classroom (or work area). **Student Tool Usage -** Students use quality tools and some are displayed in the student data folder or in the classroom (or work area).					

Quality Processes	**Standardized Processes** - Key processes are standardized and communicated to stakeholders. Flow charts or other organizers of key processes are displayed in the classroom (or work area). **Quality Work** - Quality student work is discussed, recognized and celebrated. Common rubrics, standards and expectations are communicated to students and parents. **Student-Led Conferences** - Student-led conferences are held in the classroom. Students share progress with their parents through the use of the student data folder.					
Future Direction	• Based on the results, what are the key areas for improvement? • What is my (teacher specific) plan to improve in the identified areas? Use an action plan template to determine next steps.					
Legend	1 No- Not Present in my classroom 2 No- Thinking about it, but not yet Implemented 3 Yes- In the beginning stages of Implementation 4 Yes- Almost completely implemented 5 Yes- Completely Implemented					

Figure 2.2. A typical measuring model

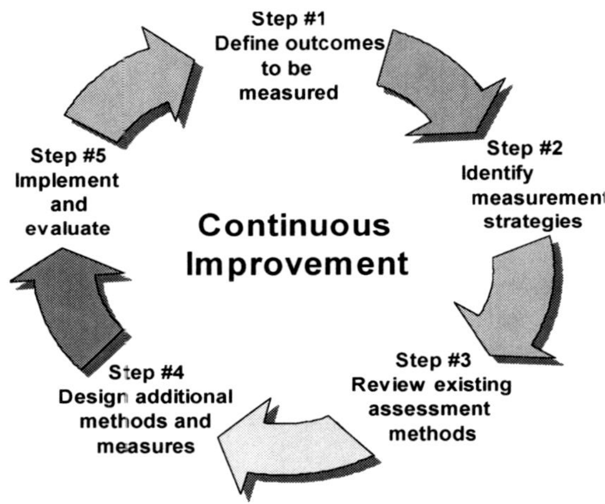

In any quality improvement initiative – especially in education - the strategic plan serves as a compass to the improvement efforts in the entire educational system whether it is a local district or college or a university. The reason for this, is because everyone works toward an aligned system that includes:

• The district's (college's or university's) strategic plan
• Department goals tied to the strategic plan
• School improvement plan (SIP) goals aligned to the district (college, university) plan
• Classroom goals aligned to the SIP goals
• Individual student goals aligned to classroom goals (see note 1)

To support systematic alignment, leaders must work to build the internal capacity to drive improvement in every corner of the district or college. Leadership teams from all schools and support departments participate in action research deployment team trainings, to learn about continuous improvement processes and tools and how to effectively manage the change process. The idea of these teams is to assist schools and departments in the use of action research as well as to facilitate sharing ideas and best practices.

16

For the systematic alignment to work effectively a variety of staff development opportunities must be offered. In addition, a heavy emphasis must be towards training in the continual improvement process using the Plan, Do, Study, Act (PDSA) cycle and other quality processes such as:

- **Analytical Skills:** *Applies logic in solving problems and analyzes problems from different points of views. Translates academic theory into practical applications and recognizes interrelationships among problems and issues.*
- **Communication:** *Articulates ideas in a clear and concise fashion and uses facts to reinforce their points. Written materials flow logically to enhance the reader's comprehension and are grammatically correct. Plans and delivers presentations effectively and uses presentation software packages to enhance their effectiveness.*
- **Creative Problem Solving:** *Develops many potential solutions while discouraging others from rushing to premature conclusions. Suggests new approaches and challenges the way things are normally done.*
- **Project Management:** *Sets goals, prioritizes tasks and meets project milestones. Seeks clarification of task requirements and takes corrective action based upon feedback from others. Creates action plans and timetables to complete assigned work.*
- **Research Skills:** *Uses computer based resources effectively thus acquiring information from multiple sources and organizes data into meaningful categories. Understands the importance of learning from work previously done.*
- **Self Learning:** *Learns independently and continuously exceeds basic requirements of an assignment. Demonstrates that they learn from their mistakes and those of others.*
- **System Thinking:** *Understands how events interrelate and demonstrates an ability to take new information and integrate it with past knowledge. Integrates and uses knowledge from various courses and sources to solve technical problems.*
- **Teamwork:** *Contributes a fair share to the completion of the project. Encourages everyone to participate, cooperates with the team members, shares information and helps reconcile differences of opinions among fellow team members.*
- **Technical Competence:** *Demonstrates a basic understanding of fundamental engineering principles and how the various engineering disciplines complement each other. Shows a basic understanding of design and manufacturing and how their classroom work applies to industry.*

A quality attitude in education is a fundamental aspect of the 21st century. It can provide a common language for comprehensive school wide improvement and systemic change. It can help in seeing what needs to be done and to promote ongoing improvement in all aspects of the educational process. Some of the specific things that it can do are:

- Continue inputting all measures of individual student learning data in the school database and utilizing the analyses at the classroom level.
- Continue to support teacher action research and peer coaching in order to implement the vision in an articulated fashion.
- Continue to measure actual student performance against the district and school standards.
- Follow the students into the middle school, high school, and beyond to ensure that their early education was as beneficial to them as it could be.
- Continue to support and implement the school wide plan, vision, shared decision making, and a continuum of learning that makes sense for all students.

- Follow and never lose sight of the guiding principles. The continual improvement and evaluation process will help us make sure we stay on target.

Note 1: A typical plan for student goals aligned to classroom goals:

- *Classroom ground rules:* Students create classroom expectations that all agree to follow in working to accomplish the mission of the classroom.
- *Classroom mission statements:* Students create a mission statement for the school year.
- *Classroom SMART goals:* Students participate in setting SMART (specific, measurable, attainable, results-oriented, and time-bound) goals that align with their school's improvement plan.
- *Classroom data centers:* Once goals are written in student-friendly language, students begin collecting data and monitoring progress.
- *Individual student data folders:* To connect every student to the classroom goals, each one maintains a data folder for tracking and measuring his or her progress toward those goals.
- *Classroom meetings:* Students use meetings as a forum to solve problems and modify the classroom system to improve results.
- *Student-led conferences:* Students are expected to be able to explain their progress by reviewing the contents of their data folders. The student, rather than the teacher, leads conferences with parents.
- *Quality tools and PDSA:* Students learn and apply quality tools and the PDSA cycle for improvement.

Summary

In this chapter we have discussed quality as it relates to education and have given examples as to where quality initiatives may be introduced at all levels of education. In the next chapter we will focus on leadership and its effect on the educational process.

References

Baldrige National Quality Program (2011-2012). *Education criteria for performance excellence: ethics, accomplishment, recognition.* National Institute of Standards and Technology. Technology Administration. Department of Commerce. Washington, DC.

Selected Bibliography

www. asq.org
www.quality.nist.gov/eBaldrige/Step_One.htm
http://www4.asq.org/ blogs/edu/.

CHAPTER 3

LEADERSHIP

In the last chapter we focused on the quality issues of education. In this chapter we focus on leadership and how it affects the educational process. Specifically we provide some guidelines for effectiveness such as innovation and Malcolm Baldrige criteria for performance excellence. In addition we provide some specific guidelines as to how a leader in education must be willing to be *bold* and *decisive in methods, policies* and *efficient ways of doing business.*

It has become common knowledge that the present conditions of our educational system (k-12 and post secondary) produce unacceptable problems which are finding greater acceptance. We are living in an ever-expanding mental, moral and social swamp. We are working from a faulty foundation consisting of evolution (man is a meaningless accident of nature, evolved from what?), communism (man is matter in motion and nothing more) and psycho-babble (man is told over and over again that he is not to be blamed for his actions; that he is not responsible). The ever-expanding swamp is further encouraged by needles for drugs, condoms for sex, counseling for irresponsibility, abortion for eliminating the unwanted, and euthanasia for removing the unneeded and mediocrity at the expense of excellence. Add to this the contamination of morality which makes for the approving of that which is wrong, attacking that which is right, abandoning historic and ethical common sense. Public laxity and apathy about the religious, educational, sexual, governmental unrealities does not encourage correcting our course. In fact, in some cases it encourages such behaviors. The result makes for frustrated and angry people who go to extreme ends to show the absence of a good societal foundation on which to stand.

To be sure, these are the ingredients for troubled people in troubling times. But then again it is the right time for *leadership*. It is time to introduce leadership in our education process that understands the problems and has a vision for a corrective course to follow. We talk about excellence but we practice mediocrity at best. We can see that in sports, academics and all social activities within our schools. We are afraid to identify excellence because someone else is going to get their feelings hurt. The absence of truth, integrity and responsibility has slipped away from a system that once was the envy of the world. Now we appease everyone by being politically correct at all costs. Everyone gets an award of sorts!

What can be done? Select individuals who administer the educational process with knowledge of leadership principles and willing to implement them, using quality principles. That means: individuals who are committed to excellence, understand the issues of education, and are responsive to learners, government, staff and society. A hundred years ago, at the dawn of the industrial revolution, public education adapted the production-line mentality to the education system with superb results (see note 2 - you will be amazed, if not shocked!). Everyone was and continuous to be expected to achieve a benchmark level of academic skills by a selected age. If they adapt, they are labeled gifted or successful, if they don't, they are labeled as having some kind of learning disability – an excuse of sorts. Somehow we have forgotten that every individual is different. It is impossible to make everyone conform to production-line standards. Today, 30% to 50% of our teenagers drop out of high school. It's not that they can't learn or don't want to. They are rejecting outdated education methods. Our education system needs to adapt to the 21st century. When motivated, people will learn and excel. Our young people are being academically stuffed while being motivationally starved. The learning disability label (in most cases) is a cover-up - boredom is the problem.

This boredom is an issue of leadership. Leadership style controls efficiency, which controls competitive value of product or service, which determines the winner. In the educational process we are stuck with an 18th century mentality focusing primarily on academic disciplines and ignoring other modes of learning.

What we need is a change in leadership that is willing to innovate and make education interesting and exiting for all learners. That leadership may be from the ranks of administrators, community, government and society at large.

The tendency to look for a leader either as a School superintendent or a president of higher learning institution from the political and the business sectors is likely to accelerate in the future. This is because the demands placed on the leadership of education have become blended between business and education policies, and outcomes. It is not uncommon for a leader to be measured based on performance based on internal policies rather than outcomes of learners. The performance based model encourages these leaders to drive up enrollments or reduce truancy, push for profitable rather than principled curricula changes, and respond to the board's or trustees concerns rather than to the voices of teachers, faculty, students in setting the agenda of their system.

We are well into an environment where the worst of corporate managerial style and strategy determines priorities in both research and teaching. Most important, the old tension between full-time administrators and full-time faculty members has become acute, and the balancing act that most presidents perform between their chief financial officers and their chief academic officers has by and large given way to rule by the CFO. As the economy spirals down, the voices of parsimony, thrift, and profit maximization will grow even stronger, and the capacity of academic leaders to shape the agenda of colleges will diminish sharply. This is a problem that local school boards, junior colleges, universities as well as private institutions face.

It is important, especially in the context of higher education, that we restore the idea that management is a tool and not an ideology. True, all our educational institutions need to be wise about long-term planning, about husbanding scarce resources, and about making wise bets about curriculum, facilities, and technology, as rapid change affects each of those matters. In fact, Appadurai (2009) suggests that it may well be time for American educational leaders to learn from the fields of design and planning, which have always had to balance the claims of art, engineering, and commerce in defining problems and crafting solutions. Planning and design may offer us more wisdom for creative educational management than the business-management ethos, which appears to have created far too much room for personal greed and the creation of socially catastrophic UFO's (unidentified financial objects).

To be sure, part of the objectives of excellent leadership is governance. In local boards most of the time we find average individuals without any background in education or finance or law or even how to run a business. However, we do find them very enthusiastic and committed to high level of excellence. The result of this lack in specific expertise about education forces them to focus their attention on the administration of the school district. As such, the community suffers and the issues turn out to be interpreted as lack of funding.

On the other hand, most college and university boards are composed largely of wealthy people, usually from the worlds of finance, law, and private enterprise. They are sometimes alumni but are often selected for their personal capacity to give, their links to other people who might give, or their historical record of having given. Many trustees today have in fact been part of the elite sectors of finance, law, and enterprise that have proven improvident, shortsighted, and badly governed. Can they be seen as the wisest of our wise that will bring both generosity and wisdom to the academy? Obviously many trustees have values and intellects that transcend their business skills. In some lucky educational institutions, those board members take care to respect the differences between the enterprises they own or manage and the educational institutions to which they serve as financial and policy stewards and, above all, as people to whom the president is accountable. But can we any more believe that the erstwhile masters of the economy are the best suited to be stewards of our most cherished educational institutions?

The exigencies of fund raising have created a gradual tendency to identify university stewardship almost completely with corporate leadership. Here colleges and universities may wish to learn something from the way American communities think about local school boards, which tends to reflect a deeper trust in the broad social intelligence of all Americans, of citizens from every walk of life who have earned the respect of their peers. After all, in aggregate, the hard-earned dollars of American parents, converted into tuition, are more vital to the overall financial health of American higher education than large private and corporate gifts, except in a small number of privileged institutions. If parents and ordinary citizens trust the leaders with their money, surely they can be expected to be as wise with the trusteeship of our colleges and universities.

Which way might we turn? It may be time to tack against the historical current by increasing the role of faculty members in hard financial decisions, by finding leaders for colleges who have a clear record of teaching and research accomplishments, and by building boards of trustees that also represent the worlds of art, public policy, medicine and foundations to temper the voices of those who come from the corporate world. It may also be time that we simply stop plotting the immediate turns in our route until we have discussed and formally agreed upon the destination of education at the level of concern (K-12, college or university). This of course, is an issue of educational strategy.

To be sure, education needs *leadership innovation*. This means that education is in dire need of *visionary leadership*. This is because *visionary leadership* increases efficiency by moving decision-making responsibility to the frontline. Efficiency is achieved with limited supervision. To make frontline responsibility effective, leadership must give to those who teach the opportunity to develop *quality decision-making skills* and learn to trust them.

One of the core values of the Baldrige Criteria for Performance Excellence is Visionary Leadership. Many educational systems have adopted this core value as their own (as for example the Cedar Rapids Community School District). However, to understand the visionary leadership, first we must define it then we can achieve it. In its simplest form it is an *educational platform* of sorts that incorporates the school's beliefs about the preferred aims, methods, and climate, thereby creating a *community of mind* that establishes behavioral norms. Another way of thinking about visionary leadership is to think of it as *an inspiring declaration of a compelling dream, accompanied by a clear scenario of how it will be accomplished.* A good vision not only has worthy goals, but also challenges and stretches everyone in the school. This aspect of visionary leadership is what makes organizations, including educational entities, advance. When a clear, widely understood vision creates tension between the real and the ideal, pushing people to work together to reduce the gap or to eliminate conflicting objectives, the result is always improvement.

Today, fast growing organizations in and out of education, are built on leadership innovation, that is, they are not built by product visionaries but by social visionaries - those who invent entirely new ways of organizing human effort, including education. When we talk about innovation in leadership we all must understand that:

- Every successful innovation is the result of a dreamer with a mission.
- Every new innovation replaces someone's previous innovation. A previous innovator may see it as a threat to their idea and work to prevent it.
- Job insecurity often kills innovation. Who in their right mind is going to innovate themselves out of a job?
- Experts who are familiar with a subject or problem often raise barriers to innovation. They tend to know all the reasons why something will not work. Their over familiarity and previous successes with a problem can blind them to seeing newer better ways to solve it. In education, perhaps this is

the most serious of all inherent problems as most of the *educators* are highly educated and offer specialized skills in their own disciplines.

- Innovators are wild ducks. When they believe in an idea, they will move impossible barriers to see their idea become a reality.
- Innovators can be impatient, nonconforming, intolerant, obnoxious, and extremely difficult to work with. Those are their good points, but they are essential to innovation.

To be sure, leadership style controls the workplace learning environment. Teachers' and administrators' attitudes towards learning affect workplace efficiency. Today's fast changing technology is forcing change in the schools, which requires learners to be in a full time learning mode. Organizations that can adapt new technology will be the leaders. Leadership in these organizations inspires *a love to learn*. These organizations have visionaries who are inventing new ways to develop and adapt employees' potential. They do not focus only on *command* and *control*, for this attitude and approach presupposes that the learners leave their brain at home and bring their body to work. Learners, who no longer have a desire to learn, control the system. All connections to expanding knowledge are broken, as they accept the status quo. They cannot adapt to changing technologies. The only connection to the knowledge base is the classroom.

Furthermore, command and control leadership produces a high level of exploding problems that no one was authorized or willing to deal with while at the basic level. The learners who are the front line, teachers who are first aware of potential problems, are not allowed to take action. Administrators are preoccupied with high priority events, usually a once minor problem that has exploded into a major event. Leaders are recognized for managing major problems, not minor ones. Leaders that spend time on basic problems get low efficiency ratings.

Leaders define their organization structure. In turn, that structure controls decision-making responsibility. Visionary leadership allows decision-making responsibility all the way down to the frontline. Standard leadership limits decision making to administrators. Leaders with vision are able to define and implement:

- *Priorities* – Organization priorities control leadership style. When priority is responsibility at the frontline, leadership will seek talent, people he can depend on to complete tasks with limited supervision. The policy will be "do it." The frontline develops quality decision-making skills that are also found in layers of management. When the priority is control, leadership will be organized in a way that all decisions must have approval. The policy will be "do not do anything until being told." Layers of management slow the final decision, while lowering efficiency.
- *Policies* - Leadership style is controlled by workplace policies. Leaders will adapt their style to the organization priorities and its goals. High efficiency workplaces are based on visionary leadership, where workplace policies authorize decision-making responsibility at the frontline. Limited supervision is needed with worker responsibility. Standard leadership is based on man's instinctive desire for control, which is leadership by default. A leader's changing mood controls policy of the moment and no one knows what the priorities are – mood-changing priorities reduce efficiency. Standard leadership requires a high level of supervision.
- *Elementary problems* - Leadership style controls the level of elementary problems, which controls workplace efficiency. Level of elementary problems is controlled, in part, by learning opportunities and leader's personal priority. Decision-making responsibility, at all levels, allows minor problems to be solved by those who are first aware of them. Management can stay focused on problems related to the organization goals. As a bonus, employee motivation is high when they feel what they are doing makes a difference. A leader's desire for control prevents minor problems from being solved, because no one can make a decision without approval. Leaders' priorities are based on high visibility events. As employees adjust work habits to minor problems, they become accepted as normal. The

volume of these problems slowly grows and the workforce slowly becomes less efficient. Administrators blame the teachers and or staff for their lack of ability to get the job done. Assigning blame without responsibility solves nothing.

- *Learning opportunity* - Quality of worker decisions is controlled by workplace learning opportunities. Learning to make quality decisions is the result of worker responsibility, resulting in the development of personal skills. An experienced workforce prevents elementary problems. Continual learning opportunity is highly motivating—it controls employee inspiration, skill level and quality. People, who only follow orders, do not have learning opportunity, do not develop personal skills and do not learn quality decision making. A workforce that is indifferent to the needs of the organization increases elementary problems. Workers learn no more than necessary to their job.

It is of paramount importance here to mention that a *Leader as Teacher* is not about "teaching" people how to achieve their vision. It is about fostering learning, for everyone. Such leaders help people throughout the organization develop systemic understandings. Accepting this responsibility is the antidote to one of the most common downfalls of otherwise gifted teachers – losing their commitment to the truth (Senge 1990).

Educators have been addressing change for a long time, and very intensively for the past 15 years. In fact, the problem is that, reform efforts have dealt with practically every instructional issue one-at-a-time and still we persist in our belief that schools are not performing as well as we would like and are in need of additional reforms. This reform cycle is jokingly referred to as "flavor of the month."

Systemic change offers an opportunity to enact change while moving beyond thinking about individuals and individual organizations, single problems and single solutions. It entails thinking about systems – policy systems, education systems, social service systems, information systems, and technology systems and so on.

Systemic change is a cyclical process in which the impact of change on all parts of the whole and their relationships to one another are taken into consideration. In the contexts of schools, it is not so much a detailed prescription for improving education as a philosophy advocating reflecting, rethinking, and restructuring – a vision of sorts by the leadership of the system. Essentially, systemic change entails working with stakeholders throughout the system to:

- Take stock of the current situation.
- Create a vision of what you want the system to look like and accomplish.
- Identify strengths and weaknesses of the current system in light of the vision.
- Target several priority items for improvement.
- Establish a plan for addressing these priority items and for measuring success.
- Assess progress regularly and revise actions as needed.
- Take stock again and use feedback to revisit vision and begin cycle again when the action cycle is completed.

An excellent leader then must be willing to be *bold* and *decisive in methods, policies* and *efficient ways of doing business*. He can accomplish these things by having:

- *Adequate yearly progress report (AYPR)*: Even though this is a government mandate it should also be an internal ritual to be used as a benchmark for any progress. (AYPR is a statewide accountability system mandated by the No Child Left Behind Act of 2001 which requires each state to ensure that all schools and districts make Adequate Yearly Progress). The overarching goal is for all students to meet or exceed standards in reading and mathematics by 2014. Each year, the state will calculate a school or district's Adequate Yearly Progress (AYP) to determine if students are improving their performance based on the established annual target. The overarching goal is for all students to meet or exceed standards in reading and mathematics by 2014.

- *Value-added assessment:* This is a way of analyzing test data that can measure teaching and learning. Based on a review of students' test score gains from previous grades, researchers can predict the amount of growth those students are likely to make in a given year. Thus, value-added assessment can show whether particular students - those taking a certain Algebra class, say - have made the expected amount of progress, have made less progress than expected, or have been stretched beyond what they could reasonably be expected to achieve. Using the same methods, one can look back over several years to measure the long-term impact that a particular teacher or school had on student achievement.
- *Program evaluation:* This is not new but is necessary for any leader in education to understand it and use it as much as possible. A change will not occur in any educational system unless the system under the guidance of its leader encourages it to transform itself into learning organization. The evaluation plan should at least embody the attributes of a learning organization as espoused by Senge and *et al.* (2000). By relying upon *formative*, as well as *summative evaluation*, the implementation process will inform the design process. The result will be a program that enables school districts to better chart their own course, while continuing to meet external expectations for progress.

The dimension that distinguishes the *new* learning from more traditional organizations is the mastery of certain basic disciplines or 'component technologies.' The five that Senge (1990, 1990a, 2000,) identifies are said to be converging to innovate learning organizations. They are:

1. *Systems thinking*: Systems thinking is a way of helping a person to view systems from a broad perspective that includes seeing overall structures, patterns and cycles in systems, rather than seeing only specific events in the system.
2. *Personal mastery*: Peter Senge says, "Personal mastery goes beyond competence and skills…it means approaching one's life as a creative work, living life from a creative as opposed to a reactive viewpoint." In a sense he links personal mastery to effective leadership stating, "The core leadership strategy is simple: be a model. Commit yourself to your own personal mastery." Personal mastery then is about creating what one wants in life and in work. Continually expanding personal mastery is a discipline based on a number of key principles and practices: personal vision, personal purpose, holding creative tension between vision and current reality, mitigating the impact of deeply rooted beliefs that are contrary to personal mastery, commitment to truth, and understanding the subconscious. Practitioners of personal mastery exhibit the following characteristics:

   - They have a sense of purpose that lies behind their goals.
   - Their vision is more like a calling than a good idea.
   - They see current reality as an ally, not an enemy.
   - They are committed to seeing reality increasingly accurately.
   - They are extremely inquisitive.
   - They do not resist, but work with, the forces of change.
   - They feel connected to others and to life itself.
   - They feel that they are part of a larger creative process that they can influence but cannot unilaterally control.

3. *Mental models*: A mental model is a visual representation of external reality, in your mind. When applied appropriately, it plays a major role in our decision-making.

24

4. *Building shared vision*: It is the leader who has the vision for the future and it is his responsibility to share it with others in the organization. Share vision, according to Senge, presumes that every organization has a destiny, a "deep purpose" that expresses the organization's reason for existence. An important element of this vision is that whereas the vision is the decision of the leader, in fact it has emerged from many people that hold similar understandings of the organization's purpose – within the organization. The leader, by asking the questions and learning to listen carefully to the answers, the sense of shared vision grows. The key is to design in a process in which people at every level of the organization, in every role, can speak openly about what really matters to them and really be heard. As this happens, a creative tension emerges between the espoused theory and the pictures of what's wanted, juxtaposed with current reality.

5. *Team learning*: Team learning focuses on the transmission of both tacit and explicit knowledge throughout the group as well as the creation of an environment in which focused creativity can flourish. It is an educational method that strives to increase student engagement (Michaelsen, *et al* 2002). I suggest the following principles guide the formation of the teams of learners in addition to what (Michaelsen, *et al.* 2002) have identified:

   - *Groups Must Be Properly Formed and Managed.* Team size should be 5-7 members with even distribution of member characteristics across groups.
   - *Students Must be Made Accountable.* "Students must be accountable for (a) individually preparing for group work, (b) devoting time and effort to completing group assignments, and (c) interacting with each other in productive ways" (Michaelsen, *et al* 2002).
   - *Team Assignments Must Promote Both Learning and Team Development.* Most of the reported "problems" with learning groups (free-riders, member conflict, etc.) are the direct result of inappropriate group assignments. Assignments that require groups to make decisions and enable them to report their decisions in a simple form, will usually generate high levels of group interaction." (Michaelsen, *et al* 2002).
   - *Students Must Receive Frequent and Immediate Feedback.* It is the feedback that is used as the correcting barometer to the appropriate learning as part of the team learning. Feedback may be use by the learners themselves or the teachers. It must be always on the issue at hand and never on the person.

Senge (1990) adds to these five the recognition that people are agents, able to act upon the structures and systems of which they are a part. All the disciplines are, in this way, concerned with a shift of mind from seeing parts to seeing wholes, from seeing people as helpless reactors to seeing them as active participants in shaping their reality, from reacting to the present to creating the future.

To be sure a good leader must be a visionary, pragmatist, knowledgeable, convincing and have authority and responsibility to carry his vision through the educational system that he is working with. So what are some of the critical issues that a good leader must possess and be knowledgeable about as far as quality is concerned? Among the many requirements we believe that the following are the core ones:

Systems thinking: A leader in the educational environment (K-12, College or University) must be able to think in a system approach. A system may be considered to be a nucleus of elements structured in such a manner as to accomplish a function to satisfy an identified need. [A system may also vary in form, fit and function. Example: a world communication network, a group of aircraft accomplishing a mission at a designated geographical location, or a small ship transporting cargo from one location to another. On the other hand, examples of a functional system are: an educational system, a financial system, a quality system, a purchasing, a design system and so on]. The elements of a system include all equipment, related facilities, material, software, data, services and personnel required for its operation and support, to the degree that it can be considered a self sufficient entity in its intended operational environment throughout its planned life cycle.

A systems approach relates all the educational activities to the support of a system and includes the elements of test and support equipment, supply support, personnel and training, transportation and material handling, special facilities, computer resources, data and so on, necessary for the accomplishment of breakthrough innovations in design of process, product and or service. In the educational system this means understanding of all pieces to make them work in the most efficient way *to produce learning at its best*. It is imperative that the experimenter; educator; administrator; legislator; board member when pursuing improvements within the educational process must have in mind that a holistic approach be taken, so that all interactions and interfaces be accounted for. The more aware the experimenter, educator, administrator, legislator, board member is about the parameters, interactions and the interfaces of the undertaken study, the greater the chance of success.

Advanced Product Quality Planning (APQP): APQP is a formal process of planning. It is also called Advanced Quality Planning (AQP). However, before we address the "why" of planning, we assume that things do go wrong. But why do they go wrong? Obviously, there are many specific answers that address this question. Often the answer falls into one of these four categories:

1. We never have enough time, so things are omitted.
2. We have done this, this way, so we minimize the effort.
3. We assume that we know what has been requested, so we do not listen carefully.
4. We assume that because we finish a project, improvement will indeed follow, so we bypass the improvement steps.

In essence then, the customer appears satisfied, but a product, service, or process is not improved at all. This is precisely why it is imperative for organizations to look at quality planning as a totally integrated activity that involves the entire organization. The organization must expect changes in its operations by employing cross-functional and mufti-disciplinary teams to exceed customer desires-not just meet requirements. A quality plan includes, but is not limited to:

- A team to manage the plan
- Timing to monitor progress
- Procedures to define operating policies
- Standards to clarify requirements
- Controls to stay on course
- Data and feedback to verify and to provide direction
- Action plan to initiate change

Advanced quality planning (AQP), then, is a methodology that yields a quality plan for the creation of a process, product, or service consistent with customer requirements. It allows for maximum quality in the workplace by planning and documenting the process of improvement (Stamatis 1998). AQP is the essential discipline that offers both the customer and the supplier a systematic approach to quality planning, to defect prevention, and to continual improvement. Some specific uses are:

- Education suppliers are expected to demonstrate the ability to participate in early design activities from concept through prototype and on to learning.
- Quality planning is initiated as early as possible, well before any implementation.

- Planning for quality is needed particularly when the educational administration and management establishes a policy of "prevention" as opposed to "detection."
- When a leader uses the principles of advanced quality planning, he provides for the organization the appropriate and applicable resources needed to accomplish the quality improvement task.
- Early planning prevents waste (scrap, rework, and repair), identifies required specification changes, improves timing for new product and or service introduction, and lowers costs.
- To facilitate communication with all individuals involved in a program and ensure that all required steps are completed on time at acceptable cost and quality levels.
- To provide a structured tool for management that enforces the inclusion of quality principles in program planning.

When do we use AQP? In our modern world we are looking for "true" breakthrough approaches for satisfying the customer with something "better" than the status quo. AQP is the vehicle for measuring this breakthrough approach from very early on (concept stage) all the way to implementation. Therefore, we use AQP when we need to meet or exceed expectations in the following situations:

- During the development of new processes and products.
- Prior to changes in processes and products.
- When reacting to processes or products with reported quality concerns.
- Before any change is transferred to new situations or new classrooms.
- Prior to process or product changes affecting product safety or compliance to regulations (if applicable).

The supplier – as in the case of certification programs like ISO 9000 - is to maintain evidence of the use of defect prevention techniques prior to production launch. The defect prevention methods used are to be implemented as soon as possible in the new product development cycle. It follows then, that the basic requirements for appropriate and complete AQP are:

1. Team approach.
2. Systematic development of products/services and processes.
3. Reduction in variation (this must be done, even before the customer requests improvement of any kind).
4. Development of a control plan.

As AQP is continuously used in a given organization, the obvious need for its implementation becomes stronger and stronger. That need may be demonstrated through:

- Minimizing the present level of problems and errors.
- Yielding a methodology that integrates customer and supplier development activities as well as concerns.
- Exceeding present reliability/durability levels to surpass the competition's and customer's expectations.
- Reinforcing the integration of quality tools with the latest management techniques for total improvement.
- Exceeding the limits set for cycle time and delivery time.
- Developing new and improving existing methods of communicating the results of quality processes for a positive impact throughout the organization.

Managing Change: Certainly an important issue in today's educational environment is change. Therefore, an excellent leader must recognize it and know how to handle it. A typical anatomy of a change for the educational leader is the following:

- *Step 1*: Identify the external and internal drivers. This means that the leader must be able to recognize the needs of the educational system and plan accordingly.
- *Step 2*: Identify the change. This means that a determination of key elements of the change must be identified and planned for. In essence this step requires: a) analysis of the current state - where we are now - through a needs assessment b) define the state where we want to be and c) assess the actual change (is it applicable, appropriate, cost effective and worth doing).
- *Step 3*: Prepare to change: This means that all key stakeholders have been accounted for as well as the sponsors, change agents (sometimes consultants) and the specific targets of change have been identified. Furthermore in this stage the determination of the degree of risk and the cost of the change is evaluated based on a) history b) culture and c) resistance.
- *Step 4*: Plan the change: This means that specific effort is taking place for designing the change system. Specific items of concern are to develop: a) communication system b) learning system and c) reward system.
- *Step 5*: Implement the change: This means that specific change strategies and tactics are indeed designed into an overall change plan for success.
- *Step 6*: Monitor the change: This means that the results of the change are being watched (monitored) and measured as the change is changing the system.

Of course, radical change was not possible until recently. There have always been inspired educator leaders who dreamed of new forms of learning. The primary reason their dreams could not be turned into practice was a lack of understanding the process of change and a suitable technology. For example as recently as five years ago, it would have been hard to imagine all children working in the spirit we see in the following scenario: A perfectly average 10-year-old, call her Jamey, is pursuing a passionate interest in creating complex computer art which she exchanges across the Internet with a small community of like-minded young people scattered across the globe. The real wonder is that she is using some very advanced mathematical principles that she learned by exchanging ideas as well as products with the same group. Today such things are beginning to happen. In five years time it will be commonplace for learning to take place through the pursuit of passionately held personal interests. Technology makes it possible to open new directions for learning. We can do it. However, there are three imperatives for this change to happen:

1. *The Economic Imperative*: Digital technology in the workplace requires a new definition of "basic skills." The transformation of work requires much more than a mastery of a fixed curriculum inherited from past centuries. Success in the slowly changing worlds of past centuries came from being able to do well what you were taught to do. Success in the rapidly changing world of the future depends on being able to do well what you were not taught to do. Already a great number of Americans are doing jobs and using skills that did not exist when they went to school - soon it will be the majority.
2. *The Social Imperative*: As the slow evolution of school lags further and further behind the rapid evolution of society, increasing numbers of students all over the world see school as irrelevant to life. Many drop out. Many more drop out mentally, emerging from school with poor skills and negative visions of themselves and the society they are entering.
3. *The Moral Imperative*: Because of our technology we can restructure our education system. Because of our commitment to democracy we must do it. The image of Jamey acquiring powerful knowledge previously inaccessible to all children puts a spotlight on new ways in which privilege breeds greater privilege. Having a personal computer and the freedom to use it to follow personal learning gives

Jamey access to a new world of knowledge. If some are left out, the gap between the "haves" and the "have nots" will grow exponentially.

Waiting to take advantage of these will only increase the difficulty and the cost. The spread of digital technology into every other sector of society makes it inevitable that it will eventually permeate school. Eventually, every student - and most pre-school children - will have more computing power than any professor of computer science has today.

Indeed, already most home computers have more power than any professor had thirty years ago. And when children grow up with this kind of knowledge - technology it is inconceivable that school will not change very radically. So the choice is not whether we will consider deep changes in school but how many children will be lost before we recognize that we have to do so. That cultural dilemma is a leadership issue, which must be solved by a strong and persuasive leader.

A successful leader must recognize and do something about the proliferation of technology but he also must be aware that *all change is a process*. Therefore, in order for that process to work he must be cognizant of all the stakeholders and always remember the following:

- *Remember the marketing basics.* Product, price, place and promotion (4Ps) are all important. All should be researched before and after the change is considered and implemented into the educational system to ensure that the value proposition meets and continues to meet the target's market needs. (Remember that the target is your specific stakeholder = customer = constituency; and market is the system that you operate *i.e.*, school district, college or university).
- *Patience.* Patience is required when applying the marketing basics to the educational system. Local stakeholders will take time to be convinced that the new change has the local credentials to meet their needs.
- *Listen.* Only by listening will you be able to understand and meet the local system's needs. Most educational stakeholders do not want to buy a product or service that has come straight off a shelf, from someone else's situation. Rather they want to be assured that they are unique and the change they are about to embark upon is "just" for them. They want to feel special and unique.
- *Relationships.* Any leader must be prepared to be "friends" with the stakeholders and specific customers within the educational system. It is imperative for change to work relationships must be developed and cultivated. Relationships build trust and integrity. However, this is as well as, not instead of, the 4Ps.
- *Be confident in your quality.* A leader must start from a strong position in the issues, quality initiatives as well as knowledge. However, the focus must always be on the value that is going to be added due to the change and he must also be prepared to explain why the change will result in a value added gain in specific terms.
- *Be methodical, but flexible.* One of the major characteristics of change is unexpected changes and or unforeseen circumstances regardless of planning. Therefore, a leader with a vision for introducing change of any kind in any environment within the educational system must be methodical but also very flexible to account for impromptu events.
- *Be prepared for plenty of negotiation.* In any educational system the leader must always remember that the majority of his stakeholders are highly educated and in some cases experts in their fields (this is true especially in the institutions of Higher Learning). This means that the leader must be able to handle and complete the deals of change based on several rounds of negotiations. This may be true due to a vast diversity of stakeholders, experiences and interests and so on. The leader should not lose faith in his vision or purpose due to small set backs (if they do happen) but rather continue

on his mission to complete the change. It is almost inconceivable that the first proposal of change will be accepted without any discussion or debate.

- *Avoid exaggeration.* In proposing a change the leader must "sell" the change but he must also be very aware of exaggerations. He should focus on his own credentials and the merits of the change proposed rather than exaggerating to make up for perceived deficiencies. All stakeholders want above all to trust their leaders. But that trust is not a given. It must be won.

Teams: An old Yiddish proverb says that "the girl who can't dance says the band can't play." In the work environment we find quite often that we project failures to anything that makes sense at the time. For some reason, we go to great lengths to find justification of failure(s) rather than look no further than the individuals involved and their behavior as a team.

Improvement in any shape or form is built upon teams. Without a team effort, nothing will be accomplished. Therefore, a team building effort must be initiated before any improvement effort takes hold of any specific project. But what is a team building? Team building is the process of taking a collection of individuals with different needs, background and expertise and transforming them by various methods into an integrated, effective work unit. This implies that developing a cohesive team requires developing a set of norms for behavior that might be different from the norms the team members are accustomed to using. That means that the team must work together to develop an initial project plan. The usual process for this development is a) initiation b) idealization c) iteration and d) implementation. While this developing is taking place, we must also recognize that the team itself is going through a transformation through the following stages: a) forming b) storming c) norming d) performing and e) closuring.

It is the responsibility of a leader to encourage the formation of teams and their cultivation throughout the system. However, as important as teams are in the educational process the leader must recognize that all project teams are transitory. That means that team members may move in and out when their assigned tasks are completed. Project teams also have structure. Team structure determines patterns of interaction among team members, with a stakeholder, with the product being developed and so on. Finally, how a team is structured determines a project's success. This is why the team formation must be designed in such a way that the team efficiency is enhanced. Efficiency, of course, is the ratio of output to input. (This may be interpreted as teams should be cross functional and multi disciplined, so that the ratio is always larger than 1.)

In a project environment input consists of team members and other resources. Output consists of work performed and goals accomplished. Inefficiency in teams is attributable to many factors, however, two of the major factors are:

1. *Poor team structure.* Projects that are organized based on the matrix structure (while offering many advantages) have built-in inefficiencies. Team membership is temporary. Time lost in learning the work done by others. (Recommendation: Keep team membership stable.) A second issue one has to be cognizant about is the fact that sometimes the specific stakeholder may not control resources directly. When that happens, more time is spent in acquiring human and material resources. (Recommendation: The leader should make it a practice to engage in pre-planning).
2. *Team friction.* By definition a team is a system comprised of many interrelated parts. Therefore, the pieces have to be brought together. If team effort is not properly integrated team inefficiencies will abound. To avoid this situation make sure that the team's configuration closely reflects the structure of the deliverable.

In both cases, poor communication is a major component of the failure. After all, information is the lifeblood of projects and communicating this information is essential to project success. There are many

30

ways of communication based friction that contribute to team inefficiency. For example: Communication as an end rather than means. In other words, in the process of communicating we use too many channels or too much time and effort at the expense of actually doing something. This of course, is indicative of a too bureaucratic system, failure to separate important from routine information, and or garbled messages.

To understand the effectiveness of a team we must understand what prevents a team from being effective. In our estimation, there are four major barriers to effective team building. They are:
1. *Differing outlooks of team members.* The strategy to eliminate or at least to minimize this barrier may be based on a) getting to know your people early in the project b) blending individual interests with team and organizational objectives c) defining responsibilities clearly and without any ambivalence and d) stressing the "team" concept.
2. *Role conflict(s).* The strategy to eliminate or at least to minimize this barrier may be based on a) asking team members where they see themselves fitting into the project b) conducting regular status meetings and c) handling any conflicts directly.
3. *Project objectives not clear.* The strategy to eliminate or at least to minimize this barrier may be based on a) developing and publicizing a clear set of project objectives b) communicating frequently with team members and c) checking for understanding
4. *Lack of management support.* The strategy to eliminate or at least to minimize this barrier may be based on a) involving management in project reviews b) keeping management well informed, not included and c) telling management what you need.

So, how then may we go about building effective teams? The following practical guidelines maybe of help (Stamatis 2003a):

- Eliminate "back home" behavior by establishing group norms.
- Develop "group mind" phenomenon common set of objectives and motives shared by the group.
- Recognize implicit contract (*i.e.* establish mutual experiences).
- Avoid "neglected resource" syndrome (*i.e.* retiring expert whose views are never heard or never noticed because participation is low. Devise ways to make participation mandatory).
- Beware of "hidden agendas" of team members.
- Build trust (in evolving a realistic plan ask each person to make trade offs, state contributions and so on. If they stay true to these contributions, it will build trust.

Communication skills: The fifth core requirement of any leader but especially one in the education system is the ability to communicate clearly. To identify effective communication skills and channels has never been more important than today in our hectic, fragmented world. While there are undoubtedly thousands of books written, papers published and philosophies espoused about how to communicate effectively, here we will try to focus on four basic items that a leader – especially in an educational environment - must understand. These four items are critical for effectiveness in any communication situation. They are: a) comprehension, b) connection, c) credibility and d) contagiousness. Together they capture what everyone connected with the project needs to know about customer response to stimuli. Separately, they provide clarity for us (as leaders) and our stakeholders, and a simple way to categorize the individual customer response. The simplicity of these four items is their power; it is easy to remember them and easy to use. It can lead to better creative executions and stronger business results.

- *Comprehension*: Here the main concern is: Is the main message clearly communicated? Simply put, do the stakeholders get it? On the surface, this is a simple assessment of whether the intended message is being understood. Simple, in theory, but not always easy to achieve, because sometimes different stakeholders have different perceptions of what they hear. The idea of comprehension from a leader's perspective is to make sure that the message is direct and easily understood without any misunderstandings or having a message with more than one interpretation. Stakeholders no matter who they are don't have the time to second guess. No matter what category of the customer we are talking about, everyone is willing to listen to the message, but they are not willing to work hard to get it.

- *Connection*: Here the main concerns are: Does the message resonate with the stakeholders? Is it persuasive? Does it communicate the specific need? Does it motivate completion of the communication agenda? These are all critical questions in determining the extent to which any form of communication connects with its intended audience. To be sure, connection is often an emotional response - something that is felt but can't be explained. For connection to take place trust, and integrity must be projected by the communicator and a genuine rapport must have been established between the communicator and the specific customer. The connection occurs when the customer perceives the message as a personal one. At this juncture connecting with the customer means that the leader has begun to establish a relationship with them via the communication tone, message itself and presentation. And how valuable is that? It means something you said or showed to them has resonated - has reached them on some internal level, whether that's - in a rational or irrational way - and so the communication resonates too.
- *Credibility*: Here the main concerns are: Does it make sense for the leader to speak to customers in a certain way? Is the tone and manner consistent with the leader's position based on their experience with and understanding of the customers needs? How do you know? If the message isn't credible, if it doesn't conform to the intent of the message and does not sound truthful, it's meaningless. The stakeholders need to believe who is saying it, what is being said and how it's being said. Otherwise any connection previously established immediately begins to break down. Credibility leads to believability and believability leads to persuasion and persuasion leads to action. So even if it's not instantly credible, it becomes credible because the audience can see a way to make the message fit. That counts too. Credibility also is an issue of:
    - *Who*: Does it make sense for the leader to speak to its audience in this way? Does it logically fit, given the equity the message has for the agenda at hand?
    - *What*: Is it something the audience expects from this message? This could be good and bad. If it's something expected, it could likely get glossed over or even ignored outright. It may fit, but if it's just "same-old," there better be enough going on in the areas of communication and connection (and contagiousness) to make up for too-smooth a fit.
    - *How*: An unexpected message or delivery can bring a lot of energy and attention to the stakeholders, especially if its history or heritage or equity gives it a flair or urgency and significance.
- *Contagiousness*: Here the main concerns are: Is there a sense of energy around the message and the way it is executed? Does it offer a new way to view the situation or category? Is it competitively differentiating? Is there something innately memorable about it? Does it evoke a vivid emotional response? Might it have talk potential (it may not always be positive talk)? Does it motivate the target to do something? Does it elicit some kind of highly-charged, demonstrable and visible reaction? When the stakeholders are responding to the message, then you know the communication is on its way to becoming an unqualified success. When a message truly resonates with its customers in a profound way, there tends to be a residual contagiousness effect. They simply can't help thinking about it or mentioning it in conversation.

Training: The final core of modern day leadership is the issue of training. In today's world training is essential. In education it is just as important for new things are always being introduced in the learning process but also in administrative, and management domains of the system. Training is an issue of leadership because it is woven into the strategic plan of the organization. The strategic plan is indeed one of

32

the functions of leadership. As such, if the mark is missed, success will be elusive. The components of the strategic training are:

1. *Goal setting and planning.* When executives decide that the specific training methodology is the "way" of doing business, everyone should know how to set goals and how those goals are related to each other. In addition, part of the planning stage in the training implementation process is to decide whether or not the training is going to be on a standard basis or an accelerated approach. It is very common that a lot of training is being conducted on an accelerated mode and quite often in split sessions rather than a continual one *e.g.* after work hours for several days or split week ends). In either case the training produces the same results.
2. *Basic business skills.* Especially the executives and champions must be aware of the consequences of selecting projects and their return on investment (ROI) so that smarter and profitable decisions may be made. (The reader must recognize here that the ROI is not only for financial returns. It can also be for effectiveness).
3. *Adaptability.* Especially for administrators and champions, cross training is a way to build respect and understanding that results in a more productive environment. Adaptability enhances creativity and encourages "outside the box" thinking.
4. *Technical skills.* Generally, this is the focal point of most training in any educational environment. Important to be sure, but not the only ones. In the educational environment, these skills are the unique requirements that will make or break the project. Without appropriate knowledge of what is available and how you can use what is available the goal will not be reached.
5. *Problem solving tools and skills.* This is the component that most organizations committed to improvement should emphasize, they should make sure that all employees have a good understanding of critical thinking, root cause analysis, and applied (basic) statistics. These skills can eliminate inertia when employees come upon obstacles that might paralyze a less educated employee.
6. *Interpersonal skills.* These are also known as *communication skills.* Speaking, listening and conflict management are the foundations of interpersonal skills and very important elements in the pursuit of the improvement process.
7. *Ability and style of mental processing and external interaction.* An effective training and development strategy without this component would be like conducting an orchestra without knowledge of which instruments the musicians play and how well they play them. It is imperative for executives and champions in the improvement process to know their players (teachers, department heads, learners, employees and so on) so that they can help not only in developing training but also in making smarter choices in terms of project assignment.

In addition to these core items the modern educational leader should be aware of the following:

Cost of quality: For the first time in our history, parents, teachers, school board members and legislators have the tools they need to make informed, fact-based choices. One of the most powerful of these tools is the Quality Education Model (QEM), which we already have mentioned. Developed in the late 1990s and recently updated and refined, the QEM provides a detailed framework for understanding what it takes - and how much it costs - to provide students with a quality education. As you recall, the Oregon's Educational Act for the 21st Century sets statewide standards for student performance and establishes high levels of accountability for schools and districts. The Oregon Constitution requires the Legislature to appropriate enough money to make sure the state's school system meets these goals. And the QEM provides the "road map" for getting there. The Quality Education Commission was formed in 1997 to answer three questions:

1. What is quality education?
2. How much does it cost?

3.   What results can we expect if we spend the money?

As important as this initiative is, leaders have also a quality tool to investigate and account for their cost in education through a Cost of Quality. The leader of the specific educational entity has the responsibility to know, allocate and evaluate costs on a priority basis. Furthermore he has the responsibility to account for inefficiencies of cost in their system. This is where Cost of Quality (COQ) plays a role.

In today's world all educational systems demand quantification of improvement. In order for that quantification to materialize there must exist in the organization a system for identifying the cost associated with problems, inefficiencies and in general customer dissatisfaction. As it turns out, the system most often responsible for such tracking is called Cost of Quality (COQ). With COQ in any organization (manufacturing and non manufacturing alike) quality and improvement may be measured at the same time. However, within the cost of quality, there are two categories that define the structure and reporting of that cost. They are:

1.   Avoidance costs
2.   Total failure costs

These two categories comprise the two operating curves used for achieving the break-even point of the quality costs. Avoidance costs and total failure costs are broken down further into two categories in each area. They are:

Avoidance costs: They are all costs associated with avoiding a failure. A failure here is anything that does not meet requirements (specifications) set by legislature, school board, administration and so on. These costs fall also into two categories. They are:

a. *Appraisal costs* - are those expenditures that an organization makes to examine the levels of quality at which products and or services are being produced. If the product or service quality level is satisfactory, the process is allowed to continue, if the quality level is unsatisfactory, the process is suspended until effective corrective action has been implemented and the process has returned to satisfactory quality level. Examples are: All inspection and associated expenses (need assessments); inspector's wages and fringe benefits; laboratory test technicians wages, salaries and fringe benefits; test samples for destructive testing; laboratory materials consumed in the process testing; laboratory tooling expenses; the portion of direct labor wages devoted to performing statistical process control (SPC), inspections and tests within the process; process capability studies.

b. *Prevention costs* - are those expenditures an organization makes to keep from producing defective or unacceptable product or service. Examples are: All training; quality assurance wages, salaries and fringe benefits; cost of design changes incurred prior to releases for production (formative evaluation); the portion of product design engineering devoted to quality assurance (summative evaluation); cost of processing changes incurred prior to releases for production (pilot studies).

These avoidance cost categories are in the case of appraisal costs expected to discover and correct problems after the problems surface. On the other hand, prevention costs are intended to be applied before the fact of producing defective product.

Total failure costs: These are costs associated with a product and or service that fails after implementation has occurred. These costs fall also into two categories. They are:

a. *Internal failure costs* - are those costs incurred by an organization while it still has ownership of the product. Examples are: Scrap; waste in process; rework charges; repair charges; learner's failures.

b. *External failure costs* - are those costs incurred by an organization after it has transferred ownership of the product to its customer, the customer has received and originally accepted the product. Examples are: Warranty costs; returned goods; design error; marketing error; cost to society associated with wrong, ineffective learning and no learning.

How does one go about starting a quality cost reporting system? It is beyond the scope of this book to address the details for constructing a quality cost reporting system, however, a simple and practical approach is to start with a review of the organization's "Chart of Accounts" to determine which of those accounts should be selected and to which quality cost category those selected accounts should be assigned. Table 3.1 gives a cursory view of the most standard form based on a typical chart of accounts. By identifying each of the accounts the reader of the report can see the influence of these costs to the total cost of the organization and as a result an appropriate management decision will take place to reduce the out of line cost. What is important about the form is the fact that it has two time periods for comparison purposes.

Table 3.1. A typical Cost of Quality Report

	Time Period A	Time Period B	Difference
Appraisal Costs			
Account 1			
Account 2			
Account 3			
Account n			
Prevention Costs			
Account 1			
Account 2			
Account 3			
Account n			
Internal Failure Costs			
Account 1			
Account 2			
Account 3			
Account n			
External Failure Costs			
Account 1			
Account 2			
Account 3			
Account n			

Systems and structures: Roles and responsibilities in any project, philosophy or even a program decisions must be made along the way. However, these decisions, more often than not, are diffused because of the complexity of the project, and its philosophy. Therefore, the implication is that control and coordination must be critical items of concern. Given that assumption then, three axioms are required for successful implementation. They are:

1. People are the project's, philosophy's and or program's most important asset

2. Focus on people more than techniques
3. Project manager is not the boss in the traditional sense – he is more of a facilitator and a coach

To facilitate and optimize these axioms every organization defines the specific roles and responsibilities for the specific project, philosophy or program implementation. In any educational system the definition of roles and responsibilities is also important. There are several levels of roles in the methodology. However, none of them are mandatory and some of them may be called by a different name in some organizations. [There is a difference between functions and titles. The functions and responsibilities are important, it is the titles that may or may not be important].

Mission: Is the purpose of the educational entity. For example: The purpose of the (name of School District) is to ensure learning for all members of the school community.

Vision: Vision is the key to how policy-makers and educators can participate in forging an education to match the needs and opportunities of the new century. But vision is also the key to what this education should be about. The primary commitment of education should be about vision. A vision is a global statement about direction and the future. In other words: "where" we want to go. It should focus on general parameters such as:

- A proud vision of self as a powerful life-long learner,
- A vibrant vision of a worth-while life ahead,
- An optimistic vision of a society to be proud of, and
- The skills and the ethic needed to follow these visions.

An example of a vision statement is: The (name of School District) will become an exemplary learning community that supports innovation and is committed to continual improvement. The (name) will be a place where a collaborative community develops curriculum, instructional strategies, and assessment to ensure all students learn. Our exemplary learning community will create:

- A collaborative culture that ensures all students learn.
- A climate that fosters instructional collaboration
- A community of trust, mutual respect, empathy
- An appreciation for diversity
- A physically safe and well-maintained learning environment

Also,
- Implement a relevant and rigorous curriculum.
  - o Lessons aligned to the current curriculum benchmarks, grade level content expectations (GLCE) or high school content expectations (HSCE)
  - o A comprehensive curriculum designed to ensure that all students have opportunities to exceed local, state, and national standards
  - o Innovative programs developed from current research and instructional trends.
- Continuously research, create, evaluate, and adapt best practice instructional strategies to ensure learning for all students.
  - o Purposeful use of instructional time
  - o Instructional strategies that meet the needs of all learners
- Use ongoing assessments as instruments to design and adapt instruction that ensures quality learning.
  - o Design formative and summative assessments based on current research.
  - o Assessments that measure the curriculum

o   Assessments that consider all learning styles
o   Assessment that include multiple levels of thinking.

Develop Strategic Goals and Objectives: Perhaps the most important step in strategic planning is to tie the strategic goals and objectives to the vision. The goals and objectives must bridge the gap between current capability and the vision. The strategic goals and objectives form the basis for the functional plans. Because of their importance, a constant vigilance through a feedback system must be in place to assure that the goals and objectives are feasible, and attainable within the constraints of the organization.

Goals: A goal is a broad statement of what the program hopes to accomplish. In fact, the Oxford Dictionary defines "goal" as the "point marking end of race; object of effort or ambition; destination;..." In the educational system a goal maybe viewed as something that it is aspired such as:

- To be a model of effective governance.
- To partner with members of the community in the support of public education.
- To pursue information and training which enhance our policy-making ability.
- To maintain our status as a (name of State) Honor Board with all members certified.
- To conduct an annual school board self-assessment

On the other hand, a goal must not be confused with an *objective*. An objective is a specific, measurable condition that must be attained in order to accomplish a particular program goal. There are many different ways to specify objectives; the program and evaluator should choose the method that works best for each situation. Program objectives include: a) condition b) criteria and c) measurement. For example: By June of 2011 50% of the Fourth Grade students will achieve "satisfactory" status on the State math test.

Develop Functional Plans: At this point your planning team coordinates with middle managers and working groups to develop the action plans. These plans must address potential problem areas and they may also include "what if" situations in case the primary plans cannot be executed. To develop action plans, you need to define the sub-processes and tasks that align with and support key processes in your organization. Do you have indicators to measure the sub-processes? If not, develop them now. The indicators should align with and support the organizational metric system. It is important that before you implement any plan that the senior planning team has a chance to review the action plans. They will check for cross-functional integration, alignment, and system optimization. This alignment is what is called *quality system documentation* (Stamatis 1996).

A quality system is the set of policies and procedures that represent the way an organization performs its process. The quality system assures that a quality program exists and is followed so that the quality of the product or service is delivered to the customer without problems or non-conformances.

The content of the quality documentation is derived from an analysis of the quality system. Quality events are identified through procedures analysis, typically using a process flow diagram. To generate the content, one must go to the source of the task. The people doing the work know what they do, and they are indeed the best source of information. Therefore, allowing the workers to be active participants in the writing and validation of the quality documentation is a means of ensuring that the documentation accurately reflects the way the firm operates. In addition, it allows employees to have ownership of the documentation, which helps promote quality and increases the intrinsic motivation of the individuals involved.

The objective of all quality documentation is to reflect accurately the way the organization operates. It should describe the current baseline and not the way things ought to be. In addition, the documentation must always be up-to-date, even though things change.

The structure of documentation: A typical structure is based on quality manual, procedures, instructions, records and forms. The records and forms are on the base of the documentation and are dependent on the representative departments of the organization. They can be arranged to suit the organization. What is important here is the notion of the involvement of the whole organization.

Even though generally there are four layers of documentation, not all organizations require the same divisions. The actual layers will depend on the complexity of the organization and its products or services. However, these four layers are quite common in most organizations, including educational systems.

1. *Quality manual.* Sometimes called the management manual, operations manual, or policy manual. The quality manual is the highest level of documentation and represents the policy of the organization.
2. *Procedures.* The procedures define the flow of the task or operation. They serve as an overview of the process, job, or task.
3. *Job/work instructions.* Sometimes these instructions are called standard operating procedures (SOPs). Job/work instructions define how the task or operation is done.
4. *Forms, records, documents, books, or files.* These are miscellaneous items that sometimes appear as single items and sometimes as part of other documentation.

Each organization defines the need for documentation, and these layers may indeed overlap from educational system to educational system. For these four levels of documentation to be fully effective, a cross-reference system must be developed to show the interrelationships between layers, and appropriate and applicable approval is required.

The approval should be at an appropriate level within the organization. Generally, the higher the level of documentation, the higher the approval authority. A rule of thumb—from the author's experience—is that documentation approval should be from two levels higher than the level seeking the approval. When the complexity of organization or product/service is high, the approval process may be assigned to more than one person. Otherwise, one person should be responsible for granting approval.

Another requirement for effective documentation is a control mechanism to ensure that only pertinent documents are used. Pertinence in this case applies to both the relevance of the subject matter of the document to the work at hand and the currency of the contents. This control entails issuing the documents needed at the correct revision level wherever and whenever they are required and ensuring that they cannot be inadvertently replaced by documents relating to another subject or to the correct subject but at a different issue. Therefore, all unnecessary documentation must be removed from the workplace without delay, and all revisions must be correct and current.

When there is a need to copy documents—perhaps for marketing or public relations purposes—control of the copies must be proportional to the risk and their use. A unique document format, special paper color, or the incorporation of a colored mark in all legitimately issued documents all make satisfactory controls.

Alteration to documents must be controlled. To prevent irrelevant changes, the document shall be reviewed and approved by the original reviewers or by other authorized people thoroughly conversant with the background information on which the original documents were based. In order to ensure that the correct documents may be issued and withdrawn, a control mechanism must exist to identify documents, revision levels, and their holders.

The Quality Manual: The purpose of the quality manual is to describe at a high level of detail (30 to 60 pages in length) the organization's quality policy, vision, and quality system in order to

- Provide a reference point from which a reader can identify and locate specific procedures and operating instructions.
- Advise the organization's staff of the full range of standards and procedures and the interrelationships among them.
- Ensure common understanding of the way the firm does its business and how it regards quality.

The quality manual is not the full documentation of the quality system. The full documentation consists of the quality manual, procedures, work instructions, and records. However, because the quality manual is an overview and the first tier in the documentation, it is likely that individual task performers will not use it very frequently. In fact, the primary readership of the quality manual is the management and staff of the organization. A typical quality manual should contain:

- The organization's principles and objectives.
- A short description of the products/services.
- A short description of the customers and suppliers.
- Organizational structure.
- Overview of the functions of the organization's executives.
- Description (one to four pages) of each functional area and its relationship to quality.
- Cross-reference between functions, procedures, and work instructions.
- Cross-reference between the organization's functions and other standards or customer conditions.
- Distribution list.
- Document change and control procedures and responsibilities.
- Copyright statement (optional).

The scope of a manual should be site specific because each site is unique and needs to be as specific as possible. Therefore, an educational quality manual may summarize the entire quality system, but when there are multiple sites, each should have its own quality manual. Sometimes, when there is a need for an abridged version to indoctrinate new employees or to brief management the quality manual is printed in a pamphlet format. When literacy is a problem in the organization, the pamphlet format allows employees to carry the document in a pocket and review it as needed.

When confidentiality is a concern, the quality manual may be published as a quality policy (same as the quality manual but with the sensitive data removed) and distributed to customers and suppliers without divulging confidential information. Such a manual may be defined as a non-controlled document. The overall structure and content of a typical format for the quality manual may be reviewed in Stamatis (1996).

Procedures: Whereas the quality manual—as already discussed—identifies the organization's policies and functions and places them in a context that describes the relationships between them, a procedure identifies the procedural steps for a function. Depending on the scope and complexity of the function(s), there may be one or more procedure manual(s). Some examples of procedure manuals are procurement manuals, operations manuals, instructional manuals, and engineering manuals. Each of these manuals relates to the procedures of a particular department. If the documentation is in an electronic form rather than on paper, it may not be necessary to divide it into separate manuals. However, access to the procedures may be restricted on a need-to-know basis.

Although there is no definite way to identify specific content, there are some generic ways to build a procedure. The following questions may help in structuring a procedure.

Purpose, objective	Why is this procedure performed?
Inputs	What materials come into this process?
	Which inputs need to be measured or evaluated?
Outputs	What specific outcomes are expected?
	Are there any interim or end product measurements?
Acceptance criteria	How are the tests, standards, or tolerance limits selected?
Procedure steps	How is the process performed?
Responsibility	Who is responsible for initiating, performing, and monitoring the process?
Audit requirements	How is the frequency of the audit determined?
	Who performs the audit? What happens to the results?
Resources	What resources (machine, method, material, manpower, measurement, environment) are required to perform the procedure?
Training requirements	What training courses, seminars, workshops, etc. are required for the operators of the particular task?
Approval authority	Who approves and authorizes the procedure?

Although all of the preceding elements are not mandatory in every procedure, the organization must define the applicability of the content and as a consequence incorporate the appropriate material. The level of detail for each procedure is unique to itself and the organization, and there is no specified length for a procedure. However, to ensure maximum applicability and appropriateness of the individual task, the operator must be included in defining the task. The following guidelines may help in procedure writing.

- Provide an overview that includes the procedure's purpose.
- Identify all materials, tools, and ingredients for the procedure.
- Identify both prerequisite and requisite skills.
- Provide an estimated time to complete the procedure.
- Do not assume. Do not skip obvious steps.
- Follow the correct order (logical, hierarchical, procedural, etc.). If order is not important, say so.
- Each step should be simple and self-contained.
- Use a hierarchical structure whenever possible. It is very easy to develop.
- Start with the most important step and keep developing them until the size and complexity of the steps give you the desired results.
- Try to start each instruction with an active (direct) verb (*e.g.*, place, drill, position) or with the prerequisite, if there is one.
- Number each of the steps and use the numbering system consistently throughout the documentation (*e.g.*, the numerical system of [#.#..#]; roman [I., II.]; alphabetical [A., B.]; combination [I. A. 1.a.i.).
- Always verify the procedure. Test it against current knowledge. Do not assume the procedure is correct because you just finished writing it.

The overall structure and content of a typical format for a procedure may be reviewed in Stamatis (1996).

Instructions: The terms *operating instructions*, *instructions*, and *standard operating procedures* are used interchangeably. They all describe details of specific steps of higher-order (less detailed) procedures. For example, classroom set up may be a step in the total instructional procedure. The SOP for the setup is the specific description (the process, the method) for this particular kind of setup.

As a general rule, instructions are at a lower level of detail than both the Quality Manual and the procedures. Instructions describe a step-by step approach to guide an operator or even a teacher through a task.

If the overall procedure is short and simple, the operating instructions may be part of the procedure manual or they may be bound separately. Because instructions are detailed and specific, they may be posted in the work station, provided to the operators as job aids, or made available on demand through electronic devices. No matter how the instructions are distributed all instructions must be available to the operators performing the task or the process and they all must be current. For more information on instructions see Wilson (1996), Brumm (1995), and Clements et al. (1995).

Auditing: ISO 8402 defines a quality audit as "a systematic and independent examination to determine whether quality activities and related results comply with planned arrangements and whether these arrangements are implemented effectively and are suitable to achieve objectives." (ANSI/ISO/ ASQC A8402-1994). Thus, an audit is a human evaluation process (assessment) to determine the degree of adherence to prescribed norms and results in a judgment. The norms, of course, are always predefined in terms of criteria, standards, or both.

To avoid confusion and misunderstandings, it must be understood from the very beginning of the audit that the norms are defined by the management of the organization and the auditor has nothing to do with evaluating the suitability of such norms. However, it is the responsibility of the auditor to evaluate the compliance of the organization to those norms. For this reason the audit is usually performed as a pass/fail evaluation rather than a point-system evaluation.

As defined then, an audit is an information gathering activity with the purpose of identifying non-compliances in the system so that improvement, corrective action, or both may be evaluated and implemented. It should be understood by all auditors and lead auditors that in a given audit there is neither a pre-established number of non-compliances nor a fair ratio of major and minor non-compliances. This is true for the first audit as well as for subsequent audits. Furthermore, audits are not public hangings.

Quality audits are neither inspection tools nor verification tools for actual acceptance or rejection of the product or service. The orientation of the quality audit is fact finding; its focus is the evaluation of the system or process. The focus of an audit is always prevention and planning, as opposed to inspections where the focus is appraising product or service quality after the fact.

Quality audits may be internal or external and take one of three forms:
- *First party audit*: This audit is conducted by an organization on itself and may be done on the entire organization or part of the organization. It is usually called an internal audit.
- *Second party audit*: This audit is conducted by one organization on another. It is usually an audit on a supplier by a customer, and it is considered an external audit.
- *Third party audit*: This audit is conducted by an independent organization (the third party) on a supplier. It can be conducted at the request of a customer or on the initiative of a supplier to gain certification. It is always an external audit. The accreditation audits are of this kind.

Regardless of the kind of audit, it is imperative that auditors and the lead auditor have no direct or indirect responsibility in the audited area or with the involved personnel. The most common types of audits are:

- *Conformity assessment*. They are developed for each new approach directive as they are being developed. In general a conformity assessment examines all activities that assure the conformity of products to a set of standards, including testing, inspection, certification, and quality system assessment. Depending on the products and health and safety risks they present, the conformity assessment can range from a full-quality assurance system guided by special requirements to manufacturer self-certification. These types of audits are voluntary.

- *Eco-management and audit scheme (EMAS).* This audit system was developed to prevent, reduce, and as far as possible eliminate pollution, particularly at its sources. It uses a polluter-pays principle that is similar to the Environmental Protection Agency program that permits companies to trade emissions allowances. The binding part of the regulations is that nations must establish methods for companies to validate the conformity and effectiveness of their environmental management systems. These types of audits are also voluntary.
- *Adequacy audit.* This audit is usually an internal audit known as a system or management audit. Its function is to determine the extent to which the documentation meets the applicable standard.
- *Compliance audit*: This audit is performed by an organization that seeks to establish the extent to which its documentation system is implemented and followed by the workforce. The focus is the system or process, not the product.
- *External audit.* This audit may be an adequacy or a compliance audit and is usually performed by the organization on its own suppliers.
- *Extrinsic audit.* This audit may be an adequacy or a compliance audit and is usually performed by an independent third party or a customer coming to look at a supplier or a supplier's supplier.
- *Internal audit.* This is perhaps the most common and most important of all audits. ISO 9001 clause 4.17 requires a company to audit its own quality system, procedures, and activities in order to establish whether they are adequate and being followed by the workforce. Furthermore, the ISO standard calls for communicating the results to management as well as for planning corrective action, if necessary. This type of audit provides excellent communication in the organization and provides management with appropriate and timely information about the quality system and its effectiveness.
- *Product/process audit.* This specialized audit examines all the systems that go into the production of a specific end product or service. It is usually called a vertical audit and should not be confused with an inspection program of an item. Product audits are applicable to auditing specific projects or contracts. A trained professional auditor should undertake the product/process audit. The auditor may be on company staff, a hired professional, or a third party. What is of paramount importance is that the auditor must be independent and not have direct or indirect responsibility for the audit area or its personnel. Whether the auditor has knowledge in the specific area or activity is not relevant because the auditor's responsibility is to look for objective evidence of conformity based on the requirements of the standard and provided by the documented system.

If the audits are done appropriately, they provide the following benefits to the organization:

- *Management orientation.* An audit will provide information on the current quality system to the management team so that appropriate evaluation can take place. The impetus for this evaluation may be the management team itself, the customer, or the competition.
- *Internal assessment.* An audit conducted as an internal assessment will provide a very good measurement of the effectiveness of the system and a strong benchmark for continuous improvement in the future.
- *External assessment.* An audit conducted as an external assessment will establish the credentials of procurement quality standard(s), that is, suitability, conformity, and effectiveness, and in addition will provide supplier certification.

For more details on the audits, the reader is encouraged to see Stamatis (1996); Keeney (1995, 1995a) and Parsowith (1995).

42

Discipline and responsibility (accountability): An issue that should concern all leaders of education is the inconsistency of discipline and responsibility. All schools have it, but all have it in different form. It is about time that we should be able all across the board to standardize the process. After all, what does each level of diploma or degree we award (high school diploma, associate's, bachelor's, master's, and doctoral) mean? What does a degree in a particular field at each of those levels mean, and what does it represent in terms of student learning? These sound like common sense questions that would have obvious and public answers. But obvious and public answers are not readily available, and that's what some of our recent arguments about accountability in the United States have been about.

A qualifications framework is a statement of learning outcomes and competencies a student must demonstrate for a diploma or degree at a specific level to be awarded. It is not a statement of objectives or goals. It is not a wish list. It is a performance criterion. When a school board or an institution of higher education is governed by a qualifications framework, it must demonstrate that its students have demonstrated some learning and worth the diploma or the degree. And that means all of its students, not just the volunteers who take a standardized test. While a qualifications framework does not dictate how that demonstration takes place or the nature and form of assessments employed, it does provide learning outcome constructs within which the demonstration when it is conducted. This is a form of accountability worth our serious consideration as part of our leadership discussion.

A second key characteristic of a qualifications framework is that the description of a diploma or a degree clearly indicates how it differs from the degree level below it and the degree level above it. The language of the framework accomplishes this differentiation by ratcheting up the benchmarks. This is called the "ratchet principle." An excellent example of this is the content challenge and performance statements of Bologna (see Note 1) —from individual courses to degrees—and penetrates the credit system as well. This principle, embodying content and performance standards, is an engine of accountability worth our serious consideration. Three levels and types of qualifications frameworks have been developed or are in the process of being developed under the Bologna Process: Transnational, National, and Disciplinary/Field.

The Transnational Qualifications Framework for the European Higher Education Area (QFEHEA) to which all Bologna participants have agreed is, of necessity, the broadest and most generic of the accountability forms. Think of our associate's, bachelor's and master's degrees. Under the QFEHEA, there are five learning outcome constructs that, in their descriptions, illustrate the "ratchet principle:"

1. Reference points of knowledge and understanding.
2. Contexts and modes of application of knowledge and understanding.
3. Fluency in the use of increasingly complex data and information.
4. Breadth and depth of topics communicated, along with the range of audiences for that communication.
5. Degree of autonomy gained for subsequent learning.

To illustrate the ratchet principle, let's take "fluency in the use of increasingly complex data and information"—watch the changes in language as one moves up the ladder from associate's to bachelor's to master's degrees (the European terms are short-cycle, first-cycle, and second-cycle):

- Short-cycle (associate's) degrees are awarded to students who "have [demonstrated] the ability to identify and use data to formulate responses to well-defined concrete and abstract problems."

- First-cycle (bachelor's) degrees are awarded to students who "have [demonstrated] the ability to gather and interpret relevant data (usually within their field of study) to inform judgments that include reflection on relevant social, scientific or ethical issues."
- Second-cycle (master's) degrees are awarded to students who "have [demonstrated] the ability to integrate knowledge and handle complexity, and formulate judgments with incomplete or limited information, but that include reflecting on social and ethical responsibilities linked to the application of their knowledge and judgments."

Draft a qualifications framework for review and public comment, revise as appropriate, and adopt as state policy. Make sure all public institutions that grant diplomas or degrees to all students who meet the qualification standards. Why go through this process? So that everyone—particularly students—understands why a bachelor's degree is different from an associate's degree in Utah or Ohio in ways other than how much time or how many credits it takes to earn it. With that clarity, these degrees will be fully respected in a global knowledge economy. And with that clarity in a few states, other states will follow.

Of course, this ratchet principle applies to K-12 systems as well. Currently we have so many standards and so many frameworks that many learners graduate from grade to grade and even high school and for all intended purposes they are functionally illiterate. The ratchet principle will allow a commonality of at least the rules of progression and it will also differentiate the learning process between grades.

"Tuning" is a methodology, including a consultation phase with recent graduates and employers, that produce reference points for teacher members who are writing criterion referenced statements of learning outcomes and competencies in the disciplines. It provides a common language for academic-subject-specific knowledge and for generic competencies or shared attributes.

Does that mean standardization of content, sequence, and delivery modes? Does it mean that the business program at the Warsaw School of Business will be a carbon copy of the business program at the University of Coimbra in Portugal or even Wayne State University in Detroit Michigan? Hardly. Tuning goes to great lengths to balance academic autonomy with the tools of transparency and comparability. They provide a common language for expressing what a curriculum at a specific institution aims to do but do not prescribe the means of doing it. Thus, the tuning notion is like convergence. It is a concept of focusing on the overall objective.

Again, the tuning principle is also applicable to the K-12 systems. It is imperative that in the years to come the educational process must be streamlined to be applicable to the needs of the modern student. Tuning in the K-12 grades will facilitate the purposeful learning and the expectations of all stakeholders in the system. It will establish strong criteria for the basic knowledge that is supposed to be learned in the K-9th grades and then the requirements for college preparation from 10th to 12th grades.

Why Does Tuning Matter to Students? Students come to college to earn a degree in anthropology, mechanical engineering, or nursing; they come to community colleges to earn degrees in medical technology or commercial art. When you ask them what they are studying, they talk about the field, the discipline. And that's the way our faculties are organized, too. So specific disciplinary content counts—a lot!—and that is a theme of most colleges and universities. When students enter a major or when they graduate, they deserve to know what they are in for and what they have accomplished. For this knowledge, as well as for guidance for faculty designing curriculum and instructional methods, Tuning suggests the following reference points—in this illustration, for the bachelor's degree. The student who is about to receive a degree in a specific major (e.g., accounting, anthropology, architecture, agricultural science, and so on) should:

- Demonstrate knowledge of the foundation and history of that major field;
- Demonstrate understanding of the overall structure of the discipline and the relationships among its subfields and to other disciplines;
- Communicate the basic knowledge of the field (information, theories) in coherent ways and in appropriate media (oral, written, graphic, etc.);
- Place and interpret new information from the field in context;
- Demonstrate understanding and execution of the methods of critical analysis in the field;
- Execute discipline-related methods and techniques accurately; and
- Demonstrate understanding

One can see that these criteria currently are not being followed and perhaps that is the reason that each college or university has their own selection of classes and most of them are not transferable to other institutions. The result is high cost to the learner and society but also high inefficiency in the educational system. The diversity is so large that each institution does not trust each other to the point where teachers, attorneys, medical doctors, nurses, engineers and many other professional disciplines before they work in their chosen field have to take a certified examination – usually given by the State.

It is time to redesign the credit system: The U.S. credit currency is a metric designed for funding and resource allocation, not as a proxy for learning. Its engine lies in the office of the vice president for finance, not the office of the vice president for academic affairs. The student is incidental. Even in the matter of time, the same faculty load serves considerable differences in student workload. Something is wrong here. If we care about accountability for student learning, perhaps we need a redesign. Perhaps the Bologna experience might help us (Adelman2008). To redesign a credit system, one needs some definitions, principles, and guidelines. The mechanical implementation of ECTS doesn't really do it. Credit should define levels of student work (time volume and intellectual demand) that render courses in different disciplines comparable. In a way, the U.S. system tries to do that now by giving extra credit for science labs or language labs, or by heavier credit weighting of externships. But we do this in a rather arbitrary fashion and wind up awarding the same number of credits for course work of widely varying intellectual demand. We give three credits for a course in econometrics and three for Introduction to Sports, and brush such dissonances under the rug. This observation is not new, but neither the Spellings Commission report nor the organized higher education community's responses attempted to deal with this core quality assurance issue—and that's what it is. If we want credits to be meaningful and indisputable in the context of transfer or for recognition of prior learning, we need consensus on student workload formulas and level descriptors together. It's not perfect, but it's a start.

After qualification frameworks, tuning, and credits and their levels, what evidence of learning and attainment might the student graduate carry forward into the world, and how is that evidence communicated? After all, isn't there a graduation ceremony at which the student receives a piece of paper on which a degree is officially recorded, stamped, and surrounded by ancient heraldic symbols? Isn't that enough? These are very fundamental questions that must be answered by the leadership of the specific institutions and more general the educational system. They are the core of the existence of education. If we are not sure as a society why we graduate students and how much they learn from our institutions of learning we have indeed lost the purpose of education. What is needed is perhaps another document, both personal and public; one that functions as an assurance for learning; perhaps something like an apprenticeship or a mentoring service.

It is time for the leaders of higher educational institutions to redesign entire programs such as the law and medical degrees. For example: Reexamine the need for a bachelor's degree in any field as a prerequisite to

Law degree. Instead, add maybe another year or two in practicum of Law classes to make the Law degree more practical. In the medical degree it is also essential to reexamine the usefulness of a full bachelor's degree. Instead, add maybe another year or two in classes that are relevant to the medical degree.

There are many other instances where true leadership can make a difference in the educational process in both academic and non-academic processes that affect all kinds of outcomes.

Note 1: The Bologna Process is a European reform process aiming at establishing a European Higher Education Area by 2010. It is an unusual process in that it is loosely structured and driven by the 46 countries participating in it in cooperation with a number of international organizations, including the Council of Europe. The Bolagna Process comes down to the following:

- It is easy to move from one country to the other (within the European Higher Education Area) – for the purpose of further study or employment;
- The attractiveness of European higher education is increased so many people from non-European countries also come to study and/or work in Europe;
- The European Higher Education Area provides Europe with a broad, high quality and advanced knowledge base, and ensures the further development of Europe as a stable, peaceful and tolerant community.

This goal is rather ambitious and it is not connected only to the Bologna Process. However, within the Process, the necessary tools for achieving these goals are being developed and implemented. Before we move further along, two things should be made clear:

1 The Bologna Process is not based on an intergovernmental treaty.
2 There are several documents that have been adopted by the ministers responsible for higher education of the countries participating in the Process, but these are not legally binding documents (as international treaties usually are). Therefore, it is the free will of every country and its higher education community to endorse or reject the principles of the Bologna Process, although the effect of "international peer pressure" should not be underestimated.

It should be noted that even though the 2010 is the deadline, it is not foreseen that all European countries should have the same higher education system by that date.

On the contrary, one of the very valued features of Europe is its balance between diversity and unity. Rather, the Bologna Process tries to establish bridges that make it easier for individuals to move from one education system or country to another.

Therefore, even if *e.g.* degree systems may become more similar, the specific nature of every higher education system should be preserved. If not, what would be the point to go somewhere else to study if what one studies is going to be the same as back home? The developments within the Bologna Process should serve to facilitate "translation" of one system to the other and therefore contribute to the increase of mobility of students and academics and to the increase of employability throughout Europe.

This is very important characteristic of the process because it can be transferred in the educational system in the US and elsewhere. It can help standardize curricula, credits and required classes for knowledge based education.

Note 2: Over 100 years ago this was a typical final examination of an 8th grader. It is amazing what a student had to know to pass this 5 hour exam. I wonder how many college graduates can pass this exam now. It gives a totally different meaning to an 8th grade education! The following eighth-grade final exam from 1895 in Salina, Kansas , USA was taken from the original document on file at the Smokey Valley Genealogical Society and Library in Salina, and reprinted by the *Salina Journal*.

8th Grade Final Exam

Grammar (Time, one hour)
1. Give nine rules for the use of capital letters.
2. Name the parts of speech and define those that have no modifications.
3. Define verse, stanza and paragraph
4. What are the principal parts of a verb? Give principal parts of 'lie,' 'play,' and 'run.'
5. Define case; illustrate each case.
6 What is punctuation? Give rules for principal marks of punctuation.
7 - 10. Write a composition of about 150 words and show therein that you understand the practical use of the rules of grammar.

Arithmetic (Time, 1 hour 15 minutes)
1. Name and define the Fundamental Rules of Arithmetic.
2. A wagon box is 2 ft. Deep, 10 feet long, and 3 ft. Wide. How many bushels of wheat will it hold?
3. If a load of wheat weighs 3,942 lbs., what is it worth at 50cts/bushel, deducting 1,050 lbs. for tare?
4. District No 33 has a valuation of $35,000. What is the necessary levy to carry on a school seven months at $50 per month, and have $104 for incidentals?
5. Find the cost of 6,720 lbs. Coal at $6.00 per ton.
6. Find the interest of $512.60 for 8 months and 18 days at 7 percent.
7. What is the cost of 40 boards 12 inches wide and 16 ft. long at $20 per metre? (I bet you are confused with this one)
8. Find bank discount on $300 for 90 days (no grace) at 10 percent.
9. What is the cost of a square farm at $15 per acre, the distance of which is 640 rods?
10. Write a Bank Check, a Promissory Note, and a Receipt

U.S. History (Time, 45 minutes)
1. Give the epochs into which U.S. History is divided
2. Give an account of the discovery of America by Columbus
3. Relate the causes and results of the Revolutionary War.
4. Show the territorial growth of the United States
5. Tell what you can of the history of Kansas
6. Describe three of the most prominent battles of the Rebellion.
7. Who were the following: Morse, Whitney, Fulton , Bell , Lincoln , Penn, and Howe?
8. Name events connected with the following dates: 1607, 1620, 1800, 1849, 1865.

Orthography (Time, one hour) [I doubt very much if most of the students know what this is?]
1. What is meant by the following: alphabet, phonetic, orthography, etymology, syllabication
2. What are elementary sounds? How classified?
3. What are the following, and give examples of each: trigraph, subvocals, diphthong, cognate letters, linguals
4. Give four substitutes for caret 'u.' (I bet most of you not only do not know what this question is much less the four substitutes).
5. Give two rules for spelling words with final 'e.' Name two exceptions under each rule.
6. Give two uses of silent letters in spelling. Illustrate each.

7. Define the following prefixes and use in connection with a word: bi, dis-mis, pre, semi, post, non, inter, mono, sup.

8. Mark diacritically and divide into syllables the following, and name the sign that indicates the sound: card, ball, mercy, sir, odd, cell, rise, blood, fare, last.

9. Use the following correctly in sentences: cite, site, sight, fane, fain, feign, vane , vain, vein, raze, raise, rays.

10. Write 10 words frequently mispronounced and indicate pronunciation by use of diacritical marks and by syllabication.

Geography (Time, one hour) [Do we even teach geography anymore?]

1 What is climate? Upon what does climate depend?

2. How do you account for the extremes of climate in Kansas ?

3. Of what use are rivers? Of what use is the ocean?

4. Describe the mountains of North America.

5. Name and describe the following: Monrovia , Odessa , Denver , Manitoba , Hecla , Yukon , St. Helena, Juan Fernandez, Aspinwall and Orinoco

6. Name and locate the principal trade centers of the U.S. Name all the republics of Europe and give the capital of each.

8. Why is the Atlantic Coast colder than the Pacific in the same latitude?

9. Describe the process by which the water of the ocean returns to the sources of rivers.

10. Describe the movements of the earth. Give the inclination of the earth.

Summary

In this chapter we have focused on the leadership of the educational process. Specifically we looked at how leadership is affecting education at all levels and recommended some specific tools and methodologies that all leaders at all levels must be familiar with for improvement and accountability. In the next chapter we will address the issue of educational methodology in education

References

Adelman C. (July 2008). "Learning Accountability from Bologna: A Higher Education Policy Primer." *Issue Brief.* Institute for Higher Education Policy. Washington, DC.

Appadurai, A. (April 10, 2009). "Higher Education's Coming Leadership Crisis." *The Chronicle of Higher Education.* P. A60.

ANSI/ASQC A8402 (1994). *Quality vocabulary.* Quality Press. Milwaukee, WI.

Arter, D. R. (1994). *Quality audits for improved performance.* 2nd ed. Quality Press. Milwaukee, WI.

Brumm, E. K. (1995). *Managing records for ISO 9000 compliance.* Quality Press. Milwaukee, WI.

Clements, R., S. Sidor and R. Winters (1995). *Preparing your company for QS-9000: A guide to automotive industry.* Quality Press. Milwaukee, WI.

Wilson, L. A. ((1996). *Eight step process to successful ISO 9000 implementation: A quality management system approach.* Quality Press. Milwaukee, WI.

Keeney, K. A. (1995). *The ISO 9000 auditor's companion.* Quality Press. Milwaukee, WI.

Keeney, K. A. (1995a). *The audit kit.* Quality Press. Milwaukee, WI.

Parsowith, B. S. (1995). *Fundamental of quality auditing.* Quality Press. Milwaukee, WI.

Michaelsen, L. K., A. B. Knight, and L. D. Fink. (2002). Team-based learning: a transformative use of small groups. Praeger. NY.

Senge, P. M. (1990). *The fifth discipline: the art and practice of the learning organization.* Doubleday/Currency. NY.

Senge, P. M. (1990a). *The Fifth Discipline. The art and practice of the learning organization.* Random House. London.

Senge, P., Kleiner, A., Roberts, C., Ross, R., Roth, G. and Smith, B. (1999) *The Dance of Change: The Challenges of Sustaining Momentum in Learning Organizations.* Doubleday/Currency). NY.

Senge, P., Cambron-McCabe, N. Lucas, T., Smith, B., Dutton, J. and Kleiner, A. (2000) *Schools That Learn. A Fifth Discipline Fieldbook for Educators, Parents, and Everyone Who Cares About Education.* Doubleday/Currency. NY.

Stamatis, D. H. (2003). *Six sigma and beyond: Statistical Process Control.* St. Lucie Press. Boca Raton, FL.

Stamatis, D. H. (2003a). *Six sigma and beyond: Foundations of excellence performance.* St. Lucie Press. Boca Raton, FL.

Stamatis, D. H. (2003b). *Failure mode effect analysis: FMEA from theory to execution.* 2nd ed. Quality Press. Milwaukee, WI.

Stamatis, D. H. (1998). *Advanced quality planning: A commonsense guide to AQP and APQP.* Quality Resources. NY.

Stamatis, D. H. (1996). *Documenting and auditing for ISO 9000 and QS 9000.* Irwin. Chicago, IL.

Selected Bibliography

Barden, D. M. (March 27, 2009). "Is It What You Know? Or Who You Know? Presidential-search Committees Increasingly Want Candidates With A Robust Personal Rolodex." *The Chronicle of Higher Education.* P A39, A41.

Haidet P, Morgan RO, O'Malley K, Moran BJ, Richards BF (2004). "A controlled trial of active versus passive learning strategies in a large group setting". *Advances in health sciences education : theory and practice* 9 (1): 15–27.

Kelly P.A., P. Haidet, V. Schneider, N. Searle, C. L. Seidel, and B. F. Richards. (2005). "A comparison of in-class learner engagement across lecture, problem-based learning, and team learning using the STROBE classroom observation tool." *Teaching and Learning in Medicine.* 17 (2). Pp. 112–118.

Michaelsen L, Richards B (2005). "Drawing conclusions from the team-learning literature in health-sciences education: a commentary." *Teaching and Learning in Medicine.* 17 (1). Pp. 85–88.

Simpson, J. (March 20, 2009). "In a Crisis, Our Nation Must Have an Ambitious Educational Strategy." *The Chronicle of Higher Education.* P. A72.

Sullivan, K. ((March 2009). "Leadership: The Next Stage." *CFO.* Pp37-39.

Some interesting web sites on visionary leadership:

    http://cepm.uoregon.edu/publications/digests/digest110.html; www.visionarylead.org; viewed on 2009-05-20; www.motivation–tools.com/workplace/visionary_leadership.htm; viewed on 2009-05-20.

CHAPTER 4

EDUCATIONAL METHODOLOGIES IN EDUCATION

In the last chapter we discussed the issue of leadership and how it affects education. In addition we recommended several tools and methodologies that all leadership positions may find useful in the pursuit of educational improvement in K-12 and post secondary levels. In this chapter we focus at the educational methodologies that are used to assimilate and infuse knowledge to students of all levels.

The way one assimilates information is not necessarily linked to his/her intellectual capacities. It is rather more dependent on environment and people who surround the person during the learning process. Sometimes ability to remember information is the result of correctly chosen method of learning.

To be sure, there are a lot of methodologies meant to help students assimilate as much information and get as much knowledge as possible. Two of the most common are the hierarchical and the elaboration approach (Stamatis 1986). One thing is known for sure: learning mostly depends on the spiritual and mental state of the person learning. In fact Stamatis (1986) has referred to it as the *intrinsic motivation* of the learner. Furthermore, day by day problems affect learning and productivity itself. That is why it is harder to study in an advanced age when an individual has a lot of questions to settle either in his personal or family life.

To effectively assimilate information there are many conditions, beyond the methodology used. However, some of the key ones are:

- all stored information regarding studied subjects should be reviewed, evaluated and synthesized or used to generate new concepts and ideas;
- proper environment for learning activity should always be appropriate for the learning at hand; exclude: continuous or annoying noise; eating during learning; too dim or bright light; rest couple of minutes each hour;
- imaginary plan of the learned theme should exist and be written down if visual memory is more developed than imaginary one;
- focus should be not on learned information itself, but on its impact, effect, affect, etc;
- assimilation, comparison, exemplifications can enforce one's learning process and help memorize more details – if needed;
- Recognition that it is normal to forget some information, but that doesn't mean it is lost forever. With a little more effort, information can be recovered.
- Focus on motivating the learner for it is the most important stimulus for knowledge and information assimilation (Stamatis 1986).

As we already mentioned the methodology plays an important role, however it is not the only factor that we should focus. Here we must emphasize and recognize that the didactic (teaching) methodology acts like a flexible process. In other words, the methodology should change to reflect changes in material, society and certainly learner make up. These changes may be both qualitative and or quantitative. This is of profound importance because our modern society is changing so fast and the educational process changes at the same rate. This of course creates a form of instability and that is why so many people in and out of the educational system always seem to call for some type of reform. The aim is stability, but it is very difficult to agree as to what is stability and for how long we should be stable, given the fact that requirements change all the time. Perhaps this is the reason (often changes) that we as a society gravitate towards the flexible road as opposed to the stable one. After all, this model (flexibility) it has served us quite well from a historical perspective but at the same time in today's world is not working as well as we have expected it too.

Depending on what methodology one uses, the didactic methodology is fundamentally a three pronged approach based on:

1. *Aspect*: This is the content for purpose issue.
2. *Dosage*: This is the amount of material presented for learning, depending on time.
3. *Combination of process*: This is the way the material is presented. It must be noted that this may in fact be a combination of processes such as hierarchical, elaboration and so on.

The complexity of these three items in the didactic methodology may be compared to an octopus, with each tentacle representing a certain direction. For example:

- practicing new methods, proceedings and techniques of education and learning to solve new phenomena in studying process;
- creating strategies and tactics that will make the educational process more flexible and efficient;
- keeping a changeable character of the learning process;
- giving priority to methods and proceedings that have an active and participating character. The emphasis here is on feedback;
- assuring a large variety of methods, rather than a dominant one. Here the teacher adjusts the method to the learners for maximum learning. It is essential that the teacher knows a variety of methods or the components of a particular method for specific application in the learning environment. In essence this applicability demands that the teaching-learning process should be based on a strong relation between student and teacher;
- assuring equality of student's access to information and self expression;
- enlarging methods and possibilities of information search and assimilation. In essence, this means a cultivation of methods that assure individual learning; it promotes self education, self evaluation, and self instruction. It is also imperative here to have the teacher encourage learners to participate in creating extracurricular activities that will strengthen and enlarge the knowledge received during curricular activities;

To be sure, the existing methodology systems have the properties of self regulation and feeling secure in the status quo. This safety, of course, means that it can work in a negative way in the sense that it may be used for a long time while not being effective. Administrators and teachers should be able to evaluate methods and approaches to learning as well as introduce new ones to the existing system without drastic consequences from the change. At a minimum level a methodology, a process, a procedure or what ever that has lost its use or is rather inefficient should be eliminated without hassles. This is very difficult in the real world because as we already have said classical methods are the main pillars of the educational system. They can suffer some structural changes or evolutional additions but their essence remains.

Now that we have talked about the value of methodology, let us discuss in a cursory form some of the approaches these methodologies may be used. The most common ones are:

Conventional learning: It is dependent on teachers and books. Also the time and place is prearranged and learning is achieved primarily with lectures from teachers and listening (from learners).

Cooperative learning: Cooperative learning is a successful teaching strategy in which small teams, each with students of different ability levels, use a variety of learning activities to improve their understanding of a subject. By using this method, each of the students will feel he or she is an important member of the class.

Discovery method: The discovery method is a teaching technique that encourages students to take a more active role in their learning process by answering a series of questions or solving problems designed to introduce a general concept (Mayer 2003). It is a method of inquiry based instruction (somewhat similar to the Socratic approach) and is considered a constructivist based approach to education. It is supported by the work of learning theorists and psychologists Jean Piaget, Jerome Bruner, and Seymour Pappet. Although this form of instruction has great popularity, there is considerable debate in the literature concerning its efficacy (Mayer, 2004). The method is claimed to be an idea of Bruner but it is quite similar to John Dewey. Bruner argues that "Practice in discovering for oneself teaches one to acquire information in a way that makes that information more readily viable in problem solving" (Bruner, 1961, p.26). This philosophy eventually became the discovery learning movement of the 1960s. The mantra of this philosophical movement suggests that we should 'learn by doing'.

Montessori approach: The Montessori approach offers a broad vision of education as an aid to life. It is designed to help children with their task of inner construction as they grow from childhood to maturity. It succeeds because it draws its principles from the natural development of the child. Its flexibility provides a matrix within which each individual child's inner directives freely guide the child toward wholesome growth.

Montessori classrooms provide a prepared environment where children are free to respond to their natural tendency to work. The children's innate passion for learning is encouraged by giving them opportunities to engage in spontaneous, purposeful activities with the guidance of a trained adult. Through their work, the children develop concentration and joyful self-discipline. Within a framework of a specific order, the learners progress at their own pace and rhythm, according to their individual capabilities.

The transformation of children from birth to adulthood occurs through a series of developmental planes. Montessori practice changes in scope and manner to embrace the child's changing characteristics and interests. They are summarized as:

- The first plane of development occurs from birth to age six. At this stage, children are sensorial explorers, constructing their intellects by absorbing every aspect of their environment, their language and their culture.
- From age 6 to 12, children become conceptual explorers. They develop their powers of abstraction and imagination, and apply their knowledge to discover and expand their worlds further.
- The years between 12 and 18 see the children become humanistic explorers, seeking to understand their place in society and their opportunity to contribute to it.
- From 18 to 24, as young adults, they become specialized explorers, seeking a niche from which to contribute to universal dialogue.

Distance learning: Distance education, or distance learning, is a field of education that focuses on both pedagogy – teaching children – and andragogy – teaching adults – as well as, technology, and instructional systems design that aim to deliver education to learners who are not physically "on site." Rather than attending courses in person, teachers and students may communicate at times of their own choosing by exchanging printed or electronic media, or through technology that allows them to communicate in real time and through other online ways. Distance education courses that require a physical on-site presence for any reason including the taking of examinations is considered to be a hybrid or blended course of study.

eLearning: This approach is based on computerized technology. However, it can provide major benefits for the organizations and individuals involved. Some of these benefits are:

- *Reducing environmental impact*: eLearning allows people to avoid travel, thus reducing the overall carbon output. The fact that it takes place in a virtual environment also allows some reduction of paper usage. With virtual notes instead of paper notes and online assessments instead of paper assessments, eLearning is a more environmentally friendly solution.
- *Quality education, made affordable*: The fact that instructors of the highest caliber can share their knowledge across borders allows students to attend courses across physical, political, and economic boundaries. Recognized experts have the opportunity of making information available internationally, to anyone interested at minimum costs. This can drastically reduce the costs of higher education, making it much more affordable and accessible to the masses. An internet connection, a computer, and a projector would allow an entire classroom in a third world university to benefit from the knowledge of an opinion leader.
- *Convenience and flexibility to learners*: In many contexts, eLearning is self-paced and the learning sessions are available 24x7. Learners are not bound to a specific day/time to physically attend classes. They can also pause learning sessions at their convenience. Alternative education, also known as non-traditional education or educational alternative, is a broad term that may be used to refer to all forms of education outside of traditional education (for all age groups and levels of education). This may include not only forms of education designed for students with special needs (ranging from teenage pregnancy to intellectual disability), but also forms of education designed for a general audience and employing alternative educational philosophies and methods.

Alternatives of the latter type are often the result of education reform and are rooted in various philosophies that are commonly fundamentally different from those of traditional compulsory education. While some have strong political, scholarly, or philosophical orientations, others are more informal associations of teachers and learners dissatisfied with certain aspects of traditional education. These alternatives, which include charter schools, alternative schools, independent schools, home based and home-based learning vary widely, but often emphasize the value of small class size, close relationships between students and teachers, and a sense of community.

Non-formal Education: This type of education consists of all kinds of deliberate influences outside formal educational institutes. It is characterized by less formal features but has the same formative predestination. Educative actions that are included in this type of education are flexible and come to meet particular interests of each individual.

Non-formal education is rooted at the beginning of education concept appearance. It is often considered an intermediary type of education as it is accessible for those who can't involve in formal education: poor, analphabets, handicapped, etc. The principles of non-formal education are following:

- Protection of the persons who want to improve in fields like: agriculture, commerce, industry;
- Motivation of individuals to rationally use intellectual and personal resources;
- Professional advancing or changing of the professional activity;
- Health education and rationalization of free time;
- Elimination of analphabetism.

All these principles can be easier achieved if the non-formal education is completed by formal education. At the same time, non-formal education is just a minor matter if removed or separated from the entire system of education.

Evaluation of the non-formal education can be effectuated observing activities like: school sport activities, interest circles, competitions, youth organizations, etc. These activities are also guided by trained persons, but their role is minimal, they usually act like moderators or coordinators. Non-formal education is also about information individuals get from broadcasting and TV. But it should be mentioned that most of the information is destructive to intellectual personality formation. Specialized school television, or some scientific programs are exceptions. Books and some magazines and papers have great impacts.

The main things that distinguish non-formal education from formal education are its content and the ways of its realization. In short, non-formal education is characterized by:

- concrete answers to fixed requirements;
- allows abstract understanding of theoretical knowledge;
- the teaching factor is excluded , while the learning factor is present and is completed by self-education.

These methodologies and others may indeed be instituted in systems such as:

Charter schools: Charter schools are nonsectarian public schools of choice that operate with freedom from many of the regulations that apply to traditional public schools. The "charter" establishing each such school is a performance contract detailing the school's mission, program, goals, students served, methods of assessment, and ways to measure success. The length of time for which charters are granted varies, but most are granted for 3-5 years. At the end of the term, the entity granting the charter may renew the school's contract. Charter schools are accountable to their sponsor- usually a state or local school board- to produce positive academic results and adhere to the charter contract. The basic concept of charter schools is that they exercise increased autonomy in return for this accountability. They are accountable for both academic results and fiscal practices to several groups: the sponsor that grants them, the parents who choose them and the public that funds them. For the legal definition of a charter school in a particular state, consult that state's charter school laws.

Charter schools are elementary or secondary schools in the United States that receive public money but have been freed from some of the rules, regulations, and statutes that apply to other public schools in exchange for some type of accountability for producing certain results, which are set forth in each school's charter.

While charter schools provide an alternative to other public schools, they are part of the public education system and are not allowed to charge tuition. Where space at a charter school is limited, admission is frequently allocated by lottery based admissions. Some charter schools provide a curriculum that specializes in a certain field - *e.g.*, arts, mathematics, etc. Others attempt to provide a better and more efficient general education than nearby public schools.

Some charter schools are founded by teachers, parents, or activists who feel restricted by traditional public schools. State-run charters (schools not affiliated with local school districts) are often established by non-profit groups, universities, and some government entities (Eskenazi 1999). Additionally, school districts sometimes permit corporations to open chains of for-profit charter schools.

To be sure people establish charter schools for a variety of reasons. However, the intention of most charter school legislation is to:

- Increase opportunities for learning and access to quality education for all students
- Create choice for parents and students within the public school system
- Provide a system of accountability for results in public education
- Encourage innovative teaching practices
- Create new professional opportunities for teachers
- Encourage community and parent involvement in public education
- Leverage improved public education broadly

Private versus public school: Public schools must follow all federal, state and local laws in educating children. Such laws usually include specifics about funding, program development and curriculum.

Private schools on the other hand, are not subject to as many state and federal regulations as public schools. Since private schools are funded independently, they are not subject to the limitations of state education budgets and have more freedom in designing curriculum and instruction.

Curriculum Public schools offer a general program, designed for all children, which usually includes math, English, reading, writing, science, history and physical education. In addition to these key subjects, many public schools offer programs in music and art. In a public school, the substance of what children learn is mandated by the state and learning is measured through state standardized tests.

There are a few fundamental differences between public and private schools, but here's the bottom line: There are great private schools and there are great public schools. The trick is finding the school that best fits your child's needs. You may also want to consider public charter schools or home-schooling. It's a good idea to research the schools that interest you and, to get a true picture of the school, visit in person.

Summary

In this chapter we discussed the educational methodologies used in the educational system for assimilating and infusing knowledge to students. We also have identified the traditional and modern ways of where and how these methodologies are used. In the next chapter we will focus on the stakeholders of all educational systems.

References

Brantlinger, E. (1997). "Using ideology: Cases of non-recognition of the politics of research and practice in special education". *Review of Educational Research*. 67 (4): 425-459.
Bruner, J. S. (1961). "The act of discovery". Harvard Educational Review 31 (1): 21–32.
Dean, D., Jr., and D. Kuhn. (2006). "Direct instruction vs. discovery: The long view". *Science Education*. 91 (3): 384-397.
Eskenazi, S. (1999). *Learning curves*. Houston Press. Houston, TX.
Fuchs, L. S., Fuchs, D., Powell, S. R., Seethaler, P. M., Cirino, P. T., and Fletcher, J. M. (2008). "Intensive intervention for students with mathematics disabilities: Seven principles of effective practice". *Learning Disability Quarterly*. 31 (2): 79-92.

Kirschner, P. A., Sweller, J., and Clark, R. E. (2006). "Why minimal guidance during instruction does not work: an analysis of the failure of constructivist, discovery, problem-based, experiential, and inquiry-based teaching". *Educational Psychologist*. 41 (2): 75–86.

Mayer, R. (2004). "Should there be a three-strikes rule against pure discovery learning? The case for guided methods of instruction". *American Psychologist*. 59 (1): 14–19.

Mayer, R.E. (2003). *Learning and Instruction*. Pearson Education, Inc: Upper Saddle River. NJ.

Stamatis, D. H. (1986). *The effects of hierarchical and elaboration theory in an adult training*. Ph.D. Dissertation. Wayne State University. Detroit, MI.

CHAPTER 5

**STAKEHOLDERS IN EDUCATION:
PARENTS, LEARNERS, ADMINISTRATION,
AND SOCIETY**

In the last chapter we discussed the educational methodologies used in the educational system for assimilating and infusing knowledge to the students. In this chapter we focus on the stakeholders of education. Specifically, we identify them and then we proceed to explain what these stakeholders expect from the educational system from K-12 and post secondary education.

Every time I think of the stakeholders in the education environment the fable of the father, son and donkey comes to mind. I love the fables of Aesop for they provide a startlingly relevant message for a variety of situations across the centuries. This one in particular illustrates most poignantly the pitfall of attempting to please everyone. The story reminds us of the difficulty of multiple stakeholders and the effect of trying to satisfy all of them.

To be sure, organizations have multiple stakeholders. There are suppliers who need to make a fair profit to remain viable, customers who want specific products at lower costs, shareholders who need to protect their investments and employees who would like a raise. While there are probably several others, these are the ones that generally come to mind. There are also the internal stakeholders vying for time, personnel, and resources. Of course, these are the traditional stakeholders in a given entity.

In an educational organization the separation of stakeholders is more complex and needs to be defined more precisely. One of the best ways to do it is to develop a quality management system that will be able to balance and effectively address the needs of the varied stakeholders. As a matter of fact, using the language in ISO 9001 will help to ensure inclusion of interested parties as fulfillment of requirements for some processes. This, in turn, will point to other requirements that facilitate the ability to manage multiple needs while dealing with various constraints.

The best example of these is the requirement in the design and development subclause 7.3.1 of ISO 9001:2008. "The organization shall manage the interfaces between different groups involved in design and development to ensure effective communication and clear assignment of responsibility." The intent of the requirement is not only to make sure that functions or activities aren't forgotten, but also that their contribution (their stake) is also properly managed.

In the education business more and more all stakeholders are increasingly recognizing what businesses have long understood. Customer satisfaction matters. But what is a stakeholder? Generally speaking, stakeholders are individuals or entities who stand to gain or lose from the success or failure of a system or an organization. A stakeholder is used interchangeably with the words: *customer* and *constituency*. The Stakeholder theory suggests that businesses need to pay attention to stakeholders by focusing on those who affect or are affected by its products or services. Stakeholder analysis creates a framework within which businesses identify, evaluate, and then incorporate these interests into their decision-making processes. Well-structured consideration of expanded interests leads to better planning, new and creative initiatives and improved resource allocation - all of which promote organizational success and curb failure. The first step of business stakeholder analysis is identifying the relevant stakeholders.

It would be true but unhelpful to say that everyone is a stakeholder in education for sustainable development. All of us will feel the impact of its relative success or failure, and all of us affect the impact of

59

Education for Sustainable Development (ESD) by our behavior which may be supportive or undermining. This generalization does not however help to identify targeted strategies of cooperation, communication or action. Particular roles and responsibilities devolve to a number of bodies and groups at different levels: local (sub-national), national, regional and international. At each level, stakeholders may be part of government (or intergovernmental at regional and international levels), civil society and non-governmental organizations, or in the private sector. The functions and roles of these categories, at each level, are complementary:

1. Governmental and intergovernmental bodies
    a. policy-making and framework-setting
    b. promoting public consultation and input
    c. national (and international) public campaigns
    d. embedding and operationalizing ESD in educational systems
    e. Civil society and non-governmental organizations
2. Public awareness-raising, advocacy, campaigns and lobbying
    a. consultancy and input into policy formulation
    b. delivering ESD, primarily in non-formal settings
    c. participatory learning and action
    d. mediation between government and people
3. Private sector
    a. entrepreneurial initiatives and training
    b. management models and approaches
    c. implementation and evaluation
    d. development and sharing of practices of sustainable production and consumption

Some functions are common to all stakeholders, including the development of ESD expertise and capacity, the production of educational and informational materials, the identification and mobilization of resources, the modeling of sustainable development practices in institutional life, the exchange of information, and the promotion of cross-sectoral cooperation.

Special mention must be made of indigenous peoples, because of their particular and long-term links to specific geo-physical environments and because of threats to their living and future. They are stakeholders both in the active and passive sense, but more especially represent a fund of knowledge in balancing the use and preservation of natural environments. Without idealizing or romanticizing this relationship of human being to nature, the intimate knowledge and sustained use of their environments gives indigenous peoples a role in informing the wider debate and offering detailed insights into practices of the 'management' of human survival and development in finely tuned and diverse environments.

Media and advertising agencies are key stakeholders in promoting the broad public awareness and ownership without which ESD will remain the concern of a few enthusiasts and be confined within the walls of educational institutions. Only a groundswell of public opinion will result in an understanding of and commitment to the principles of sustainable development and therefore an engagement with educational and informational initiatives.

So, can we be specific as to who the stakeholders are and how they fit in the educational system? Yes, we can. They are:

- *Investors – society*: An organization promises the investors an income that is better than what they could get from any other place. As a result, they invest their hard-earned money in the organization. In education, society at large is investing their tax dollars in expecting a better world for everyone.

One may also consider as investors the local *community*: An organization needs the community to survive because the community builds roads, provides electricity, police protection, and so on. In turn, organizations are obliged to keep the community's environment clean, to pay taxes, and to support and participate in school and community activities. In education the community is the immediate input to the educational system especially for the K-12 as well as community colleges.

- *Management - Administrators*: Managers are promised a good income if they can develop the organization and make it profitable. They often work 50 to 60 hours a week, giving up a lot of their family life. Certainly the organization has an obligation to its managers to provide them financial security and give them meaningful work assignments. In education the administrators develop the strategy and structure for the educational entity to plan and implement systems which assure that learning takes place.

- *Employees - teachers/staff*: The employees produce and sell the products and services to the external customers. Essentially, employees are selling a big part of their lives and must receive equitable pay. In education the teachers and staff are the ones that carry out the policies of the administration and they also do the teaching to the students.

- *Customers – students*: The customers provide the money that allows an organization to meet its obligations to the first three stakeholders. An organization must have satisfied customers to meet those obligations. In education the students are viewed as the primary customers of the educational system and therefore they have to be provided with a product that is wanted, understood and applicable to their life. In other words the students must be given a "value added" product.

- *Suppliers - book publishers and others*: I can't think of any organization that can exist without good suppliers. Organizations must work with their suppliers and pay them a fair price for their products and services. In education suppliers may be the book publishers, suppliers of food, cleaning material, facility equipment or general supplies for educational usage on the daily routine of education.

- *Employees' and teacher's/staff's families - Parents*: An organization uses about 40 percent of the family breadwinner's waking hours per week even if he or she puts in no overtime. Employees must have enough time to meet their obligations to their families—time to take care of running a home and time to spend with their spouses and children. In education the parents are indeed very formidable for all levels of education. They are the ones that they do the selection of the specific school, they are the ones that pay the fees through taxation or tuition for services rendered and they are the ones that do voluntary work in all sorts of ways to support programs and initiatives for the specific school.

- *Special interest groups*: Special interest groups provide a special service to the community. Whether their services seem worthy or not, organizations need to work with the special interest groups that are in keeping with the best interests of the nation. In education the special interests are many and quite diverse. They could represent different groups or business with specific agendas for the curriculum.

To be sure the educational environment has its own nomenclature and sometimes it may be confusing. Tables 5.1 and 5.2 provide a summary and an explanation of some of these terms that one may have a difficulty translating from the quality jargon to the educational language.

Table 5.1. The core seven difficult definitions

Classical terminology	Definition in Educational nomenclature
Supplier	Developer or provider of education or training
Customers	Students for education; employers; trainees for training; parents; other educational institutions; society
Product	Course, education or training program; education or training material
Executive management	General Director; Headmaster; Rector; President; Superintendent; Committee of directors…
Purchasing	Acquisition of necessary goods and services, including the use of temporary, free-lance or external teachers; trainers; lecturers.
Processes	Refer to the development, planning, delivery of education and training, including any assessment of students; trainees; pupils.
Training	Training and professional development of the staff of the education or training organization

Table 5.2. The most common difficult quality words associated with education

Classical Terminology	Definition in Educational nomenclature	Other possible interpretations
General	The education and training services offered, including: Associated tools and services.	Product=the acquisition of learning; the student, trainee, pupil; the degree qualification obtained.
Contract	Contact review only covers agreements with customers. However, all types of agreements with customers – also implicit ones – from the registration of students for a course, to a negotiated agreement and evaluation instruments for students; trainees; pupils may be covered.	Contract review also covers contracts with suppliers, subcontractors or external trainers.
Design	Design does not include (or only marginally) development of education and training (designs stops at the specification of program content). Definition of education or training specifications; design of course programs and curricula; specification of the content of education or training material; design assessment and evaluation instruments for students or learners in specific environments.	Design includes substantial elements of development, up close before delivery stage.
Design Validation	Design validation of a course happens just before it is released.	Validation of the course design happens after the first run of the course.
Documents	External documents need minimal document control, unless when they critically affect the	Most external documents should be controlled much the same way as internal documents.

	quality of the education or training.	
Others	Part-time teachers should be considered as other staff (unless their input is very limited or irregular).	Part-time teachers are to be considered as sub-contractors.
Customer's products	Supervision of students, welfare, care is to be considered (where relevant).	Supervision of students, welfare, care should be considered when appropriate.
Identification	Identification and traceability refers to the education and training services.	Identification and traceability applies to the student/learner.
Calibration	Calibration is only required for the equipment of which the accuracy is critical for the learning process, and for any equipment needed for testing the performance of trainees. It refers mainly to the validity of the assessment and evaluation tools used.	Calibration is needed for all equipment used for the purpose of developing and delivering education or training.
Inspection	Test and inspection concerns the monitoring and evaluation of the education and training services offered, including tangible items produced for it. The assessment and evaluation of the courses; programs; materials by the students; trainees; pupils; employers.	Test and inspection cover all aspects of assessments which take place, including those concerning students. Test and inspection only refer to the tangible items used for the education and training service.
Inspection	Receiving inspection is impossible for services; these aspects may only be applicable for certain goods purchased	Receiving inspection and test cover the need to establish the level and needs of incoming students

Test Status	Inspection and test status refers to the stage at which education, training programs (and all their components) are.	Inspection and test status only applies to equipment. Inspection and test status also applies to learners.
Non conformities	The definition of non-conforming "product" should be extended to include the services as well. Any problem occurring during the development and delivery of education and training.	The control of non-conforming products only refers to faulty tangible items.
Handling	Only applicable to tangible goods (in as far as these are used).	This should be also interpreted for services, and thus cover items like student care, counseling etc.
Statistics	For simple statistics (sums, averages, tables) evidence of the correctness of the figures are OK; for more advanced computations evidence is needed of understanding of the techniques adopted.	This applies to all stages where at least sums or averages are computed

Parents: Any reform that empowers parents, that creates a democratic process or allows more decision making on the local level are all positive things. The involvement of parents in the K-12 educational process has been documented and reinforced in many studies over many years. In fact, it has become one of the most important things that they can do to influence local boards and to keep in touch with their own children. This involvement however, does not stop with the graduation at the high school level. It continues to the college and university life of their children. Two of the biggest concerns parents have when they send their sons and daughters to college are whether they will be safe, and whether they will do well academically. Both of those concerns are legitimate, and both are closely related to alcohol and other drugs, whether used by the student or by their fellow students. Parents deserve to know what schools are doing to curb alcohol and other drug use, and college administrators must be prepared to answer tough questions about their alcohol and other drug abuse prevention policies and programs.

Starting with the college selection process, parents can take note of physical indicators and other signs that show the extent of the "party culture" on campus. Parents should be aware of the campus alcohol and other drug (AOD) policies, including the campus code of conduct and student alcohol policy, and to what extent each is enforced. Additionally, prior to their own student's college experience, parents can ensure they send the appropriate messages of what college is all about – pursuing a first-rate education and opening one's horizons – as opposed to exposing their children to stories of their own high-risk behaviors while a college student. Reinforcing expectations and norms of a party culture is an inaccurate portrayal of campus life and can lead students to make unhealthy, and in some instances dangerous, decisions about AOD use.

Once their children are in college, parents can play an active role in the prevention of college student AOD use by joining a campus and community coalition or a campus task force. Parental notification policies are also effective methods for formally including parents in enforcing healthy choices and deterring high-risk behavior. In issues related to college student mental health and well-being, parents can voice their concerns to be notified as soon as possible if their student displays signs of distress or crisis. Parents can cultivate open and clear lines of communication with campus administrators, and also be clear with their students about their expectations.

Perhaps the most important thing parents can do to help ensure their children make healthy, informed decisions while in college is to stay involved in their children's lives. Parents should play an active role with their college-age children by talking to them about their academic and social lives. Phone calls and e-mails are easy mechanisms to remain engaged, especially during the first few weeks and months of college life when students are most vulnerable and are at greatest risk of making high-risk decisions. Research has shown that the more involved parents are, the more likely their children are to make safe choices about their AOD use.

With a thorough understanding of the full range of forces that effect student high-risk behaviors and well-being, parents can exert a positive and powerful influence on campus administrators to provide comprehensive policies, programs, and services to support their students through a healthy college learning experience. When parents are involved in their children's education, both children and parents are likely to benefit. Researchers report that parent participation in their children's schooling frequently:

- Enhances children's self-esteem
- Improves children's academic achievement
- Improves parent-child relationships
- Helps parents develop positive attitudes towards school
- Helps parents develop a better understanding of the schooling process.

Despite these advantages, it is not always easy for parents to find time and energy to become involved or to coordinate with schedules for school events. For some parents, a visit to school is perceived as an uncomfortable experience, perhaps a holdover from their own school days. Others may have their hands full with a job and other children. The availability and cost of babysitters are other factors. Recently, teachers and other school staff have made special efforts to increase communication with parents and encourage involvement in children's learning experiences.

Ways to Involve Parents: One kind of parental involvement is school-based and includes participating in parent-teacher conferences and functions, and receiving and responding to written communications from the teacher. Parents can also serve as school volunteers for the library or lunchroom, or as classroom aides. In one survey, almost all teachers reported talking with children's parents - either in person, by phone, or on open school nights - and sending notices home (Becker and Epstein, 1982). These methods, along with requests for parents to review and sign homework, were most frequently used to involve parents.

Parents can participate in their children's schools by joining Parent Teacher Associations (PTAs) or Parent Teacher Organizations (PTOs) and getting involved in decision-making about the educational services their children receive. Almost all schools have a PTA or PTO, but often only a small number of parents are active in these groups.

Another kind of involvement is home-based and focuses on activities that parents can do with their children at home or on the teacher's visits to the child's home. However, few teachers involve parents through home-based activities, partly because of the amount of time involved in developing activities or visiting and partly because of the difficulty of coordinating parents' and teachers' schedules.

Ways to Reach Parents: Some programs aim to reach parents who do not usually participate in their children's education. Such programs provide flexible scheduling for school events and parent-teacher conferences, inform parents about what their children are learning, and help parents create a supportive environment for children's learning at home.

Many schools have responded to the needs of working parents by scheduling conferences in the evening as well as during the day, and by scheduling school events at different times of the day throughout the year. It is important for teachers to keep the lines of communication open. This involves not only sending regular newsletters and notes, but also obtaining information from parents. Phone calls are a greatly under-used technique for keeping in touch. A teacher usually calls a parent to report a child's inappropriate behavior or academic failure. But teachers can use phone calls to let parents know about positive behavior and to get input. Parents justifiably become defensive if they think that every phone call will bring a bad report. If teachers accustom parents to receiving regular calls just for keeping in touch, it is easier to discuss problems when they occur.

Teachers need to consider families' lifestyles and cultural backgrounds when planning home activities. However, some activities can be adapted to almost any home situation. These are activities that parents or children engage in on a day-to-day basis. Teachers can encourage parents and children to do these activities together, and can focus on the opportunities that the activities provide for learning. For example, although television viewing is a pastime for most children and adults, they do not often watch shows together. Teachers can suggest appropriate programs and send home questions for families to discuss. This discussion can be carried over into class.

Busy parents can include children in such everyday activities as preparing a meal or grocery shopping. Teachers can also suggest that parents set aside a time each day to talk with their children about school. Parents may find this difficult if they have little idea of what occurs in school. Notes on what the children have been working on are helpful. Parents and children can discuss current events using teacher-provided questions. Teachers often suggest the activity of reading aloud to children. Reading to children is an important factor in increasing their interest and ability in reading. Teachers can also encourage children to read to parents. In areas where children may not have many books, schools can lend books, and teachers can provide questions for parents and children to discuss.

Home activities allow parents flexibility in scheduling, provide opportunities for parents and children to spend time together, and offer a relaxed setting. To be most beneficial, home activities should be interesting and meaningful - not trivial tasks that parents and children have to "get through." When teachers plan home activities, they often think in terms of worksheets or homework that will reinforce skills learned in school. But parents often grow tired of the endless stream of papers to be checked and the time spent on "busywork." Another danger of promoting home activities is the possibility that there may arise an unclear distinction of roles, with teachers expecting parents to "teach" at home. Teachers and parents need to understand that their roles are different, and that their activities with children should be different.

Difficulties in Involving Parents: All teachers experience the frustration of trying to involve parents and getting little response. Teachers complain that parents do not come to conferences or school open houses, check homework, or answer notes. This leads some teachers to conclude that parents do not care about their children's education. While it is true that the emotional problems of a few parents may be so great as to prevent them from becoming involved with their children's education, most parents do care a great deal. This caring is not, however, always evidenced by parent attendance at school events. There are a number of reasons why these parents may not become involved, and teachers need to consider these before dismissing parents as uninterested.

For many parents, a major impediment to becoming involved is lack of time. Working parents are often unable to attend school events during the day. In addition, evenings are the only time these parents have to spend with their children, and they may choose to spend time with their family rather than attend meetings at school.

For many apparently uninvolved parents school was not a positive experience and they feel inadequate in a school setting. Parents may also feel uneasy if their cultural style or socioeconomic level differs from those of teachers (Greenberg, 1989). Some parents who are uninvolved in school may not understand the importance of parent involvement or may think they do not have the skills to be able to help. Even parents who are confident and willing to help may hesitate to become involved for fear of overstepping their bounds. It is the responsibility of teachers and administrators to encourage such parents to become involved.

Students: Like most adults, children (yes, even adolescents) will live up to (or down to) whatever expectations are set for them. Researchers such as Davis, Murrell (1991), Bonwell and Eison (1991) and many others have emphasized the importance of student effort and involvement in their academic and co-curricular activities as the decisive elements in promoting positive educational outcomes. To be sure many schools have struggled to extend opportunities and accompanying expectation for students to assume responsibility for their own education often has been lacking. Educational entities must work to create a climate in which all students feel welcome and able to fully participate. It is equally important to nurture an ethic that demands student commitment and promotes student responsibility. Students can contribute to their own learning and to the development of a campus climate in which all can grow and learn.

What Is Student Responsibility? Schools of all kinds are learning communities, and individuals accepted into these communities have the privileges and responsibilities of membership. If we are to communicate our expectations, we must offer a set of standards and examples that moves our discussion from generality to practice. Pace (1980) has offered such a set of standards and has embedded them in the College Student Experience Questionnaire (CSEQ).

The CSEQ is based on the proposition that all learning and development requires an investment of time and effort by the student. At the heart of the CSEQ is a set of scales which defines the dimensions of student responsibility. These scales are called "Quality of Effort" scales in that they assess the degree to which students are extending themselves in their college activities. The domains include the use of classrooms, libraries, residence halls, student unions, athletic facilities, laboratories, and studios and galleries. The social dimension is reflected in scales that tap contacts with faculty, informal student friendships, clubs and organizations, and student conversations. Pace's work gives the academic community a map of the terrain of student responsibility and suggests concrete activities that contribute directly to student growth and learning.

Why Is Student Responsibility Important? First, student responsibility is the key to all development and learning. In fact, all educational outcomes are tied to the effort that students put into their work and the degree to which they are involved with their studies and campus life.

Second, irresponsible students diminish our collective academic life. Within an individual classroom, the behavior of even a few highly irresponsible students or, worse, a large number of passive, disaffected students can drag a class down to its lowest common denominator. For an institution, the erosion of an academic ethos can lead to a culture that is stagnant, divisive, and anti-intellectual.

68

Third, the habits of responsible civic and personal life are sharpened and refined in late high school or during college. Will employers, international economic competitors, or future history itself be tolerant of students who fail to develop sufficient self-control and initiative to study for tests or participate in academic life?

Finally, if educational institutions are to reclaim the public trust, they must learn not to make promises that cannot be kept. All educational institutions regardless of their rank have responsibilities to students and society. Yet, primary schools, high schools or colleges are not solely responsible for the outcomes of their students. A clear acknowledgment of the mutual obligations of all members of the academic community is a prerequisite to restoring the education's balance and clarity of purpose.

What Are The Foundations Of Student Responsibility? Stratton, Rombach, and Shi (2007), Pace (1990), Tinto (1997, 1997a), Pascarella (1991), and Astin (1993) have offered explicit theories about how colleges [and by extrapolation other educational institutions] can promote student learning and growth. Despite different uses of terms, these approaches have much in common. First, each theorist recognizes that the student's background plays a role in shaping educational outcomes. This role is largely indirect and is moderated by the school environment and a student's interactions with faculty and peers. Second, each theorist sees the campus environment exerting an enabling effect on school outcomes. Last, all emphasize the importance of a partnership between the school and the student. Schools alone cannot "produce" student learning. Schools provide opportunities for interaction and involvement and establish a climate conducive to responsible participation. Each approach reflects the centrality of what we call student responsibility.

The body of research derived from the work of these theorists represents one of the strongest and most sustained accounts of what it takes to succeed in any school environment. The review indicates that the effects of initial group differences on school outcomes are relatively slight and largely mediated by the manner in which the student engages the school experience. Generally, students appear more alike than different. The differences however, follow two elements: 1) the structural features of the organization and 2) the climate or "ethos."

Structural features that tend to isolate students and promote an ethos of anonymity produce poor school outcomes. School climates characterized by a strong sense of direction and which build student involvement tend to promote favorable outcomes by promoting student-faculty and student-peer relations, as well as establishing an expectation that students will behave responsibly. Finally, the decisive single factor in affecting school outcomes is the degree to which students are integrated into the life of the campus, interact with faculty and peers, and are involved in their studies.

How Can We Encourage Responsible Student Behavior? Institutional policies and practices must be oriented toward developing a climate in which students' responsibility and active participation in their own schooling experience are promoted. Policies that stress the importance of student achievement and in-class and co-curricular challenge and support are essential for student growth. The institutional culture clearly must convey the institution's purpose in an unambiguous manner, and the ethos of the campus must be one in which students believe they are members of a larger community. As student culture serves as a filter for students entering a school, care must be taken to ensure that students who are prepared inadequately understand the nature of any school life and what is expected to attain satisfactory academic and developmental gains.

Small-scale, human environments must be built in which students and faculty collectively can engage in the process of teaching and learning. As learning is the process through which development occurs, it is crucial for students to be *actively engaged* in the classroom. Course activities are the vehicle through which students may become more fully engaged with academic material. The literature clearly indicates that the quality of effort that a student expends in interactions with peers and faculty is the single most important determinate in college outcomes.

If we want to teach children to be responsible, we have to trust them with responsibilities. Classroom jobs are an effective way to enlist students in the duties of running a classroom. Obviously, the jobs have to be reflected on the level that they are. For example: In the primary classes maybe an assignment of drawing or describing a visit to the supermarket. In the junior high school maybe an assignment of describing a trip to the zoo or something else that they would be interested in. In high school they maybe involved with a project of balancing a check book or filling out an employment application. In college they may be involved with some kind of debate or research and so on. All these activities should be planned for a 10 to 15 minute participation in classroom at the end of the class.

The important thing about this practice is to make sure that the learners are involved. Key things to keep in mind are the following:

- *Pitch Your Idea*: Tell the students that, soon, they will have the opportunity to apply for classroom jobs. Give them a few examples of the types of jobs that are available and watch their eyes light up as they imagine themselves as the little kings or queens of a certain domain of the classroom. Make it clear that, when they accept a job, they will have to take it very seriously and if they do not meet their commitments, they can and will be "fired" from the job. Make this announcement a few days before your plan to formally introduce the job program so that you can build anticipation and portray the importance of classroom jobs.
- *Decide on the Duties*: There are hundreds of things that need to be done to run a successful and efficient classroom, but only a couple dozen that you can trust the students to handle. Thus, you need to decide how many and which jobs to have available. Ideally, you should have one job for each student in your class. In classes of 20 or fewer, this will be relatively easy. If you have many more students, it will be more challenging and you may decide to have a few students without jobs at any given time. You will be rotating jobs on a regular basis, so every one will have a chance to participate eventually. You also have to consider your own personal comfort level, the maturity level of your class, and other factors when you decide how much responsibility you are ready to give your students.
- *Design an Application*: Using a formal job application (a project charter with specific objectives) is a fun opportunity for you to get each student's commitment in writing that they will perform any job to the best of their abilities. Ask students to list their first, second, and third choice jobs.
- *Make the Assignments*: Before you assign the jobs in your classroom, hold a class meeting where you announce and describe each job, collect applications, and emphasize the importance of each and every duty. Promise to give each child his or her first or second choice job some time throughout the school year. You will need to decide and announce how often the jobs will be changing. After you assign the jobs, give each student a job description about their assignment. They will use this to learn what they need to do, so be explicit!
- *Monitor their Job Performance*: Just because your students now have jobs doesn't mean you can just sit back and take it easy while they perform their duties. Watch their behavior closely. If a student is not performing the job properly, conference with him or her and tell the student exactly what you need to see in their performance. If things don't improve, it might be time to consider "firing" them. If their job is essential, you will need to find a replacement. Otherwise, simply give the "fired" student another chance during the next cycle of job assignments. Don't forget to schedule a certain time each day for the jobs to be performed.

That's about it! As you can see, classroom jobs are a wonderful way to teach responsibility and build a sense of classroom community. With the use of job applications, you are also giving the students practice at filling out forms, which is an academic standard in many districts.

Administrators: These individuals are the visionaries of any educational institution and they set the direction of the learning process in their own jurisdiction whether it is a primary school, middle school, high school, college, university or whatever. The responsibilities that they have are enormous. In fact, is this responsibility that is causing so many executives (department heads, principals), especially new CEOs (Superintendents, Presidents), to want to reorganize right away. And why do they go to the white board and start drawing boxes and placing peoples names in them? They think the exercise is simple and can be done one afternoon between meetings…or maybe even in a meeting on another subject. Back of the envelope organizational design will lead to even more chaos than they can imagine. What some executive don't understand is that organization redesign is as critical as strategy development and needs the proper thoughtfulness.

While administrative responsibility for general education (in all tiers of the education ladder) most often falls within the purview of the School board in K-12, faculty senate or to a Dean of undergraduate studies in colleges and universities, responsibility for the academic and curricular integrity of general education is more dispersed. The typical general education program does not have its own teacher/faculty community that engages in regular reflection upon a body of collective knowledge, appropriate procedures for discovery, shared curricular goals, and peer review. Instead, the general education mosaic has many tiles, each laid down by individual artisans. The artisans of course, are the individual teachers/faculty members who offer their specialty knowledge and take individual responsibility for the academic quality of their own specialties such as: science, mathematics, humanities and so on. Each of these components may be very well made, but students and teachers/faculty alike tend to perceive them as individual course requirements only, rather than to perceive the shading, outline, contour, and contrast of the mosaic as a whole.

If organizational realignment or design doesn't start with a strategic plan (this is part of the APQP that we discussed in the leadership chapter), it is already off the rails. Structure must follow strategy! Why are you realigning? Just to shift people around? How ridiculous is that? But the reality is that it happens far more often than you'd think. And as CEO, if you don't have the patience for a full blown plan, then at least have a vision of the future so you can redesign to an aspirational image of your organization down the road. Be smart about it to avoid mistakes. The mistakes may take the form of the following:

- Not assessing the strategic needs of the organization - short term or long term
- Aligning to no particular strategy or vision for the organization
- Just moving people around in boxes
- Not considering modern management techniques and restructuring around older concepts - functional versus market or customer segments
- Doing what's easy versus what's right for the organization
- Restructuring to fit people's personal needs not the business needs
- Restructuring without the benefit of proper job profiles making people wonder what their new job really is
- Abdicating organization realignment to the HR department to design

These are only some of the worst ones. But we're all guilty of this. Now in doing it right, I'm not talking about a big bureaucratic process. I am suggesting be patient, do the plan or your vision properly, and then align your resources to suit the needs of the plan or the challenges of the future. The main objective is to do it for a reason and not randomly or in a self serving manner.

To be sure organizational realignment is a way to reposition or reengineer the direction of the educational institution and it is the CEO's responsibility. However, it must be understood that any change of that magnitude will affect people's performance in two major ways:

1. **Organizational realignment can motivate behavior.** Through the definition of jobs, the creation of goals, the development of measures, and the use of reward systems, people can be directed and energized to behave in certain ways.
2. **Organizational realignment can facilitate behavior.** Once someone is motivated to behave in a certain way, the realignment (renewal) can help them do so. By providing methods and procedures, by placing the person in proximity to others with whom the person needs to communicate, and by providing necessary information, the formal organization can help people perform tasks better by having a clear set of organizational realignment objectives such as:
   a. Drive the organization toward a customer focus
   b. Reduce the hierarchy
   c. Minimize organizational boundaries
   d. Achieve deep change throughout the organization
   e. Reduce the cost structure

To determine future needs, the existing organization needs to be assessed in terms of its effectiveness and efficiency. This must be done objectively or change simply for the sake of change will occur. At the same time looking at current priorities and the needs for the future must be taken into account. Normally, this requires a complete organizational audit or review of the structure, people and manner in which the business is done. This need not be lengthy, bureaucratic or excessive. But the facts need to be placed out in the open followed by an objective pros and cons analysis.

Many administrators through organizational change processes do not consider the following two major aspects:

1. Identification of existing organizational synergies across organizational boundaries, and
2. Cultural implications of any redesign changes that could affect transition. It is imperative that with appropriate and applicable preparation, an effective process should allow for a number of organizational options to emerge and be considered. Each option should include the following:
   a. Ability to implement the strategy
   b. Clear function definitions
   c. Role alignment within each function and across each functional group
   d. Clear role definition in terms of a job profile

The pros and cons of each realignment option should be evaluated and compared to each other with one option emerging as the most viable strategically, best suited for the organization and its times, and one that can be implemented with the least disruption.
Disruption is inevitable but it should be minimized with a stage rollout plan. Too fast is as bad as too slow.

Taken together motivation and facilitation offer powerful tools for influencing individual behavior. When combined in a thoughtful, systematic way the formal realignment can have a positive effect on culture and have an immense impact on the performance of the educational institution but also for the learners. So, the moral for the administrators here is to get "the" directional strategy right and then get their respective organization lined up behind it. Don't rush it and don't cut corners. Done properly, your people will embrace the changes and be energized about making the vision come to life. Moreover, you will be positioned to achieve your goals and be a better institutional entity.

Teachers/Faculty: Teachers for sure have an impact on students but they also involve parents who might not otherwise be involved. While it is possible for a teacher to implement such a parent involvement program alone, it is much easier if the school as a whole is committed to the program. Administrative staff can relieve some of the burden of implementing a comprehensive parent involvement program, and can offer help and support to teachers.

Staff/Employees' families: Arguably both have high interest in the business of their institutions. However, they both have low influence. This signals the importance of communicating with this constituency but not necessarily involving them directly in the organization – unless, of course, the staff is unionized. In contrast, customers (the ultimate end-user of the institution's product) may have both high interest in and influence on this particular institution's outcome since their views directly affect the businesses (and their own) success. Their views need to play a central role in planning.

Employers: The role of employers is not so easily addressed. Attempts have been made by many institutions to place employers in quadrants of low interest and influence to high interest and influence but that is not exactly optimal. Surely the employers of recent graduates (whether from high school, undergraduate or graduate school) are stakeholders.

In a perfectly synergistic environment, prospective employers would have both high interest in and influence on educational institutions. This is how they will ensure the graduates they hire will be well-prepared for the workplace, and employers will not be required to provide additional and expensive retraining. Correspondingly, academic institutions will recognize and value employers who both hire and are happy with their graduates and immediately include them in institutional thinking. On the other hand, if that is the case that would imply that educational institutions are strictly training entities and not academic organizations in pursuit of "pure knowledge."

Many employers would suggest quite rightly that they have little influence in any tier of the educational process but in a real sense, they - the employers - are a critical customer. To be fair, many employers have shown little interest in educational institutions, preferring to do their own training. Correspondingly, academic institutions, with the growing exception of some professional schools and other schools with extensive externships and other outreach programs, have not exactly welcomed employers as key participants in the academic enterprise. What students do on campus (both within and outside the classroom) is generally divorced from their prospective work environment.

This approach needs to change, in all educational tiers. If a graduating student is unemployable or only employable with extensive retraining, then the educational institution, in essence, has failed. The employers will be disturbed - as will the students and their families. Stakeholder analysis signals that both employers and educational institutions are missing their important interrelationship. If educational institutions have a better sense of what employers want in their future employees and businesses have opportunities to share their needs and obtain graduates who are better workers, then both enterprises benefit. Employers should, then, move from being in the low interest/low influence quadrant into the high interest/high influence quadrant. To fit there comfortably, both groups must change.

Society at large: Some of the same arguments used for the employers in the last section apply to the society as a stakeholder. Whenever we speak of the society as a stakeholder of education we introduce what is known as 'The skills paradox.' The skills paradox tells us that as the jobs market becomes more competitive adults with poor basic skills will suffer most. Yet, the least skilled workers remain the least likely to receive training. This is where life learning for all may be an option. It could be financed by credits to the individual for pursuing education and or training at his own institutional choice. This program may be similar to what the Europeans are planning with their concept of 'knowledge-based' society. The big challenge will be to ensure that people who currently have only basic skills are not left behind. To be sure, 'Skills for the future,' is a very tricky proposition and it may be successful by overcoming resistance to continual learning. This is vey important and critical for a learning society and adult learning practices have a critical role to play in the rapidly changing landscape of local government, not least in developing the essential tools of participative and representative democracy. Of course, society is very demanding on many fronts especially in diversity. Diversity accepts and promotes differences. Therefore, both education and training should accommodate its objectives not only in theory but also in reality. The right to be different is essential as we move into the new century and adult learning theory and approaches to learning should be incorporated in the learning process.

Our modern society as a stakeholder of education and training is indeed very demanding in the qualifications of the graduates of our institutions to do tasks and be involved with projects that are quite advanced in relationship to the past several years. It is important then for our institutions of learning to make sure that the basics are learned and then progressively add topics and disciplines that will make learners functional in our society.

As a society we must have faith in institutions of learning. For example when we have a high school graduate we expect certain outcomes as part of their learning. As we progressively move to technical schools, junior colleges and universities these outcomes become more prominent as well as more specific. It is a shame that we have lost our trust in many of our professional education and training institutions and their validity for their graduates to the point where we have to depend on State or Professional groups for additional certifications. As a result teachers, nurses go to a university for four years but then they have to be certified. Why? Didn't their school provide the appropriate knowledge to practice their discipline? The same for attorneys, medical doctors, professional engineers, accountants, Real Estate professional and the list is getting longer every day. Why this unnecessary parade of certifications? If the institutions do not provide the appropriate and applicable education and or training then they should revamp their curricula to reflect the demand of the society at large.

Obviously, society as a stakeholder is very complicated but if the institutions do their job right the first time by developing the appropriate strategic approach and implement their objectives correctly some, if not all of the difficulties will be minimized if not eliminated.

Summary

In this chapter we have focused on the need to define and identify the stakeholders and provide some of their specific needs in the educational process. In the next chapter we will address the customer satisfaction and service for any educational entity

References

Astin, A. (1993). *What Matters in College: Four Critical Years Revisited*. Jossey-Bass. San Francisco, CA.
Bonwell, C. and J. Eison. (1991). "Active Learning: Creating Excitement in the Classroom." *ASHE-ERIC Higher Education Report No. 1*. Washington, D.C. The George Washington University, School of Education and Human Development. ED 336 049. 121 pp. PC-05; MF-01.
Davis, T. M. and P. H. Murrell. (1991). "Turning Teaching Into Learning: The Role of Student Responsibility in the Collegiate Experience." *ASHE-ERIC Higher Education Report*. Series 93-8 (Volume 22-8). Retrieved from www.gwu.edu/~eriche. On April 4, 2009.
Gross, K. and P. Goldwin. (September 2005). "Education's Many Stakeholders." *University Business*. Pp. 1-3.
Kuh, G., J. Schuh, E. Whitt and Associates. (1991). *Involving Colleges*. Jossey-Bass. San Francisco, CA.

Pace, R. 1990. *The Undergraduates: A Report of Their Activities and Progress in College in the 1980s.* UCLA Center for the Study of Evaluation. Los Angeles, CA.

Pascarella, E., and P. Terenzini. 1991. *How College Affects Students.* Jossey-Bass. San Francisco, CA.

Stratton, S., K. Rombach, and S. Shi. (2007). "Facilitating Simultaneous Learning and Growth: A Model of Preservice and In-service Teachers' Professional Development." In C. Crawford et al. (Eds.), *Proceedings of Society for Information Technology and Teacher Education International Conference 2007* (pp. 3150-3156). AACE. Chesapeake, VA.

Tinto, V. (1997). "Facilitating Simultaneous Learning and Growth." *Thought and Action.* 13(1). Pp. 58-62.

Tinto, V. (1997a). "Enhancing Learning Via Community." *Thought and Action,* 13(1), 53-8.

Selected Bibliography

Becher, R. (1987). "Parent Involvement: A Review Of Research And Principles Of Successful Practice." *ED.* 247 032.

Becker, H. J. and J. L. Epstein. (1982). "Parent Involvement: A Survey of Teacher Practices." *Elementary School Journal.* 83, 2, 85-102.

Brown, P. C. (N.D.). "Involving Parents in the Education of Their Children." ED308988 89 ERIC Digest.

DeKanter, A., Ginsburg, A., and A. Milne. (1986). *"Parent Involvement Strategies: A New Emphasis On Traditional Parent. Roles." ED.* 293 919.

Greenberg, P. (1989). "Parents As Partners in Young Children's Development and Education: A New American Fad? Why Does It Matter?" *Young Children.* 44, 4, 61-75.

McLaughlin, M. and P. Shields. (1986). "Involving Parents In The Schools: Lessons For Policy." *ED.* 293 920.

Stevenson, D. and D. Baker (1987). "The Family-School Relation and the Child's School Performance." *Child Development.* 58, 5, 1348-57.

CHAPTER 6

CUSTOMER SATISFACTION AND SERVICE

In the last chapter we addressed the need for defining and identifying the stakeholders in the educational process. In this chapter we will address customer satisfaction and how it applies to any educational environment.

When we think of "accountability" in education, we usually envision standards (written by school systems, states, or the federal government), combined with measures to see if schools are meeting those standards - *e.g.*, exam results, graduation rates, per/pupil spending, and teachers' qualifications. This is "external" accountability because it comes from outside of each school. Most people think such pressure is necessary and appropriate.

For schools that are public institutions, they should be accountable to the public through its elected representatives. For private institutions the accountability is towards parents who should be vigil in their son's and daughter's progress. This accountability is a device of sorts for keeping educators honest and up-to-speed. It is a reflection of how the stakeholder – the customer is satisfied. The main alternative to external accountability is market discipline (*i.e.*, letting parents decide which schools are working best). There may be a place for some market discipline in education, but it has severe limitations. Thus legally-mandated standards and tests seem necessary.

It must be noted here that "external" standards demonstrate a lack of trust for teachers if not a failure by the individual institution. I know from my personal experience as well as the experience and testimony of friends and close relatives who are classroom teachers that this lack of trust is hard to accept, especially when a person is a good educator and the standards and exams are at least partly foolish (as they tend to be, primarily because they lack validity and reliability). Moreover, "external" accountability measures are always blunt or crude, whether they are used in business, medicine, education, or any field. Any such measures will apply unjustly or inappropriately in certain particular circumstances. And if people want to resist them, they can - by shifting blame, "working to rule," or even cheating.

Therefore, we shouldn't forget about "internal" accountability. For example, a good teacher feels that she doesn't want to let her learners down or disappoint their parents, her peers, or her principal. "Internal" accountability is also what drives really successful students. It's not the grade they care about, ultimately, but what their teacher and parents think about their work. So the question becomes: How can we increase "internal" accountability in schools? Some ideas are:

- Dramatically shorten the list of "external" standards and yardsticks, but make the ones that remain really count. For example, school systems should be held strictly accountable for their graduation rates and the basic literacy and numeracy of their students at specific grades. However, state assessments should not measure students' mastery of long and heterogeneous lists of facts. For the most part, teachers and schools should decide how to assess their students' knowledge of "content" areas, with some non-binding guidance from the state about what is important.
- Make schools smaller, so that faculty can't as easily hide their performance from their colleagues. To be sure there's a lack of hard data that correlates school size to academic performance. Nevertheless, Gross and Godwin (2005) believe that small schools represent a promising development.

- Use juries to assess some student work, and put several teachers as well as community members on each of these juries. That way, colleagues will be able to assess the work that's going on in other classrooms.
- Pay for time during the day when faculty can meet to discuss issues with students. Not only will such planning time allow them to develop appropriate responses to kids' problems; it will also help each teacher to see what the others are doing - or failing to do.
- Without necessarily reducing class size at the high school level, reduce the number of kids who are in contact with each teacher during their four-year school careers. The goal is to strengthen relationships and prevent students and adults from hiding from one another.

Yet another aspect of internal accountability for the post high school learner would be more student control and decision making within schools. Perhaps even include some student-centered "market accountability." Students are a lot smarter than people give them credit for, and they can sniff out bad teachers vs. good teachers much easier than politicians, administrators, parents, or even other faculty. Empowering students with greater control over what classes they take, and which professors they take them with could demonstrate quite clearly who the good and bad teachers are.

As we discussed in the last chapter *customer* can be any recipient of a service outside of the work group, whether internal or external. In an educational system we have several customers or stakeholders. They are both internal and external. The internal customers are easy to identify as they are the teachers, students, staff and administrators. The external ones are as diverse as the society at large, parents as well as colleges and universities.

To satisfy the internal customers is easier than the external because the internal ones are generally more homogeneous and therefore the needs and expectations can indeed be identified and planned for in a formal process. In essence, a good start is to have a good management system in place and recognize that satisfaction is a goal of the entity at hand which is based on recognizing prevention methods to problems and or issues, understand the process itself and have a formal problem solving system to deal with problems and or issues if they do occur. A typical model showing this relationship is shown in Figure 6.1. The external ones are more difficult and demand understanding and follow up. Specifically, to understand the external customer:

- You see yourself as a part of the team
- You accept responsibilities and ownership for problems
- You see yourself as a part of the solution

No mantra in business is more sacred than "you must listen to your customer." Yet a company can land in a deep trouble by listening single mindedly to its customers, to the exclusion of others who may be speaking solid, good sense. Examples are everywhere, but one of the most recent and famous is the case of Apple Computers (Levin, 1996). For years, everyone—outside consultants, strategists, analysts—told the company executives to license their technology to the makers of clones, just as IBM did with its PC. The idea was to drive down machine prices and make Apple's computing style the standard for the masses. Apple had developed some truly innovative concepts: a graphical user interface, plug-and-play capability, easy networking, and so on. In the early days, these concepts made Apple machines easier to use than IBM machines. By the logic of cloning, the more people who become wedded to Apple's standards, the more would eventually buy its software.

Time and again Apple declined to license. The company feared cheaper imitations would drive machine prices down and ruin their profit margins (which is what happened to IBM). Apple drew support for its noncloning strategy from its highly loyal customers.

Whether they realized it or not, the devoted customers must have helped reinforce Apple's hope that customers would continue to pay premium prices for Apple technology and spurn less expensive IBM clones. If this is the message that Apple executives were hearing and believing—and I can only speculate that it was—it is not hard to understand why Apple delayed granting licenses to clonemakers.

Such issues are not simple. With hindsight it is not hard to see that Apple blundered badly by delaying the decision to license. For most of its history the company was posting solid profits, holding a solid share of the market and above all it had a very satisfied customer base. It is easy to understand how licensing clones might have seemed like a radical course. But that is why directors pay chief executives the big salaries and that is why they fire them.

Knowing the customer is no substitute for maintaining a keen strategic sense of the industry. No one knew their customers better than old line department stores; yet somehow department stores were caught flatfooted by catalog companies, factory outlets, home shopping networks, and discounters. Newspaper subscribers may love their morning papers, but the industry struggles to stem declining readership.

The moral of the story? Yes, do listen to the customer. However, know your business first and apply the knowledge to satisfy the current customer as well as the future customer. This is shown in Figure 6.1. The reader will notice that customer satisfaction for internal accountability is based on the overall management system of the educational entity with understanding of prevention of problems, understanding the process and having a problem solving mechanism to solve the problems and or issues if the occur.

The growing popularity of customer satisfaction has given rise to the development of different programs for measuring it. Although these programs vary widely in scope and methodology, most are designed to produce a single satisfaction metric based on random sampling of customers at a single point in time. This common approach ignores the fact that in many cases (*e.g.*, equipment and other durable products) customers use products over a relatively long life cycle made up of a sequence of distinct phases. These products may require the investment of significant resources by the customers and the longer the life of the product the greater the potential for customer satisfaction to change (usually decrease) over time. These aspects tend to increase a customer's recollections of his or her experiences with the product throughout its life.

Taking a page out of business management strategies, many educational institutions have participated in student satisfaction surveys and have brought in experts to train departments dealing directly with students to be more "consumer friendly." But, these efforts alone are not enough in today's competitive and costly educational environment, as a small but increasing number of institutions have come to recognize.

Academic institutions as we discussed in the last chapter need to expand their definition of "customer" beyond on-campus students. They need to recognize and incorporate into their thinking - both within and outside the classroom - other key stakeholders in the academic enterprise: parents, communities, and employers. Satisfying this new triumvirate of interests is not simple and requires that those within institutions change how they approach their day-to-day activities.

Figure 6.1. A basic model for customer satisfaction

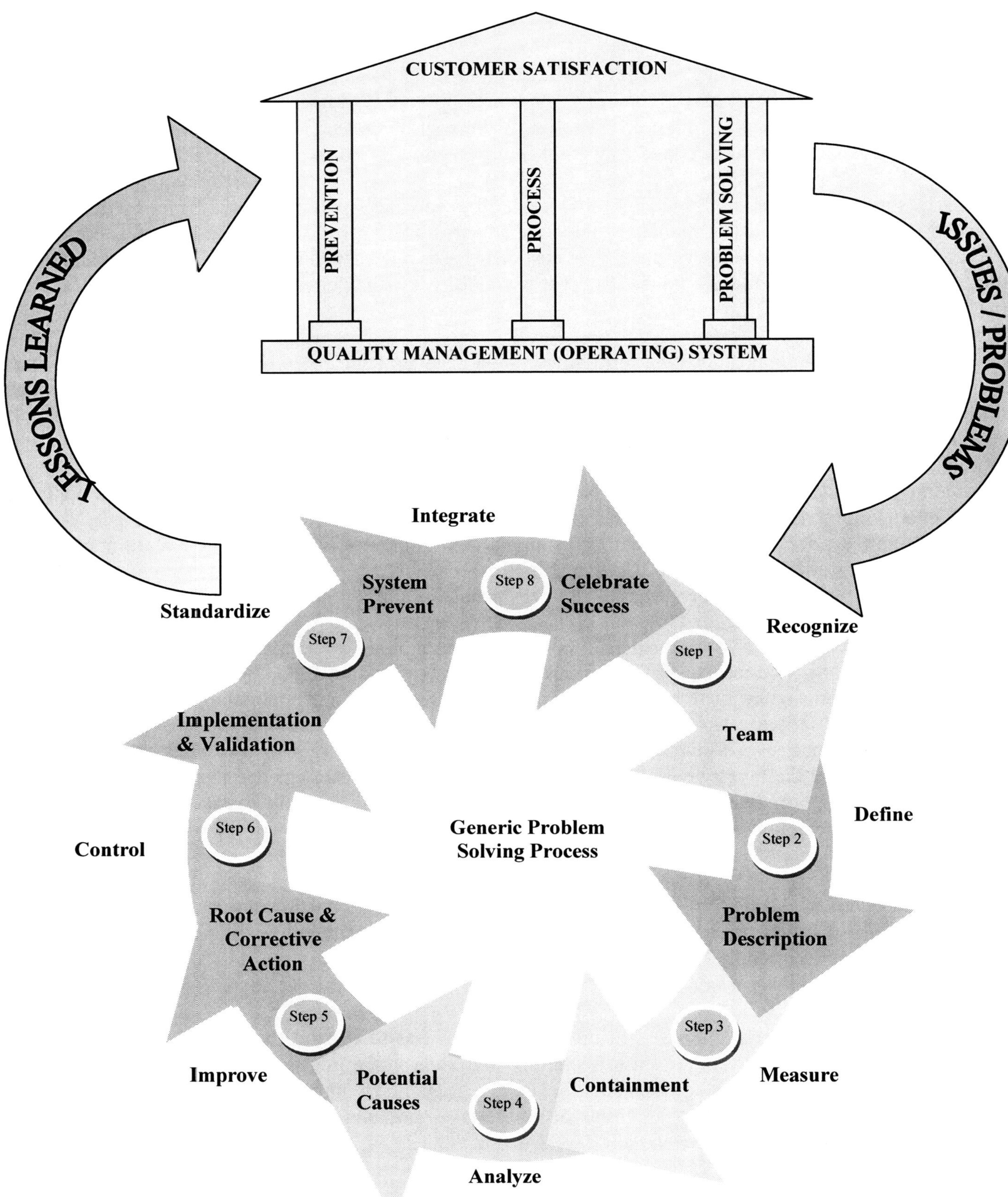

Generally speaking, stakeholders are individuals or entities who stand to gain or lose from the success or failure of a system or an organization. Stakeholder theory suggests that businesses need to pay attention to stakeholders by focusing on those who affect or are affected by its products or services. Stakeholder analysis creates a framework within which businesses identify, evaluate, and then incorporate these interests into their decision-making processes. Well-structured consideration of expanded interests leads to better planning, new and creative initiatives and improved resource allocation - all of which promote organizational success and curb failure.

Although academic institutions have been loath to employ business strategies into their operational thinking, there is one approach that begs to be transported into the academic arena - business stakeholder analysis (BSA) (Gross and Godwin 2005). BSA is a useful tool for learning how to think more expansively about stakeholders, and then actively to incorporate these newly identified stakeholders into the corporate decision-making process without sacrificing institutional values.

In an educational institution, a stakeholder analysis would start by identifying the obvious and well-known stakeholders: parents, students, faculty, and administrators. Parents are very interested in the educational institution, but have little influence on the enterprise. On the other hand, students, faculty, administrators, employers and society at large include people and entities within and outside the business itself. But the assessment would not stop there. For example, just like in a business that produces consumer products cares about its customers but also its suppliers, its prospective customers, its employers, and its community, so and the educational institutions of all levels need to consider, among others, their alumni, the parent body, the community where they are located, and the entities - both public and private - that will be employing their graduating students. Ideally, educators would also consider the ultimate consumer of the employer's products; for example, a law school would consider the ultimate consumer of legal services in addition to the law firm itself, and a medical school would consider the patients in addition to the hospitals.

In an organization, customer satisfaction should be a system that involves everyone. Customer satisfaction is a systematic process for collecting customer data (*e.g.*, surveys, complaints, audits, and so on), analyzing this data to make it into actionable information, driving the results throughout an organization, and implementing satisfaction improvement plans. Therefore, the main components of a customer satisfaction system are the measurement programs coupled with other information provided by the customer (*e.g.*, customer complaints, service information, and so on) and customer satisfaction improvement plans. The measurement programs should be designed to assess satisfaction levels at different periods during the life cycle of a customer and should clearly point out what aspects of the business need to be improved. The satisfaction measures and analysis obtained are then used to create close-looped customer satisfaction improvement plans which should be devised and implemented by the different functions in an organization. Once improvement plans are implemented, follow-up surveys should be done to track progress. For the construction of a survey instrument see Stamatis (1996) and Kerlinger (1973).

In the education arena we have many customers which we addressed as stakeholders in the last chapter. However, the same requirements apply here as we mentioned in the last paragraphs. That is: Each customer, parent, student, administrator, board member, business community and society at large has to be satisfied with the product and service that they receive form the educational process. Of curse, in the case of the educational process the product (learner) goes through different phases during its life: the learning process, use of the learning ability, and an improvement or replacement decision for the learning. At the end of the product's life, society at large decides whether or not to replace the product with the same or another learning requirement. One can then think of the customer as having a "life cycle" which ends and may be renewed when the product's life ends. The events preceding the replacement phase can strongly influence customer satisfaction and a customer's willingness to repurchase a company's products.

In the second phase of stakeholder analysis, just like business leaders prioritize among the stakeholders by assessing both their relative interest in and influence on (power within) the organization, so too the educational entity must reevaluate the prioritization of their own stakeholders. This prioritization should be based on a simple chart of high and low scales. An example is shown in Table 6.1.

Table 6.1. Prioritization scale

	Influence	
	High	Low
Interest	Low	High

Once the scale has been agreed upon and all stakeholders appear on this prioritization chart, the decision for high priority concern becomes quite obvious as one follows the priorities of the resultant quadrants high/high, high/low, low/high, and low/low. Those with both the greatest interest and influence are of the highest priority. Those with the least interest and least influence may be worth cultivating prospectively but need not have a mainstream role in business planning.

With priorities established, stakeholder analysis turns to understanding the stakeholder interests within each quadrant, often through detailed interviews with them. After careful evaluation, stakeholder analysis actually moves to incorporating the gathered information into the design and function of the business enterprise.

In the business context, stakeholder analysis might include market research, such as interviewing customers to determine what the customer wants and needs in a new product, or what would make an existing product work better. In other words, instead of companies pre-guessing what their customers want, they ask them. Based on the responses they proceed with particular offerings in products or services. The rationale here is that as customers sense that businesses are responsive to them will be more loyal purchasers.

This approach may be applied to educational institutions. However one must be very careful because the results may be counter productive. Let us see an example starting with the role of parents. Suppose an institution interviewed select members of the parent body to determine what would most benefit them in terms of their child's educational experience. The results could produce changes in how parents are treated on campus and the communications they receive between visits. It could influence the content of events for families at orientation, lead to the creation of family days during the semester, and foster frequent correspondence and e-mail access to applicable administrators so questions can be answered and natural concerns assuaged.

Educational institutions could also start listening to employers. Given the diversity among employers and the wide-ranging jobs into which graduates will be placed, this is no small task. But, it is worth understanding what employers want in their employees and then seeing if those skills are ones that can be integrated into the academic experience without undermining the academic enterprise. It is certainly premature to assume that the skills that employers want are antithetic to a thoughtful educational enterprise. Suppose, by way of example, that employers want employees who are computer literate, and who can read and assess data, call out important information, and write clearly and persuasively. In addition, perhaps employers want employees who are comfortable with multiple cultures and diverse languages. Employers may also be seeking employees with strong oral communication skills. Perhaps employers want graduates with excellent research skills, too.

Rather than guess about employer needs, educational institutions should inquire about them. Once armed with the data, institutional leaders can assess how those skills might be incorporated into the classroom and campus experience. Just imagine introducing a greater number of oral, rather than written, final examinations if verbal communication skills were highly valued in certain fields.

Obviously, not every class can teach every skill that every employer wants or every request that a parent may have. Nor should they. But, educational institutions that listen to parents, employers and other constituents that are willing to think through with them how needed "skill sets" can find a home within their school will have accomplished several critical goals. They will have created graduates who will be satisfied and gainfully employed. And, they will have created relationships with employers who are willing to employ their students, as well as be willing to work with educators to achieve a match between what academia can provide and what the workplace demands. A new, yet a classic example of this, is the introduction of Six Sigma training in many universities.

As has occurred repeatedly in business, success comes to those who identify, learn from, and involve their stakeholders. Educators should take their cue from business' successes. It is time to identify, listen to, and involve more stakeholders in the academic enterprise and to do so continually. It is imperative that we adapt the success lessons from business to educational environments so that the better results can be implemented. One way of learning and adopting these lessons is through Benchmarking.

A good tool to use in order to optimize customer satisfaction is the six sigma methodology. The reason for being a good tool is that especially in any educational environment, customer satisfaction is the driving force behind the improvement initiative of excellence. Customer satisfaction is the organization's knowledge of the customer, overall customer service systems, responsiveness, and its ability to meet their functionality in terms of requirements and expectations.

The basic aim of quality process is the delivery of ever improving value to customers. To identify this "value" we also must identify the types of customer. A customer is someone who is impacted by the product (goods or service). Therefore, within any company there are departments and persons (internal customer) that supply products of services to each other. If service to internal customer is unsatisfactory it is unlikely that the expectation of external customer will be met. On the other hand, clients who buy the product or service are the external customers. Products or services may be sold to end users by intermediaries such as dealers, retail stores, distributors and so on, thus determining the ultimate customer. [Organizations should take into account both intermediaries and end users when defining their "customer."]

But that is not enough. In the educational system – at all levels – we are also interested in customer expectations and priorities of needs as they are essential in product development. Product development translates customer expectations for functional requirements into specific specifications and quality characteristics. This means starting with desired product and then identifying the necessary characteristics for raw materials, parts, assemblies and process steps. This is where the six sigma methodology may play a role in helping the institution to select and evaluate the best alternatives.

In addition to the six sigma methodology two common techniques documenting the voice of the customer in their own terms and incorporated in the six sigma methodology are the Kano model and Quality Function Deployment (QFD). Whereas the Kano model allows us to identify and differentiate the basic, performance and excitement items that the customer perceives as important, the QFD is a specific technique consisting of a series of interlocking matrices that translate customer functionality into product or service or process characteristics. Specifically, it provides a systematic methodology that helps the organization to:

- Thoroughly define customer functionalities into requirements

- Prioritize those requirements
- Benchmark characteristics against competition and best practices
- Decide how to meet or exceed the requirements by designing those features into the product or process or service

We all must remember that if the appropriate and applicable definition of quality (as it relates to customer expectation) is not introduced early in the concept or design phase, there is a risk that design error will be discovered by the customer, in the market place. Because of this importance, it is imperative that management commitment must exist and continually review the process. This means, that management must always be in tune with how the company provides effective management of its interactions and relationships with customers and uses information gained from customers to improve products/process/service, as well as its customer relationship management process. Management can do that by:

- Ensuring easy access for customers to seek assistance, to comment and to complain
- Follow up with customers on products to determine satisfaction with recent transactions to seek feedback and to help build relationships
- Customer-contact employees (selection; special training – knowledge of product; empowerment and decision making; technology and logistics support for reliable and responsive service satisfaction)
- Analysis of feedback and complaint data for policy development, planning and resource allocations. In other words, a commitment to customers by the organization to promote trust and
    - Confidence in its product, when failure occurs
    - Free from unusual conditions and or exceptions
    - Open and honest communications
    - Comparison with competitors commitment

Why such a fuss about satisfaction in the six sigma methodology? Because, as we remove the dissatisfaction we decrease variation, and thereby increase satisfaction. But what is the source of dissatisfaction? Simply stated, it is a "complaint." It is an assertion of the quality defiance. The complaint may concern the product or it may concern other activities such as incorrect invoicing or shipment of incorrect goods, or discipline issues or even behavior and policy concerns. As the number of complaints increases a systematic approach to use centralized location to a) Register all complaints b) Summarize the complaints and c) Route the complaint to the concerned department, must be an issue. The information gained should be viewed as a feedback and appropriate and applicable action should be taken to "fix" the problem(s). To facilitate an optimum access for customers to comment on an organization's product/process/service is to have a company representative visit each customer frequently or ask the customer for their feedback on frequent intervals. The key here is to make sure that the feedback is easy for the customer. Typical items are:

- Provide personnel with well designed data sheets for easy and accurate recording
- Provide incentive to encourage adequate feedback
- Provide a glossary of terms to improve communications and code number to simplify the data entry analysis
- Provide training in "how" and "why"
- Conduct audits of the data feedback process
- Make use of modern technology to collect the field information and analysis to provide managers with summaries and decision making
- Make use of the "sample" concept

- Make use of the "control" concept

Furthermore, information about satisfaction may be obtained through warranty records. A warranty is a form of assurance that a product/process/service is fit for use or failing this "use," that the user will receive some kind of compensation. In most situations there are two kinds of warranties a) a general warranty of "merchantability" – fitness for the customary use of such product and b) special warranty for the specific use to which product will be put (used), provided the seller knows these special conditions.

These special conditions may be identified or planned as:

- Comprehensiveness of warranty coverage
- Terms and conditions of warranties, including exclusions and the like
- Clarity and understandability of written warranties. Keep both the legal jargon and fine print (footnotes) to a minimum
- How customers value the extra commitments the organization makes for customer satisfaction
- How the organization compares to competitors or Best Class leaders
- How innovative the organization's effort is for its commitment to customer. [Remember that written guarantees are especially helpful to customer because: a) they protect the buyer by selling out the seller's obligations to customer and b) they protect the seller by spelling out the limit of the seller's obligation].

In addition to feedback and warranties an organization must "know" their customer. This is done with the proper and applicable segmentation strategy. The organization should know the current and potential customers. (Some organizations differentiate this by calling them "customer" and "consumer" respectively.) Next step is to divide the customer into different market segments. While it is true that all of the customers have some common requirements and expectations about the products, those in different markets have their own unique requirement as well. For example: in a local school district there is an unusual high demographic of say Greek immigrants. The segmentation policy that perhaps the school district might consider is to offer bilingual teaching to the students of that particular group. In a college environment if the majority of the students come from a heavy automotive region, and they are interested in automotive related topics, then the segmentation policy could be a) automotive and b) non automotive. Once this differentiation has taken place, now each customer is considered unique. Some of the considerations should be the following:

- Thoroughness of process identifying market segments and potential customers
- Degree to which customer requirements have been identified for each market segment
- Identification of the common and unique requirements and expectation for each market segment
- Frequency of data collection on each market segment

To be sure, customer understanding and satisfaction are of great interest. However, suppliers play a major role in customer satisfaction as well. The relationship obviously varies from adversarial to teamwork and everything else in between, but the fact remains unless organizations have a good relationship with their supplier base their customer satisfaction will be short lived or not present at all. It is imperative that the relationship must be cultivated and developed to the point where the organization and the supplier see it as a "win-win" relationship. To do that, some of the following concepts and principles must be followed:

- The supplier becomes an extension of the buyer's organization
- Working closely together for the mutual benefit of both parties
- Long term purchase agreement

- Joint quality related activities (training, planning and so on)

It is obvious from this short list of requirements that communication and teamwork are essential. So let us look at some communication techniques that may help the process:

- Warrant cards: Upon purchase of the product, the purchaser is asked to return a card stating the condition of the product when it was received.
- Telephone calls: Here, customers are called and asked for impressions on the quality of the item they purchased
- Visit individual customers: Another form of collecting data is the periodic visit to major customers by a marketing or engineering representative of the company
- Mail survey: For most of the questions, the customer is asked to respond by checking off excellent, very good, good, fair or poor
- Special arrangement(s) with individual customers: A simple but effective approach for gaining field intelligence is to establish a special arrangement with a few customers to obtain information in depth. Fundamentally, this approach is heavily based on interviewing skills on a one-to-one basis.
- Focus group: This technique is conducted in order to better understand customer's perception of a company's product. It consists of about eight to ten current and potential customers who meet for a few hours to discuss a specific product. [Depending on the goals, the participants of a focus group may be average customers, non customers or special customers]. Some key features of a focus group are:

  - The discussion can focus on current products, proposed products or future products
  - A moderator who is skilled on group dynamics, guides and or facilitates the discussion
  - The moderator has a clear goal as to the information needed and a plan for guiding a discussion
  - Often a company personnel observes and listens in an adjacent room shielded by a one way mirror.

In the discussion of customer satisfaction we will be amiss if we do not recognize that conflicts arise. For example: How customer related data and results are aggregated with other key data to analyses into actionable information and develop priorities for prompt solutions to customer related problems? Or, how do we interpret and analyze the data? Or, what data is appropriate? When these types of questions arise, conflict exists, and it should be handled professionally as a data driven application with appropriate and applicable conflict resolution practices. There are three minimum requirements of conflict resolution. They are:

1. Existence of a formula and logical process for resolving customer complaints
2. Clearly define escalation procedure for situations in which customers do not feel their complaint has been resolved by lower level personnel
3. Level of empowerment

So, how can six sigma help in customer satisfaction? Or better yet, what are some of the specific items that six sigma may provide that will benefit the organization and will increase customer satisfaction and loyalty? We believe that at least the following outcomes will be directly related to the effort of implementing six sigma:

- Product and service planning: Long term focus; prevention based; customer driven strategic planning process

- Measured performance: Customer satisfaction; market share; long term profitability; total productivity
- Attitude toward customers: Recognition and importance of the voice of the customer; professional treatment and attention to customers needs, wants and expectations
- Quality of products and services: Provided according to customer requirements and needs
- Marketing focus: Increased market share and financial growth achieved through customer satisfaction
- Process management approach: Focus on error and defect prevention rather than appraisal techniques and justification; product and service delivery attitude – realization that fast time to market is important; people orientation – customer driven and management by data; mode of operation – management supported improvement through teamwork between suppliers, process owners and customers; improvement strategy – total process management and focus on continual improvement.

Summary

In this chapter we have attempted to explain the issue of customer satisfaction in the educational process by focusing on each of the stakeholders. In the next chapter we will focus on specific tools of improvement.

References

Ford, C. (January 1996). Partnership offers process manufacturing solution. *Managing Automation*. Pp. 24-25.

Greene, A. (January 1996). Looking beyond ERP for a supply chain advantage. *Managing Automation*. P. 6.

Levin, D. (February 8, 1996). Apple took advice from wrong group. *Detroit Free Press*. P. 1E.

Kerlinger, F. N. (1973). *Foundations of behavioral research*. 2nd ed. Holt, Rinehart and Winston. New York.

Stamatis, D. H. (1996). *Total quality service*. St. Lucie Press. Delray Beach, FL.

CHAPTER 7

TOOLS FOR IMPROVEMENT

In the last chapter we discussed customer satisfaction and how it applies to the educational process. In this chapter we will identify some common yet powerful tools for improvement in the educational process.

It is beyond the scope of this book to address in detail all the methodologies and specific tools available for anyone practicing quality. However, here we present a plethora of both basic and advanced items that may be used in pursuing improvement in an educational environment. In addition, the tools that we have selected are frequently used, and simple. Because of the cursory approach to each one of them, the reader is highly encouraged to see other references, such as Mizuno (1988), Brassard and Ritter (1994, 1988), Gitlow, Gitlow and Openheimer (1989), Grant and Leavenworth (1980), Gulezian (1991), Ishicawa (1982), Kerzner (1995), Tague (1995) and many others in the references and selected bibliography.

As in any discipline, in quality we also have specific tools for improvement. Fundamentally, that improvement begins by preventing problems from happening and if they do happen to find the root cause and solve it. In other words, we use specific tools in a very structured and documented approach to either prevent or solve a problem at its root cause and provide an *actionable solution*. Of course, since the root cause analysis is a process in itself, the individuals who are involved with the process must know its components. Generally, this process involves a variation of seven stages. They are:

1. *Problem Description*: here we must differentiate between symptom and problem. A symptom is a sign, evidence, indicator, or manifestation of a primary or secondary issue root cause. A problem on the other hand is a concern that is currently causing difficulties. Sometimes we must be careful because the way we define a symptom may in fact be the problem and the way we define the problem may indeed be a symptom. For example, if we had a nonconformance (a deviation from what is expected) – say absenteeism - and asked WHY we have this situation?; then, in seeking an answer to the "WHY?", we found that absenteeism is caused by lack of transportation availability; the transportation issue here may be because the parents do not have a vehicle, the school does not provide bussing or it may be that education in the family is not held in high esteem and the person who misses school is interested in a job to support the family. As we can see from this simple example it can be a very convoluted process to find the real problem. That is why in the process of identifying what is the true problem description may be somewhat time consuming and difficult to isolate. Therefore, we want to continue to ask WHY, until we are certain of all the root causes including, most importantly, the primary root cause. If the problem definition cannot be articulated with specificity, then a request from the contact initiator for further clarification of the Who?, What?, When?, Where?, Why?, How? and How Many?, is required.
2. *Interim Action/Containment and Effective Date*: Here we try to isolate the problem as much as we can in order to minimize the effects to the customer, by putting a temporary action in the system to prevent further damage.
3. *Root Cause*: Here we move forward with specific analysis to resolve the problem. It is vital to emphasize the importance of capturing all the root causes of the nonconformance, during root cause analysis. If all the root causes are not captured, the problem may seem to have been corrected; only to surprise us by reappearing in the future. There are many tools that one may use but the most common ones are: a) Time line analysis: Identifying events that occurred shortly before, during, and after the problem developed, to identify potential root causes b) Brain storming: An activity in which team members give their ideas of potential root causes and solutions. The intent is to generate several initial ideas, without criticism. Then, to seek a team consensus on the most likely root causes

and solutions, from the ideas given c) Is/Is not: Review problem description; then describe where problem's "symptoms" are observed (IS) and where problem's "symptoms" could be, but are not observed (IS NOT). Then the contrast between the corresponding IS and IS NOT statements are examined to identify potential root causes of the problem d) Cause and effect diagram: It is also called a fishbone diagram. A brief problem description is placed at the right end (the effect) of a horizontal line on the diagram, and various branches and sub-branches come off this horizontal line (the causes). The main branches typically represent Man, Method, Machine, Material, Measurement, and Mother Nature (Environment), known as the 6Ms or 5M&E e) Flow chart and FMEA: A Flow Chart represents in a visual way the flow of the current process. The FMEA on the other hand is a way to identify potential problems and offer a solution given a set of priority items f) Pareto chart: A Pareto chart ranking may be applicable, and if so, would provide insight into potential root causes. It is a way of prioritizing causes g) 5Ws: A technique used to identify potential root causes by asking as many questions as necessary, even more than 5 if necessary, to identify potential root causes.

4. *Permanent Action and Effective Date*: Here we identify the permanent solution that we found in the analysis stage and the effective date of the implementation.
5. *Verification*: Perhaps one of the most critical stages. Here we verify whether or not the "fix" that we identified in our analysis is indeed a *true fix*. Sometimes this is called as the turn on/turn off stage: This technique is used, when economically practical, to test a root cause. If the root cause has been accurately identified and is reintroduced to the process, the problem will return. Then when the root cause is removed, the problem will go away. (Note that the "Before" refers to "close to" but before the root causes are corrected. The "After" refers to after the root causes are corrected).
6. *Control*: This is the monitoring of the process after the problem has been fixed. The control makes sure that the problem does not repeat again.
7. *Prevention*: Here we plan for prevention of problems and improvement of the process.

In the classical sense the tools are categorized into two categories: a) Basic tools and b) Advanced or Management tools. In our discussion however, we are going to address some additional methodologies and tools that may be used in the educational institutions from K-12 and colleges and universities.

Basic tools

Brainstorming: By far the most frequently used tool. This is a group decision-making technique designed to generate a large number of creative ideas through an interactive process. Brainstorming can be used to get the ideas of the team and or group organized into a process flow diagram or a cause-and-effect diagram. It is perhaps one of the most common and first tools used in quality initiatives.

Questions to use during brainstorming sessions: Often the question regarding brainstorming is: "How do we begin?" The following basic four questions pose a good beginning.

1. What are the organization's three most important unsolved and or recurrent quality problems as you see them?
2. What kind of action plan is needed to solve these problems?
3. Which areas are most in need of such action? (Try to be as specific as possible.)
4. What are some major obstacles in the way of improving our quality?

Even though this is a creative session we must follow specific rules:

1. Clearly define the goal of the brainstorming session. This is very important. If the definition is not clear, then the participants will be discussing different problems.
2. Try to have all people give their ideas in three words or less.

3. Write down all ideas. Some may seem silly, but they may lead in an idea that could help solve the problem.
4. Generate a large number of ideas. Quantity, not quality is important here. The greater the "idea count" the better! Combinations of ideas are alright, too.
5. Do not allow one or two individuals to dominate the session.
6. Make the ideas visible so that everyone can easily see them; use an overhead projector or a flip chart to list the ideas.

Brainstorming Procedure: In addition to the rules, there are appropriate procedures that must be followed in order for an optimum resolution. These procedures are divided into two categories which are:

1. Creating the ideas
- The leader asks each person to list his/her ideas on a piece of paper.
- The leader then solicits everyone's contribution. This is done by going from person to person in rotation. If a member does not have an idea on a particular round, he/she simply says "I pass." However, he/she is asked on every round.
- As ideas are given they should be listed on a transparency or a flip chart.
- Omit only ideas that have been listed and that have already been contributed by someone else.
- After each person has contributed their individual list, the leader asks for any additional ideas which may have been generated during the contribution process.
- A final point. The human mind thinks at two different levels, the conscious and the unconscious. After a good brainstorming session everyone's mind will be spinning with all new, wild ideas. The unconscious mind will continue brainstorming even after you have stopped thinking about it at a conscious level. Thus the team should continue the brainstorming after an incubation period has passed.

2. Evaluating the ideas that were contributed
- Each of the ideas should be evaluated. Some ideas will be scrapped right away without a detailed discussion.
- The evaluation should be pointed towards the idea and never towards the person who suggested it.

Check sheet: Check sheets are forms that guide the experimenter in categorizing the data as they are being collected (Stamatis 1997). Its construction is very simple and is as follows:
- Agree on the item being observed
- Decide on a time period to collect data.
- Design a form that is clear and easy to understand.
- Collect the data honestly and consistently

5W: When identifying underlying causes, it can also be useful to ask five sequential "Whys" to get to the heart of a problem. For example: What is the problem? "Deliveries not complete by 4:00 p.m." Why does this happen? The routing of trucks is not optimized. Why? Goods are loaded in the trucks based on size rather than location of delivery. Why? The computer automatically defines the order based on large items first. Why? Large items are delivered first. Why? Current workflow prioritization puts large items first on the delivery schedule, regardless of location and proximity.

Cause and effect diagram: This diagram is a method of organizing information about a problem or a goal (Stamatis 1997). It is a visual representation of what people think is the cause of a particular problem. In its simplest form it is a method used to help decide what to do to achieve a goal; it is based on the relationship among the variables of: manpower, machine, method, material, measurement, and environment. With the analysis of the relationships between these variables an isolated cause and effect resolution is identified. There are three basic rules in constructing a cause-and-effect diagram:

1. Start with a clear definition of the problem or goal. Put this in a box on the right side of the paper.
2. Draw arrows using the "five Ms and E" (*i.e.*, manpower, machine, method, material, measurement, and environment). Other labels may be used if appropriate and applicable.
3. Begin to fill in all the things that you think will cause the problem or help to achieve the goal.

A typical cause-and-effect diagram looks like a fishbone and that is why some call it as such. Because this diagram is very popular in the quality improvement process, let us also address some issues in the construction process.

1. A cause-and-effect diagram may be constructed at the same time as the brainstorming is being conducted, or after a process flow diagram is completed, or even independently from either one of them.
2. Write down in the applicable category everything people suggest. Do not judge.
3. Remember, the information is important, not the form.
4. Where causes are put in the diagram is not important at first. They can go under any of the headings or even under multiple headings.
5. There is nothing wrong with placing the same cause in different places on the diagram, if people want it that way. If you find that a cause is recurring under different headings, it may be an indication of obvious trouble.
6. It is important for all persons to help in adding causes to the diagram.
7. If the diagram is not finished at the end of the meeting, you or others can add to it later.
8. Some companies post cause-and-effect diagrams so that their employees can add to them. They serve as displays rather than tools to identify problems and improvements.

Dispersion Analysis Cause-and-Effect Diagram: A major disadvantage of the cause-and-effect (C&E) diagram is that many major causes for a quality problem could appear on a single branch (Stamatis 1997). This makes the diagram difficult to develop and use. A slightly different C&E diagram is a *dispersion analysis diagram* where all the major sources of variability are listed as branches. (Quite often the cause-and-effect diagram is used first and then a dispersion analysis diagram is used to identify and expand on the major causes).

In choosing to use a C&E diagram versus other types of diagram, consider the following:

- *Advantages*: 1) There is a clear grouping of potential causes which enables effective later analysis, and 2) the resulting diagram is not too complex.
- *Disadvantages*: 1) Major causes can be easily overlooked, if the 5M&E method is not used first; 2) it is sometimes difficult to classify major causes; and 3) the greatest knowledge of potential causes is required.

In essence then the construction question is: "Why is there variability in major cause (#) that could cause a quality problem (X)?"

There are many ways that the C&E diagram may be used. For an effective and efficient use in the workplace the following seven rules should be followed:

1. Develop a process flow diagram for the part of the process you want to improve.
2. Isolate and clearly define the problem to be solved.
3. Use the brainstorming technique to find all possible causes of the quality problem.

4. Organize the brainstorming results into logical categories.
5. Construct the appropriate cause-and-effect diagram that clearly and accurately displays the relationship of all the data in each category.
6. Explore and implement solutions to assess improvement.
7. Use statistical methods to assess improvement.

A C&E diagram is used to identify and categorize problems. Therefore, the person who is using it must be cognizant of some basic information as far as selecting a solution is concerned. The information is gained through a series of questions, and the following questions may serve as samples.

- Will the solution solve our problem and is there information existing to improve this?
- How long is it going to take to make the necessary changes and to see some signs of reducing or eliminating the problem?
- What monetary investment will be needed?
- What quality improvements will be achieved?
- How many people/jobs are affected by the quality improvement solution?
- How will the improvement affect people? Will they need to make changes?
- Will they choose to accept the changes?
- What technical changes are needed? Will these changes have an impact on the 5M&E?
- How much change can the company absorb at one time? How quickly can the changes be made and who is needed to help make the changes?

In addition to these questions, the team must use some rules for selecting a solution and then move to the approval process. The rules are indeed very basic, however, and are very important in the process. They provide consistency as well as a systematic approach to the C&E process. On the other hand, the approval process provides a sort of checklist of how the solution is approved and then implemented. To monitor the process, an action plan is used. A typical action plan is shown in Figure 7.1.

Figure 7.1. A typical action plan

Action Plan Process: ____________ Date: ____________				
Significant Characteristics	Evaluation Method	Frequency	Analysis of Result	Reaction and or Responsibility of Action

The Basic Rules
- Decide your goal (what you want to accomplish) and the method you are going to use to solve the problem.
- Be sure to let all the people who are affected by the problem be involved in selecting and planning its solution.
- Evaluate the costs, benefits, and time involved to implement the solution.

- Decide the steps that are necessary to implement the solution.
- Create a formal presentation for choosing the problem and your suggested solution(s).

The Approval Process
- Introduce what you are going to talk about.
- Clearly define the problem.
- Show the importance of the problem and its related costs (use evidence).
- Clearly state your proposed solution.
- Talk about the benefits of solving this problem (use evidence).
- State what is needed to solve the problem.
- Prepare a checklist to cover anticipated questions, objections, etc.

Implementing the Solution
- Clarify all tasks to be completed.
- Define the order of completion of the tasks.
- List the resources needed to complete each task. Who does what? How long will it take?
- Give the time frame for completion of task.
- Assign responsibility for each task.
- Assign how results will be measured and monitored.
- Set up procedures for measuring results of each task.
- Evaluate the effectiveness of solution.

Team Responsibilities for an Effective Solution
- Do not take anything for granted.
- Do not assume anything—ask questions.
- Tell each person what they are responsible for doing.
- Ensure that everyone works to complete and follow through with the action plan.
- Make sure completion of assignments are monitored.
- Remove any barriers to successfully implementing the solution.
- Be sure everyone affected by the solution is in the final process of implementation.

Histogram: This is a bar graph that gives a historical and pictorial representation of a set of data (Stamatis 1997). It is used to determine:

1. the shape of a series of data values
2. the readiness of a process to undergo a capability study
3. the dispersion and central tendency of the data (quick analysis)
4. the relationship of machines, customers, suppliers, etc. (quick analysis)

To construct a histogram,
- Determine how many data values to use.
- Determine the width of the data by computing the range.
- Select the number of cells for the histogram.
- Determine the width of each cell.
- Determine the starting number for the first interval.
- Calculate the intervals.
- Assign data values to the appropriate intervals.
- Construct the histogram by drawing bars to represent the cell frequencies.

Process flow chart: One of the most often used and powerful tools in the quality improvement process. A process flow diagram is a road map of the process (Stamatis 1997). Specifically, a process flow diagram illustrates and or clarifies events/tasks in a process and the events/tasks between them. It assists in highlighting: 1) the present situation, 2) the differences between what should/is thought to be happening and the actual situation, 3) the proposed situation, and 4) any potential problem areas. It can be used to facilitate effectiveness during brainstorming, constructing a cause-and-effect diagram, and in every other situation where there is ambivalence about what the present state is. To construct a process flow chart, the following are important.

- Assemble all the appropriate people.
- Define the process and its boundaries.
- Brainstorm the process.
- Use the simplest symbols possible (*i.e.,* O, operations; D, delay, -->, flow; ∇, inventory; $\square$, inspection). Decisions are usually shown as diamonds or O since they are activities (operations).
- Draw the steps the process actually follows.
- Make sure each feedback loop is accounted for.
- Draw the steps the process should follow.
- Compare the two, and make the appropriate adjustments.

Pareto diagram: The Pareto analysis is a chart based on the Pareto principle (Stamatis 1997). This principle was named for an Italian economist who, in the late 1800s, found that most of the wealth in Italy was owned by a few of the people. Today we find that 80% of our problems in any environment can be traced to 20% of the causes. The Pareto analysis is a process of ranking opportunities so we can determine which should be pursued first. In essence, the Pareto analysis allows us to examine the vital few from the trivial many.

Pareto analysis should be used at various stages in a quality improvement program to determine which step to take next. Pareto analysis is used to answer such questions as "What department should have the next team?" or "On what problem should we concentrate our efforts?" The chart itself is a graph that ranks factors in descending order of frequency or magnitude from left to right. The following steps are necessary to construct a Pareto chart:

- Decide the appropriate time interval.
- Decide the number of classifications.
- Decide the total number of occurrences for each category using primary or secondary data.
- Calculate category percentage.
- Rank categories in descending order.
- Calculate the cumulative percentage.
- Construct a Pareto chart for magnitudes and cumulative percentages.

Scatter diagram: If one is interested in finding out if there is a relationship between variables, then the scatter plot is a useful tool for finding that relationship (Stamatis 1996, 1997). Regardless of what the relationship is, the scatter plot cannot prove that one variable causes the other. What it shows in a graphical form is that a relationship exists and how strong that relationship is.

One of the shortcomings of the scatter plot is that it is not always possible to describe a relationship with a mathematical formula (*i.e.,* it is a pictorial relationship); however, statistics can numerically describe the relationship between two sets of data. The methods used to do this are too difficult to present here, but we can gain an idea of the end result of the methods. The actual mathematical relationship between sets of data is called a correlation.

To construct a scatter plot:
- Collect at least 50 paired samples of data.
- Draw horizontal and vertical axes, making sure that the values on each axes become higher as you move away from the origin (as you move up and to the right in the vertical and horizontal axes respectively.) As a general rule the expected "cause" is the horizontal axes, where the "effect" is the vertical axes.
- Plot the data.

Statistical process control (SPC): A key aspect of defect prevention is using "the voice of the process" *(i.e.* data from process and product measurements analyzed by appropriate statistical methods) to indicate when actions are necessary (*e.g.* adjustments, tool changes) and conversely, when the process should be left alone (Stamatis 2003, Montgomery 1985). The approaches to gathering data and analyzing it will vary according to the type of process and such other factors as degree of automation, process capability, and production volume. The launching of SPC and the development of existing programs require the expertise of people trained in the use of statistical methods. While the preferred method is to have such people on the organization's staff, there are situations where outside consultants can be of service.

The process parameters and/or product characteristics to be controlled using SPC are taken directly from the control plan and also incorporate all that has been learned from the AQP process. As more experience is gained through operation of the process, the need for SPC on certain characteristics may decrease. Upstream controls may reduce or eliminate the need to control certain characteristics. Alternatively, customer use of the products may suggest additional characteristics requiring control. In all cases, the control plan should be updated and submitted to the customer for approval.

When one speaks of SPC one really addresses three distinct items. They are: statistics, process and control. To appreciate the essence of "Statistical Process Control," one must think of employing the language of statistics, focused on a process for the purpose of control. An overview of what each aspect contributes to the total concept will prove helpful. (The reader should keep in mind that the SPC is really a methodology to study the behavior of the process rather than controlling anything.)

Statistics has frequently been described in a broad sense as a universal language, which is most useful in describing physical variability. Any group of data or numbers can be described and analyzed through statistical methods. Effective use of the language is enhanced by choosing the most pertinent data and handling it in the most efficient manner to best describe the physical variability of interest.

A familiar analogy involves engineering drawing as a universal language employed in describing the physical shape of a product. A blueprint is a document utilizing engineering drawing to describe the physical shape of a product. In an analogous sense, a control chart [a central tool of SPC] is a document utilizing statistics as a universal language to describe the physical variability of a process.

On the other hand, a *process* may be defined as a combination of inputs, both durable and convertible resources, for the purpose of obtaining desired quality outputs. The transformation (value added) of the inputs into the output(s) is the process. The convertible resources are the inputs: materials, energy and information. Traditionally speaking, they have been called: manpower, machine, material, method, measurement and environment. Output, on the other hand, indicates: products, information and services.

96

The transformation itself may be part of the durable resources or a combination of the durable as well as the convertible resources including environment.

Using this definition, a process may be thought of in global terms as all the operations of a business collectively or in a much more narrow sense as a particular operation of a specific machine. Both views are appropriate. Typically, opportunities for improvement are illuminated by removing as much of the noise as possible by narrowing the focus to smaller elements of the total process.

Control, the final word of "SPC," is frequently misconstrued as a misnomer. The question arises, "Does SPC control anything?" Strictly speaking, SPC does not control anything. However, a little thought leads one to the conclusion that control is not only an appropriate term but also the key to successful implementation of SPC. The classical control cycle consists of at least four actions: observing or measuring, comparing, diagnosing and correcting. Any time these four actions are successfully accomplished, a control cycle may be applied to many different systems in various ways.

The issue for organizational improvement strategies reduces to two generic applications of such a control cycle: Product Control and Process Control. Successful completion in either case may lead to improvement; however, it is significantly more improved through process control. To optimize this improvement in any process, process variation must be understood.

Process variation: The purpose of a control chart is to view **over** time the behavior of the process. [This must be emphasized over and over again, because we can also view the behavior of a process in specific time *i.e.* with a histogram].That behavior may be due to either a common or special cause. In either case, improvement in quality (reduction in variation) of the output may come as a result of either removing or reducing either or both types of causes.

1. Special cause: A source of variation which influences some (or all) of the measurements but in different ways. (If special causes of variation are present… The output of a process will not be stable over time…and is not predictable). Therefore, special causes are: assignable, chaotic and unnatural.

2. Common cause: A source of variation which influences all of the measurements in the same way. (If only common causes of variation are present… the output of a process forms a distribution pattern that is stable over time… and that pattern is predictable). Therefore, common causes are: random, natural and chance.

Quite often, one wonders what is the problem with variation? The answer, of course, is that when one wants to determine from the variability pattern in the data which deviations from the target have likely been produced by special causes and which have probably been produced by just the common causes. Why is this important? Because the responsibility for corrective actions rests with different authority levels. In the case of Special cause: Local fault which frequently can be corrected at the process by the operator and/or the supervisor are sufficient to correct the issues and concerns. On the other hand, common cause: system fault, which requires the attention of management to affect improvement of the process is necessary.

At this juncture, the reader may wonder as to how can this be done since all the data comes from the same process? The answer is to apply appropriate and applicable statistical techniques which have the ability to separate the presence of special causes in light of the ever present common causes. When this is done, improvement is the result. For more information on SPC see Stamatis (2003).

Since the purpose of SPC in problem solving and Process Control is to continually improve quality, productivity and costs, let us identify the elements that should facilitate this continual improvement. They are:

1. Top Management Commitment
2. Top Management Involvement
3. Team Approaches To Problem Identification and Solving
4. Statistical Training at all Levels
5. Implementation Plans with Supportive Resources

Perhaps, the most important requirement in any organization that embarks on any improvement initiative is the organization itself. That means its culture; attitude and approach are items of concern. The reason for this is that a total SPC approach stresses statistical thinking as a management tool but combines that with substantive knowledge of the processes to yield improvement results. A coordinated effort to identify and to appropriately act upon sources of variability is paramount. Proper organization is the starting point; while a number of scenarios might accomplish the objectives, a model which has performed well in various industries will be discussed. The model follows the following five stages/steps:

The first is to set up a *steering committee*: This group has the authority to designate and oversee SPC efforts. Setting the structure for efficient closure of the process control loop should be an aggressive goal. This group should be active in setting goals, monitoring progress, assuring efforts are directed in a useful manner and in making sure the various SPC efforts of different departments or groups are compatible. Specific responsibilities are:

- Decide on what areas should be addressed
- Ensure smooth movement of implementation
- Facilitate momentum building by ensuring timely and appropriate follow-up action to requests
- Involve each in following the reports
- Recognize accomplishments

The second is to recognize the use of *process teams*: Teams vertically integrated around the processes work most efficiently. Collection and analysis of data, conducting of experiments, and general steering of the pursuit of improvement for a particular process are all responsibilities of these groups. Specifically, responsibilities are:

- Planning the process control charts, proper type and logistics
- Installing the control charts, training and providing suitable materials and routines for the production personnel
- Monitoring the process control data collection and process information gathering to ensure smooth and effective use of the tools
- Acting upon instabilities, or creating the structure for the same.
- Monitoring and reporting progress, inhibitors, etc.

The third stage/step is to institute an *educational phase*. No one is born with all the knowledge that is needed to improve any process. That knowledge is learned. Therefore, the goals of this effort are to:

- Familiarize many with the common language
- Provide many with some basic knowledge
- Provoke thinking on an individual basis as to how this fits into one's daily work
- Provoke thinking of implications on a system basis
- The prerequisites for this knowledge are:
- Management awareness / understanding of basic philosophy
- Commitment of resources

- Organization for implementation

The fourth stage/step of the model is the *utilization phase*. It would not do anybody any good until what has been learned has been (or is in the process of being) implemented. Therefore, the goals in this phase are to:

a) Goals of the pilot application stage:

- Build technical confidence and maturity in the critical mass that is responsible for implementation
- Demonstrate utility of the techniques to many
- Bring more structure / order to problem solving

b) Goals of the mature utilization stage:

- Bring statistical / process thinking on board with new products and processes
- Solve some major problems
- Realize some major gains
- Integrate improvement programs
- Transfer ownership to the system as a whole

The fifth and final stage/step is the *institutionalization phase*. This means what has been learned, must become part of the organizational culture and must be done as an automatic response. It becomes the new status quo for improvement. Specifically, institutionalization means:

- Gathering data, charting, analysis and appropriate actions are a daily discipline
- Relying on facts and statistical data are natural reactions
- Everyone speaks the common language of SPC
- SPC is an integral part of conducting business
- Process control thinking is everyone's job every day.
- Statistical process control is perpetual because the benefits are recognized by all

While some elements that need to be in place before an organization moves into this phase can be (and have been) enumerated, timing of so doing is difficult to assess. With a clear vision as to where the organization is headed, efforts for attaining the goal can be better placed.

Whereas the use of SPC is an important element in the improvement process, it must be realized that there are also some common problems that one should be aware. Some of these problems are:

- Misunderstanding of the concepts of process control versus product control as they relate to both quality and productivity.
- Misconception of the physical difference between special and common causes as they relate to process performance.
- Lack of understanding concerning what control charts are informing an operator versus what they are telling management.
- Absence of a framework and methodology which rigorously identifies where statistical charting can best be employed for the most pertinent process diagnostic information.
- Failure to accept the absolute importance of closing the process control loop…diagnosing root causes, following through with appropriate countermeasures and solidifying the improvement gains.

- Luck of understanding the concept of loss function. [Use of the Loss Function Concept to serve as a means: a) To evaluate quality in terms of loss due to variation in function on economic grounds, b) To articulate the economic interpretation of a specification limit and c) To assess the economic performance of a process].

From this cursory overview one can see that SPC is a bundle of techniques that identify random (common) causes versus identifiable (special) causes in a process. Both of these are potential sources for improvement. The amount of random variation affects the capability of a process to produce within a desired range of requirements. Hence, SPC could be performed to determine processing capabilities and how to achieve those levels. The determination and correction of recurring systematic changes is also a possibility (Stamatis 1997, 2003).

The reduction of the random variation or the uncertainty of a process and the identification and correction of special causes are critical aspects of the total quality management process. Correction often requires a change in the total process and quite often multiple changes at the same time.

The first step of process improvement is to control the environment and the components of the system so that variations are within natural predictable limits. The second step is to reduce the underlying variation of the process. The undertaking of both of these is the issue of control charting.

A control chart is a pictorial representation of the process variation over time. A control chart identifies the changes in the process and unless the characteristic of the process is known, the change cannot be determined. All control charts are fundamentally based on the normal distribution, with statistical limits. The limits (upper and lower) are calculated and are drawn on either side of the process average. Do not confuse limits with specifications. Limits are calculated based on data from the process. Specifications are given by the customer and are the requirements we are expected to meet as a very minimum.

In a sense, a control chart is a tool which sends a signal making possible the distinction between abnormal and normal variation. In addition, one of the very fundamental concepts in all control charts is the notion of control.

Control does not necessarily mean that the product/service will meet your needs. It only means that the process is consistent and even then, it may be consistently bad or good. For a detailed discussion on control theory and application see Montgomery (1985) and Duncan (1986). For the constant values used in the construction phase of control charts, for the appropriate formulae used in the construction of control limits, capability, and basic descriptive statistics see Stamatis (2003) and many other references in the bibliography.

Types of Control Charts: There are many types of control charts. However, their selection depends on the kind of data available. There are two kinds of data: variable and attribute. When variable data are available, a range of powerful charts are available. Variable control charts monitor or measure things that are actually measurable on a continuous scale, such as temperature, pressure, acidity, time, and so on. For example, typical charts that may be used in monitoring variable data are:

$\overline{X}$ *and R chart*. These charts require a number of consecutive units be taken n times per work period and analyzed for specific criteria; they display graphically the process stability and show data in terms of spread (piece-to-piece variability) and its location (process average). $\overline{X}$ charts cover averages of values in small subgroups (sample taken), which is known as the measure of location. R charts deal with range of values within each sample (highest minus lowest), which is known as measure of spread. To construct $\overline{X}$ and R charts:

1. Select the size, frequency, and number of subgroups.
2. Subgroups.
3. Select and record the raw data.
4. Calculate the average of each of the subgroups as well as the range.
5. Calculate the overall average of the process as well as the average range.
6. Construct control chart scale. (A good rule of thumb in constructing the scale is as follows. For the range chart, take 2-3 times the largest range average. For the average chart, identify the largest and the smallest average of each of the subgroups, then take the difference of these two, multiply the difference by 2, and add it to the grand average.)
7. Plot the averages and ranges on the chart.
8. Calculate the control limits for the range chart, using appropriate formulae and constants.
9. Calculate the control limits for the average chart, using appropriate formulae and constants.
10. Interpret the range chart.
11. Interpret the average chart.

If process is consistent and repeatable then,

12. Calculate the process capability.
13. Continue to monitor the process.

If process is not consistent and repeatable then,

11a. Identify the cause(s) of inconsistency.
11b. Remove the cause(s).
11c. Continue to monitor until the process is consistent and repeatable.
11d. Move to steps 10 and 11 as needed.

Individual and Moving Range Chart. These are standard control charts that require less samples than the $\overline{X}$ and/or R charts to establish stability. Even with one sample one can use this chart to establish trends and identify the variation between batches and or individual items. Other than the level of sampling, this chart is very similar to the $\overline{X}$ and R charts. To construct an individual and moving range chart:

1. Collect and record the raw data.
2. Select an appropriate interval of samples.
3. Calculate the range of each of the interval subgroups.
4. Calculate the overall average of the process and average range.
5. Construct the control chart scale.
6. Plot averages and ranges on the chart. (A good rule of thumb in constructing the scale is as follows. For the range chart, take 2-3 times the largest range average. For the individual chart, identify the largest and the smallest value, then take the difference of these two, multiply the difference by 2, and add it to the grand average.)
7. Calculate the control limits for the range chart, using appropriate formulae and constants.
8. Calculate the control limits for the average chart, using appropriate formulae and constants.
9. Interpret the range chart.
10. Interpret the average chart.

If process is consistent and repeatable then,

11. Calculate the process capability.
12. Continue to monitor the process.

If process is not consistent and repeatable then,

10a. Identify the cause(s) of inconsistency.
10b. Remove the cause(s).
10c. Continue to monitor until the process is consistent and repeatable.
10d. Move to steps 9 and 10 as needed.

Median and R chart. This is a standard chart that is an alternative to the $\overline{X}$ and R charts for the control of processes. It is less sensitive to trends, however, and under some circumstances is considered to be more difficult to construct. It graphically displays the stability of a process, and yields similar information to $\overline{X}$ and R charts, but has several advantages.

1. It is easier to use since daily calculations are not required.
2. Individual values and medians are plotted, so the median chart shows the spread of process output and gives an ongoing view of process variation.
3. It shows where nonconformities are scattered through a more or less continuous flow of a function.
4. It shows where nonconformities from different areas may be evident.

To construct a median and range chart:

1. Select the size, frequency, and number of subgroups.
2. Select and record the raw data.
3. Select the median of each of the subgroups as well as the range.
4. Select the overall median of the process and the average range.
5. Construct control chart scale. (A good rule of thumb in constructing the scale is as follows. For the range chart, take 2-3 times the largest range average. For the median chart, identify the largest and the smallest median of each of the subgroups, then take the difference of these two, multiply the difference by 2, and add it to the grand median.)
6. Plot the median values and ranges on the chart.
7. Calculate the control limits for the range chart, using appropriate formulae and constants.
8. Calculate the control limits for the median chart, using appropriate formulae and constants.
9. Interpret the range chart.
10. Interpret the median chart.

If process is consistent and repeatable then,

11. Calculate the process capability.
12. Continue to monitor the process.

If the process is not consistent and repeatable then,

10 a. Identify the cause(s) of inconsistency.
10b. Remove the cause(s).
10c. Continue to monitor until the process is consistent and repeatable.
10d. Move to steps 9 or 10 as needed.

$\overline{X}$ *and s charts.* These are standard control charts that are similar to $\overline{X}$ and R charts, however, the s part of chart considers standard deviation (SD) and is more complicated to calculate. Because of the standard deviation, it is more sensitive to the process variation, especially with larger samples. On the other hand, it is less sensitive in detecting special causes of variation that produce only one value in a subgroup as unusual. To construct an average and standard deviation chart:

1. Select the size, frequency, and number of subgroups.
2. Select and record the raw data.
3. Calculate the average of each of the subgroups as well as the range.
    3a. Calculate the standard deviation for each subgroup.
4. Calculate the overall average of the process and the average range.
    4a. Calculate the average standard deviation of the process.

5. Construct control chart scale. (A good rule of thumb in constructing the scale is as follows. For the standard deviation (SD) chart, take 2-3 times the largest SD average. For the average chart, identify the largest and the smallest average of each of the subgroups, then take the difference of these two, multiply the difference by 2, and add it to the grand average.)
6. Plot the averages and ranges on the chart.
7. Calculate the control limits for the standard deviation chart, using appropriate formulae and constants.
8. Calculate the control limits for the average chart, using appropriate formulae and constants.
9. Interpret the standard deviation chart.
10. Interpret the average chart.

If the process is consistent and repeatable then,
11. Calculate the process capability.
12. Continue to monitor the process.

If the process is not consistent and repeatable then,
10a. Identify the cause(s) of inconsistency.
10b. Remove the cause(s).
10c. Continue to monitor until the process is consistent and repeatable.
10d. Move to steps 9 and 10 as needed.

Conversely, attribute control charts result from counting; they monitor or measure whether variables do or do not have certain characteristics or how often characteristics are present in a process. Examples are: percent defects, percent of nonconformities, and so on. Basically, these control monitor pass/fail or go/no go situations. When the data is attribute in nature, then different charts are used. Typical charts are:

p chart. This is a standard control chart that requires a variable sample size, and charts either conforming or nonconforming items. Graphically, it displays stability of process, and it measures the actual number of conforming and nonconforming items rather than total number of faults. It expresses numbers in either fractional or percentile terms (whether conforming or nonconforming items are used) of total sample. (For example, total number of faulty forms in a batch irrespective of number of faults in any one form.) To construct a p chart:

1. Select the size, frequency, and number of subgroups.
2. Collect and record the raw data.
3. Calculate the proportion for each subgroup.
4. Calculate the average proportion as well as the average number of defectives.
5. Construct control chart scale. (A good rule of thumb in constructing the scale is as follows. For the p chart, identify the largest and the smallest proportion of each of the subgroups, then take the difference of these two, multiply the difference by 2, and add it to the grand average.)
6. Plot the individual proportions.
7. Calculate the control limits using appropriate formulae.
8. Interpret the p chart.

If the process is consistent and repeatable then,
9. Calculate the process capability.
10. Continue to monitor the process.

If process is not consistent and repeatable then,
8a. Identify the cause(s) of inconsistency.
8b. Remove the cause(s).
8c. Continue to monitor and watch for process change.
8d. Move to step 8.

np chart. This is a standard control chart that is similar to the *p* chart, but must be used if the sample sizes are the same. Graphically, it displays stability of process, and it measures the number of nonconforming items rather than total number of faults (e.g., the total number of faulty forms in a batch irrespective of faults in any one form.) To construct an np chart:

1. Select the size, frequency, and number of subgroups.
2. Collect and record the raw data.
3. Calculate the process average number of nonconforming items.
4. Construct the control chart scale. (A good rule of thumb in constructing the scale is as follows. For the np chart, identify the largest and the smallest proportion of each of the subgroups, then take the difference of these two, multiply the difference by 2, and add it to the grand proportion).
5. Calculate the control limits, using appropriate formulae.
6. Interpret the control chart.

If process is consistent then,

7. Calculate the process capability.

If the process is not consistent then,

    6a. Identify the inconsistencies.
    6b. Remove the inconsistencies.
    6c. Continue to monitor and watch for changes in the process.
    6d. Move to step 6

c chart. This is a standard control chart for the total number of non-conformities, based on a constant sample size. Graphically, this chart displays stability of the process (*e.g.*, the total number of errors in a batch of 100 forms rather than just the number of faulty forms.) To construct a c chart:

1. Select the size, frequency, and number of subgroups.
2. Collect and record the raw data.
3. Calculate the process average number nonconforming items.
4. Construct the control chart scale. (A good rule of thumb in constructing the scale is as follows. For the c chart, identify the largest and the smallest defectives of each of the subgroups, then take the difference of these two, multiply the difference by 2, and add it to the grand average defective.)
5. Calculate the control limits based on appropriate formulae.
6. Interpret the control chart.

If the process is consistent then,

7. Calculate the process capability.

If process is not consistent then,

    6a. Identify the inconsistencies.
    6b. Remove the inconsistencies.
    6c. Continue to monitor and watch for changes in the process.
    6d. Move to step 6

u chart. This is a standard control chart that is similar to the *c* chart, but must be used if the sample sizes vary. Graphically, it displays the stability of process (*e.g.*, the total number of errors in a batch of 100 forms rather than just the number of faulty forms.) To construct a u chart:

1. Select the size, frequency, and number of subgroups.
2. Collect and record the raw data.
3. Record and plot the nonconformities per unit in each subgroup.
4. Calculate the process average of nonconforming items per unit.

5. Construct the control chart scale. (A good rule of thumb in constructing the scale is as follows. For the u chart, identify the largest and the smallest nonconformities of each of the subgroups, then take the difference of these two, multiply the difference by 2, and add it to the grand average nonconformities).
6. Calculate the control limits based on appropriate formulae.
7. Interpret the control chart.

If the process is consistent then,

8. Calculate the process capability.

If the process is not consistent then,

    7a. Identify the inconsistencies.
    7b. Remove the inconsistencies.
    7c. Continue to monitor and watch for changes in the process.
    7d. Move to step 7

Control Chart Interpretation: A process with only *common variation* is predictable, consistent, and stable. The process under these conditions is said to be in control. Detailed examples of all condition in control chart interpretations may be reviewed in Stamatis (2003, Chapters 9-11). As one looks at a control chart with common variation it is easy to spot that all points are within the control limits and they follow a random pattern. This is the ideal and very sought after condition in every control chart.

Unlike the common (inherent) variation a process may also have undue variation due to some *special variation* (*i.e.*, due to assignable cause). That means that some part of the operation has changed in some degree and/or fashion. In other words, the present process is not part of the old one. The behavior of this change is shown in the control chart by the following signals:

1. *Points beyond control limits.* When this is shown in the chart, it means that the sample was collected from at least two different distributions of the process. Again, note that a change in the process may in fact be an improvement. The point is that this condition should be investigated and appropriately recorded in the process log. This is the most simplest signal to detect because it is obvious to see on the chart without any effort.
2. *Run of seven (7) points.* Even though all the points of the distribution are within the limits, this condition when present in the control chart shows that the process has a shift of the process average. That shift may be above or below the average and it must contain at least seven points in a row. When this happens, it is called a *run*. This is a special case and it should be highlighted in the control chart itself. It continues for at least twenty-five (25) subgroups, this means that the process has changed enough to recalculate the limits and the process average. It should be noted that the change should NOT be carried out unless the reason for the change has been identified.
3. *Trend of seven points.* A trend is a special run of seven points that increase or decrease steadily. Think of it as drift in the process setting. Depending on the drift one may call an increasing trend a "run-up," while a decreasing trend one may call a "run down." Note that in this special cause there are two signals of concern: the downward trend and the run below the process average. It is not uncommon to have more than one signal in a control chart.
4. *Cycle of points.* A cycle is a repetition of a pattern. It may have more than one cause and they are very easy to spot as well as correct. One of the easiest methods to solve a cycling problem may be to study the process through a process flow chart or a team effort approach.
5. *Unusual variation or stratification of hugging.* This is one of the most difficult signals to spot because it is easy to misinterpret as a good chart. The cause of this signal is not in the variation of the process, but rather it may be in the sampling itself or the scale of plotting. It is very important to note that as one looks at the chart the first impression is that it is "too good to be true" or "something is just not right." From a statistical point of view when this happens, it is referred to as a zone control

problem. There are two main reasons for this unusual variation and they are: 1) basic changes have occurred in the process, and 2) process streams have had an effect on the overall process.

When one talks about zone control it is a reference to a control chart divided into three equal zones (each zone is one standard deviation). In analyzing a zone control chart, one should take note and examine what has changed and possibly make a process adjustment if:

1. Two out of three successive points are on the same side of the centerline in zone A or beyond.
2. Four out of five successive points on the same side of the centerline in zone B or beyond.
3. Seven successive points are on one side of the centerline.
4. Seven successive points are increasing or decreasing.
5. Fourteen points in a row are alternating up and down.
6. Fifteen points in a row are within zone C (above and below centerline).

A general algorithm to recalculate the control limits for any control chart is:

1. Does the process have enough points (usually 25) to generate a pattern?
    a. If yes, go to Step 2.
    b. If no, do not recalculate limits. The data is not sufficient.
2. Is there a pattern present on the control chart?
    a. If yes, go to step 3.
    b. If no, do not recalculate limits.
3. Do you know what is causing the pattern?
    a. If yes, go to step 4.
    b. If no, do not recalculate limits; focus the effort in identifying root cause(s) for patterns.
4. Do you like the pattern, as it appears?
    a. If yes, recalculate appropriate limits based on the formulae in Appendix D.
    b. If no, do not recalculate limits. Go to Step 3.

Advanced tools

Activity network diagram: The activity network diagram (AND) is also known as the Program Evaluation Review Technique (PERT). It is used to find the most efficient path - critical path—and a realistic schedule for the completion of any project by graphically showing the total completion time, the necessary sequence of tasks, those tasks that can be done simultaneously, the critical tasks to monitor, and the slack time of tasks within the project.

Process and Decision Program Chart: The Process and Decision Program Chart (PDPC) is also a tool for improving implementation through contingency planning. It is fundamentally a tree diagram, but it is much simpler. To construct this chart:

*   Select a team closest to the implementation project.
*   Determine proposed implementation steps.
*   Identify as many as possible and likely problems of each step.
*   Identify as many as possible and reasonable responses of each likely problem.
*   Choose the most effective countermeasures and build them into a revised plan.

Affinity diagram: An affinity diagram is the organized output from a team brainstorming session. It is a creative process and expresses data in the form of language without quantifying it. The purpose of an affinity diagram is to generate, organize, and consolidate information concerning a product, process, or complex issue or problem. The steps for constructing one are:

1. Choose a group leader.
2. State the issue or problem.
3. Brainstorm and record ideas.
4. Write each idea on a card.
5. Move the cards into like piles.
6. Name each pile with a title card.
7. Draw the affinity diagram. (Draw a circle or square around each group of like cards.)
8. Discuss the piles.

Priority Matrix: This approach is used when one wants to use a systematic approach to weigh the present options. Specifically, this approach helps at least in the following ways:

1. It quickly identifies basic disagreements.
2. It forces a team to focus on the best things to do, rather than everything they could do.
3. It limits private agendas since all the criteria identified are team generated.
4. It educes the chances of selecting someone's pet project.
5. It increases participation and ownership of both problems and solutions.
6. It increases morale and communication in the team and the organization.

The approach to constructing the prioritization matrices is dependent upon the notion that the team is willing to decide based on a consensus. Unless consensus is understood and utilized in the decision process, this approach to prioritization will not be effective. Assuming that consensus is utilized, there are six required steps:

1. Agree on the goal to be achieved; the agreement must be clear, concise, and exact.
2. Create the list of criteria.
3. Using an L-shaped matrix that reflects the needs of the group. See (Stamatis 1997).
4. Compare all options relative to each criteria.
5. Using the L-shaped summary matrix, compare each option based on all criteria combined.
6. Choose the best option(s) across all criteria.

Force field analysis: Force field analysis (FFA) is a systematic way of identifying and portraying the forces (quite often people) for or against change in an organization. The specific forces will be different depending upon the area where they are applied. Typical steps in conducting a FFA are:

1. Identify the actual driving forces or factors working for change. (Define the current situation.)
2. Prioritize driving forces by voting or use of some consensus achieving technique. (Define/base the desired position on the results of an FFA.)
3. Identify current restraining forces or factors working against change. (Define the worst possible situation.)
4. Prioritize restraining forces. (What are the forces for change? What is their relative strength?)
5. Identify potential driving forces or factors that realistically favor change but are not yet currently operating. (What are the forces against change? What is their relative strength?)
6. Identify potential restraining forces or realistically possible forces that would work against change if they were present. (What forces can you influence?)
7. Determine if there are actions that can be taken to:
    a. increase the effect of the current driving forces

b. add to the driving forces or cause potential driving forces to happen

c. decrease or eliminate the current restraining forces

d. ensure that the potential restraining forces do not occur or do not impact the issue being investigated

e. eliminate specific action that can be taken relative to each of these forces that you cannot influence

8. Begin to develop some strategy statements about proposed actions. Statements should begin to answer: Who, What, When, Where, How, How much, and What are the expected results?

Matrix diagram: The matrix diagram method is designed to clarify problematic spots through multidimensional thinking. Specifically, it is designed to seek out principal factors from many characteristics concerning a subject under study. The matrix diagram helps to expedite the process of problem solving by indicating the presence and degree of strength of a relationship between two sets of factors. By using the intersecting points of the factors, the experimenter may determine the strength of the relationship. There are many different types of matrix diagrams, however, they all focus on identifying the relationship(s) of the factors. Some of the most typical types are:

- *The T-type matrix.* It is a matrix of A factors corresponding to B and C factors, respectively. This type may be used when there is a need for defect-reducing activities. Also, it may be utilized when exploring a new use of materials. In this case, the T-type matrix may be used to analyze ingredients and components of the material by characteristics and usage.

- *The Y-type matrix.* This type of matrix is a combination of three L-type matrices: A factors and B factors, B factors and C factors, C factors and A factors. The intent of this matrix is to show how these factors correspond to each other. It can be used anytime there is a concern of optimizing three factors.

- *The X-type matrix.* This type of matrix is a combination of four L-type matrices. This matrix shows the correspondence of four sets of factors: A and B, and AB and D; B and A, and BA and C; C and B, and CB and D; and D and A, and DA and C. Applications of this matrix are limited, but it can be used to consider the correspondence of management functions, management inputs, output data and input data.

- *The C-type matrix.* This type of matrix is expressed in a rectangular cube whose sides are represented by three elements, A, B, and C. The main feature of this cubic type of matrix is the "point of conception of the idea," which is determined by three elements of A, B, and C in three-dimensional space.

Nominal group technique: The nominal group technique (NGT) is one of many structured group processes that have been designed and developed. It is a special-purpose technique that is useful for situations where individual judgments must be tapped and combined to arrive at decisions that cannot be reached by one person. The NGT is a problem-solving or idea-generating strategy, and is not typically used for routine meetings.

The NGT was developed by Andre L. Delbecq and Andrew H. Van de Ven in 1968. It was derived from social-psychological studies of decision conferences, management—science studies of aggregating group judgments, and social-work studies of problems surrounding citizen participation in program planning. Since that time, the NGT has gained extensive recognition and has been widely applied.

The NGT takes its name from the fact that it is a carefully designed, structured, group process that involves carefully selected participants as independent individuals rather than in the usual interactive mode of conventional groups. It is a well-developed and tested method that is fully presented in the work of Delbeck, Van de Ven, and Gusstafson (1975), and Delbeck and Van de Ven (1986).

The NGT has four phases in addition to an introduction and a conclusion. The participants are physically present in groups of 8-12 and the session is controlled by a process consultant (facilitator) and an assistant. During the introduction, the facilitator attempts to familiarize the participants with the process and make them feel at ease with what will transpire during the meeting. The facilitator usually discusses very briefly at least the following:

1. the purpose of the session and the importance of the process
2. the steps of the NGT
3. how the results will be used and the next steps

The facilitator then reads a carefully worded task statement. This is the task that the participants should respond to during the structured group session. It is usually simple and direct. If the facilitator is asked what is meant by the task statement, he or she usually avoids introducing bias that occurs by giving examples. Instead, the facilitator often asks several participants to give their interpretation of the task statement. Additionally, the facilitator often asks several participants to directly respond to the task statement. The process of forcing the participants to clarify the task statement themselves is called self-priming and can be very effective. When the responses appear to coincide with the objective and the remainder of the participants appear to have grasped the task, the facilitator proceeds to the first basic step of the NGT.

The first phase is called *silent generation* and typically takes about 10-15 minutes. During this phase, the group members are instructed to write their responses to the task statement. Both the facilitator and the assistant also write during this period. Even if a majority of participants appear to stop writing before ten minutes has elapsed, the period is not shortened. If some talking occurs, the facilitator tactfully asks for cooperation in permitting others to think through their ideas.

Like each of the steps in the NGT process, silence is purposefully designed. It is based on the notion that a) silent generation focuses attention on a specific task, b) frees the participants from distractions, and c) provides them with an opportunity to think through their ideas rather than simply to react to the comments of others. In this sense, it is a search process that yields contributions of greater quality and variety. Participants are motivated by the tension of seeing those around them working hard at the group task.

They are forced to attend for a longer time to the task, rather than rushing immediately to consider the first idea that is suggested to the group. They are freed from all of the inhibiting effects of the usual face-to-face interaction of unstructured groups. Judgment of ideas cannot take place during this early and crucial portion of the group process.

Next comes the *round-robin* phase. The facilitator interrupts the process, yet emphasizes that there is no need to stop generating. (Any additional ideas should be added to the silent generation lists.) The facilitator calls on participants one-by-one to state one of the responses they have written. Participants may pass at any time and may also join in on any subsequent round. A participant may propose only one item at a time, and either the facilitator or an assistant records each item as it is offered. The only discussion allowed is between the facilitator and the participant who proposed the item. The discussion is limited to seeking a concise rephrasing for ease of recording. As each participant responds, the facilitator repeats verbatim what has been said and the assistant records the concise phrase on a sheet. This phrase goes on until all the ideas generated by the group are listed and displayed.

The round-robin phase permits the leader to establish an atmosphere of acceptance and trust. He or she does not unduly rephrase or evaluate the contributions, and they are equally and prominently displayed before the group. It is essential that the leader be open and that there is no *valuative behavior*. Each idea and each participant should receive equal attention and acceptance. There is little opportunity for the process to be dominated by strong personalities, to be inhibited by possible sanctions or conflicts, or to be suppressed by status differences. The process separates ideas from their authors and permits conflicting and incompatible ideas to be explicitly tolerated. It provides a written record of the group's efforts as a basis for the next step.

The third phase is called *clarification*. Once all the items have been recorded, the facilitator goes over each one in order to ascertain that all participants understand the item as it has been recorded. Any participant may offer clarification or may suggest combination, modification, deletion, and so forth of items. However, evaluation is avoided. The facilitator moves rapidly from one measure to the next, keeping up the pace of the process. During this step, the underlying logic behind items may be brought out, there may be some expressions of life references of opinion, and the group may conclude that some items can be eliminated or combined because of duplication.

Pace is important to this step and the facilitator's job is to keep the group moving rapidly through the list of items. Although in this phase the group is more like an interacting one, the facilitator seeks to control lengthy discussions, arguments, and "speech making." Again the effort is to separate ideas from their authors, to clarify rather than to evaluate, and to ensure full opportunities for participation. It is important to point out that the clarification aspect of the NGT is perhaps the primary determinant for the resulting quality of the list of items. If there is a great deal of overlap from item to item and if there is ambiguity on the part of the group members as to exactly what each item means, the next step, which involves voting and ranking, will be invalid. Experience has shown that a certain amount of combination is necessary.

The fourth phase—*voting and ranking*—provides the participants with an opportunity to select the most important items and to rank those items. The participants are provided with between five and nine blank 3'x5' cards (post-it notes may also be used). Usually, participants are provided with eight cards, but the number can vary depending on how many responses are generated during the round-robin phase. Each participant is asked to select the eight most important items from the list displayed before him or her. Typically, the list will contain 20-30 items. To avoid any confusion in handling their judgments, participants are asked to write the items out, one per card, in an abbreviated fashion, in the center of the blank cards. They are also asked to write the sequential list number of the item in the upper left-hand corner of the card. When all have completed this step, they are asked to spread the eight cards out in front of them and to rank and weight the items. Typically, they are given the following instruction: *From the eight cards, choose the most important item, write the number 8 with a circle around it in the lower right-hand corner of the card, and set the card aside.* Another way of phrasing this to assist some in deciding which in most important is: *Which of the eight items would you use to guide future actions relative to this topic if you could only use one?*

After the first pass of ranking, the ranking process continues thusly: From the remaining seven cards, choose the least important item, write the number 1 with a circle around it in the lower right-hand corner of the card, and set the card aside. Another way of phrasing this to assist some in choosing the least important item is: If you could use only six of the seven items in front of you, which one would you drop off? The process continues in this fashion until all the cards have been ranked. At this point of the process, tabulation of the votes takes place. The tabulation process involves sorting the cards by sequential item number from the original list and recording the weight given to each. At the end, the facilitator has three alternatives:

1. Invite the participants to take a ten-minute break (possibly for refreshment) while the facilitator and the assistant tabulate and display the results.
2. Invite the participants to watch the tabulation process take place.
3. Invite the participants to fill out a brief questionnaire that has been prepared by the coordinator for the specific purpose of evaluating the reaction of the participants to the process, obtaining

suggestions from the participants as to next steps, determining the likelihood of implementation, and so on.

The fourth step in the NGT process permits the participants to express their individual evaluations of the items in a way that is free of social pressure. It provides a constructive method for dealing with conflicts, and leads to a clear expression.

Tree (function) diagram: A tree diagram (sometimes called a systematic diagram) is a graphic representation of the different levels of actions used to accomplish a broad goal. The purpose of making a tree diagram is to generate the most specific level of action items that can be implemented to accomplish a broader goal. The steps to construct the tree diagram are:
1. Record the problem or goal statement.
2. Generate the first level of items by asking questions like: "What needs to happen to achieve this goal or solve this problem?" This level of questioning is considered to be the means to achieve the end or main goal.
3. Complete the systematic diagram under each major path by asking the question "What needs to happen to achieve this goal or solve this problem?" Notice at this stage as you move from left to right in the diagram, the tasks are getting more specific. Of course, each level is the new means to accomplish the end (*i.e.*, the prior level item).
4. Study the tree diagram. In reviewing the diagram, start with the last level on the far right and ask: "Will this set of items achieve the next higher level?" If the answer is yes for every level, then the diagram is complete. If not, then redo the diagram.

Interrelationship diagram: An interrelationship diagram is a pictorial representation of the cause-and-effect relationships among the elements of a problem or issue. The purpose of making an interrelationship diagram is to identify the root causes and root effects of a problem. Root causes are those factors or aspects of a problem which primarily influence other factors. Root effects are those factors of a problem which are primarily influenced by other factors. The steps of constructing an interrelationship diagram are:

1. Clearly define the issue or problem.
2. Generate an affinity diagram. (If the affinity diagram has already been generated, go to Step 3.)
3. Construct the diagram layout. Write the problem statement at the center of a piece of paper and draw a circle around it. Then place the header cards from the affinity diagram in a circular pattern around the problem statement. Draw a circle around each header card.
4. Analyze the relations. If a relationship does not exist, do not draw a line between circles. If a relationship exists, draw a line between the two categories. Place an arrow at only one end of the line. The arrow indicates the category which is the effect and away from the category which is the cause.
5. Count the arrows. Once the analysis stage is complete, count the number of arrows going in and out of each category. Write the numbers above each category in the form number in/number out.
6. Identify the root causes and effects. The root causes are the categories with the greatest number of arrows going out and the root effects are the categories with the greatest number of arrows going in.
7. Study the final diagram. The focus on the quality improvement efforts will be cased on the analysis of the root causes.

Special Methodologies/tools

Gap Analysis: It is a methodology that helps to identify the current capabilities of each key process result area to the future customer requirements spelled out in the most probable future scenario. Do you have gaps in capability? If you do, they are critical issues and need action. In fact, it is these gaps that will serve as the basis for near- and long-term goal setting.

The gap analysis also provides the organization with a reality check of the planning process up to this point. A careful study of the gap will help the organization to achieve their goals more in a more realistic manner. For example, if the gap between present capability and the future state is small and easily achievable, then the planning team probably did not stretch enough in visualizing the future. On the other hand, if the gap is large and overwhelming, maybe the team needs to readjust the future state.

A third possibility exists in which the gaps are all achievable, but there are too many to address them simultaneously. If that is the case, then the team may go back and prioritize key result areas, values, and environmental factors to set reasonable goals.

Needs Assessment: The organizational needs (of both the organization and employees) in a given organization are not static, but undergo change over time. Therefore, it is important that management periodically review these needs. The forces for change are many and are constantly with us, occurring as a result of changes in employee and/or corporate expectations, changes in technology, changes in knowledge, and a variety of changing social patterns. To adequately assess the perceived needs of a system requires the involvement of representative segments of the corporate culture. By seeking needs information from the representative groups, management can be more responsive to the "wishes" and real "needs" of all the employees.

The identification of needs involves a discrepancy analysis, sometimes called a gap analysis, which identifies two opposite positions and the difference, if any, between them. An example will clarify the point. A discrepancy analysis might use either of the following two questions: 1) Where are we now and where should we be? or 2) How important is this and how well do you feel this is being done? By comparing the answers to these questions it is possible to ascertain where significant discrepancies exist and where they do not exist.

Obtaining organizational needs from the employees is not an end in itself, but instead represents a very valuable source of information regarding the current status of the organizational system. A needs assessment can provide the organization system with some of the best available information on the immediate characteristics of the organizational quality system, training programs, and those areas where attention and resources should be directed, both internally and externally to the system. For a detailed concept and application explanation see Kaufman (1979). Here, however, a simpler model for needs assessment is presented based on four distinct phases (Stamatis 1997).

Phase 1. *The Needs Assessment Framework*: Here the corporate goals and objectives are set. The existence of the goals and objectives are the primary function of this phase.

Phase 2. *Determine Discrepancies*: Essentially this process involves a comparison of "what is" with "what should be" in the organization, process, and in the three areas of the training setting. For the components of the organization and the process, the discrepancy phase identifies the current operational status and the expected operational status. The most important guideline in determining such discrepancies is to insure an unbiased objective accounting and an active participation of all involved. On the other hand, in the areas of training setting, Phase 2 focuses on employee achievement, program and/or training operations, and preference assessment.

Phase 3. *Setting Tentative Goal Statements*: Given the information collected and analyzed in Phase 2, Management must analyze and interpret this data within the goal framework. Some of the alternatives are:

1. Validate existing goal statements.
2. Develop new goals as indicated and supported by the discrepancy analysis.

3. Refine or revise existing goal statements.
4. Eliminate outmoded or outdated goals.

Phase 4. *Rank Order the Goals*: The final phase of the process involves determining the priority of goal statements. Essential to the effective conduct of the needs assessment is the sincere commitment of management at all levels. It is this commitment that facilitates the process and brings it to closure. The preference assessment is designed to gather a reasonable amount of judgmental input from the various employee groups, processes, and systems. The instrument used for such a task is usually a survey instrument asking questions relative to the concern of the management team. The questions focus on "what is" and "what should be." The actual development of the questions must utilize a cross-sectional or cross-functional team of employees for a correct and valid content.

Once the needs assessment has taken place and the priorities have been determined, the next step is evaluation. There are many models one can follow in evaluating a program evaluation. Excellent sources are Madaus, Scriven, and Stufflebeam (1983); Bank, Henderson, and Eu (1981); and Scriven (1991). For our purposes Brinkerhoff's (1987) model will be used with some minor modifications. The essence of the model is that it corresponds to the decisions necessary for programs to proceed productively and defensibly through the stages, thereby enabling and facilitating quality efforts.

- Stage 1 evaluates the value and importance of problems and/or opportunities in the organization.
- Stage 2 aims at the production of a defensible program design and might access a given design's practicality.
- Stage 3 assesses the significance of planned and unplanned departures from the design.
- Stage 4 reveals that sufficient skill, knowledge, and attitude were in fact acquired.
- Stage 5 assesses how much and how well the acquired skill, knowledge, and attitude are being translated into intended on-job behavior changes.
- Stage 6 shows the value of organizational effects and their relationship to training.

In order to implement this six-stage model a series of relevant questions must be asked. For typical questions and concerns that may help in the process see Stamatis (1997).

Kano model: It is a simple model that forces the experimenter, educator, administrator, legislator, board member and so on to take into account the "basic," "performance" and "excitement" characteristics of the customer. It is an essential early step of understanding the "customer" and how the functionality of the particular design may effect the customer satisfaction. Ultimately the understanding gained by the Kano model is used in the QFD analysis to define and redefine customer requirements.

Ideation: Educational leadership by definition (almost) demands "out of the box" thinking. A long standing tool to inspire creativity, in the world of quality, in fact in all team activities, has been the use of the brainstorming technique. In the last several years, however, a new twist of the brainstorming methodology has been utilized and it is called *Ideation*.

The brainstorming activity focuses on the process. However, that focus sometimes created a problem in the creativity process. Ideation on the other hand, focuses on the results and as a consequence, eliminates the confusion of the process. Whereas brainstorming breaks down barriers and allows participation from all the involved participants, based on a ritualistic approach, ideation goes a step further in the sense that it comes up with ideas without worrying about the process. In fact, because ideation does not worry about the process, the participants are more likely to push the development of ideas into concepts.

Ideation is very flexible, and uses fewer rubrics in deciding on a particular result. It is more efficient than the brainstorming and thus may be used in a variety of activities. The actual application of ideation is the same as the brainstorming minus the rules. While brainstorming typically involves a facilitator and the employees, in a typical ideation approach outsiders may be involved. These outsiders may be from cross-functional and multi-disciplined areas. Their function is to give their perspective and to break as many barriers as possible.

To have excellent results in any ideation process, the make up of the participants should have at least the following profile characteristics:

- *Those who envision*: These people add direction, inspiration and momentum to the discussion. They focus on the end result and present a vision of what they want to create. They are very good for strategic planning activities, since they are capable of describing the ideal future in 5 to 10 years.
- *Those who modify*: These people examine the components of problems and bring stability and thoroughness to the process. They prefer to take things one step at a time and build on what they already know.
- *Those who experiment*: These people like to test carefully and receive input to confirm ideas. They like to trouble shoot and answer questions on how to use products within their intended markets and how to find other possible uses.
- *Those who explore*: These people would excel in taking a product and incorporate new ideas for improvement or enhancement of the product. They thrive on the unknown and have a sense of adventure.

A typical creative usage analysis using ideation may be the TRIZ (The theory for inventive problem solving).

Quality function deployment (QFD): Quality function deployment (QFD) is difficult to define for many reasons. It is sometimes narrowly defined and sometimes broadly defined. Although it was introduced as a concept over 20 years ago, it is not yet fully systemized. It is used in different ways in different organizations. Some organizations, like Bell Labs, are calling it matrix product planning, but there are some very successful projects with no matrices. Let me suggest a working definition. QFD is a philosophy and strategy which enables all members of the organization to participate in the design process in understanding and fulfilling the requirements of their customer. In the educational environment, QFD is a methodology to bring together the various departments within an educational system in a planned manner and cause them to focus on the "voice of the customer."

As a philosophy, QFD teaches that all design of product and process should be rooted in the needs of the customer and that the design should be accomplished efficiently and accurately before offering a service on a regular basis. As an organizational strategy, QFD involves all segments of the organization in the design of product and process, thus reducing the chances of design errors and assuring the optimal design possible.

As a collection of tools, QFD may include quality tables, matrices, value engineering, fractional factorial experimentation, FMEAs, SPC data, finite element analysis, simulation studies, planning tools, reviewed dendrograms (a chart presenting thought patterns in a design improvement effort), bottleneck engineering (a group of schematic presentations of design improvements such as the dendrogram), and other tools that enhance and document design efforts.

QFD can help us shore up our weaknesses while building on our strengths. It encourages a comprehensive, holistic approach to product development that are generally found lacking in American industry (Eureka and Ryan, 1988) and especially in educational institutions. QFD's primary goal is the overcoming of three major problems (Eureka and Ryan, 1988), namely:

114

- disregarding the voice of the customer
- losing information
- preventing different individuals and groups from working to different requirements

The implementation of QFD can provide the organization with both strategic benefits as well as operational benefits. Strategic benefits include, but are not limited to: larger market share (as in community colleges, universities, private or public institutions and others), improved quality, shortened cycle time, fewer requirement changes, lowered manpower, reduced cost, increased reliability and validity of the programs offered, and reduced process variation. On the other hand, operational benefits include, but are not limited to: combination with other quality technologies, increased process efficiencies, encouragement of a new way of thinking and/or changing paradigms, improved participation, systematic approach to analysis, improved group and team interactions, and product organizations (Sullivan, 1987), enhanced communication, identification of conflicting requirements, and most importantly, it preserves information for the future.

Whereas it is beyond the scope of this book to define and explain the detail implementation process for a QFD, the reader is encouraged to see Cohen (1995), Day (1993), Akao (1990), Bossert (1990), Sullivan (1986), Eureka (1987), and American Supplier Institute (1987, 1989) for a detailed implementation methodology and actual case studies from U.S. companies. However, because QFD is such a powerful tool and its use is being expanded in all kinds of industries, including all educational systems, the process is summarized here.

The QFD approach translates the customer's requirements, characteristics, operations, and requirements. The QFD approach in education does not differ much from the classical approach. Its function is to translate the "raw" customer's requirements, specific characteristics, operations, and implementation requirements into satisfaction deliverables to the identified customer. Each step is interrelated and tracked through the House of Quality matrix. QFD matrices and charts deploy the customer's requirements from the product planning stage all the way to the classroom. The QFD methodology involves translating a list of loosely stated customer objectives into "what."

These "whats" are the items we wish to accomplish (*i.e.*, the basic customer requirements). Each "what" is then broken down into "how" or the method required achieving each "what." The "what" and "how" can then be listed. Although the "how" list represents greater detail than the "what" list, they are often not directly actionable and require yet further definition.

Unfortunately, this process is complicated by the fact that through each level of refinement some of the "how" affect more than one "what." Attempting to clearly trace the relationships of the "what" and "how" becomes confusing at this point. However, by restructuring the "what" and "how" lists perpendicular to each other the relationship can be observed clearly and then rated. At this point, it becomes necessary to establish "how much" for each "how." This interrelationship is elaborated much more in the above sources and Stamatis (1997).

The flow of information is from "what" to the "how" through the relationship matrix, then to the "how much." The "how" and "how much" are then translated into "what" for the next chart, ensuring that the objective values are not lost. This process continuous until each objective is refined to an actionable level. This process continues until all operations and requirements are defined.

By using the QFD methodology, one can indeed prevent "things from falling through the cracks" by forcing interrelationships between each discipline. In fact, both detail and functions now have clear line of responsibility and accountability. As designers and management change assignments the QFD charts remain with the product and/or process, informing the incoming group how the product was developed and produced. This also provides a marshaling point for similar designs, reducing turn around time to develop new products. This in fact may be the greatest advantage of using QFD as it really preserves knowledge for the organization.

Clausing (1988) summed up the concept of QFD as: ... the voice of the customer to the factory floor. It brings all the corporate wisdom, including all the specialized knowledge of the many and diverse corporate specialists, to bear on the product. And it achieves multifunctional consensus, which results in a product that's best for the customer and the corporation. QFD is a major operational practice that helps achieve products that are higher in quality, lower in cost, and developed much faster, and that contain features that are better matched to customer requirements. By using QFD to achieve products that strongly appeal to potential customers, organizations will experience increased market share and growth and improved quality of work life.

QFD then in the educational process may be viewed as a systematic way of assuring that the development of product or service features, characteristics and specifications, as well as the selection and development of process equipment, methods and controls are driven by the demands of the customer or marketplace. The terms "development of a product" include several things, including: a) Applying new technology b) combining existing and new technology and c) improving quality of performance.

From a QFD perspective, planning is determining *what* to make and designing is deciding *how* to make it. In the educational process we can use QFD to identify what is needed for each stakeholder and then follow up with designing a system to either close the gap or implant a new innovative system. Both are important and both depend on the level and the degree of understanding the relationship of customer's wants, needs and the product or service in question. Whereas the traditional approach of transferring the customer's wants into requirements has been to use the "House of Quality" approach, for the educational systems we recommend the detailed methodology, yet systematic approach based on the work of Clausing and Hauser (1988) as well as the work of Akao (1990). This is so, because with this type of approach the QFD can actually be used not only in the appraisal mode of quality but also in the planning mode of quality.

The value of this approach is in its ability to trace the wants of the customer all the way to the classroom. The classical approach may be shown in Figure 7.2 and the educational adaptation is shown in Figure 7.3. Both are similar and are summarized in four stages. They are:

Figure 7.2. A generic QFD process

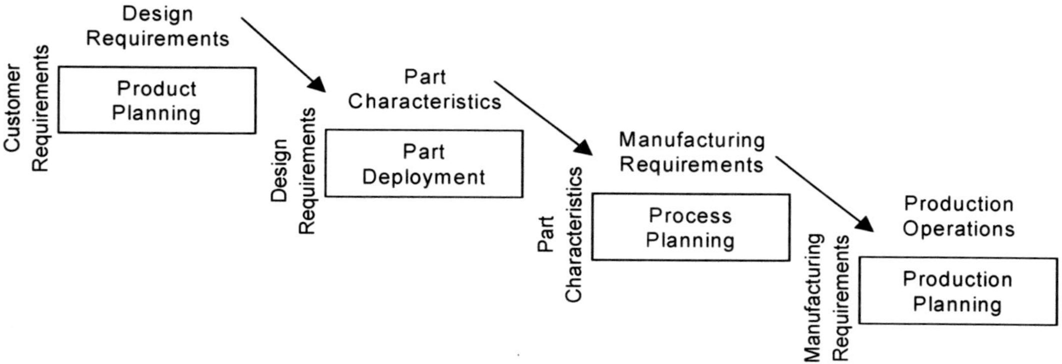

Figure 7.3. The QFD model in the educational process

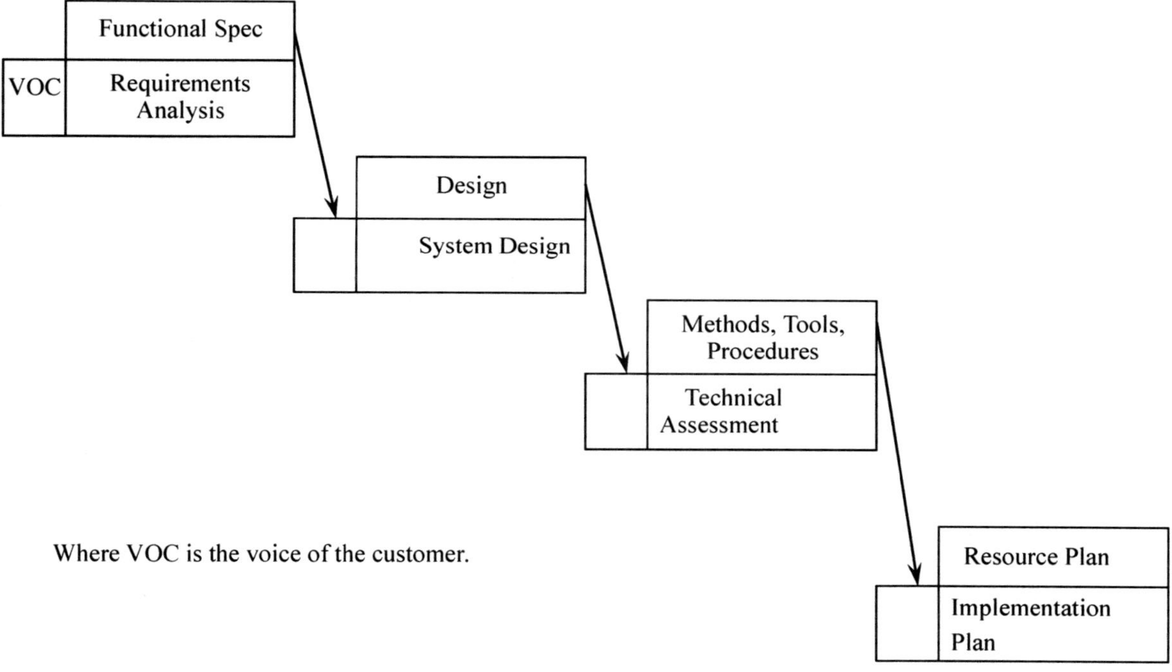

- *Stage 1*: Establish targets. This is where the first quality management meeting is held to critique the design concept and target setting. Two major items are of concern.
    - o Develop a planning matrix (multiple functions) in which the following are identified:
        - ▪ Recognize the voice of the customer
        - ▪ Analyze major product features
        - ▪ Perform market and technical evaluation of competitive products/services
        - ▪ Establish targets for major features
    - o Evaluate strengths and weaknesses of your product/service offering
        - ▪ Design, technology, reliability, cost
        - ▪ Identify major selling features, critical targets, necessary breakthroughs
- *Stage 2*: Finalize design timetables and prototype plans. The major issue of concern is.
    - o Discuss/evaluate all possible means of achieving important characteristics
        - ▪ Decision on technology to be used

- Targets and tolerances for critical components identified
    - Fault tree analysis/design FMEA/Taguchi optimization methods used (if applicable and appropriate)
    - Final characteristic deployment matrix generated
- *Stage 3*: Establish conditions of production. This is where a thorough discussion of the process of targeting and mass production planning takes place. Two major items are of concern.
  - Primary emphasis is process design
    - Relate critical component targets and tolerances to prototype processing conditions
    - Optimization experiments performed as needed
  - Leadership of the QFD process is transferred from designers to practitioners when the decision to go ahead with mass delivery (production) is made.
    - Significant control items and means of control established
    - Process FMEA/FTA/Poka Yoke methods established
    - Further need for breakthroughs defined
    - Trial runs used to verify forecasted process stability, capability, adequacy of control points and product quality
    - Output should provide excellent results with minimum effort
    - Process quality planning matrices generated
- *Stage 4*: Mass implementation (delivery) start-up. This is where the final quality management meeting is held, approximately 3 to 6 months after start up of production. The discussion is lead by practitioners but the designers are active participants. Items of discussion may be issues of actual performance and data to be integrated in current and or future QFDs and whether or not, additional study is needed for more detailed information and whether or not additional or clarified commitments must be made. The major items of concern in the overall discussion are.
  - Develop data base on mass implementation versus plan
  - Identify problems and areas for further improvement
  - Integrate operator suggested efficiency or effectiveness improvements into plan
  - Identify additional customer valued inputs

Surveys: Survey research studies large and small populations by selecting and studying samples chosen from the interested populations to discover the relative incidence, distribution and interrelations of the selected variables. This type of survey is called a sample survey.

Surveys are not new. They have been around since the eighteenth century (Campbell and Katona 1953 chap. 1). However, surveys in the scientific sense, are a twentieth century development. To be sure, survey is considered to be a branch of social scientific research, which immediately distinguishes survey research from the status survey. The procedures and methods of survey research have been developed mostly by psychologists, sociologists, anthropologists, economists, political scientists and statisticians. All of them have a tremendous influence in how we perceive the social sciences.

In the quality profession, on the other hand, even though we use survey instruments, the process of surveying is not quite clear. To be sure, a survey, by definition links populations and samples. Therefore, the experimenter is interested in the accurate assessment of the characteristics of whole populations. For example a typical survey study may be conducted to investigate how many suppliers of type A material qualify for the approved supplier list, given characteristics such as: delivery, price, quality, capability and so on. Another example where a survey may be used by the quality professional is in the area of identifying and or measuring the current culture, attitude and general perception of quality in a given organization. Furthermore, we may use surveys to identify the attitudes about different courses, comparisons between curricula, school districts, methods of teaching, and in so many other applications.

In using a survey, it must be understood that the experimenter uses samples - very rarely, if ever, they will use populations - by which they will infer the characteristics of the defined universe. To be successful, such undertaking must depend on random samples and unbias questions. For the mechanics on how to construct a questionnaire see Stamatis (1996) and Kerlinger (1973). Surveys can be classified by the following methods of obtaining information:

- *Interviews*. They are very expensive, however, they do provide for individualized responses to questions as well as the opportunity to learn the reasons for doing or even believing something.
- *Panel technique*. A sample of respondents is selected and interviewed, and then re-interviewed and studied at later times. This technique is used primarily when one wants to study changes in behavior and or attitudes over time.
- *Telephone survey*. At least from a quality application, they have little to offer other than speed and low cost.
- *Mail questionnaire*. Quite popular in the quality field. It is used to self evaluate your own quality system, culture of the organization and so on. Its drawback, unless used in conjunction with other techniques, is the lack of response, inappropriate (leading, bias, ambiguous, and so on) questions, and the inability to verify the responses given.

Benchmarking: An additional tool in the tool box of improvement in any educational environment is benchmarking. Benchmarking is a way of comparing the practices of an organization with that of another, with the intent of learning about the process(es) and improving the results of the organization. A generic model is shown in Figure 7.4. Its basic assumption is a win-win situation for all the parties participating. It is beyond the scope of the book to address all the issues and methodological characteristics of benchmarking; however, we give an overview of the fundamentals. For more information see Watson (1992), Spendolini (1992), Camp (1989, 1995), and Stamatis (1996, 1997).

Benchmarking is an approach that when used appropriately one may examine both internal and external excellent performance for both understanding and improvement of a process and/or the entire organization. Formally, benchmarking has been defined a number of ways (Adam and Vande Water, 1995) including:

- as a process for identifying and learning from the best practices in the world
- as a search for and application of significantly better practices that lead to superior competitive performance
- as a process of comparing the business of one organization against another to gain information about "best practices" that when creatively adapted, can lead to superior performance

The performance analysis demanded by the benchmarking process may take a variety of approaches; however, the most common, effective and simple to understand is the hierarchical approach (top - bottom). The top being best in class practices, followed by industry practices and the lowest being your own organization. The most effective is the best in class (top) whereas the most difficult is your own organization (bottom). The lowest level indicates an internal comparison of best practices. This activity typically involves comparing functions of departments or business units within the same organization. On the other hand, the top level is reached when organizations throughout the world are considered as potential bench-marking partners.

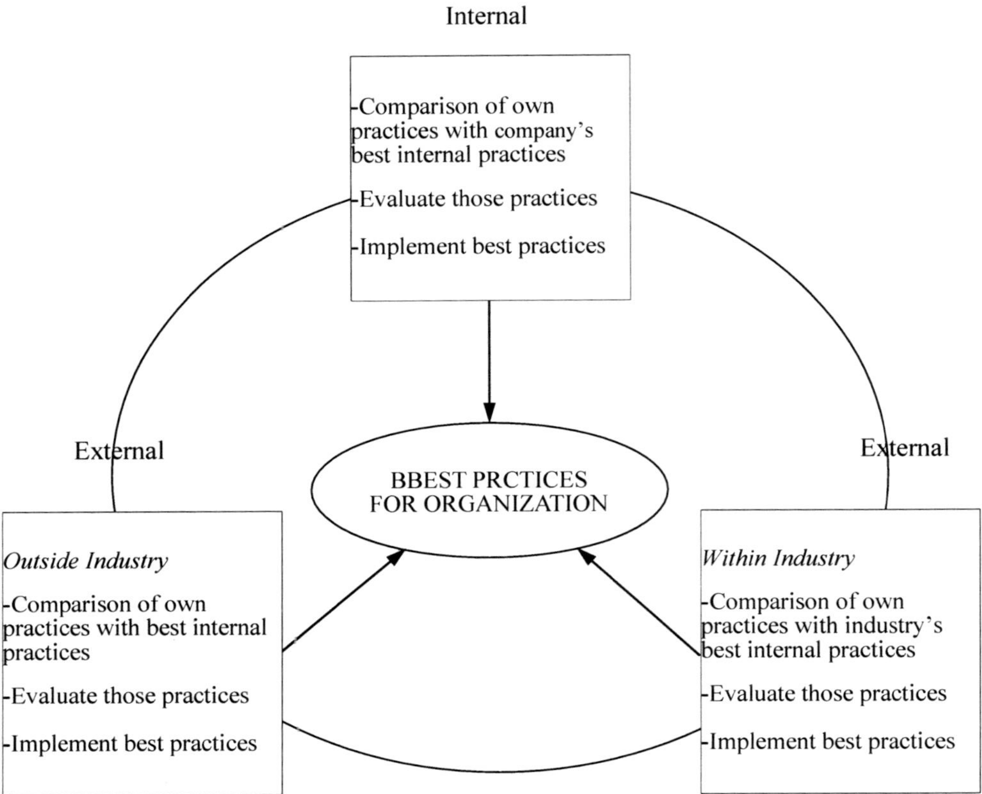

The creation of a profitable and sustainable competitive advantage should be the focus of any business process. Future growth and market share allocations are dependent on management's ability to identify positive and negative aspects of the competition's product or service, as well as the customer's likes and dislikes. Benchmarking is the vehicle to understand and facilitate this competitive advantage. As a result of benchmarking the organization may continue on the path of continual improvement (the Kaizen approach), or pursue a more dynamic approach to change (the reengineering approach), or pursue a combination of both. No matter what the selection is, it is important that the organization sooner or later focus on an operating strategy. The basic questions of operating strategy then become a function of one of the three strategies:

- The organization can pursue a cost strategy by being the low cost provider with a standard level of quality.
- The organization can embrace a value strategy by offering more value to the customer than the competition is able or willing to provide while maintaining proximity on cost and quality.
- A niche strategy that is a hybrid of one of the first two paths.

A typical process for conducting a benchmarking is the following:

1. Identify those processes needing improvement.
2. Identify a department within your company that conducts the process better than your department.
    a. Identify a firm that is the world leader in performing the process.
3. Contact the internal manager and arrange for a physical visit of the process in question and/or an interview with appropriate and applicable personnel.

a. Contact the manager of the organization you are benchmarking and arrange for a physical visit of the process in question and/or an interview with appropriate and applicable personnel.
4. Collect the data.
5. Analyze the data.
6. Take action.
7. Evaluate action.

This seven-step process should provide for a customer-focused benchmarking activity that produces deliverables for customers. Underlying the structure is the fundamental requirement of identifying the customer of the process for the subject being benchmarked and identifying this customer's needs. A customer is a person or activity that may benefit from information, a product, or a service. Customers may be internal to the organization, or they may be external to the organization. Regardless of the internal/external relationship, the needs, wants, and expectations of the customer must be targeted for achievement.

Finally, it is because of this customer-driven focus that organizations should target their benchmarking activities based on priorities within:

- the organization's core competencies
- significant problem areas
- areas of specific customer satisfaction and dissatisfaction
- the organization's core processes

Benchmarking is a continuous, systematic process that uses metrics in the search for best practices that will enable and direct real change, leading to Best-in-Class (BIC) performance. In addition, benchmarking is recognized as a proactive, positive, structured process that affords value to the company, its employees, customers and shareholders.

Benchmarking is a recurring process of defining Critical Success Factors (CSFs), comparing CSFs with the toughest competitors or BIC performers, and using comparison results to develop strategies and plans to change.

The objective of benchmarking is to make real changes that achieve *Best in Class* (BIC) performance. By placing metrics on project items, you know where you stand. Large improvements of 25-50-100% can be realized. If you have a specific problem, it may already have a solution. Find and apply the solution FAST and reduce cycle time. Change is accepted more readily when benchmarking metrics prove that techniques, methods and processes are being used successfully in BIC organizations. Good leaders realize benchmarking is not a delegated process, but consider it an energizing learning event, especially when done as a team.

The expected results from applying successful benchmarking processes include:
- Gaining valuable information knowledge and insight to appraise business decisions, strategic options and business opportunities that impact shareholder value.
- Identifying the gaps between your performance and BIC organizations' performance. This result should support the organization's objective of comparing key business indicators to those of competitors and other non-competitive organizations. The comparison helps to determine the organizations position in the industry and marketplace.
- Identifying ways to close the gaps through improved knowledge, process and practices that support the overall organizational Strategy - fastest time to market and quickest implementation of new ideas in the industry.

A Benchmarking process to close the identified gap requires a commitment from management and organization, and the participation of employees. An aggregate of management, organization and employees is critical to achieving the superior performance necessary for a true *commitment to change.*

The Benchmarking process and findings must be understood by the entire organization to obtain a *commitment to change.* Organized management support and careful communication are essential to successful Benchmarking. Employee involvement is needed to smoothly implement the findings. These criteria lead to excellence and superior performance.

It is of paramount importance to recognize that BIC is not necessarily referring to your competitors. Rather, Best-in-Class Achievement is defined as the reference metric that best describes the appropriate level of achievement for a project. Therefore, in Benchmarking we may pursue the BIC in a variety of situations and sources, such as in:

- Best-in-City
- Best-in-Company
- Best-in-Industry
- Best-in-Country
- Best-in-World

For Benchmarking to be effective it must support the effort to compare the organization's key business indicators to those of competitors and best-in-class performers, and identify in-house performance by comparing business practices to best practices within the institution and other organizations. Ultimately, to realize overall value, best practices and lessons learned must be shared continuously with others throughout the educational entity.

Why would anybody use Benchmarking? Because by learning from several BIC organizations and adding your own innovative ideas, it is possible to surpass the current BIC performance. By using Benchmarking an organization may become more flexible, learn to use less, to do more, become faster, more agile and more predatory. And, what better way to accomplish this strategy than by identifying and implementing the best practices within the organization and those employed by best-in-class organizations. [It is important to recognize that the Benchmarking process is learning and doing things that other BIC organizations are currently doing. There is nothing theoretical or futuristic here. Remember, many of the "answers" you need are in another organization, perhaps another industry. It is faster to find these proven solutions and add your innovative ideas than to reinvent. Therefore, the power of Benchmarking is truly on the application and transferring knowledge from other BICs to your own organization].

In addition to the obvious benefits, benchmarking can also contribute to the following:

- Assists in achieving organizational strategies
- Establishes baseline measurements
- Helps us meet and exceed competitor's strengths
- Brings best practices into the company… Fast
- Stimulates and motivates learning from outside the company
- Helps break down barriers to change

Benchmarking types: Different situations require different benchmarking processes to attain reliable results, best practices, and a commitment for change from the team. The following benchmarking process types may be used individually or combined as necessary:

1. *Process/Generic Benchmarking* - Focuses on improving processes, practices, methods and techniques. Projects are customer driven and linked to organizational strategies. The range of application is wide and may produce large, value-added improvements.
2. *Specialized Types* - Use as steps similar to Process Benchmarking and are defined as follows:
   - **Strategic** helps with strategic decisions (high level).
   - **Functional** usually looks only within a specific function of an organization (similar to Process Benchmarking).
   - **Competitive** is product or process focused, but only competitors are looked at.
   - **Performance** is comparing usually product or service performance with competitors.
   - **Best Practices** is similar to Process Benchmarking, and is sometimes used synonymously. Also, it sometimes focuses on management practices that allow for superior processes.
   - **Internal** looks at other internal operations to find Best-in-Company.
   - **Product** is a form of Performance or Competitive benchmarking which concentrates on product design evaluations, and manufacturing and assembly methods.
   - **Camera** uses photography to obtain product ideas and competitive information.

Benchmarking model: Benchmarking encourages systemic thinking by recognizing the importance of interdependencies and aspects of the process to attain Best-in-Class status. Benchmarking allows individuals and teams to identify the most critical things to change. Ultimately, it encourages new ideas and motivates people to take an innovative approach to business problems.

There are several models to follow. However, here we will only describe one of the most common models, known as the Motorola model. (Actually, the model was developed by DEC, Motorola, Boeing and XEROX.) The model has Five Phases, and begins with deciding what to benchmark and concludes with the actual implementation of change.

- *Phases 1 and 2* discern what to benchmark and how to do it. These phases entail the selection of a focused project and studying the current process or project.

1. What to Benchmark?

  Goal: Select a Benchmarking topic.
   - List the Critical Success Factors (CSFs).
   - Review the strategic plan. (Identify elements in it.)
   - Can the team link the CSFs to elements in the strategic plat
   - Choose an area of strength/weakness to focus on.
   - List the CSFs by priority.
   - Divide the highest priority CSFs into components and prioritize-if necessary
   - Has the team agreed upon a Benchmarking topic.

- *Phase 2* may take 40% or more of the total project time.

2. How do "we" do it?

  Goal: Analyze the internal process data.
   - Identify the people who are critical to the Benchmark process.
   - Get team agreement on definitions.
   - Contact people critical to project.
   - Define the process (through documentation, flowcharting, organizational mapping . . .).
   - Define at least two different ways to quantify the internal data and break into smallest pieces.
   - Normalize data and apply over time.

- Contact internal people to verify internal data.
  - Has the team agreed on how the process is defined?
- *Phase 3* involves finding the Best-in-Class process and setting up learning partnerships. Corporate values are paramount, especially during this phase. You must be above-board, ethical and open about your motives.

3. Who is best?

Goal: Select benchmarking partners
  - Create a list of criteria (for selection of potential Benchmark partners).
  - Select a pool of partner candidates.
  - Secure preliminary data.
  - Narrow candidate pool (to between three to five candidates).
  - Has the team agreed upon the selection of Benchmark partners?

- *Phase 4* is determining why their performance is superior. This phase applies the comparison of our methods and practices against the Best-in-Class.

4. How do "they" do it?

Goal: Determine what enables the Benchmarking partner to be BIC

- Review the DOs and DON'Ts and the legal considerations for information exchange.
- Gather public information.
- Create a partner profile.
- Generate a list of questions to drive the Benchmark project (using documentation).
- Has the team answered all the questions with public information?
- Determine methods needed to gather non-public information.
- Create project plan to gather information.
- Do you need help to create tools?
- Pilot the tools internally.
- Create a contingency plan.
- Gather data, debrief, and finalize data gathering.
- Normalize the BIC data to your process.
- Identify the gap and calculate.
- Has the team agreed on what enables the BIC to create and maintain the gap?

- *Phase 5* involves analyzing the enablers, adding your own innovations, setting improvement goals, and developing action plans to achieve them. This phase deals with the implementation of best practices discovered as a result of a benchmarking process. The strategy is to create and follow through on an action plan to close the gaps the benchmarking team identified.

5. Analysis and Implementation for change.

Goal: Create an Action Plan.
  - What; When; Who
  - List the recommendations to close the gap.
  - Select a method to close the gap.
  - Implement the action plan.
  - Measure the results.
  - Recalibrate. (Determine if the changes targeted in the action plan are taking place.)
  - Is the partner(s) performing as predicted?
  - Are there new performers? (Recycle).

Benchmarking Project Partners: Here are some tips to help you convince a Best In Class (BIC) organization to partner with you on a benchmarking project:

- Find the person that can approve your request - large projects usually require higher level of authorization.
- They will learn by participating.
- Advise them that someday they might want to benchmark your organization - reciprocity
- Tell them you anticipate a long term relationship - people with common interests.
- Tell them why this project is important to your organization.
- Take advantage of any connections between the organizations, such as customer, supplier, and subsidiary.
- Tell them what disciplines you would anticipate being involved and for how long.
- Make sure they know that you have a benchmarking process, and that you will be considerate of their time - that you will be focused and surgical.
- Make sure they understand that you will act as project manager and provide to them all data collected from all the benchmarking partners during the project. This includes your own answers to any questions the partners are asked.

Verify that all the benchmarking partners being considered can work together - there might be competitive or other reasons why the BIC candidate list will have to be adjusted.

In the educational process every discipline stakes its turf and tells people what it is in accessible language relying on advisory committees from the fields addressed. Bringing accessible language to bear facilitates the on setting boundaries for designing, modifying, and evaluating the presentation of disciplines in the educational systems (institutions) either individually or in groups of peer institutions. At that point of course, Benchmarking statements maybe publicly accessible so that:

- Teachers are reminded of what they have committed themselves to doing in the matter of distribution of knowledge and skills;
- Students can see in advance—and while it is in progress—what their academic journey is about and what levels of performance and understanding are expected; and
- External observers with a constitutive interest in the outcome of students' study (employers, governance authorities, public policymakers) have an important set of guidelines (though not the only set available to them) for judging the quality of education and training provided by institutions in that discipline.

In essence then, Benchmarking in education is another road to accountability. For a concrete case, let's pick a difficult discipline–history. A bachelor's degree program in history does not produce practitioners of a regulated occupation in the same way that a program in accounting does, so benchmarking statements do not refer to the discrete practices even of professional historians. Instead, a history advisory committee to the institution may specify six parameters for the content of a bachelor's level program in history, thus benchmarking the delivery of the program:

  - *Time Depth*: One doesn't see continuity and change in human affairs unless the temporal breadth of one's historical study is considerable.
  - *Geographical Range*: History cannot promote intercultural understanding without requiring its graduates to have studied more than one society or culture.

- o *Contemporary Sources*: The discovery, identification, and use of materials contemporary to the historical periods studied. These are research skills, and they are transferable.
- o *Reflexivity*: Something born in historiography and methods courses: critical reflection on the nature of the historical enterprise, its "social rationale," and its "theoretical underpinnings."
- o *Diversity of the Discipline*: Think of economic, social, political, environmental, or cultural history; or topics in women's history; or quantitative methods in history. The benchmarking here says that a graduate should have been "introduced to some of these varieties of approach."
- o A major independent *written project* such as an undergraduate thesis using original sources or an evaluation of conflicting historical interpretations of a major controversy.

All aspects of this presentation—generic and content—are then wrapped up in statements of learning outcomes subject to assessment, for example:

- Demonstrable command of a substantial body of historical knowledge;
- Demonstrable ability to develop and sustain historical arguments in a variety of forms, formulating appropriate questions and utilizing valid evidence;
- Demonstrable ability to gather and deploy evidence and data to find, retrieve, sort, and exchange new information; and
- Demonstrable command of comparative perspectives, which includes the ability to articulate analogies in the histories of different countries, societies, or cultures.

A department can select a configuration from these learning outcomes to determine the knowledge and competence of its students. Assessment (how "demonstrable" is executed) and the judgment of performance plays a significant role in the history benchmarks statement, and the committee is very clear that a student who has not met threshold performance criteria "is likely to have failed to progress at an earlier stage" and, thus, will not receive the degree.

What do we learn from benchmarking and what do we suggest? When U.S. educational institutions (K-12, colleges, community colleges, and universities) describe what students must do to earn a diploma or a degree in their institution or a specific field, they list courses (required and suggested), credits, and minimum grade point average, not learning outcomes. Sometimes, departments issue a statement of the purpose of the degree in terms of the careers to which it traditionally leads or careers in which its subject may be useful. Sometimes one finds flowery mission statements extolling the vision or heritage or human benefits of the field. But rarely is there an attempt to provide a statement of the summative knowledge, skills, and capacities expected of graduates—let alone criterion-referenced performance criteria.

Students themselves thus have little idea of the meaning of either their learning or the credential they receive. Benchmarking is a way to fix that problem.

Measurement System Analysis (MSA): People measure product characteristics or process parameters so they can assess the performance of the system of interest. The measured values provide feedback of the process, so that people may adjust settings, replace tools, redesign fixtures, or allow the operation to continue on its current course. The measurements are indeed the data that will allow people to make decisions critical to improvement efforts.

As critical as these measurements are, no measurement process is a set of perfect activities. Sometimes different numbers or readings result when the same part or sample is measured a second time. Different readings may be made by different people, gauges, or by the same person using the same gauge. The difference in successive measurements of the same item is called measurement error. This source of variation must be analyzed because the validity of the data directly affects the validity of process improvement decisions.

The purpose of performing a Measurement System Analysis (MSA) is to ensure the information collected is a true representation of what is occurring in the process. Perhaps the most important item to remember is that total variation in a process is equal to the sum of the process variation and the measurement system variation. Therefore, minimizing measurement variation ensures that variation reflected by the data collected represents only process variation. As a consequence, MSA is performed on a regular basis to ensure that data is valid and reliable. Typical information gained by conducting MSA is:

- Is the measurement system capable for this study?
- How big is the measurement error?
- How much uncertainty should be attached to a measurement when interpreting it?
- Are the measurements being made with measurement units that are small enough to properly reflect the variation present?
- What are the sources of measurement error?
- Can we detect process improvement if and when it happens?
- Is the measurement system stable over time?

To be sure, measurement system is a major component of the process. In fact, studying variation within the parameters of the measurement system is of paramount importance because:

1. Measurement error contributes to process variation and has a negative influence upon the process capability level.
2. Measurement error is present whenever measurements are made. The effects of measurement error influence the assessment of all other items of the process.

In addition to being a part of the process or system, measurement activities also may form a process. It must be emphasized, that it is totally inappropriate to view measurement error as merely a function of measurement hardware or instruments. Other components of the measurement process are equally important to measurement error or validity. For example people contribute to measurement error by having different levels of tactile, auditory, or visual perception. These characteristics account for calibration and or interpretation differences.

Another example in measurement error is the contribution of a "method" change. This kind of error is one of the largest sources of variation in the measurement process. The significance of this is compounded when different people or instruments are used to evaluate the same item or process. Obviously, a standard procedure is needed for every measurement activity. Only this procedure should be used by all people who operate test equipment. Measurement errors that are sometime attributed to differences in people are actually due to differences in methodology. People are usually able to produce similar readings when they use the same methods for operating the measurement equipment. Other examples where measurement error may be introduced are: Changes in environment, changes in test equipment, and changes in standards and so on.

Failure mode and effect analysis (FMEA): An FMEA is a technique of a very strict methodology to evaluate a system, a design and or a process for possible ways in which failures can occur. For each failure that can be a real or a potential failure, an estimate is made of its effect on the total system and of its seriousness. In addition, a review is made of the action being taken (or planned) to minimize the probability of failure or to minimize the effect of failure. For a very detailed explanation see Stamatis (2003a, 1995).

This simple but straight forward approach can be very technical (quantitative) or very non-technical (qualitative), utilizing three main factors for the identification of the specific failure. The three factors are the occurrence - how often the failure occurs, severity - how serious the failure is, and detection - how easy or difficult is to detect the failure.

The complication of the approach is always dependent on the complexity of the problem as defined by the following:

1. **Safety.** Injury is the most serious of all failure effects. In fact, in some cases, it is of unquestionable priority and of course, at this point it must be handled either with a Hazard Analysis and or Failure Mode and Critical Analysis (FMCA).
2. **Effects on downtime.** How are repairs made? Can repairs be made while the machine is off - duty time or while the machine is operating?
3. **Access.** What hardware items must be removed to get at the failed component? This area will be of great importance as environmental laws are changed to reflect world conditions for disassembly.
4. **Repair planning.** Repair time, Maintainability, Repair tools, Cost, Recommendation(s) for changes in design specifications. Here, The Shingo approach, DOE or Design for Manufacturability may be considered.

In the educational system we may extend these four principles to include:

- Implementation of learning methodologies
- Implementation of new technologies in the classroom
- Implementation of new approaches to curricula
- Implementation of new programs and services in the non-educational activities

To carry this methodology to its proper conclusion the following prerequisites in understanding are necessary.

1. **Not all problems are important.** This is very fundamental to the entire concept of FMEA, because unless internalized we are going to "chase fires" in the organization. We must recognize that some problems are more important than others for whatever the reason. The fact is that some problems have indeed higher priority than others. FMEA helps identify this priority.
2. **You must know the customer.** The definition of "customer" normally is thought of as the "end user." However, a customer may also be defined as a subsequent or downstream operation, as well as, a service operation. When using the term customer from an FMEA perspective the definition plays a very major role in addressing problems. For example, as a general rule in the design FMEA one views the "customer" as the end user, while in the process FMEA the "customer" is viewed as the "next operation in line. This "next" operation may indeed be the end user but it does not have to be. Once you define your customer (internal, intermediate or external) you may not change it - at least not for the problem at hand - unless you recognize that by changing it you may indeed have changed your problem and or consequences.
3. **You must know the function.** It is imperative to know the function, purpose, objective of what you are trying to accomplish, otherwise you are going to waste time and effort in redefining your problem based on situations. If you have to, take extra time to make sure you understand the function or purpose of what you are trying to accomplish.

4. **You must be prevention oriented.** Unless you recognize that continual improvement is in your best interest the FMEA is going to be a "static" document to satisfy your customer or market requirements. The push for this continual improvement makes the FMEA a "dynamic" document changing as the design and or process changes with the intent ALWAYS to make a better design and or process.

Why do we do FMEAs?

The propensity of our managers and engineers to minimize the risk in a particular design and or process has forced us to look at Reliability Engineering to not only minimize but also to define the risk. Perceived risk is driven by the following factors:

- Competition
- Warranty and service costs
- Development technical risks
- Market pressure
- Management emphasis
- Customer requirements
- Safety
- Legal , Statutory requirements
- Public liability
- Others

These risks can be measured by reliability engineering and or statistical analyses. However, because of their complexity, the FMEA has extracted the basic principles without the technical mathematics and has provided us with a tool that anybody committed to continual improvement can utilize.

Statistical Process Control (SPC) is another tool that provides the impetus for the FMEA, especially for a process FMEA. SPC provides information about the process in regards to changes. These changes are called common and special causes. From an FMEA perspective we may look at the common causes as failures that are the result of inherent failure mechanisms and as such, they can affect the entire population. In this case, this is a cause for examining the design.

On the other hand, special causes are looked at as failures that result from part defects and or manufacturing problems and as such, they can affect a relatively small population. In this case, there is cause for examining the process.

- Customer requisition is of course a very strong influence as to why we may be doing an FMEA. For example: All educational institutions are required to be certified by a third party entity. That certification serves as a notice to the customer that the institution fulfils minimum requirements of education.
- Courts and or government may require some substantiation as to what level of safety and reliability you provide in the institution.
- International standards such as the ISO-9000 series may define for you the program of documentation in your design. For example: Quality systems incorporating specific tools such as FMEA or Fault Tree Analysis (FTA) or Failure Mode and Critical Analysis (FMCA) with safety prevention provisions will be particularly important in protecting a company from unfounded liability claims. Furthermore, proposed safety directives would oblige educational institutions to monitor the safety of their students, employees and facilities.

Other benefits (partial list) of the FMEA are:

- Improves the quality, reliability and safety of the products
- Improves the institution's image and competitiveness
- Helps increase customer satisfaction
- Reduces product development time and COSTS
- Helps select the optimum system design
- Helps determine the redundancy of the system
- Helps identify diagnostic procedures
- Establishes a priority for design improvement actions
- Helps identify critical and/or significant characteristics
- Helps in the analysis of new processes and methods of teaching in the educational environment

Even though all the above reasons are legitimate, the most important reason for writing an FMEA is the need to improve. Unless this need is part of the culture of the organization, the FMEA program is not going to be successful.

The Process of Doing an FMEA

To do an FMEA effectively one must follow a systematic approach. The recommended approach is an eight-step method that facilitates the system, the design, the process and the service FMEAs.

1. *Brainstorm.* Try to identify in what direction you want to go. Is it system, design, process, or service? What kind of problems are you having with a particular situation? Is the customer involved or are you pursuing continual improvement on your own? If the customer has identified specific failures, then your job is much easier, because you already have the direction identified. On the other hand, if you are trying on your own the brainstorm and/or the cause-and-effect diagram may prove to be the best tools to identify your direction of attack.
2. *Block diagram* (used only for system and design). Make sure everyone on the team is on the same wavelength. Does everyone understand the same problem? The block diagram will focus the discussion. If nothing else, it will create a baseline of understanding for the problem at hand.
   - *Process flow chart* (used only for process and service). Make sure everyone in the team is on the same wavelength. Does everyone understand the same problem? The process flow chart will focus the discussion. If nothing else, it will create a baseline of understanding for the problem at hand.
3. *Prioritize.* Once you understand the problem and its relationship to other problems, the team must begin the plan for action. For example, in one problem there may be subproblems or areas that need to be addressed first. More often than not, a thorough study of the block diagram or the process flow chart will indicate the appropriate action. This is the stage where we really begin to focus on the problem.
4. *Data collection.* Begin to collect data of the failures and start filling out the appropriate form.
5. *Analysis.* Focus on the data and perform the appropriate analysis. Everything is fair, provided it is appropriate and applicable. Here, QFD, DOE, another FMEA, SPC, and anything else may be used to provide the appropriate results.
6. *Results.* Based on the analysis, the results are derived. The results must be data driven; nothing else will do.
7. *Confirm/evaluate/measure.* Once the results have been recorded, it is the time to confirm, evaluate, and measure the success or failure of the recommended action taken. This evolution takes the form of three basic questions:
   a. Are we better off than before?

b. Are we worse off than before?

c. Are we the same as before?

8. *Do it all over again.* Regardless of how you answer Step 6, you must pursue improvement all over again because of the continual improvement philosophy. Your long-range goal is to eliminate completely all failures and your short-term goal is to minimize your failures if not eliminate them. Of course, the perseverance for those goals have to be taken into consideration in relationship to the needs of the organization, cost, customer, and competition.

Affinity Chart: An affinity chart is the organized output from a team brainstorming session. (It differs from brainstorming in that the affinity chart uses cards as headers that can be changed and organized in piles for discussion.) It was created by Kawakita Jiro and is also known as the KJ method. The purpose of an affinity chart is to generate, organize, and consolidate information concerning a product, process, service, and/or complex issue or problem. The chart is used when the answer to the following three questions is a positive "yes."

- Is the issue complex and hard to understand?
- Is the problem uncertain, disorganized, or overwhelming?
- Does the problem require the involvement and support of a group or a team?

The actual construction of the chart takes seven basic steps:

1. Choose a group leader.
2. Choose the problem and if possible state it in a question form.
3. Brainstorm and record all ideas. Each idea should be written on its own index card or note.
4. Arrange the cards into like categories.
5. Name each category with a header card.
6. Draw the affinity chart. Arrange headers with the appropriate generated ideas and circle or box them together.
7. Discuss the categories.

Storyboard: Quality improvement storyboards and storybooks use the steps in the FOCUS/PDCA strategy to help teams organize their work and their presentations so others can more readily learn from them. They reduce variation in the process by focusing the learning experience on the content rather than the method of telling. For a very detailed discussion see Forsha (1995a,b). In addition, storyboards form a permanent record of a team's actions and achievements, and all the data generated and storyboards can function as the working minutes of the team.

Electronic learning (or e-Learning or eLearning) is a type of technology supported education/learning (TSL) where the medium of instruction is through computer technology, particularly involving digital technologies. E-learning has been defined by Nichols (2008) as pedagogy empowered by digital technology. In some instances, no face- to- face interaction takes place. E-learning is used interchangeably in a wide variety of contexts. In companies, it refers to the strategies that use the company network to deliver training courses to employees. In the United States (See note 1), it is defined as a planned teaching/learning experience that uses a wide spectrum of technologies, mainly internet or computer-based, to reach learners. Lately in most universities, e-learning is used to define a specific mode to attend a course or programs of study where the students rarely, if ever, attend face-to-face for on-campus access to educational facilities, because they study online. Benefits of e-Learning versus traditional classroom settings e-Learning can provide for major benefits for the organizations and individuals involved.

1. Reducing environmental impact: e-Learning allows people to avoid travel, thus reducing the overall carbon output. The fact that it takes place in a virtual environment also allows some reduction of

paper usage. With virtual notes instead of paper notes and online assessments instead of paper assessments, e-Learning is a more environmentally friendly solution.

2. Quality education, made affordable: The fact that instructors of the highest caliber can share their knowledge across borders allows students to attend courses across physical, political, and economic boundaries. Recognized experts have the opportunity of making information available internationally, to anyone interested at minimum costs. This can drastically reduce the costs of higher education, making it much more affordable and accessible to the masses. An internet connection, a computer, and a projector would allow an entire classroom in a third world university to benefit from the knowledge of an opinion leader.

3. Convenience and flexibility to learners: in many contexts, e-Learning is self-paced and the learning sessions are available 24x7. Learners are not bound to a specific day/time to physically attend classes. They can also pause learning sessions at their convenience.

Note 1: American public education is operated by state and local governments, regulated by the United States Department of Education through restrictions on federal grants. Children are required in most states to attend school from the age of six or seven (generally, kindergarten or first grade) until they turn eighteen (generally bringing them through twelfth grade, the end of high school); some states allow students to leave school at sixteen or seventeen (United States 2007). About 12% of children are enrolled in parochial or nonsectarian private schools nonsectarian private schools. Just over 2% of children are home schooled.(United States 2003). The United States has many competitive private and public institutions of higher education, as well as local community colleges with open admission policies. Of Americans twenty-five and older, 84.6% graduated from high school, 52.6% attended some college, 27.2% earned a bachelor's degree, and 9.6% earned graduate degrees (United States 2003a). The basic literacy rate literacy rate is approximately 99% (United States 2007a, 2005; The United Nations assigns the United States an Education Index of 0.97, tying it for 12th in the world (United States 2006).

Summary

In this chapter we have addressed some of the most common yet powerful tools for improvement. Specifically we have divided them into three categories for easier application. That is: a) basic tools b) advanced tools and special methodologies/tools. In the next chapter we address the six sigma methodology for improvement.

References

Adam, P. and Vande Water, R. (February 1995). "Benchmarking and the bottom line: Translating business reengineering into bottom-line results." *Industrial Engineering*. Pp. 24-26.

Akao, Y. (Ed.). 1990. *Quality function deployment: Integrating customer requirements into product design.* Productivity Press. Cambridge, MA.

American Supplier Institute (ASI). (1987). *Quality function deployment: A collection of presentations and QFD case studies.* ASI. Dearborn, MI.

American Supplier Institute. (1989). *A symposium on quality function deployment.* ASI. Dearborn, MI.

Bank, A., Henderson, M., and Eu, L. (1981). *A practical guide to program planning: A teaching models approach.* Teachers College, Columbia University. New York.

Brinkerhoff, R.O. (1987). *Achieving results from training.* Jossey Bass. San Francisco. CA.

Bossert, J. L. (1990). *Quality function deployment: A practitioner's approach.* Quality Press. Milwaukee, WI.

Brassard, M. and Ritter, D. (1988). *The memory jogger.* GOAL/QPC. Methuen, MA.

Brassard, M. and Ritter, D. (1994). *The memory jogger II.* GOAL/QPC. Methuen, MA.

Brinkerhoff, R. 0. (1987). *Achieving results from training.* Jossey Bass. San Francisco.

Duncan, A. J. (1986). *Quality control and industrial statistics*. 5th Ed. Irwin. Home-wood, IL.

Camp, R. C. (1995). *Business process benchmarking: Finding and implementing best practices*. Quality Press. Milwaukee, WI.

Camp, R. C. (1989). *Benchmarking: The search for industry best practices that lead to superior performance*. Quality Press. Milwaukee, WI.

Campbell, A. and Katona, G. (1953). "The sample survey: A technique for social-science research." In: L. Festiger and D. Katz, *Research methods in the behavioral science*. Holt, Reinhart, and Winston, New York.

Clausing, D. (1988). "Quality function deployment." In: N. E. Ryan. (Ed.). *Taguchi methods and QFD: Hows and whys for management*. American Supplier Institute. Dearborn, MI.

Cohen, L. (1995). *Quality function deployment: How to make QFD work for you*. Quality Press. Milwaukee, WI.

Day, R. G. (1993). *Quality function deployment: Linking a company with its customers*. Quality Press. Milwaukee, WI.

Delbecq, A. L. and Van de Ven, A. H. (1986). *Group techniques for program planning*. Green Briar Press. Middleton, WI.

Delbecq, A. L., Van de Ven, A. H., and Gustafson, D. H. (1975). *Group techniques for program planning: A guide for nominal and delphi processes*. Scott Foresman. Glenview, IL.

Eureka, W. E. (1987). *Introduction to quality function deployment*. Paper presented in a training class offered by American Supplier Institute. Dearborn, MI.

Forsha, H. I. (1995a). *Show me: The complete guide to storyboarding and problem solving*. Quality Press. Milwaukee, WI.

Forsha, H. I. (1995b). *Show me: Storyboard workbook and template*. Quality Press. Milwaukee, WI.

Gitlow, H., Gitlow, S., Oppenheim A., and Oppenheim, R. (1989). *Tools and methods for the improvement of quality*. Irwin. Homewood, IL.

Grant, E. L. and Leavenworth, R. S. (1980). *Statistical quality control*. 5th ed. McGraw-Hill Book Co. New York.

Gulezian, R. (1991). *Process control statistical principles and tools*. Quality Alert Institute, Inc. New York.

Ishikawa, K. (1982). *Guide to quality control*. Asian Productivity Organization. Kraus International Publications. White Plains, NY.

Kaufman, R., and English, F. W. (1979) *Needs assessment: Concept and application*. Educational Technology Publications, Englewood Cliffs, NJ.

Kerlinger, F. N. (1973). *Foundations of behavioral research*. 2nd ed. Holt, Reinhart and Winston, Inc. New York.

Kerzner, H. (1995). *Project management: A systems approach to planning, scheduling, and controlling*. 5th ed. Van Nostrand Reinhold. New York.

Madaus, G. F., Scriven, M., and Stufflebeam, D. L. (Eds.). (1983). *Evaluation models*. Kluwer-Nijhoff Publishing. Boston.

Mizuno, S. (Ed.). (1988). *Management for quality improvement: The 7 new QC tools*. Productivity Press. Portland, OR.

Montgomery, D. C. (1985). *Introduction to statistical quality control*. John Wiley and Sons. New York.

Nichols, M. (2008). E-Learning in context. http://akoaotearoa.ac.nz/sites/default/files/ng/group-661/n877-1---e-learning-in-context.pdf

Scriven, M. (1991). *Evaluation Thesaurus*. 4th ed. Sage Publications. Newbury Park, CA.

Spendolini, M. J. (1992). *The benchmarking book*. Quality Press. Milwaukee, WI.

Stamatis, D. H. (2003). *Six sigma and beyond: Statistical process control*. St. Lucie. Boca Raton. FL.

Stamatis, D. H. (2003a) Failure Mode Effect analysis: FMEA from theory to execution. 2nd ed. Revised and expanded ASQ Quality Press. Milwaukee, WI.

Stamatis, D. H. (1997). *TQM engineering handbook*. Marcel Dekker. NY.

Stamatis, D. H. (1996a). *Total quality service*. St. Lucie Press. Delray Beach, FL.

Stamatis, D. H. (1996b). *Documenting and auditing for ISO 9000 and QS-9000*. Irwin Professional. Burr Ridge, IL.

Stamatis, D. H. (1995). *Failure mode and effect analysis. FMEA from theory to execution*. Quality Press. Milwaukee, WI.

Sullivan, L. P. (1987). *The company-wide benefits of QFD*. Video tape. American Supplier Institute. Dearborn, MI.

Sullivan, L. P. (June 1986). Quality function deployment. *Quality Progress*. Pp. 39-50.

Tague, N. R. (1995). *The quality tool box*. Quality Press. Milwaukee, WI.

United States (2007). *Statistics About Non-Public Education in the United States*. U.S. Dept. of Education, Office of Non-Public Education. Washington, D.C. http://www.ed.gov/about/offices/list/oii/nonpublic/statistics.html. Retrieved on 06/05/2007.

United States (May 31, 2007a). *The World Factbook*. CIA. 05/31/2007. https://www..cia.gov/library/publications/the-world-factbook/geos/us.html. Retrieved on 10/14/2008.

United States (November 2006). *Health, United States, 2006*. Centers for Disease Control and Prevention, National Center for Health Statistics. http://www.cdc.gov/nchs/data/hus/hus06.pdf#027. Retrieved on 08/15/2007.

United States (2003). *Educational Attainment in the United States: 2003*. U.S. Census Bureau. http://www.census.gov/prod/2004pubs/p20-550.pdf. Retrieved on 08/01/2006.

United States (2003a). *A First Look at the Literacy of America's Adults in the 21st Century*. U.S. Department of Education. Washington, D.C.

United States (2005). *Human Development Indicators*. United Nations Development Programme, Human Development Reports. 2005. Archived from the original on 06/20/2007. http://web.archive.org/web/20070620235428/http://hdr.undp.org/reports/global/2005/pdf/HDR05_H DI.pdf. Retrieved on 01/14/2008.

Watson, G. H. (1992). The benchmarking workbook: Adapting best practices for performance improvement. *Quality Press*. Milwaukee, WI.

Selected Bibliography

ANSI/ISO/ASQC A8402. (1994). *Quality vocabulary*. ASQC. Milwaukee, WI.

Arter, D. R. (1994). *Quality audits for improved performance*. 2nd ed. Quality Press. Milwaukee, WI.

Eureka, W. E. and Ryan N. E. (1988). *The customer-driven company: Managerial perspective on QFD*. American Supplier Institute. Dearborn, MI.

Keeney, K. A. (1995a). *The ISO9000 auditor's companion*. Quality Press. Milwaukee, WI.

Keeney, K. A. (1995b). *The audit kit*. Quality Press. Milwaukee, WI.

Kish, L. (1965). *Survey sampling*. John Wiley and Sons. New York.

Kuzela, L. (November 12, 1984). "Here's how to put quality control to work for you." *Industry Week*. P. 21.

Miller, W. H. (August 1, 1988). "Changed focus: Technology fix to cost of quality control." *Industry Week*. P.16.

Mills, C. A. (1989). *The quality audit*. Quality Press. Milwaukee, WI.

Parsowith, B. S. (1995). *Fundamentals of quality auditing*. Quality Press. Milwaukee, WI.

Rosenstone, Steven J. (2009-03-06). "Public Education for the Common Good." University of Minnesota. http://cla.umn.edu/news/clatoday/summer2002/dean.php. Retrieved on 2009-12-17.

Russell, J. P. (1995). *Quality management benchmark assessment*. 2nd ed. Quality Press. Milwaukee, WI.

U. S. Department of Education (N.D.)"Ages for Compulsory School Attendance...". U.S. Dept. of Education, National Center for Education Statistics. http://nces.ed.gov/programs/digest/d02/dt150.asp. Retrieved on 2007-06-10.

CHAPTER 8

SIX SIGMA IN EDUCATION

In the last chapter we introduced some very common and powerful tools for anyone in the educational system to use if they are really interested in process improvement. In this chapter we will discuss the six sigma methodology and how it may be used to improve the educational process. We will address both DMAIC and DCOV models.

Every methodology has a conceptual approach to work with. Six Sgma is no different and, in fact, has two lines of approach. The first is to address existing (current) problems, and the second, to prevent problems from happening to begin with. The second one is also called Design for Six Sigma (DFSS). In both approaches, the methodology attempts to bring harmony between Technology, People and Business Strategy and at the same time optimize each and every one of these three items with the total organization in mind. These two models are known as: 1) the Define, Measure, Analyze, Improve and Control (DMAIC) and 2) Define, Characterize, Optimize, and Verify (DCOV).

The six sigma methodology has adopted the old plan-do-study-(check)-act (PDS(C)A) approach, with some very subtle variations in that breakthrough strategy. This approach is a functional one—it clearly shows the correct path to follow once a project has been selected. It is beyond the scope of this book to discuss all the details of the six sigma methodology, however, for a very detailed discussion and implementation strategy the reader is encouraged to see Pyzdek (2001), Breyfogle (2003), Stamatis (2004, 2002-2003). Here we will summarize both models with their essential elements. For specific tools and forms used in the six sigma methodology see Appendix B.

The DMAIC model

Define: The first stage—define—serves as the platform for the team to get organized, determine the roles and responsibilities of each member of the team, establish team goals and milestones and review the process steps. The key points to be defined at this stage are the voice of the customer, the scope of the project, the cause and effect prioritization (a list that the team creates for pursuing the specific project based on cause and effect criteria) and project planning. The intent is to align the business strategy and the preliminary definition of the project.

Each of these points can be linked to the customer (some are quite obvious and others not so), and it is essential to appreciate and understand this link to the customer before and during this stage of the model. The following are the steps to take to complete the define phase of the DMAIC model:

- *Define the problem.* The problem is based on available data, is measurable and excludes any assumptions about possible causes or solutions. It must be specific and attainable. It also must address some type of a customer concern or importance to the customer. This is called critical to customer (CTC) characteristics. Sometimes this identification may occur concurrently with the identification of the customer or may be postponed until the customer is identified.
- *Identify the customer.* This is more demanding as we systematically begin the process of analysis. We must identify who is directly impacted by the problem and at what cost. We begin by conducting a random sample analysis to identify the overall impact and then we proceed with a detailed analysis of the cost of poor quality (COPQ). The focus of the team here is to identify a large base of people affected by poor quality.

- *Identify critical to quality (CTQ) characteristics.* By identifying CTQ characteristics, the project team determines what is important to each customer from the customer's point of view. Identification of CTQ characteristics ascertains how these particular features appear when meeting customer expectations. Typical questions here are: What is "good condition?" and What is "on time?"
- *Map the process.* Mapping of the process in this stage of the define phase of the six sigma methodology is nothing more than a high level visual representation of the current process steps leading up to fulfillment of the identified CTQ characteristics. This "as is" process map will be useful throughout the process as:
  - A method for segmenting complex processes into manageable portions.
  - A way to identify process inputs and outputs.
  - A technique to identify areas of rework.
  - A way to identify bottlenecks, breakdowns and non-value added steps.
  - A benchmark against which future improvements can be compared with the original process.

  Any organization is a collection of processes, and these processes are the natural business activities you perform that produce value, serve customers and generate income. Managing these processes is the key to the success of the organization. Process mapping is a simple yet powerful method of looking beyond functional activities and rediscovering core processes. Process maps enable you to peel away the complexity of your organizational structure and focus on the processes that are truly the heart of your business. Armed with a thorough understanding of the inputs, outputs and interrelationships of each process, you and your organization can understand how processes interact in a system, evaluate which activities add value for the customer and mobilize teams to streamline and improve processes in the "should be" and "could be" categories. It should be noted that understanding the process is an important objective of the process map. However, something that is just as important, and usually undervalued from constructing a process map, is the benefit of the alignment of the team to the process at hand. Once this alignment occurs, and everyone in the team understands what is expected, the conclusion of a successful project is a high probability.
- *Scoping the project.* The last step of the define stage is scoping the project and if necessary, updating the project charter. During this step the team members will further specify project issues, develop a refined problem statement and brainstorm suspected sources of variation. The focus of this step is to reduce the scope of the project to a level that ensures the problem is within the team's area of control that data can be collected to show both the current and improved states and that improvements can be made within the project's timeframe.

At the end of this stage, it is not uncommon to revisit the original problem statement and refine it in such a way that the new problem statement is a highly defined description of the problem. Beginning with the general problem statement and applying what has been learned through further scoping, the team writes a refined problem statement that describes the problem in narrow terms and indicates the entry point where the team will begin its work. In addition, a considerable amount of time is taken at this step to identify the extent of the problem and how it is measured.

Ultimately, the purpose of this stage is to set the foundations for the work ahead in solving a problem. This means that an excellent understanding of the process must exist for all team members, as well as complete understanding of the CTQ characteristics. After CTQ factors are identified, everyone in the team must agree on developing an operational definition for each CTQ aspect. Effective operational definitions:

- Describe the critical to quality characteristics accurately.
- Are specific so that the customer expectation is captured correctly.
- Are always written to ensure consistent interpretation and measurement by multiple people.

Whereas typical methods of identifying CTQ characteristics include but are not limited to focus groups, surveys and interviews, the outputs are CTQ characteristics, operational definitions and parameters for measuring.

Measure: The second stage of the DMAIC model—measure—is when the team establishes the techniques for collecting data about current performance that highlights project opportunities and provides a structure for monitoring subsequent improvements. Upon completing this stage, we expect to have a plan for collecting data that specifies the data type and collection technique, a validated measurement system that ensures accuracy and consistency, a sufficient sample of data for analysis, a set of preliminary analysis results that provides project direction and baseline measurements of current performance.

The focus of this stage is to develop a sound data collection plan, identify key process input variables (KPIV), display variation using Pareto charts, histograms, run charts, and baseline measures of process capability and process sigma level. The steps to carry through this stage are:

- *Identify measurement and variation.* The measure subsets establish the requirements of measurement and variation, including: a) the types and sources of variation and the impact of variation on process performance, b) the different types of measures for variance and the criteria for establishing good process measures, and c) the different types of data that can be collected and the important characteristics of each data type. As part of this step the types of variation must be defined. There are two types of causes of variation:
    - *Common causes.* These are conditions in a process that generate variation through the interaction of the 5Ms (machine, material, method, measurement, manpower) and 1E (environment). Common causes affect everyone working in the process, and affect all of the outcomes. They are always present and thus are generally predictable. They are generally accepted sources of variation and offer opportunities for process improvement.
    - *Special causes.* These are items in a process that generate variation due to extraordinary circumstances related to one of the 5Ms or 1E. Special causes are not always present, do not affect everyone working in the process and do not affect all of the outcomes. Special causes are not predictable.
- *Determine data type.* In this step the team must be able to answer the question, "What do we want to know?" Reviewing materials developed during the previous stage, the team determines what process or product characteristics they need to learn more about. A good start is the definition of the data type. This is determined by what is measured. Two types of data can be collected by measuring:
    - *Attribute data.* One way to collect data is to merely count the frequency of occurrence for a given process characteristic (*e.g.* the number of times something happens or fails to happen). Data collected in this manner is known as attribute data. Attribute data cannot be meaningfully subdivided into more precise increments and is discrete by nature. "Go/no go" and "pass/fail" data are examples of this category.
    - *Variable data.* A different way to look at data is to describe the process characteristic in terms of its weight, voltage or size. Data collected in this manner is known as variable data. With this type of data, the measurement scale is continuous-it can be meaningfully divided into finer and finer increments of precision.
- *Develop a data collection plan.* In developing and documenting a data collection plan the team should consider:
    - What the team wants to know about the process.
    - The potential sources of variation in the process (Xs).
    - Whether there are cycles in the process and how long data must be collected to obtain a true picture of the process.

- o   Who will collect the data.
  - o   How the measurement system will be tested.
  - o   Whether operational definitions contain enough detail.
  - o   How data will be displayed once collected.
  - o   Whether data is currently available, and what data collection tools will be used if current data does not provide enough information.
  - o   Where errors in data collection might occur and how errors can be avoided or corrected.
- *Perform measurement system analysis.* This step involves performing graphical analysis and conducting baseline analysis. During this step, the team verifies the data collection plan once it is complete and before the actual data is collected. This type of analysis is called a measurement system analysis (MSA). A typical MSA indicates whether the variation measured is from the process or the measurement tool. The MSA should begin with the data collection plan and should end when a high level of confidence is reached that the data collected will accurately depict the variation in the process. By way of a definition, MSA is a quantitative evaluation of the tools and processes used in making data observations. Perhaps the most important concept in any MSA study is that if the measurement system fails to pass analysis before collecting data, then further data should not be collected. Rather, the gauge should be fixed, the measurement system should be fixed and the measurement takers should be trained.
- *Collect the data.* During this step, the team must make sure that the collected data is appropriate, applicable and accurate, and that it provides enough information to identify the potential root cause of the problem. It is not enough to plan carefully before actually collecting the data and then assume that everything will go smoothly. It is important to make sure that the data continues to be consistent and stable as it is collected. The critical rules of data collection are:
  - o   Be there as the data is collected.
  - o   Do not turn over data collection to others.
  - o   Plan for data collection, design data collection sheets and train data collectors.
  - o   Stay involved throughout the data collection process.

The outcome of this step must be an adequate data set to carry into the analyze stage.

Analyze: The third stage—analyze—serves as an outcome of the measure stage. The team at this stage should begin streamlining its focus on a distinct group of project issues and opportunities. In other words, this stage allows the team to further target improvement opportunities by taking a closer look at the data. We must remember that the measure, analyze and improve stages quite frequently work hand in hand to target a particular improvement opportunity. For example, the analyze stage might simply serve to confirm opportunities identified by graphical analysis in the measurement stage. Conversely, the analyze stage might uncover a gap in the data collection plan that requires the team to collect additional information. Therefore, the team makes sure the appropriate recognition of data is given and applicable utilization is functional, as well as correct. Yet another important aspect of this stage is the introduction of the hypothesis testing for attribute data. On the other hand, in the case of variable data we may want to use: analysis of means (1 sample t-test or 2 sample t-test), analysis of variance for means, analysis of variance (F-test, homogeneity of variance), correlation, regression and so on.

At the end of this stage the team should be able to answer the following questions:

- What was the improvement opportunity?
- What was the approach to analyzing the data?
- What are the root causes [there may be more than one root cuse] contributing to the improvement opportunity?
- How was the data analyzed to identify sources of variation?
- Did analysis result in any changes to the problem statement or scope?

We are able to do this by performing the following specific sequence of tasks:

- *Perform capability analysis.* This is a process for establishing the current performance level of the process being. This baseline capability will be used to verify process improvements through the "improve" and "control" phases. Capability is stated as a short-term sigma value so that comparisons between processes can be made.
- *Select analysis tools.* This step allows the team to look at the complete set of graphical analysis tools to determine how each tool may be used to reveal details about process performance and variation.
- *Apply graphical analysis tools.* This refers to the technique of applying a set of basic graphical analysis tools to data to produce a visual indication of performance,
- *Identify sources of variation.* This refers to the process of identifying the sources of variation in the process under study, using statistical techniques, so that significant variation is identified and eliminated.

The analyze stage continues the process of streamlining and focusing that began with project selection. The team will use the results produced by graphical analysis to target specific sources of variation.

As an outcome of the analyze stage, the team should have a strong understanding of the factors impacting their project including:
- Key process input variables (the vital few Xs that impact the Y).
- Sources of variation—where the greatest degree of variation exists.

Improve: The fourth stage—improve—aims to generate ideas; design, pilot and implement improvements; and validate the improvements. Perhaps the most important items in this stage are the process of brainstorming, the development of the "should be" process map, the review and/or generation of the current FMEA (failure mode and effect analysis), a preliminary cost/benefit analysis, a pilot of the recommended action and the preliminary implementation process. Design of experiments (DOE) is an effective methodology that may be used in both the "analyze" and "improve" stages. However, DOE can be a difficult tool to use outside a manufacturing environment, where small adjustments can be made to input factors and output can be monitored in real time. In non-manufacturing, other creative methods are frequently required to discover and validate improvements. The following steps should be taken at this stage:

- *Generate improvement alternatives.* The emphasis here is to generate alternatives to be tested as product or process improvements. The basic tools to be used here are brainstorming and DOE. With either tool, a three-step process is followed:

    o Define improvement criteria—develop CTQ characteristics.
    o Generate possible improvements—the best potential improvements are best evaluated based on the criteria matrix.
    o Evaluate improvements and make the best choice.

- As a result of these steps, several alternatives may be found and posted in a matrix formation. The matrix should have at least the following criteria: "must" criteria (the basic items without which satisfaction will not occur) and "desirable" criteria (items that are beyond the basic criteria and do contribute to performance improvement). Once these are identified a weight for each is determined, either through historical or empirical knowledge, and appropriately posted in the matrix. At that point each criterion is cross-multiplied by the weight and the appropriate prioritization takes place.

This is just one of many prioritization methods. Other prioritization methods may be based on cost, frequency, effect on customer and other factors.

- *Create a "should be" process map.* This map represents the best possible improvement the project team is able to implement. It is possible that a number of changes could be made to improve a process. The individual process map steps will serve as the input function of the FMEA.
- *Conduct FMEA (failure mode and effect analysis).* The FMEA is meant to be a "before the failure" action, not an "after the fact" reaction. Perhaps the most important factor in any FMEA is the fact that it is a living document and therefore it should be continually updated as changes occur or more information is gained.
- *Perform a cost/benefit analysis.* This analysis is a structured process for determining the trade-off between implementation costs and anticipated benefits of potential improvements.
- *Conduct a pilot implementation.* This step is a trial implementation of a proposed improvement, conducted on a small scale under close observation.
- *Validate improvement.* One of the ways to validate the effectiveness of the changes made is to compare the sigma values before and after the changes have been made. Remember, this means to compare the same defects per million opportunities.

Control: The fifth stage—control—is to institutionalize process or product improvements and monitor ongoing performance. This stage is the place where the transition from improvement to controlling the process and ensuring that the new improvement takes place. Of course, the transition is the transferring of the process from the project team to the original owner. The success of this transfer depends upon an effective and very detailed control plan. The objective of the control plan is to document all pertinent information regarding the following:

- Who is responsible for monitoring and controlling the process?
- What is being measured?
- What are the performance parameters?
- What are the corrective measures?

To make the control effective, several factors must be identified and addressed. Some of the most critical are:

- *Mistake-proofing.* This is to remove the opportunity for error before it happens. Mistake-proofing is a way to detect and correct an error where it occurs and avoid passing the error to the next worker or the next operation. This keeps the error from becoming a defect in the process and potentially impacting the customer CTQ characteristics.
- *Long-term MSA (measurement system analysis) plan.* Similar to the original MSA conducted in the measure stage, the long-term MSA looks at all aspects of data collection relating to the ongoing measurement of the Xs and high level monitoring of the Ys. Specifically, the long term MSA documents how process measurements will be managed over time to maintain desired levels of performance.
- *Appropriate and applicable charts (statistical process control).* A control is simply a run chart with upper and lower control limit lines drawn on either side of the process average. Another way to view the control chart is to see it as a graphical representation of the behavior of a process over time.
- *Reaction plan.* A reaction plan provides details on actions to be taken should control charts indicate the revised process is no longer in control. Therefore, having a reaction plan helps ensure that control issues are addressed quickly and that corrective actions are taken.
- *The new or revised standard operating procedures (SOPs).* Updating SOPs and training plans is the practice of revising existing documentation to reflect the process improvements.

At the end of the control stage, the process owner will understand performance expectations, how to measure and monitor Xs to ensure performance of the Y, and what corrective actions should be executed if measurements drop below the desired and anticipated levels. Furthermore, the team is disbanded while the black belt begins the next project with a new team.

A summary of the DCOV model follows

One of the most predominant ideas for design for six sigma is the notion of historical perspective and paradigm change. Our commitment to solving our problems must be based on the precept that we want to avoid problems rather than fix them. To do that we must recognize that old Einstein saying paraphrased here: You cannot solve problems with the same level of knowledge that created them. In other words, we have to look elsewhere for our answers. We cannot always depend on history. We have to look beyond our current status and capability if we are indeed committed to continual improvement.

To fix problems before they happen is an issue of planning and design. It certainly goes beyond the current knowledge and quite often beyond the current modus operandi of a given organization. It forces one to think of future designs. Design for six sigma (DFSS) is a proactive approach to preventing problems from occurring. That is a design issue. Therefore, the power of the six sigma methodology is in the design for six sigma.

As powerful as DFSS is to problem resolution and avoidance, it must also be recognized that there are some problems that do not need to be fixed. Simply stated: Some problems are not worth solving. Some issues may seem like they should be problems, but are not problems at all. A problem may be an inherited part of the way you do business and you may not want to change. Or the problem may be part of everyday variability. Trying to solve it is like trying to stop the tides. Trying to fix it wastes effort, and your misguided efforts might make things worse.

Some problems are not worth solving because their consequences are too small to worry about. Your focus should instead be to attack the problems that cumulatively cause enough loss to worry about. Also, some problems are blessings in disguise—problems that, if solved, would allow an even bigger problem to cause a real disaster. On the other hand, for problems that really need to be fixed, design for six sigma is the only way. For the problems that should be investigated, a rigorous approach is recommended, such as the design for six sigma process, using the define, characterize, optimize and verify (DCOV) model. The minimum effort required to solve problems using the DCOV model is as follows:

- Completely understand what happened.
- Identify the causal factors that led to the problem.
- Systematically find the root causes of each causal factor.
- Develop and implement solutions to eliminate the root causes.

To be sure, design for six sigma is very demanding, and yet the opportunity for true improvement and real customer satisfaction lies only with a systematic study up front (in the design). The goal is to improve customer functionality through customer satisfaction and customer loyalty. The process of improvement then is to:

- Establish a functional relationship between customer satisfaction drivers (dependent variables) and specific design parameters, Critical to quality (CTQ) characteristics (independent variables). By reducing the sensitivity of the associated system to noise factors and then manufacturing the independent variables at the 6 (six standard deviations) level, the performance that drives customer satisfaction and ultimately loyalty will be more consistently achieved over time.

- While the DFSS process steps are presented in a sequential flow, process execution is not necessarily sequential. For example, the capturing of the voice of the customer, system design and functional mapping are typically iterative processes. On the other hand, design for robustness and for productivity is both simultaneous and iterative.
- The DFSS process may become generic and can also be applied during any of the following phases (i.e., advanced project, forward product and ongoing).

To apply these principles to a successful design, these items must be followed:

- Understand the fundamental ideas underlying the notion of manufacturability or the service at hand.
- Understand how statistically designed experiments can be used to identify leverage variables, establish sensitivities, and define tolerances.
- Understand how product and process complexity impacts design performance.
- Explain the concept of error propagation (both linear and nonlinear) and what role product/process complexity plays.
- Describe how reverse error propagation can be employed during system design.
- Explain why process shift and drift must be considered in the analysis of a design and how it can be factored into design optimization.
- Describe how six sigma tools and methods can be applied to the design process in and of itself.
- Discuss the pros and cons of the classical approach to product/ process design relative to that of the six sigma approach.

The define stage: In the first phase of the DCOV model, the define stage is first explored. The purpose of this stage is to identify the critical to satisfaction (CTS) drivers, Y, and to establish an operating window for chosen Ys for new and aged conditions. The define stage is divided into three areas:

- *Inputs*. These are the activities that are the initiators for further evaluation. Typical activities are: researching the quality and customer satisfaction history; evaluating warranty data; benchmarking; checking functional, serviceability, corporate and regulatory requirements; evaluating the process in integrating targets; conducting surveys; auditing the current design or process; profiling the brand; performing a Kano analysis; undergoing quality function deployment (QFD); and defining design specifications.
- *Action*. These are the activities that actually help in the selection of the Ys. Typical activities are definition of customer and/or product requirements, relating requirements to customer satisfaction, and conducting peer review.
- *Output*. These are the results of the action. Typical results are projected targets and a preliminary model of understanding.

The characterize stage: In the second phase of the DCOV model, the characterize stage is explored. This stage is generally completed through a two-step approach. The first is the system design and the second is the functional mapping. In both cases, the goal is to characterize the robustness of the design. Therefore, the purpose of the first step is to flow CTS Ys down to lower y's ($Y = f(y_1, y_2, y_3, y_n)$) and to characterize robustness opportunities ($Y = f(x,n)$). The purpose of the second step is to relate CTS ys to CTQ design parameters (xs) and to optimize the strategy to deliver this robustness.

1. System design. The process for exploring the first step of the characterize stage is divided into three areas:

a. *Inputs*. These are the activities that will generate the action of this step. Typical actions are creating functional boundaries and interface matrices as applicable, function trees ($Y \rightarrow y$), a P-diagram; and robustness and/or reliability checklists.
   b. *Action*. These are the activities that help the decomposition of Y into contributing elements, y_1; obtain ($Y = f(y_1, y_2, y_3, ... y_n)$) through modeling, such as DOE, using CAE or hardware (if applicable), experience or prior knowledge and peer review.
   c. *Output*. This is the result of the action. Typical results are Pareto diagrams, benchmarked CTS factors and the target range of y.
2. Functional mapping. The process for exploring the second step of the characterize stage is divided into three areas:
   a. *Inputs*. These are the activities that will generate the activity of this step. Typical activities are creating functional boundaries and interfaces of system design specification (SDS), a functional tree ($y \rightarrow x$), P-diagrams and a robustness and/or reliability checklist.
   b. *Action*. These are the activities that actually help the decomposition of y, into contributing elements, x_1. Typical activities are: relate independent ys to xs (modeling) or relate correlated ys to xs (modeling, axiomatic design); choose robustness strategy; innovate using structured inventive thinking (SIT) or the theory of inventive problem-solving (TRIZ), understand the process capability and conduct peer review.
   c. *Output*. This is the result of the action. Typical results are results of screening experiments and prior engineering/organizational knowledge, a Pareto diagram, preliminary target and/or range estimates of x, and internal and/or external benchmark of manufacturing capability of xs.

The optimize stage: In the third phase of the DCOV model, the optimize stage is explored. This stage is also generally completed through a two-step approach. The first is the design for robust performance and the second is the design for productivity. In both cases, the goal is to improve robustness. Therefore, the purpose of the first step is to characterize the present long time in service robustness for the product, and improve robustness by further minimizing product sensitivity to manufacturing and usage conditions, as required. The purpose of the second step is to characterize capability and stability of the present process. This is done simultaneously with the first step. Furthermore, in this step we are also interested in minimizing process sensitivity to product and service variations, as required.

1. Design for robust performance. The process for exploring the first step of the optimize stage is divided into three areas:
   a. *Inputs*. These are the activities that will generate the activity of this step. Typical activities are completing a P-diagram (important y_is), determining what to measure, control factors (xs), noise factors and error states; conducting an experimental plan (two-step optimization with confirmation run); devising a robustness and reliability checklist; perform a design FMEA (including noise factor analysis) and determining process capability.
   b. *Action*. These are the activities that actually help find nominals (targets) for xs that minimize variability. In other words, specify tolerances. Typical activities are reducing sensitivity to noise (parameter design, robustness assessment, reliability and robustness), determining tolerances (tolerance design, statistical tolerance, reliability and robustness), eliminating specific failure modes using strategies such as redundancy, eliminating noise and compensating.
   c. *Output*. These are the results of the action. Typical results are variability metric for CTS or related function (*i.e.*, range, standard deviation, signal to noise (S/N) ratio improvement) and target and tolerances specified for specific characteristics.
2. Design for productivity. The process for exploring the second step of the optimize stage is divided into three areas:

a. *Inputs.* These are the activities that will generate the activity of this step. Typical activities are to present process capability, historical process data (model, surrogate), assembly and manufacturing process flow diagrams (process mapping), reference gauge repeatability and reproducibility (R&R) capability studies [if they exist] and a process FMEA, including noise factor analysis.

b. *Action.* These are the activities that actually help the optimization process to produce x_is nominal with 6σ capability by applying robustness methods to the process (using two-step optimization: reduce variability and then shift to target); using appropriate error-proofing such as DFA, DFM, service and or assembly sequence [if applicable], poka-yoke, etc.; update the control plan; conduct peer review.

c. *Output.* This is the results of the action. Typical results are short-term capability, long-term capability and an updated control plan.

The verify stage: In the fourth phase of the DCOV model, the verify stage is explored. This stage is also typically completed through a two-step approach. The first is the overall DFSS assessment and the second is the test and verify. In both cases the goal is to verify that the capability and product integrity over time is as it was designed and as the customer is expecting it to be. Therefore, the purpose of the first step is to estimate for process capability and product function over time. The purpose of the second step is to assess actual performance, reliability and service capability, as well as to demonstrate customer correlated (real world) performance over time. If the results of design for robust performance, design for productivity, assessment and testing are not satisfactory, the model action may revert back to the previous stage, or even as far back as the functional mapping stage. Furthermore, in every one of these stages, a trade-off analysis will be performed to ensure all CTSs factors are met.

- *Overall DFSS assessment.* The process for exploring the first step of the verify stage is divided into three areas:
    - *Inputs.* These are the activities that will generate the activity of this step. Typical activity is evaluating data from previous steps.
    - *Action.* These are the activities that actually help the DFSS overall assessment. Four predominant activities are conducted here: a) determine the CTS/CTQ characteristic/measure and conduct a comparison between the $Z_{estimate}$ and Z_{actual}, b) conduct sub-assessments, as needed, c) perform tests and simulation as well as a comparison between the $Z_{estimate}$ and Z_{actual}, and d) conduct a variability study over time for both product and process.
    - *Output.* This is the results of the action. Typical results are an overall review of assessments for previous steps with the champion or appropriate management.
- *Test and verify.* The process for exploring the second step of the verify stage is divided into three areas:
    - *Inputs.* The activities that will generate the activity of this step. Typical activities are developing a reliability and/or robustness plan and designing a verification plan with key noises.
    - *Action.* These are the activities that actually help to conduct physical, analytical performance tests enhanced with appropriate noise factors. Typical activities are correlating tests to customer usage; improving ability of tests to discriminate good/bad parts, subsystems and systems; and conducting peer review.
    - *Output.* This is the results of the action. Typical results are testing results such as key life testing; accelerated tests; long-term process capabilities; product performance over time (e.g., Weibull test and survival plot); and a reliability/robustness demonstration matrix.

Optimization of both models

To optimize the technology, people and business strategy using either the DMAIC or DCOV models we must above all focus on the customer functionality and in turn customer satisfaction. How? By following at least seven principles:

1. Always do right. This will gratify some people and astonish the rest, including the competition. The value of customer satisfaction already has been proven in many studies, so much so, that doing right by customers is correct and profitable. To do this, we must understand the functionality that the customer is seeking from our products and or services.
2. It is noble to be good, and it is nobler to teach others to be good and less trouble. It is imperative that we must teach the employees of our organization that keeping existing customers is less trouble and expensive than finding new customers. Part of the training must be a daily dosage of continual support of customer satisfaction initiatives including but not limiting to customer recognition.
3. When in doubt, tell the truth. Indeed, a novel idea. However, unless there is an aura of trust in the culture of the organization, do not expect miracles. It is of paramount significance that employees should be trained to do this and something like a simple job aid may be all that is needed. This may help to remind us that we all exist to "please" the customer. Without a customer, we do not exist!
4. It is better to keep your mouth closed and let people think you are a fool than to open it and remove all doubt. We must be cognizant of the old Spartan saying; "to speak less is true philosophy." It is indeed silence that speaks volumes in some situations. Train your employees to listen to their customer and respond appropriately. That means body language may be just as acceptable as verbal signals.
5. Few things are harder to put up with than the annoyance of a good example. Employees and customers both constantly appraise your demeanor; the former will take it at face value, one hopes, emulate it while the latter will appreciate it and ultimately repay it with more business. Setting standards always is a challenging task; not setting standards is failure. However, remember that standards no matter what form they appear as, are always indicative of minimum performance.
6. A complement ought always to precede a complaint, where one is possible, because it softens resentment and ensures for the complaint a courteous and gentle reception. To be sure, we all know that the customer quite often is wrong, unreasonable and difficult to deal with. However, it is not smart to make that distinction immediately; rather, when appropriate the customer should be retrained to your organization's values. For any change to be successful, the customer must be on your side first.
7. Do not let schooling interfere with education. In the final analysis you are responsible for the success of your organization, the one that has to decide what level of customer satisfaction is required, how to train for it and how to nurture it. It usually requires a generous serving of knowledge learned in formal education and informal education - real world experiences. The mix of appropriateness depends on you, the occasion and the specific goal you have set for satisfaction. [An analogy may prove the point; in a horse race both the "jockey" and the "horse" are important. So much so, that a winner is declared when both of them cross the finish line at the same time. At different races we see a different combination. For example in the Kentucky Derby we see a new horse and an experienced jockey. Conversely in local races we see older horses with younger jockeys. You see the experience is the 'horse and the education is the jockey." Both are important and yet the mix is always situation dependent. (A hint: The truly educated know that education alone is not enough.)]

In our modern world, one can see that businesses (financial, services, education, health care, manufacturing and non manufacturing alike) are being put to the test. The test of pursuing customer satisfaction is through quality initiatives, yet at the same time contributes to the organization's bottom line. It turns out that six sigma may help in this initiative because it focuses on "real" improvement, rather than scapegoats. It forces us to look at "real" situation with "real" potential of improvement for the entire organization rather than sub-optimizing the organization.

Sub-optimization can be a real threat for the viability of Six Sigma programs. Organizations embarking on Six Sigma need a methodology to understand the global dynamics of the larger system to facilitate global optimization through local projects. If that does not happen the result is negative leverage projects. It occurs when a part of the system is optimized but the larger system is worse off as a result. A well-known example of this in the Lean literature is over-production. Over-production is the result of efforts by a part of the organization to optimize its processes without realizing that the larger system has no immediate use for the additional production.

Systems thinking in education has the potential for some interesting applications during the Six Sigma journey:

- An organization's leadership team can use systems thinking in order to kickoff a high-impact initiative by focusing on real root cause areas rather than the symptoms of high level problems.
- A Master Black Belt can use systems thinking to map out the system dynamics around a mission critical to the overall system (in the language of 6 sigma, the Big Y) that he or she has been tasked to optimize, and then identify the various high-leverage daughter projects (in the language of the 6 sigma the Critical Xs).
- A Black Belt or Green Belt can use systems thinking during the Define phase to identify the possible negative consequences of optimizing the project Y. By doing so, the project team can strategize how to avoid, eliminate or minimize these negative consequences. For instance, when trying to optimize end-to-end process flow time, one typical negative consequence is the reduction of quality.
- A Black Belt or Green Belt can use systems thinking during the Measure or Analyze phases to identify the system dynamics of the critical Xs that affect the project Y that the team has been tasked to optimize.

Six Sigma programs can avoid irrelevance by addressing the real issues of an organization with the use of systems thinking. It would be another step in integrating successful management practices into a single management system which wisely uses resources while focusing on what is important for customers, shareholders and employees.

In order for six sigma to survive, quality needs and overall strategic plans must exist in the organization. That means that there is a system in the organization where the following are addressed:

1. *Linkage between Quality Function Needs and Overall Strategic Plan*: Perhaps this is the most important issue in six sigma but also in any endeavor that is trying to address improvement of any kind. The focus here is on the quality function needs and the plan to support such needs currently but also in the future. Of course, these needs have to be in line with the organizational aims, policies, and plans. Some key considerations are in the areas of: competition, cost, differentiation of product and usage of appropriate tools.
2. *Linkage between Strategic Plan and Quality Plan*: The second most important issue in six sigma methodology is to correlate the strategic plans with an actual quality plan. That means that the organization either has or is willing to develop programs that deal with feedback, corrective action, data collection, processing and analysis and process and product development. In addition it means that the organization has or is willing to develop infrastructure to address issues like organization, administrative support, control processes, internal audits, processes that identify customer needs and policies for inspection and testing.

3. *Theory of Variation (common and special causes)*: It is beyond the scope of this book to have a lengthy discussion on variation; however, it is imperative that common (inherent) variation and special (assignable) variation are understood. We associate common variation with (random, material, prevalent, or normal variation; stable process; predictable; and process improvement is through management intervention. On the other hand, we associate special variation with (abnormal activity; unpredictability; and or specific knowable causes). To understand variation we must also understand the components of variation. That is: Total variation = Variation due to factor A + Variation due to factor B + Variation due to interaction AB + variation due to sampling error. Typical examples of common and special cause variation are:

Common causes of variation.

- o Slight variation in raw material
- o Slight machine vibration
- o Lack of human perfection
- o Variation in measurement readings
- o Variation in tooling.
- o Variation in operator skills

Special cause variation
- o Difference in machines or processes
- o Batch of defective raw material
- o Faulty machine set-up
- o Test equipment out of calibration
- o Unqualified operator
- o Part-time seasonal help
- o Variable work force

Sometimes, it is possible to have variation due to a combination of both types as for example:

- o Major recession
- o Equipment failure
- o Price roll-back
- o Employee downsizing

Typical basic problems that the six sigma methodology may tackle which confirm Deming's intuitive knowledge about variation and system thinking.

- o Poor design of product.
- o Poor instruction and poor supervision
- o Failure to measure the effects of common causes, and to reduce them
- o Failure to provide the production workers with information in statistical form
- o Procedures not suited to the requirements
- o Machines not suited to the requirements
- o Settings of the machines chronically inaccurate
- o Poor lighting
- o Vibration
- o Mixing product from streams of production
- o Uncomfortable working condition
- o Shift of managements emphasis from *quality* to *quantity*

    o   Managements failure to face the problem of inherited defective material

4. Quality Function Mission: The mission is a very important characteristic in the totality of strategic planning. The focus here is to make sure that the mission is aligned with the business strategy of the organization. In other words, to establish an organizational mission in clear simple language, so that it is understood by everyone in the organization (and by others) that the appropriate and applicable key driving forces to satisfy the customer are identified in such a way that the start of improvement must begin with:

- o Establishing priorities
- o Defining organizational policies
- o Trade off analysis to resolve: Conflict with cost, delivery dates, and other parameters
- o Maintain continual improvement activity

To appreciate even further the power and influence of the mission, let us look at its hierarchy:

- o Mission - broad policy of what the organization is existing for, The focus is on:
    - o defining the quality mission and policy, and provide quality awareness in the organization
    - o setting goal to meet mission
    - o training and team concept
    - o measuring mission accomplishments
    - o relationship with vision, values, and goals
- o Vision - the key processes that assist in fulfilling this mission
- o Values - the key indicators to affirm the vision and the mission
- o Goals - the reinforcement to accomplish the mission

In the context of six sigma methodology, it is imperative to recognize that NO organization can function without some (written or unwritten) quality principles and policies. That means that management must champion, if not outright direct, the "key" principles and policies for the entire organization. Typical issues are:

- the need for quality principles and the right policies (creed, beliefs, truths, rules, moral and ethical standards as they relate to the uniqueness of the organization's history, management, and state of development)
- appropriate approval from executive management (practiced by everyone)
- participation by key managers
- understanding the need for customer relations (internal and external)
- understanding need for continual improvement
- understanding that everyone should be involved and concerned
- understanding the importance of quality
- understanding the importance of planning and organization

5. Metrics and Goals that Drive Organizational Performance: We cannot talk about performance in the abstract. Performance is always an output of a function – see Figure 8.1. Therefore, for performance to be of value, the organization must have metrics and goals. The goals of course should be attainable, realistic, measurable and related to customer usage. The metrics, on the other hand, must be identified as "real" measures for these goals. [Do not be afraid to take risk if the risk is commensurable with the anticipated benefit]. Typical samples of some basic requirements are considerations about:

- o Customer satisfaction

148

o   The voice of the customer
o   Economic ramifications
o   Environmental and legal impact
o   Worthiness
o   Applicability

Figure 8.1. A visual representation of the goals to results flow

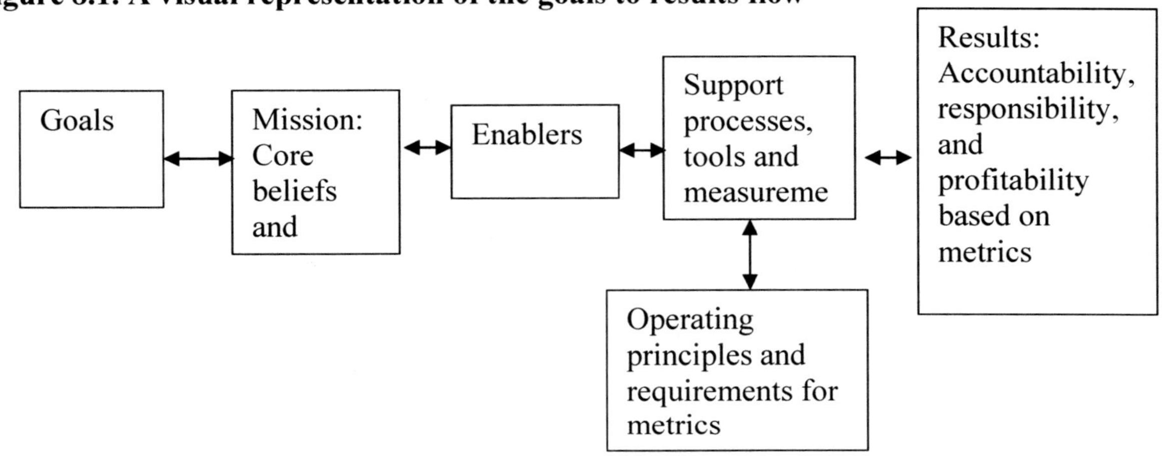

Goals → Mission: Core beliefs and → Enablers → Support processes, tools and measureme → Results: Accountability, responsibility, and profitability based on metrics

Operating principles and requirements for metrics

6. Resource Requirements to Manage the Quality Function: The last item in strategic planning as it concerns the six sigma methodology is the issue of resources. It must be recognized and understood that a typical organization that embraces the six sigma philosophy requires for everyone who is involved directly, especially the managerial levels, to be appropriately trained. So the issues associated with resource requirements are quite important for the organization. Typical items of concern are:

- Appropriate and applicable training
- Knowledgeable personnel
- Adequate leadership commitment
- Inspection and testing availability
- Work performance personnel
- Verification capability

Roles in Six Sigma

In the six sigma methodology, all the roles and responsibilities – see Table 8.1 - for all levels presuppose several prerequisites. The specificity for the prerequisites, of course, depends on the level. However, there are some prerequisites that are common to all levels and they are:

- Process/Product Knowledge
- Willing and able to learn mathematical concepts
- Knows the Organization
- Communication Skill

- Self Starter/Motivated
- Open-Minded
- Eager to Learn New Ideas
- Desire to Drive Change
- Project Leadership Skills
- Team Player
- Respected by Others
- Track Record on Results

Table 8.1. Different "role" names used in the six sigma methodology

Generic name	Other name
Process owner	Sponsor or Champion
Team member	Team member or Green Belt
Team leader	Black Belt or Green Belt or Project manager
Coach	Master Black Belt or Black Belt
Implementation leader	Six Sigma director, Quality leader, Master Black Belt
Sponsor	Champion or process owner
Executive management	Six sigma steering committee, Quality Council, Leadership Council

In conjunction with the above prerequisites, there is also an implied responsibility that is of paramount importance as it relates to the executives. After all, it is the executives who are in charge of the change! Therefore, it is very important for them to accelerate the change process by being visible advocates of the six sigma methodology. Specifically, the executives must be committed to improvement and not just get involved! That means, that they have to work closely with the Champions and the Master Black Belts to mobilize commitment and make change last. The commitment must be translated into the following actions:

- *Identify and remove the barriers* and *roadblocks* to achieving high performance with Six Sigma.
- Ensure that *only the best* are nominated to be Black Belts.
- Ask Black Belts many *questions* to ensure that they are focused appropriately.
- Demand **follow-up** and **monitoring** activities.
- *Establish the Six Sigma scorecard.* Make Six Sigma reviews a regular part of your management process.
- Align Six Sigma results and business *strategic objectives*
- Drive *functional ownership* and accountability
- *Manage your attention.* Be proactive to assure that the change is real.
- Develop and demonstrate *personal competence* with the *Breakthrough Strategy*
- *Celebrate successes*, recognize accomplishments

Now let us look at the five key roles and their specific contribution to the six sigma methodology.

Executives: The executives legitimize the changes about to happen because of the six sigma implementation methodology through their actions to:

- ***Establish the Vision*** - Why are we doing Six Sigma?
- Articulate the ***business strategy*** - How does Six Sigma support the business strategy?
- Provide resources
- ***Remove Roadblocks***/Buffer conflicts
- Support the ***culture change*** by encouraging others to take the risk and make the change
- Monitor the results by ***defining the scorecard*** for six sigma and hold others accountable for the results
- Align the ***systems and structures*** with the changes taking place
- Participate with the Black Belts through ***project reviews*** and recognition of results

Champions: The champions implement the changes as a result of the six sigma methodology by taking action to:

- Develop a ***vision*** for the organization
- Create and maintain ***passion***
- Develop a ***model*** for a perfect organization
- Facilitate the ***identification*** and ***prioritization*** of projects
- Develop the ***strategic decisions*** in the deployment of Six Sigma around timing and sequencing of manufacturing, transactional and new product focus
- ***Extend project benefits*** to additional areas
- ***Communicate*** and market the *Breakthrough Strategy* process and results
- Share ***best practices***
- Establish and ***monitor*** a team process for optimum results
- Recruit, inspire and "free up" Black Belts – ***pick the best people***
- Develop the reward and ***recognition program*** for Black Belts
- ***Remove barriers*** for Black Belts
- ***Coach and develop*** Black Belts
- Provide the ***drum beat*** for results by a) reviewing projects and b) keeping score through metrics
- Develop a ***comprehensive training*** plan for implementing the *breakthrough strategy*

Key attributes and qualifications are:

- Select projects and monitor performance
- Set project goals
- Select Black Belt candidates
- Provide customer focus
- Provides timing and sequence for projects
- Ensure that the project is kept on schedule
- Identify key metrics
- Monitor business results
- Deploy Six Sigma in areas for best results
- Must understand the strategy and discipline of Six Sigma
- Transfer results into other areas
- Remove barriers
- Assist with resources as needed
- Eliminate barriers for the project

Master Black Belts (MBB): He or she is the expert and facilitator in the organization regarding problem solving and Six Sigma methodology. Some of the attributes and qualifications are:

- Successfully completed key Six Sigma projects
- Ability to facilitate problem solving
- Provides guidance, coaching for champions, black belts and green belts
- Understand the big picture

- Partner with the Champions
- Assist in the identification of projects
- Expert in the tools and concepts of the six sigma methodology
- Develop and deliver training to various levels of the organization
- Have a passion for six sigma and cycle time improvement
- Land a hand when necessary to do the project
- Certify the black belts
- Take on leadership of major programs

- Coach and support BB in project work
- Facilitate sharing of best practices across the organization
- Provide in time training and or technical resources as needed
- Develop new tools and or applications or modify old tools for specific application and be able to teach
- Participate in project reviews to offer technical expertise

Black Belts (BB): He or she is the project manager of the project. Projects under his guidance are typically over $100,000/project and they are of about six months duration per project. Some of the attributes and qualifications are:

- Work full-time on selected projects
- Team leaders of Six Sigma projects
- Knowledge in Six Sigma methods and techniques
- Have a track record of results using Six Sigma methodology
- Complete formal Six Sigma training
- Train and certify green belts
- Successfully lead a project that results in significant improvements
- Have a basic knowledge of statistics
- Knows the organization

- Have knowledge of the product or process
- Be a self starter and motivated
- Have excellent communication skills
- Have excellent interpersonal skills
- Be open minded
- Team player
- Respected by others
- Eager to learn new ideas, tools and approaches
- Desire to drive change

Green Belts (GB): They are closest to the process and always work under the direction of the BB. They are the ones who do the majority of work in investigating the problem(s), and in some cases strictly under the guide of a BB will pursue a project on their own with a magnitude of savings no more than 10 – 20 thousand dollars. The length of a typical project for a GB is between 30 - 45 days. Some of the attributes and qualifications are:

- Assist the Black Belts
- Work on projects part-time
- Be familiar with simple statistical tools
- Apply Six Sigma tools to solve chronic problems
- Help collect and analyze data, run experiments and perform other tasks associated with the project

Projects and Six Sigma

Project Management: Project Management is the application of functional (and other) management skills under time limited, goal directed conditions. The success of the Six Sigma methodology, many have suggested, depends on the selection of the appropriate and applicable project and its completion. We agree with this assessment and we suggest that all concerned should be at least familiar with some basic concepts of Project Management. In the Six Sigma methodology the key project manager is the Black Belt. As such, to assure effectiveness in their projects they must avoid pitfalls although that is not enough. To be truly effective, the Black Belt must guide the project forward in the best possible manner. Guiding the project has to do with leadership and entrepreneurship. Black Belts must be able to influence people.

But what is a project? It involves (effective) utilization of human and non human (technological, financial, informational and material) resources to achieve a specific purpose, such as:

- Set of well defined, related and controllable tasks
- Extended period of time
- Relatively longer/shorter duration
- Culminates in a major output

In the Six Sigma methodology by a project we mean elimination of a problem in a process or preventing the problem from entering the process. In other words, there are unique aspects of project management as we try to implement it within the Six Sigma methodology. Some of that uniqueness is in the areas of:
- When something new, or never has been done quite like this before
- Need to deal with diverse people in a team setting
- Strict time deadlines and performance expectations that are highly visible
- Need to manage interface problems – especially in cross functional departments

When "uniqueness" is present in a project, the implication is that we cannot count on past experience risk and uncertainty. When "interrelatedness" is present in a project, the implication is that we need a broader perspectives (system view, schedule adherence, need for replanning flexibility). When "goal orientation" is present in a project, the implications are that we deal with a set of interrelated goals. This is very important because it implies that we a) must zero in on the goal definition and operational definition(s) that we are dealing with b) need to control group processes – preferably isolate each one as much as possible, and c) success/failure is highly visible. When "resources" are present in a project, the implications are that we need some form of negotiation and a strong leadership for support. Under this condition the Champion's contribution is of paramount importance.

Project management depends, therefore, on three items: 1) *People*: This means that the person in charge should be very familiar with the concept of team, conflict management, project organization and managing for task accomplishment. 2) *Planning*: this means, that the person in charge should be very familiar with statement of work, project planning, work breakdown structures, project risk analysis and responsibility charts, and 3) *Control*: This means, that the person in charge should have at least a basic knowledge of critical path of a project, costs and budgets, project scheduling, project control and replanning.

Typical tools used in the Six Sigma model

There are many tools one may use in the Six Sigma methodology. It is beyond the scope of this book to identify and explain all the tools. However, Table 8.2 shows the most common ones for the DMAIC and Table 8.3 for the DCOV model:

Table 8.2. The DMAIC model and some tools and outputs

Model	Steps	Tools	Outputs
Define	Initiate the project	Project charter Meeting effectiveness	Project charter Project team formed Clear customer requirements
	Define the process	SIPOC map Value stream map	
	Determine customer requirements	Brainstorming Affinity diagram Murphy's analysis Interviews Surveys Customer requirements test	
	Define key process output variables	Project charter KPOVs	
Measure	Understand the process	SIPOC/VSM Input/Output analysis C&E matrix Detailed Process map	Current state Process map Identified and measured Xs (KPIVs) Measurement system verified
	Evaluate risks on process inputs	FMEA	Current capability of Ys (KPOVs)
	Develop and evaluate measurement systems	Data collection plans Data integrity audits Continuous MSA Attribute MSA	
	Measure current performance	Process capability OEE	
Analyze	Analyze data to prioritize key input variables	Basic statistics Basic graphs Statistical process control t-tests	Root causes of defects identified and reduced to vital few Prioritized list of potential Key inputs
	Identify waste	ANOVA Non-parametrics Chi-square Regression Multi-vari studies	Waste identified
Improve	Verify critical inputs	Design of experiments	Finalize list of KPIVs Action plan for improvement
	Design improvements	Kanban/Pull Mistake proofing Quick change over Workplace organization Process mapping Process documentation	Future state process map, FMEA, control plans New process design/documentation Pilot study plan
	Pilot new process	Training plans Statistical process control FMEA Control plans	
Control	Finalize the control plan	Control plans Process documentation Training plans	Control system in place Improvements validated long term

| | | Communication plans
Statistical process control
Documentation | Continuous improvements,
opportunities identified
New process handed off
Team recognition |
| | Verify long term
capability | Statistical process control
Process Capability | |

Table 8.3. The DCOV model and some tools and outputs

Model	Tools/methodology	Deliverables
Define	• Kano model • Quality function deployment • Regression • Conjoint analysis	• Kano diagram • CTS scorecard • Y relationship to customer satisfaction • Benchmarked CTSs • Target and ranges for CTS Vs

Characterize	• Functional structures
	• Axiomatic designs
	• TRIZ
	• P-diagram
	• R&R checklist
	• DOE
		• Function diagrams
		• Mapping of Y—> critical function —> y_s
		• P-diagram, including Critical Technical metrics, y_s
		  • Control factors, x_s
		  • Noise factors, n_s
		• Transfer function
		• Scorecard with target and range for y_s and x_s
		• Plan for optimization and verification
		  • R&R checklist

Optimize	• Design FMEA • Process FMEA • Experimental design—response surface • Parameter design—two step optimization • Tolerance design • Simulation tools • Error prevention—compensation, estimate noise, mistake-proofing • Gage R&R • Control plan	• Transfer function • Scorecard with estimate of σ_y • Target nominal values identified for x_s • Variability metric for CTS, Y or related function (e.g., range, standard deviation, S/N ratio improvement) • Tolerance specified for important characteristics • Short-term capability, "z" score • Long-term capability • Updated verification plans: robustness and reliability checklist (if available) • Updated control plan
Verify	• Reliability methods • Design reviews • Customer requirements, including governmental requirements	• Reliability testing • Specific testing based on requirements • Customer functionality • Product and/or service as designed

Summary

In this chapter we discussed the Six igma methodology as it may be applied in the educational system. We discussed both DMAIC and DCOV models. In the next chapter we will discuss the lean approach to education.

References

Breyfogle, F. W. III. (2003). *Implementing six sigma.* 2nd ed. J. Wiley and Sons, Inc. NY.
Pyzdek, T. (2001). *The six sigma handbook.* McGraw-Hill. NY.
Stamatis, D. H. (2004). *Six sigma fundamentals.* Productivity Press. NY.
Stamatis, D. H. (2002-2003). *Six sigma and beyond.* Vol.1-Vol. 7. St. Lucie Press. Boca Raton, FL.

CHAPTER 9

LEAN APPROACHES TO EDUCATION

In the last chapter we discussed Six Sigma and how it may be used in education. In this chapter we introduce the concept of lean and suggest ideas as to how any educational system may indeed use its concepts and tools to reduce waste and become more lean and effective in satisfying their several customers.

In these fiscally demanding times, declining resources compounded with increasing demands for higher levels of performance often hinder schools from achieving a proactive position in the knowledge economy. School administrators show great commitment to student achievement, but are often beset by obstacles in the quest for academic and organizational distinction.

I recently asked a successful school administrator from a top-performing school district in Michigan to describe what specific problem was preventing his building and district from engaging in *continual improvement*. He told me, "The problem as I see it is not that the work is too hard or that there is too much; it will always seem that way. The problem is that all the tricks in our bags that at one time worked, may not work as effectively now."

Implied in his concern is a shared sense most school districts in the state of Michigan and the nation at large, hold. That is, commonly used solutions are at capacity because cost cutting is at its limit. There is a clear awareness among superintendents that schools cannot cost cut their way to improvement. Yet, many districts find they are making choices between the dichotomous forces of budget reductions and reform.

There is a 60-year-old established system for institutional development well known in other sectors, called the lean enterprise. "Lean" packages both philosophical views and operational tools in original and customized ways through a simple notion: continual improvement and innovation leads to *value creation* and the *elimination of waste*.

The lean system provides a good model for education, as it integrates well with the work of professional learning communities that bring together educators and school leaders in an ongoing basis for collective problem identification and problem solving. Similarly, "lean approaches" impact the way people think about and carry out work throughout an organization. This means that familiar processes, such as budget planning or instructional technology support, come under continual corporate examination with the intention of improvement. Lean is not a theory, but a system that targets one or more organizational processes for improvement, specifically selected based on key principles and using key tools. For specific selected tools and methodologies used in lean see Appendix C.

Schools – in all educational levels - are in a good position to consider lean thinking and applications. In fact, it is relatively easy to produce a lean process improvement system benchmarked for schools. For instance, if instructional delivery, the core business of schools, were placed into a lean system, then lean thinking would be promoted by leadership and several improvement tools would be used. One such tool is value stream mapping. This analysis solicits the views of key stakeholders — students, teachers, parents, policy makers, administrators and board members — in regard to what is of value. A student's instructional day is then mapped out, looking at allocations of time and resources for various activities. Based on the views of the stakeholders, decisions would be made as to what is of value during that instructional day and what is not. What is of value is kept and what is not is either improved so that it becomes valuable, or it is eliminated.

In addition to value stream mapping, other lean tools would be used to facilitate continual improvement of instructional delivery. The idea is not to improve a process once and then leave it alone, but rather to set up the dynamics and protocols for continuous improvement. For some additional tools see Appendix C.

Many schools are wholeheartedly and sincerely engaged in school reform. Just as the building principal observed, schools unequivocally understand what needs to be done on this front. It is in the area of how to reform that uncertainties arise. The educational leader struggling with how to stop wasting resources and how to engage in spot-on organizational development will find lean process thinking helpful. Using lean tools to carry out initiatives will equip the educational leader to lead a lean culture. Through lean thinking and applications, the process of continuous improvement will no longer seem overwhelming and out of context from the daily work of school officials, but actionable and scalable. The first step is to formalize the focus of the improvement and then ask strategic questions. A typical approach is the one formalized by Peavey (1995). The idea is to have a vision of where you want to go and by that vision you should plan the direction of the improvement. Peavey focuses on seven specific directions of questioning and they are:

1. Creates motion - Gears to "How can we move?"
2. Creates options - Instead of "Why don't you ..?", asks "Where would you ...?"
3. Digs deeper - "What needs to be changed?" "What is the meaning of this?"
4. Avoids "why."
5. Avoids "yes" and "no" questions - These leave the presenter in a passive or uncreative state.
6. Empowers - "What would you like to do?"
7. Asks the unaskable questions.

Examples of typical powerful questions to ask are:

1. How important is this?
2. Where do you feel stuck?
3. What is the intent of what you're saying?
4. What can we do for you?
5. What do you think the problem is?
6. What's your role in this issue?
7. What have you tried so far? What worked? What didn't?
8. Have you experienced anything like this before? (If so, what did you do?)
9. What can you do for yourself?
10. What do you hope for?
11. What's preventing you from ..."
12. What would you be willing to give up for that?
13. If you could change one thing, what would it be?
14. Imagine a point in the future where your issue is resolved. How did you get there?
15. What would you like us to ask?
16. What have you learned?

Key methodologies and tools that may be used in the lean approach to education are:
- Team building
- Managing change
- Root cause analysis
- Problem solving techniques (SPC, Pareto diagram, Histogram, Check sheets, Relationship diagrams, Affinity diagrams, Cause and effect diagrams and others)
- Brainstorming

- Process flow diagrams
- Value stream analysis
- Efficiency and effectiveness analysis
- And others

Efficiency and effectiveness

The concept of efficiency is often connected to a moral imperative to obtain more desired results from fewer resources. Efficiency needs to be thought of as a matter of degree. Efficiency is not a "yes/no" kind of phenomenon. It is instead better thought of in relative or comparative terms. One operation may be more efficient than another. This said, the more efficient of the two operations could become even more efficient. The quest for greater efficiency is never over, and this sense of a perennially unfinished agenda is one source of the generalized sense of anxiety that tends to surround the efficiency concept.

If the goal is to obtain more desired results from fewer resources, then it is important to be clear about what is being sought. Society might have a very efficient system because a large amount of outcome is being obtained relative to the resources being spent or invested, but if the outcomes are out of sync with what is truly desired, there is a real sense in which the system is not very efficient. Of course, this invites important questions about who gets to decide what counts as a desirable outcome, and in education there are longstanding and ongoing debates over what the educational system ought to be accomplishing.

Therefore, the focus of any lean undertaking in any organization, including educational institutions, is to optimize the resources internally and satisfy the customer. Another way of saying this is to minimize - if not completely eliminate – waste. As originally developed and refined by economists, the concept of *efficiency* refers to the relationship between the inputs into a system (be it agricultural, industrial or educational), and the outputs from that system (be it wheat, vehicles or educated individuals).

It is a disarmingly simple idea that presupposes a *transformation* of some kind. One can think in terms of what was in hand before the transformation, what was in hand after the transformation, and one can also think about the transformation process itself. The before elements are commonly referred to as ingredients, inputs, or resources while the after elements are called results, outputs, or outcomes. The transformation process is sometimes less obvious and can become confused with ingredients. For example, in an educational setting, a teacher can be thought of as an ingredient while teaching is an important part of the actual transformation process.

An education system is said to be efficient if maximum output is obtained from a given input, or if a given output is obtained with minimum possible input. Inputs and outputs have somehow to be valued so that they may be aggregated; and usually prices are used to perform this valuation function. The problems of measuring efficiency in education, however, are considerable. They stem mainly from difficulties in measuring educational output, as well as from quantifying the relationship between inputs and outputs. How educational output is measured depends, of course, on the nature of the objectives of the educational system. Depending on the philosophical, political or analytical viewpoint adopted, the objectives may differ considerably. (Some of this material has been adopted and downloaded on April 20, 2009 from http://www.uis.unesco.org/i_pages/indspec/efficiency.htm).

Effectiveness, on the other hand, deals with satisfaction of customers. In other words, how the output relates to what the customers want. (The reader should remember that the educational system has many customers. Therefore, the objective of satisfaction will be different for each customer and more likely for each institution). This diversity of objectives presents a monumental problem for measuring effectiveness.

Nevertheless many have suggested a simple way and that is the output of a given cycle of education as the number of pupils who complete this cycle (the graduates). As simple as this output is, it presents some fundamental problems one of which is the lack of recognition that even the drop outs have learned something from the system that attempted to teach them something. In a more complete definition of output, perhaps the educational attainment of the students dropping out, as well as the level of educational achievement of the graduates should therefore be taken into account. This way of measuring output still gives us some useful insights into the functioning of an educational system.

Educational inputs comprise the buildings, teachers, books, teaching-materials, etc. which may be aggregated financially in terms of expenditures per pupil-year. However, the number of pupil-years used by a cohort of pupils to graduate constitutes an input indicator appropriate for the measure of efficiency in education. One pupil who spends one year at school is said to have spent one pupil-year. In this way, we can relate efficiency to the amount of inputs expressed in monetary terms through the number of pupil-years used.

Internal efficiency can be derived, in a quantifiable way by considering the relationship between inputs and outputs when students flow through the grade structure of an educational cycle. For example, in a school cycle of, say, six years, a successful completer would require at least six pupil-years to go through the education process; it would take at least 12 pupil-years to produce 2 successful completers, 18 to produce 3, etc. In other words, if all goes well and no pupil drops out or has to repeat, the ideal average number of pupil-years per successful completer should be equal to the duration of the school cycle. The most common indicator used to assess the educational efficiency is the coefficient of efficiency (or its reciprocal referred to as the input-output ratio). The coefficient of efficiency is calculated by dividing the optimal (ideal) number of pupil-years (i.e. in absence of repetition and drop-out) by the number of pupil-years actually spent by a cohort of pupils. In a 'perfectly efficient' system, this coefficient would equal 100%, and inefficiency arises when it is lesser than 100% (If the input-output ratio is used instead, the perfect state would be 1, and inefficiency arises from any point which is greater than 1).

Since it is often costly and difficult to generalize the school-record system based on reliable individualized pupil information, educational internal efficiency is assessed using the reconstructed cohort method. The indicators derived naturally are subject to the limitations and/or assumptions related to this *cohort analysis method* (see note 1).

The concept of internal efficiency has two main advantages (measurability and analytical clarity) as a tool of educational diagnosis. However, it can easily lend itself to over-interpretation. The limitations of the educational internal efficiency must therefore be recognized and respected. These limitations are related to the weaknesses of some of the key-concepts used to define efficiency and effectiveness in education, such as:

- *Inputs*: the pupil-year is a non monetary measure of input, which fails to take into account the concepts and findings of educational cost analysis. Costs of education are not a simple linear function of the number of pupils. The pupil-year concept fails to grasp the many different determinants of educational costs.
- *Outputs*: 1) the fact that the output is equated with the number of graduates makes for a very narrow view of the education process and its contribution to economy and society; 2) the fact that grade repetition is considered as wasteful (and automatic promotion accordingly as raising efficiency) is not entirely justified by insights into the positive and negative effects of repetition; 3) the fact that no output value whatsoever is accorded to the years spent by drop-outs in school, ignores research on

162

the threshold of literacy retention; for secondary education, this assumption is particularly unrealistic.

- *Process*: the concept of internal efficiency in education is applicable only to those educational processes which follow the age/grade-pattern of conventional formal schooling.
- *Efficiency*: 1) internal efficiency does not necessarily ensure external efficiency; in reality, the two concepts frequently militate against each other; 2) the reduction of educational wastage through higher internal efficiency will not necessarily, contrary to popular beliefs, entail any budgetary savings: if the elimination of grade repetition happens by decree, it will remain ineffective in terms of learning achievement; if it is backed up by remedial teaching, unit costs of education may be increased; 3) where drop-out is to be reduced through lowering drop-out rates, the accommodation capacity of school systems will have to be increased accordingly, particularly in the higher grades: educational budgets will rise as a consequence.

Special considerations on efficiency and effectiveness

In the United States, education is viewed as a responsibility of the individual states rather than the national government, and the states have made efforts to define the outcomes they seek from their educational systems. These efforts have come to be known as standards-driven initiatives, where the standards constitute pronouncements from the states about the collective expectations for what the schools need to accomplish. The idea has been for each state to articulate the desired outcomes and then provide flexibility to the districts, schools, administrators, teachers, and students to meet the standards in ways that make the most sense given local circumstances.

States have handled this in different ways and there are interesting deeper questions about how to balance state judgments with judgments that are made at more localized levels. How, for example, should a disagreement between a duly constituted local school board and the state be settled? Going further, how should the views of local boards be considered as the state sets its standards? What is the proper role for minority views? And how should revisions be handled as time passes?

It is customary to think of the state's setting minimum standards that can be exceeded by individual localities if a locality resolves to do so and can muster the necessary resources. This thinking presupposes a hierarchical view of educational outcomes in the sense that outcome "C" builds upon outcome "B" while outcome "B" builds upon outcome "A." A problem is that outcomes may not always have this kind of hierarchical nature. Suppose a school wants to provide a high degree of personalized attention as part of its program. Is this an input or an outcome? Let us suppose that this is a costly thing to do. The school that pursues this strategy is going to consume more ingredients and if only the standard outcomes are looked at, this school is going to look like costs are high relative to the outcomes that are realized. Hence, the school could look inefficient for the simple reason that it has chosen to pursue a different set of educational goals. There is also the possibility that a locally selected goal can interfere with or undermine one of the state selected goals.

In addition to reaching agreement about the mix of outcomes to pursue, there are important measurement issues to consider. An interest in efficiency is frequently accompanied by an interest in measuring magnitudes. If one is seeking more out of less, one frequently wants to know "how much more," and the result has been a boom in the efforts by educational psychologists and others to develop valid and reliable measures of the learning gains of students. Critics of efficiency analysis in education worry that ease of measurement can unduly influence the selection of the outcomes that the system will be structured to achieve. In other words, the worry is that the drive for efficiency will lead, perhaps inadvertently, toward the use of educational outcomes that are chosen more because they are easy to measure than because of their intrinsic long-term value for either individual students or the larger society. Standardized tests of various kinds have been relied upon as measures of the outcomes of schooling and have been criticized on these grounds.

Sometimes there is interest in the economic consequences of schooling, and this interest has prompted analysts to use earnings as a measure of schooling outcomes. A rich literature has developed in the economics of education where efforts have been made to estimate the economic rate of return to different levels and types of schooling. This is a challenging area of research because earnings are influenced by many factors and it is difficult to isolate the effects of schooling. The goal of this research is to capture the value added by schooling activities.

The relevance of the value-added concept is not limited to economists' studies of rates of return. Even in cases where the focus is on learning outcomes as measured by tests or other psychometric instruments, there are questions to answer about the effects of schooling activities relative to the effects of other potentially quite significant influences on gains in students' capabilities. Serious studies of the efficiency of educational systems measure educational outcomes in value-added terms.

Measurement issues also arise from the collective nature of schooling. The results gained from schooling experiences are likely to vary among individual students and this prompts questions about how best to examine the result for the group in contrast to an individual student. Is one primarily interested in, say, the average performance level, or is there a parallel and perhaps even more important concern with what is happening to the level of variation that exists across all of the students within the unit, be it a classroom, grade level within a school, a school, a district, a state, or a nation? The early research on educational efficiency in the 1960s placed a heavy emphasis on average test score results for relatively large units like school districts. More recent work demonstrates greater interest in measures of inequality among students. The standards-driven reform movement includes a considerable amount of rhetoric about all students reaching high standards; the analysis of efficiency presupposes an ability to move beyond the easy rhetoric to make clear decisions about how uniform performance expectations are for students.

In addition, there is an important distinction to maintain between the levels at which a system operates and the rate at which inputs are being transformed into outcomes. One can "get the outputs right" so that the desired items are being taught/learned in the correct proportion to one another. In such a case, gains in the understanding of mathematics are occurring in the correct proportion to, say, gains in language capabilities. But this says nothing about the absolute level at which the system is operating. The naive view might be that the system should operate at 100 percent of its capacity, but this overlooks the fact that scarce resources are needed to operate at this level and that education is not the only worthy use of these precious resources. Policy-makers must make often difficult trade-off decisions about the level at which the educational system will operate relative to the level of other competing social services. The early twenty-first century is witnessing a considerable amount of debate over the proper level at which to set the educational system, often as part of an effort to define what counts as an "adequate" education.

With respect to outcomes, the goal is to reach agreement about (1) the relative mix of performance outcomes to realize; (2) the degree of uniformity of performance across students; and (3) the level of capacity at which the system should operate. In addition, there needs to be an ability to measure what is being accomplished.

The Choice of Inputs

The outcomes that are selected drive the entire system. Input issues, in contrast, are more straightforward and almost mechanical in nature. Once what is to be accomplished is known, at what level, and for whom, society can then turn to the challenge of doing so in as economical a way as is possible. In other words the goal is to accomplish the desired results for as little cost as possible, and this involves making the best possible use of whatever ingredients or resources that are available.

Although this seems straightforward, there are a number of complexities that need to be considered:

- **First**, there is the dynamic nature of the process. As time passes, more is learned about how to make better and better use of the available resources and new resources may also become available. A good example of a new resource lies in the area of telecommunication and computing technology.
- **Second**, there is the technical versus cost dimension to consider. A particular resource or input might be highly productive in the sense that a small amount could make a significant difference, but this same highly productive resource might be extraordinarily costly.
- **Third**, in addition to making sense of benefits relative to costs, there is also the challenge of making the best possible use of whatever resource is being employed. The quest for greater efficiency requires the parties to make the best possible use of whatever resources come into their possession.
- **Finally**, there is the potential for the costs of inputs to influence the selection of outcomes. Some outcomes are more costly to produce than others. For example, a student who finds it difficult to learn will, by definition, be relatively costly to educate, and these extra costs could influence decisions that are made about how uniform to make the learning outcome standards. And thus, the distinction between outcomes and inputs begins to break down.

The Transformation Process and Implications for Policy

Policymakers are very interested in assessing the degree of efficiency in educational systems. One difficulty arises when indicators are used that fail to provide accurate information. For example, a widely available statistic is the level of spending on education expressed on a per pupil basis. At first glance, this looks like an efficiency indicator since it provides insight into the commitment of resources (the expenditure figure) and the result (the number of students being served by the system). Critics note that this statistic has been rising over time and conclude that the system is becoming less efficient. There are many reasons to be wary of using the expenditure per pupil statistic and its changes over time to reach such a conclusion. Even with a control for the effects of inflation, there remains a fundamental problem on the outcome side of the analysis since there is no direct measure of what the schools are accomplishing and how this might have changed over the period.

Even if accurate, noncontroversial measures of efficiency and its changes over time can be obtained, it is difficult to obtain clear insight into what policies should be developed to ensure gains in efficiency without undermining other key social goals like fairness and freedom of choice. Much of the challenge here depends on the fundamental nature of the transformation process that is presupposed as part of the efficiency concept. The efficiency concept derives from the field of economics where it was initially applied to industrial production processes such as the manufacture of automobiles. These industrial manufacturing processes involve the combination of numerous nonhuman ingredients such as lengths of steel, aluminum, glass, chrome, and so forth. These ingredients are transformed thanks to various physical and chemical processes whose scientific properties are relatively well understood, making the results quite predictable.

For a manager whose goal is to improve efficiency, this kind of information is invaluable. With this information the manager can compare higher performing units with lower performing units and make a diagnosis about the source of the inefficiency in the underperforming units. There may be problems with a unit's ability to get the most out of the inputs it is using; there may be a less than optimal mix of inputs being used; and/or the mix of outputs being produced may be misaligned. The "efficiency expert" in such a situation is able to pinpoint the source of the difficulty and can prescribe steps for improvements.

In contrast, the educational process is heavily committed to the use of human resources and the various inputs are brought together and transformed in ways that are sometimes difficult to predict. Without denying the significance of the human dimension within industrial manufacturing processes, it stands to reason that the production or transformation process that lies at the center of educational systems is fundamentally more complex and less well-understood than production in the industrial sector. A better comparison comes from studies of efficiency in crop production in the field of agricultural economics. But even here, the production process for growing a particular plant is better understood than is the process through which human minds mature and acquire knowledge and understanding. Indeed, it is possible to question whether the educational process really lends itself to the input-output, mechanical formulation that lies at the heart of the efficiency concept. According to this view, educational growth is inherently unpredictable, and the teacher is better thought of as a creative artist than as a productive input whose impact can be measured and predicted in a rigorous and scientific way.

While it is clear that knowledge of the technical properties of the educational process is more limited than what exists, say, in the area of automobile manufacturing, it does not follow that the educational process is inherently unknowable in this sense. In other words, the lack of progress to date in coming to grips with the technical properties of the education transformation process does not mean the process is inherently unpredictable and unmanageable. A more prudent conclusion is that care needs to be exercised in efforts to assess the efficiency of educational systems. It also follows that care needs to be exercised in the use of the efficiency assessment data that are gathered.

Consider the following example of how the results of an efficiency analysis in education can be misapplied. Suppose an analysis goes forward that suggests that a particular school or school district is less efficient than most others. Suppose the response is to penalize the less efficient unit by reducing the flow of state or federal resources. A byproduct of such a policy is a reduction in the funding of the education being provided to students who through no fault of their own find themselves located within an inefficient educational system. Those who work to improve the efficiency of educational systems must guard against this potential to "blame the ultimate victim" of the situation. Similarly, the use of incentives to encourage greater efficiency runs the risk of rewarding those who are already enjoying considerable success. If the problem lies with the unknown nature of the production process, it is perverse to be implicitly penalizing the underperforming districts because they do not have knowledge that is lacking elsewhere. Penalizing underperformers makes sense only if the knowledge is available and the penalties are meant to provide greater incentive to find it. States sometimes handle this by providing technical assistance but technical assistance really works only when it is based on bona fide knowledge, something which is not always possible, given the continued limited understanding of the properties of educational production under a wide range of circumstances.

At this stage of development in efforts to apply the efficiency concept to the field of education several conclusions can be reached.

- It is important to make sure that the comparative information suggesting that one educational unit is more or less efficient than another is accurate.
- This accurate comparative information needs to be used as a set of guidelines/suggestions and needs to stop short of becoming overly rigid and prescriptive.
- Efforts need to be made to monitor very carefully the results of attempts to improve the efficiency of educational systems that are perceived to be below expectations.
- Additional research efforts need to be made to better understand the technical properties of the transformation process that gives rise to desired educational results.

166

- The results of this continuing research will be instrumental in future efforts to make further efficiency improvements in education and can go far toward reducing the ambivalence that historically has characterized educators' reaction to the efficiency concept and its application to the field of education.

Note 1: The following is from http://www.uis.unesco.org/i_pages/indspec/cohorte.htm
Downloaded on May 31, 2009. The assessment of internal efficiency and wastage in education uses techniques similar to those from cohort analysis in demography. A cohort is defined as a group of persons who jointly experience a series of specific events over a period of time. Accordingly, we may define a 'school cohort' as a 'group of pupils (students) who join the first grade of a given cycle in the same school year, and subsequently experience the events of promotion, repetition, dropout or successful completion of the final grade, each in his/her own way'.

There are three ways to analyze educational internal efficiency by means of the cohort student flow method, depending on the type of data collected. These methods are as follows: true cohort, apparent cohort, and reconstructed cohort.

- The ideal way to obtain a precise assessment of wastage is through the use of the *true cohort method*, which involves either longitudinal study in monitoring the progress of a selected cohort of pupils through the educational cycle, or through retrospective study of school records in order to retrace the flows of pupils through the grades in past years. This method, however, is more costly and time-consuming and requires a good and reliable school-records system based on some sort of individualized pupil/student information. For this reason, this method is not yet generalized.

  In the absence of individualized pupil/student information internal efficiency in education can be assessed based on data for repeaters by grade together with enrolment by grade for at least two consecutive years using either the apparent or reconstructed cohort method.
- The *apparent cohort* method is applied when there is no data on repeaters. Then the enrolment in grade 1 in a particular year is compared with enrolment in successive grades during successive years and it is assumed that the decrease from each grade to the next corresponds to wastage. This method, the most commonly used so far, produces estimates of drop-out, and its main weakness is that it assumes that pupils are either promoted or else drop-out of the school system. Repetition as a factor of paramount importance is overlooked. This method is nevertheless appropriate for institutions in countries applying automatic promotion.
- A more pertinent and commonly used method is the *reconstructed cohort* method which places less demand on the availability of detailed data over time. To apply this method, data on enrolment by grade for two consecutive years and on repeaters by grade from the first to second year will be sufficient to enable the estimation of three main flow-rates: promotion, repetition and drop-out. Once obtained, these rates may be analyzed first of all by grade to study the patterns of repetition and drop-out. Then, they are used in a reconstructed pupil-cohort flow to derive other indicators of internal efficiency. A good example of this may be seen in http://www.uis.unesco.org/i_pages/indspec/cohorte.htm

Summary

In this chapter we discussed the concept of lean and how it is used to reduce waste. Specifically we made the distinction between efficiency and effectiveness and how these two basic concepts may be used to satisfy the stakeholders of education. In the next chapter we focus on reform at all levels of education.

References

Peavey, F. (1995). "Strategic Questioning." *In Context*. No. 40.

Selected Bibliography

Becker, Gary S. (1975). *Human Capital*. 2nd edition. New York: Columbia University Press.
Fuhrman, Susan H. (January 1999). "The New Accountability." *CPRE Policy Briefs RB–27* January. Consortium for Policy Research in Education, Graduate School of Education, University of Pennsylvania.
Ladd, Helen F. (Ed). (1996). *Holding Schools Accountable*. Washington, DC: The Brookings Institution.
Levin, Henry M. and Mcewan, Patrick J. (2001). *Cost-Effectiveness Analysis*. 2nd edition. Thousand Oaks, CA: Sage.
Monk, David H. (1992). "Education Productivity Research: An Update and Assessment of its Role in Education Finance Reform." *Educational Evaluation and Policy Analysis*. 14 (4):307–332.
Monk, David H., and Walberg, Herbert J. (Eds.). 2001. *Improving Educational Productivity*. Greenwich, CT: Information Age.
Murnane, Richard J. and Levy, Frank. (1996). *Teaching the New Basic Skills: Principles of Educating Children to Thrive in a Challenging Economy*. New York: Martin Kessler Books, The Free Press.
Monk, D. H. <a href="http://education.stateuniversity.com/pages/1945/Efficiency-in-Education.html">Efficiency in Education - The Choice of Outcomes, The Choice of Inputs, The Transformation Process and Implications for Policy</a>
Read more: http://education.stateuniversity.com/pages/1945/Efficiency-in-Education.html#ixzz0HTIB5FS0&B

CHAPTER 10

EDUCATIONAL REFORM

In the last chapter we discussed lean and how it may be used to improve education by minimizing waste. In this chapter we address educational reform at all levels. Some of these reforms have been proposed and discussed before (by many educators and organizations) but here we take the position that reform is eminent and has to be implemented as soon as possible. We all have a stake in it. It is our future. We cannot stand by and complain that the education is a "failure" and be complacent with doing nothing.

It was Margaret Mead who said (I paraphrase) if we are to achieve a richer culture, rich in contrasting values, we must recognize the whole gamut of human potentialities, and so weave a less arbitrary social fabric, one in which each diverse human gift will find a fitting place. Indeed the fitting place for recognizing and I may add cultivate human potentialities is education.

Most states and districts in the 1990s adopted outcome-based education (OBE) (see note 1) in some form or another. A state would create a committee to adopt standards, and choose a performance-based assessment to assess whether the students knew the required content or could perform the required tasks.

OBE reforms usually had other disputed methods, such as constructivist mathematics and whole language, larded onto them. Some proponents advocated replacing the traditional high school diploma with a Certificate of Initial Mastery. Other reform movements were school-to-work, which would require all students except those in a university track to spend substantial class time on a job site.

In recent years, new definitions of intelligence have gained acceptance and have dramatically enhanced the appraisal of human competencies. Gardner (1983, 1993, 2000) suggests that there are at least eight human intelligences. They are:

1. words (linguistic intelligence)
2. numbers or logic (logical-mathematical intelligence)
3. pictures (spatial intelligence)
4. music (musical intelligence)
5. self-reflection (intrapersonal intelligence)
6. a physical experience (bodily-kinesthetic intelligence)
7. a social experience (interpersonal intelligence), and/or
8. an experience in the natural world. (naturalist intelligence)

Two of these, verbal/linguistic intelligence and logical/mathematical intelligence, have dominated the traditional pedagogy of western societies. The other six non-traditional intelligences, spatial, musical, kinesthetic, interpersonal, intrapersonal and naturalist have generally been overlooked in education. However, if we can develop ways to teach and learn by engaging all eight intelligences, we will increase the possibilities for student success and create the opportunity to, in Margaret Mead's words, "weave a social fabric in which each diverse human gift will find a fitting place."

Learning success for all learners depends on the active involvement of at least four factors:

1. *Assessment*: Unless one is able to assess the learning that takes place in different domains, and by different cognitive processes, even superior curricular innovations are destined to remain unutilized. In this country, assessment drives instruction. We must devise procedures and instruments which are

"intelligence-fair" and which allow us to look directly at the kinds of learning in which we are interested. We must begin to develop intelligence mastery assessment especially in a world in which self teaching is one of the ways of learning.

2. *Curriculum*: Far too much of what is taught today is included primarily for historical reasons. Even teachers, not to mention students, often cannot explain why a certain topic needs to be covered in school. We need to reconfigure curricula so that they focus on skills, knowledge, and above all, understandings that are truly desirable in our country today. And we need to adapt those curricula as much as possible to the particular learning styles and strengths of students.

3. *Teacher Education*: While most teacher education institutions make an honest effort to produce teaching candidates of high quality, these institutions have not been at the forefront of efforts at educational improvement. Too often they are weighted down by students of indifferent quality and by excessive - and often counterproductive - requirements which surround training and certification. We need to attract stronger individuals into teaching, improve conditions so that they will remain in teaching, and use our master teachers to help train the next generation of students and teachers.

4. *Community Participation*: In the past, Americans have been content to place most educational burdens on the schools. This is no longer a viable option. The increasing cognitive demands of schooling, the severe problems in our society today, and the need for support of students which extends well beyond the 9-3 period each day, all make it essential that other individuals and institutions contribute to the educational process. In addition to support from family members and other mentoring adults, such institutions as business, the professions, and especially museums need to be involved much more intimately in the educational process.

Too often, Americans have responded to educational needs only in times of crisis. This is an unacceptable approach. Education works effectively only when responsibility is assumed over the long run. We have made significant progress in this regard over the past decade. There is reason to be optimistic for students of the future, as dedicated individuals continue to collaborate in solving the challenging educational problems of our time.

So reform is definitely in the air all over the country, but the question is what kind of reform are we talking about? Where is that reform to begin? How do we go about any reform? Who initiates this reform? And when should we start? Of course, these are all relevant questions and demand answers. The easy way to answer all of them is that reform must begin now and in all areas of education. It must involve all stakeholders and recognize that their needs are quite different but all have a common thread which is improvement of outcome. There are many ways to reform education but here we will focus on some critical ones.

General education: At best, most students consider general education an obstacle to be gotten out of the way as soon as possible on a mad dash to major courses; at worst, they consider it a devious plot on the part of colleges and universities to ensure that unpopular and irrelevant courses are filled. Thus, regardless of how compelling the imperatives driving it, general education reform-resulting in a new set of courses, new modes of instruction, new themes, or any combination of these-is unlikely to have much of an impact on students, most of whom remain unaware of the reasons for the changes.

More generally, most students do not understand the need for a general education component, which may comprise as much as one-third of their entire education. This lack of awareness is compounded by the belief, reinforced by our own practices, that a diploma or even a degree represents no more than the accumulation of a specified number of credits. Given that general education typically is presented to students as a subset of the total curriculum (*e.g.,* six credits in the arts, nine credits of sciences, six credits in social sciences, and so on), is it any wonder that students approach their educations without clear, well-informed intentions?

170

Notwithstanding the ubiquitous talk of paradigms shifting to embrace active and engaged learning, we continue to use the most sterile and abstract language in explaining the general education program to our students. The traditional approach is to communicate through pamphlets or booklets that have all the imagination of a computer usage manual and enough educational jargon to challenge even the most informed among us. In some cases, education provides students with a list of acceptable courses, thus reinforcing the notion that a diploma or a degree is no more than an accumulation of credits.

Yet, we still believe our students will come to some profound understanding of the purposes of general education. The assumption that, by simply experiencing the designated courses, students come to appreciate the notion of general education and to understand its importance simply does not hold up in practice. In fact, this approach almost guarantees that any intended outcomes of general education reform will be lost on the recipients. Instead, students need structured opportunities to understand, plan, and implement their own general education program.

This dilemma may be somewhat corrected if students and their counselors and or advisors meet regularly to discuss how best to craft the available options - and how best to see general education not only within the context of the diploma or degree but also as a foundation for lifelong learning. This approach requires both the active involvement of knowledgeable counselors and or advisors who are sympathetic to the goals of general education and a structured format for student reflection on individual courses of action.

Students should be required to complete a general education plan, specifying which courses they will take and, more importantly, why. One reason, for example, might be to create a specific theme within the general education categories (such as science, technology, humanities, society interactions, or methods of communication and so many others). Drawing from these general themes, would fulfill some of the purposes of general education, while also allowing students to craft for themselves - and to explain to themselves and to their counselors or advisers - their own rationales for their choices.

Choice schools: It is about time to allow parents to choose their school. Let the market dictate what schools should be the winners and which will be the losers. The idea was first introduced by M. Friedman who first advanced the concept of educational vouchers nearly half a century ago. Few people heard his call and fewer still took him seriously. The overwhelming majority of Americans had become accustomed to government assigning their children to government schools by virtue of their residence, and even when they were unhappy with the results they rarely thought of "choice" as a solution. The deplorable outcome of those empty notions is defended by the vested interests whose pockets are lined by the status quo. Parents, taxpayers, and others who are serious about educational quality know better. What is now up for grabs is the practical implementation side of the choice issue.

The empowerment and transformation of parents into active agents is the foundation of educational choice theory. For a hundred years or more, governments have assigned our children to local public schools based where our homes are; and we pay for those schools whether or not we're able to choose an alternative. That's a strong financial incentive to stay put. The very nature of public, monopolistic bureaucracies is such that raising objections to what the government offers is frustrating, time-consuming and often futile. But when parents are able to say "no, thanks" with speed and ease, they can and will step up to the plate and behave like real consumers of education who are empowered to start shopping around. We have seen this with some parents. For example, the very wealthy and most politicians have always had school choice. They simply pay twice—once in private school tuition and then in taxes for the public system they indeed have rejected. They have realized and are able to support a strong education for their children.

Their commitment is supported by a strong correlation between parental involvement and the success of children in school. The concept of choice takes full advantage of parents' valuable knowledge about their children and their respective talents, abilities, and learning styles. This information equips parents to make optimal choices about where their children should attend school and what kind of school might best suit their children's needs and temperaments.

Unfortunately, a surprising number of poor, inner city families opt for nonpublic alternatives too, but only at enormous sacrifice. Sadly for millions of low-income Americans, education for their children means being stuck with failing and dangerous public schools that spend too much to achieve too little.

Free market education benefits everybody including those who choose not to fully employ it themselves. That's the magic that has made American free markets the envy of the world. Education will not be any different!

Rules based reforms: These include such things as extending school days and the school year, changing teacher certification and school accreditation requirements, imposing national and state testing, enacting stricter dress codes, and the like. Research has shown that these reforms, while causing marginal improvements, have failed to turn around a large-scale decline in education. More drastic city or state "takeovers" of failing schools and districts and legislative proposals such as "Outcome-Based Education," "Goals 2000," and other regulatory regimes have been and still are being tried, with the same disappointing results.

Resource-based reforms: These include such measures as increased funding, new textbooks, wiring schools for internet access, renovating or updating school facilities, reducing class sizes (fewer pupils per teacher), and other measures that require greater financial expenditures. Scholars have studied the relationship between per-student spending and achievement test scores since the publication of "Equality of Educational Opportunity" (better known as "The Coleman Report") in 1966. Author James Coleman, a leading sociologist, concluded that factors such as per-pupil spending and class size do not have a significant impact on student achievement scores.

Economist Erik Hanushek and others have replicated Coleman's study and even extended it to international studies of student achievement. The finding of over 30 years of their research is clear: *More money does not equal better education.* There are schools, states, and countries that spend a great deal of money per pupil with poor results, while others spend much less and get much better results. Yet, despite this and subsequent findings, many lawmakers and educators continue to believe that additional resources and funding will somehow solve the problems within the government education system.

The Kansas City (Missouri) School District provides the perfect illustration of the inefficacy of increasing resources to improve academic and social outcomes. In 1985, a federal judge directed the district to devise a "money-is-no-object" educational plan to improve the education of black students and encourage desegregation. Local and state taxpayers were ordered to fund this experiment. The result: Kansas City ended up spending annually more money per pupil, on a cost-of-living adjusted basis, than any of the 280 largest school districts in the United States. The money bought 15 new schools, an Olympic-sized swimming pool with an underwater viewing room, television and animation studios, a 25-acre wildlife sanctuary, a zoo, a robotics lab, field trips to Mexico and Senegal, and higher teacher salaries. The student-to-teacher ratio was the lowest of any major school district in the nation at 13-to-1. By the time the experiment ended in 1997, costs had mounted to nearly $2 billion. Yet, test scores did not rise. And there was even less student integration than before the spending spree, not more.

In May 2000, the Missouri Board of Education officially removed accreditation status from the district for failing to meet any of 11 performance standards. The loss of accreditation means the district has two years to raise test scores, improve graduation rates, and make progress in other areas or face the prospect of a takeover by the state. On March 10, 2010 the Board of Education decided (on a 5-4 decision) to close 29 out of 61 schools in the district because a) there was no more money and b) the student population has decreased. Similarly, the Detroit School District has decided to close half of the schools due to budget constraints.

The cost issue in all tiers of education is indeed very important and timely. However, whereas Breneman and Haarlow (1998) estimate that the cost nationally of addressing the lack of basic skills in public higher education is approximately $1 billion, Phipps (1998) puts the figure at about $2 billion annually. But these figures are only the costs of remedial or developmental education in higher education paid by the government. They do not include several types of costs that are included in our calculations, such as: higher education costs paid by the recipients of remedial education; remedial education costs paid by privately operated higher education; expenditures by employers to teach basic skills to employees; expenditures by employers to purchase technology that substitutes for the lack of basic skills among employees; lost productivity in the workplace caused by the lack of basic skills; and the cost of government programs to address problems caused by the lack of basic skills (including welfare, criminal justice, etc.).

One way to calculate the economic cost of students leaving high school without having acquired basic skills is to identify the direct expenditures made by employers and institutions of higher learning to remediate those students' lack of basic skills. State government gave community colleges $21,824,016 for "developmental and preparatory" instruction. But state monies represent only 33 percent of community college revenues, with the other two-thirds coming from tuition, local property taxes, the federal government and grants and donations. If state money covers one-third of community college remedial education expenditures, as the Michigan Department of Education estimates, then community colleges in Michigan spend a total of $65.4 million on teaching students basic skills (Ladner and Brouillette 2000).

Michigan public universities spend $17.9 million and Michigan private universities spend $5.9 million every year to offer remedial courses. This total of $23.8 million spent by four-year institutions in Michigan also is likely to be a conservative estimate of the cost of remedial education in those institutions (Green 2000).

1. Public school districts and private schools should implement a rigorous test that students must pass before graduating from high school. At the very least, this would re-enforce the idea that there is an academic standard high school students are expected to attain in order to graduate. While it is no panacea, a graduation test would help to shore up the integrity of a high school diploma and give high schools a greater incentive to ensure that their students acquired basic skills.
2. Public school districts and private schools should shoulder at least some of the financial burden of addressing the lack of basic skills among their graduates. A number of organizations have proposed some sort of "money-back guarantee" for high school diplomas. In other words, if high school graduates are unable to demonstrate mastery of basic skills, schools would have to pay for at least some of the cost of remedial education for those students. This financial responsibility would provide a further incentive to schools to ensure that their graduates were minimally competent.
3. Allow families to choose the elementary and secondary schools their children attend. Parents should be able to choose alternative schools for their children when a school or district fails to provide an adequate education. One of the reasons that America's system of higher education attracts the best students from all over the world is the presence of a competitive system that provides students with choices. Post-secondary students can choose among a large number of community colleges, public universities, private colleges, or vocational schools. Meanwhile, elementary and secondary students

are assigned to their schools, and are unable to escape poor performing schools unless they possess the financial wherewithal to relocate to a better public school district or pay tuition at a private school. Offering K-12 student the same kind of school choices that we already provide college students will create a more competitive elementary and secondary system that delivers higher quality and greater opportunities.

There is a final note on cost. Per-pupil spending today is roughly double (in inflation-adjusted terms) what it was in 1983, when the U.S. was declared "a nation at risk." That huge increase in public outlays has funded all manner of questionable practices, including ever-shrinking class sizes (popular with parents and teachers, but mostly unrelated to student achievement), an ever-growing number of teachers and other school employees, a uniform salary schedule that treats incompetents and all-stars identically, an unsustainable pension-and-benefits system, and a tenure system that protects instructional dysfunction. In other words, taxpayers have spent decades funding an enormous, inefficient jobs program (Petrilli, Finn and Hess 2009).

We have all but exhausted the "rules" and "resources" approaches to education reform, with little to show for our time and money. The one promising category left is "incentives."

Incentive reform: Merit pay for teachers is one incentive-style reform. Parental choice is the centerpiece of this strategy. The dramatic growth of charter schools and both intra-district and cross-district public schools-of-choice programs all represent recent introductions of incentive-based reforms. These measures are beginning to replace the rigid assignment system with some important but rather limited choice opportunities.

Giving parents the opportunity to buy their education from the *best* is the true and correct approach to incentive reform. Full educational choice implies the freedom of parents to pick the best and safest schools—public or private. Parents who place a high priority on education for their children would be empowered or incentivized, not penalized.

Vouchers: Whereas the vision of full educational choice was envisioned by M. Friedman – the free market economist over 40 years ago – the vehicle of achieving it is the voucher. Public, tax-funded vouchers are simply direct payments from the government to individuals to enable them to purchase a particular good or service—in this case, education—in the open market. Those payments can be in the form of a check that the beneficiary deposits in his bank account and draws upon to pay for the vouchered item. Or, they can be a coupon that the beneficiary gives to the private provider of the vouchered item, who then redeems it for cash from the government. The voucher system in education is analogous to the food stamp.

We should note that vouchers aren't always creatures of government. Pioneered by such philanthropists as Peter Flanigan and J. Patrick Rooney, privately funded vouchers (sometimes called scholarship programs) are now making it possible for tens of thousands of children to opt out of bad public schools and into good private ones. Such programs have the inherent virtue of being entirely voluntary every step of the way. Bureaucracy for its own sake doesn't exist within such programs. And because no tax money enters the picture, there are no politicians piling on the paperwork, meddling with the schools, or otherwise using the education of the children involved as a political football. But the real debate over vouchers for school choice centers on publicly funded ones.

Public voucher programs are in place in Milwaukee, Cleveland, certain rural communities within the state of Vermont, and in a very limited way in Florida. Parental satisfaction is high and studies are beginning to show that the programs are yielding improvements in student performance. But at the same time, the future of the voucher option is cloudy and uncertain. Legal and constitutional challenges are numerous. The opposition has succeeded in stigmatizing vouchers to the point where "the V-word" is shunned even by proponents. President Bush could not get the Congress to fund even a tiny voucher program. A significant number of private schools that would be eligible for vouchers don't want to touch them with the proverbial 10-foot pole, in fear of the attached strings.

And it's becoming abundantly evident that while vouchers may be politically feasible in a few legislatures, they are dead-on-arrival when attempted at the ballot box. No voucher initiative—and there have been many of them—has ever secured much more than 30 percent of any popular vote, even as polls show strong majority support for the general concept of choice at the same time.

Increasingly within the school reform movement, vouchers are no longer seen as the one and only way, or even the best way, to realize full educational choice. There is, in my view, a superior option that is not only better policy but is more politically viable as well. That option is tax credits.

Tax Credits: Tax credits are designed to provide parents with tax relief linked to expenses incurred when they select a school other than the government-assigned one for their children. That typically means a private school, but tax credits can also apply to tuition charged by a public school that accepts a student from outside its regular jurisdiction. The credit is usually a dollar-for-dollar reduction in taxes owed (whereas a tax deduction is merely a reduction in taxable income). For example, if a taxpayer has a pre-credit tax liability of $2,000 and a tuition tax credit of $1,500, the taxpayer would pay a tax of only $500.

Tax credits are typically applied against only state and/or federal income taxes, but property tax credits have been proposed as well. For the purposes of school choice, tax credits might be allowed for any or all out-of-pocket educational expenses incurred by an individual, from tuition to textbooks to transportation to extracurricular fees—though tuition is the most common expense allowed in practice. Private schools usually charge tuition and/or fees, and government schools often charge tuition to nonresident students and fees for extracurricular activities. These expenditures are also creditable items under many tax credit proposals.

Many proponents of educational tax credits prefer them to vouchers on the grounds that they entail less government regulation of private schools and less risk of entanglement between church and state because of their indirect nature. Credits, unlike vouchers, do not transfer any money from the state to schools or taxpayers. There's no need to launder anybody's money through a public bureaucracy first before it pays for a child's schooling.

Indeed, because vouchers are funded out of the pool of taxpayer funds, some citizens will always argue that "Some of my money will be going to send your child to a school I don't like." Those citizens will want government to regulate how, when, and where their tax money can be used by other people. The legislators who appropriate it and the bureaucracy that dispenses it will be more than happy to oblige.

Because of the prospect of regulation, some private schools will surely not accept vouchers—at first. But over time, it will become very difficult for them to pass up the allure of "free" money and the opportunity to make schooling less expensive for their families. Government shackles will follow government shekels, as they always do sooner or later. With private schools increasingly dependent on voucher revenue, few will be able to wean themselves away when regulation becomes invasive. The initial benefit of competition between schools due to vouchers will diminish as regulation homogenizes all schools into an amorphous blob feeding at the public trough.

Tax credits, on the other hand, don't represent a claim by anyone on someone else's wallet. You don't get the credit if you don't pay tuition or if you don't pay taxes. A credit on your taxes represents your own money, period.

Education researcher and author Andrew Coulson notes that a significant advantage tax credits have over vouchers is that they restore to the family the direct financial responsibility for educating their children. He writes, "Since all the money involved in these [tax credit] programs is privately and voluntarily spent, issues of church-state entanglement and necessary public oversight of public spending are rendered moot. Because of the greater resistance to regulation that follows from the absence of state funding under tax-credit programs, those programs do a better job . . . ." Coulson argues that tax credits are superior to vouchers because they more effectively promote and protect the conditions that have historically produced educational excellence: parental choice, direct parental financial responsibility, freedom for educators, competition among schools, financial incentive for educators, and universal access to the education marketplace.

Here's another way to see this crucial difference: Vouchers are food stamps for education, a mechanism for the forcible redistribution of wealth from all citizens to some citizens. Tax credits are mechanisms for fairness, an accounting device that permits people to keep at least some of their own money that they would otherwise pay for the government-assigned school they are not using. Moreover, if the credit allowed is a modest one—half, for example, of what the government spends per pupil in the public system—then an actual savings for the public system and for all taxpayers is generated every time a child migrates from a public school to a private one. All of that makes it impossible for opponents to argue honestly that the tax credit is "draining" funds from the public system, though the more dishonest among them will say that anyway.

In the long run, vouchers may not diminish the role of government and politics in education. Tax credits are much more likely to reduce that role and to put private institutions and private individuals—parents in particular—in charge once again. But while both mechanisms are worth the risk to escape the intolerable status quo, both still require vigilance to keep the government at bay.

Political Viability: Friedman has said he prefers vouchers over tax credits because we should not use the tax system as a social engineering tool. But a tax credit for education is fundamentally different from a tax credit for solar panels or electric cars or any other politically correct gimmick *du jour*. That's because not only is education itself mandatory, but taxes to pay for it are as well, and that's not likely to change any time soon. A tax credit designed to get you to change your behavior (to buy a solar panel, for instance) is just not the same as a tax credit that refunds some of what government charged you for something you don't want to buy.

Instinctively, most people seem to understand this distinction. They are naturally more sympathetic to the fairness of a tax credit than the redistribution of a voucher. They are much more familiar with tax credits and their kissing cousin—tax deductions—because they've used them again and again year after year. When a survey of congressional and state legislative candidates was done in Michigan in 1998, it was found that there were many incumbents and challengers who favored tax credits for education but not vouchers, and none who favored vouchers but not tax credits.

When a voucher plan was on the ballot in Michigan in November 2000, yard signs popped up all over the state declaring "No Vouchers!" It's hard to imagine a similar proliferation of "No Tax Credits!" signs, had that been the choice before voters. Even liberal Democrats like Bill Clinton, Al Gore, and our new U.S. Sen. Debbie Stabenow support tax credits for preschool and post-grade 12 education.

Not surprisingly, of all the many statewide ballot initiatives for educational choice across the nation in the past 30 years, the one that holds the record for securing the greatest percentage of the popular vote is the 1998 Colorado tax credit initiative (about 41 percent). It was poorly crafted, vastly under-funded, and it came out way too late for its proponents to have enough time to inform the public. But it still beat by a good margin the highest vote percentage any voucher plan has ever won.

Yes, any tax credit adds a complication (a line or two) to our tax forms, and thereby takes us a step away from a less complicated flat tax. As a staunch advocate of limited government, free markets, and a flatter income tax if we're going to have one at all, I confess to a small strategic compromise there. But our voucher friends need to acknowledge that vouchers are a whale of bigger fudge than any tax credit. Most voucher proponents don't advocate food stamps, redistribution, or government subsidies for any other business or enterprise. A tax credit for education is not so much a compromise as it is simply the best mechanism we're likely to get for letting people keep what's theirs when they are paying taxes for education but don't want to buy it from the government.

Tax credits for education can assume different shapes. Under a traditional credit plan, only a parent who pays private educational expenses (like tuition) for his child and who has a tax liability greater than the amount of the allowable credit will qualify. The problem with a traditional tax credit is that low-income parents who don't have the money to pay for a private school or have little or no tax liability will be left out in the cold. That deficiency could be remedied partially by making the credit "refundable," meaning the credit could result in a refund check from the government if your tax liability is low. But that would effectively voucherize the tax credit insofar as low-income parents are concerned, which would introduce some of the political and economic baggage of vouchers that I've already mentioned.

The form of tax credit that solves these problems is one for which the Mackinac Center for Public Policy, is nationally known for pioneering as early as 1996. They were the first to give it the name, *Universal Tuition Tax Credit* and the first to design such a plan for an entire state—Michigan. It requires an amendment to our state constitution, which will happen in the future, but until that day comes I'm happy to report that the concept is catching on elsewhere.

In states like Virginia, Utah, and Idaho, groups have copied or adapted the Mackinac plan to their particular state's tax and education funding infrastructures, and are gaining public and legislative attention for these adaptations. The center through the chief architect of the plan, Joseph Overton, predicts this approach will eventually eclipse all others as the preferred vehicle for achieving full educational choice. The Cato Institute in Washington has endorsed the basic framework of the Mackinac plan and is working with the center to get it a wider hearing nationally.

Key to the "universal" tax credit concept is that it allows any taxpayer—individual or corporate, parent or grandparent, neighbor or friend—to contribute to the education of any elementary or secondary child and then qualify for a dollar-for-dollar credit against certain taxes owed. The maximum credit is equal to half what the government spends per pupil in the public schools, which is more than enough to cover educational expenses at 90 percent or more of private schools. It envisions scholarship funds supplied with private tax credit monies. These scholarship funds would be established by schools, companies, churches, and myriad private groups—spurred on by individuals and companies who want to help children get their schooling in the best and safest schools of their choice.

The popularity of tax credits among parents has exploded throughout the country in recent years. K-12 tax credits have passed state legislatures in Arizona, Minnesota, Iowa, and Illinois. Arizona expanded parental school choice in 1998 to include tax credits for donations to both private scholarship programs and government schools. Former Gov. Fife Symington signed into law a bill in April 1997 granting an income tax credit of up to $500 for people who donate to nonprofit groups that distribute private scholarships to students. The law also offers taxpayers a credit of up to $200 for money given to government schools to support extracurricular activities.

On the national level, Michigan congressman Peter Hoekstra has proposed federal legislation that would permit a universal education tax credit of up to $500 against federal income taxes owed. That would keep billions of dollars from ever going to Washington in the first place, which is a virtue in itself. But education is still overwhelmingly a state and local matter, and that's where groups must work to craft a universal tax credit plan onto their existing tax and education infrastructure.

One final thought: Any school choice plan should start with the recognition that private schools are not the problem we face today. They are an important part of the solution. We must not bargain away their independence to get choice even if it's in the form of a universal tax credit. We must not burden them with new government mandates cloaked in the guise of "accountability." Private schools are already accountable—they have customers who can take a walk, not captives who have no real options.

Educational choice is an idea whose time has come, and the universal education tax credit is an idea whose time is about to arrive. It can get the job done and avoid many of the problems inherent in the voucher approach. It will minimize the danger of intrusive government, though private schools will always have to be vigilant under any system. It will galvanize and strengthen civil society by giving individuals and companies new incentive to assist the educational dreams of their fellow citizens. It will bolster the incentives of existing public schools to improve. And perhaps most importantly, it will put choice and responsibility back in the laps of parents from whom such things should never have been taken in the first place.

529 Plans: A 529 Plan is an education savings plan operated by a state or educational institution designed to help families set aside funds for future college costs. It is named after Section 529 of the Internal Revenue Code which created these types of savings plans in 1996. These plans are also OK for out of state colleges. This is a big boost for choice since the 529 plans can be used to meet costs of qualified colleges nationwide. In most plans, your choice of school is not affected by the state your 529 savings plan is from. You can be a CA resident, invest in a VT plan and send your student to college in NC. As of this writing every state now has at least one 529 plan available. However, it's up to each state to decide whether it will offer a 529 plan (possibly more than one) and what it will look like, meaning 529 plans can differ from state to state.

As long as the plan satisfies a few basic requirements, the federal tax law provides special tax benefits to you, the plan participant. 529 plans are usually categorized as either prepaid or savings plans.

> *1. Savings Plans* work much like a 401K or IRA by investing your contributions in mutual funds or similar investments. The plan will offer you several investment options from which to choose. Your account will go up or down in value based on the performance of the particular option you select.
> *2. Prepaid Plans* let you pre-pay all or part of the costs of an in-state public college education. They may also be converted for use at private and out-of-state colleges.

The Independent 529 Plan is a separate prepaid plan for private colleges. Educational institutions can offer a 529 prepaid plan but not a 529 savings plan (the private-college Independent 529 Plan is the only institution-sponsored 529 plan thus far).

Reform the strategy of the boards (on the local or college level): Boards have got to come to grips with their financial model going forward. We are perhaps in the worst time that we have ever been. Institutions all around the country are facing some real challenges to their own finances, their own budgets, both in terms of revenue and the ability to address the question of costs, and expenses. Historically, boards don't get the kinds of comparative data, don't have the amount of time to really look at some of these challenges in a rigorous and strategic manner. However, now and in the future, they need to understand the questions that they need to ask. So when it comes to institutional strategic finance, the first thing they need to know is that

178

when we talk about costs, we're not talking about price. We're talking about where our institutional revenues are allocated, and how are they allocated. They need to have a clear understanding of their institution's mission. And they need to have a clear understanding of where the institution's priorities are headed.

In essence all boards must get more active in controlling the mission of their school environment. Obviously, they cannot do it alone because of lack of both time and expertise but they can ask probing questions that others cannot. Above all boards must work on projects and agendas that are strategic in nature and for the betterment of their institutions in the long term.

Internal reform for colleges and universities: Both colleges and universities need internal reform in their faculty status. The current relegation of adjuncts to what seems a second class academic citizenship is a toxic structure far more disabling for the educational system than any other visible concern in the campus. All educational institutions (K-12, junior, senior colleges and universities) have differences and some are better than others. Therefore, competition for the best students and faculty members must be a way to compete in the future. Another consideration may be for teachers and faculty to have a mobile tenure to make sure that the "best" will go to the "best educational" environment.

Yet another reform must be in the area of junior colleges. The overarching goal of national higher education policy is (at least we claim as a society) to effectively educate students at the postsecondary level. While colleges should focus on the needs of their students, it is important that they also have clearly defined goals along those lines, with incentives to match. Success in a new system must be measured by progress. Right now appropriations to community colleges are primarily based on enrollment, without regard to whether their students earn degrees or get good jobs. That gears incentives toward inputs and process, rather than outcomes.

To avoid the trap of appropriations we must 1) Develop national goals and a performance-measurement system: Perhaps one of the priority items must be the issue of transferring credits and defining what is acceptable performance and 2) funding must be increased directly from either the State or Federal government: The state and federal government should invest resources specifically to promote greater access and success for students. As the money flows into these institutions they should be required to track and report student results, consistent with the metrics that the college has defined. Typical metrics may be: completion of a minimum number of credits, transferred credits, or earned a degree. The government support will help with specific resources in enhancing both quality and innovation as well as making these colleges accountable through common student data systems.

Reform curriculum: Higher institutions have come of age to begin introducing innovation, agility and ethical behavior as part of their teaching. The focus of excellence in all forms of educational systems must once again return to be part of the American culture. Mediocrity is not the way to go. Grade inflation must stop. Average performance is a killer to education, and society at large. Not recognizing and encouraging excellence is even worse. In fact it is a sure thing to destroy education as we know it.

What makes the task so challenging is that this generation of students is perhaps more diverse than any previous generation, not only in race and ethnicity, but skills, characteristics and experiences. For example, the days of the "traditional" student, or school homogeneity, are long past. Higher education is no more the domain of the 18 year old, fresh out of high school, supported by parents, concerned only with studying and socializing. In fact, according to figures from the National Center for Education Statistics, the "traditional" undergraduate has become the exception rather than the rule. Now, 73 percent of all undergraduates are in some way "nontraditional" —and 39 percent are 25 years or older.

So modern day students are individuals who for whatever reason have delayed their pursuit of a college degree; some have a GED only; others started college years ago but suspended their studies. Some work full-time, have spouses and children. They're sons and daughters of immigrants, first generation Americans. They're underemployed or out of work family providers seeking to build new careers out of necessity. They're struggling to surmount not only economic obstacles, but barriers of language, culture, even basic academic and social skills.

As a result of all these characteristics the curriculum must be reflective of the student's needs. Therefore, it is imperative that a review of the course offerings is conducted in order to evaluate the learners who come to school with widely varying levels of preparedness.

That relevancy begins with an individual assessment of a student's prior knowledge and current abilities—an essential first step to engage students for learning. Furthermore, to keep students interested and motivated, the school needs to continue to be innovative in its delivery of education, to adopt multiple modes of assessing progress and forge new ways to reinforce successes. Above all, the institution must continually balance the need to invest in its future transformation with the necessity to fulfill its present promise to students of a life-changing education.

In the case of high school students, boards and administrators in conjunction with colleges and universities must develop curricula that are innovative and present interest as well as challenge to the students. One of the ways that this may be accomplished is through offering advanced placement (AP) classes. The AP program is intended to provide high-school students with an academic college experience, typically at the level of an introductory college course. As such, most AP courses cover a wide breadth of topics, which necessitates sacrificing some depth. That, however, is also true of the typical introductory college course.

AP credit broadens, not narrows, the college experience for its recipients. While it's true that some students might use their credits to graduate early, AP credit—and particularly its related perk of placing out of survey courses—is likely to enhance, rather than truncate, students' academic experience. When we become proficient in a subject, our tendency is to delve further into it. Students are free to pursue their AP subjects in more advanced courses in college without having to take prerequisites that might not interest them. The opportunity offers rigorous, college-level education to motivated students, and offers the benefit of college credit. While it is true that not all students who are encouraged to take AP are ready, and that not all courses at all schools meet the college-level standard, AP is a valuable program worthy of attention and, when required, correction and improvement.

A second way is to be more cognizant of the pedagogy we use in the classroom. Especially for the unmotivated student we must use methods that will entice the learners early on in their learning process and create an internal enthusiasm for learning. In other words we must instill confidence to the students for success. To do that we must cultivate the students to appreciate the learning process with challenging assignments so that they can experience the satisfaction of intellectual engagement. This means that in the process of learning we have to teach them that sometimes the only way to move forward is to destroy something and that is part of learning as well.

A third way in the modern world is to begin teaching ethical behavior as early as possible. It is very important to recognize that we may have smart and knowledgeable learners that graduate from our institutions of learning but ethically challenged. To be sure teaching ethical behavior is much easier than practicing *the* ethical behavior. Teaching must be done in a manner of steps and each step must be completed and understood. These steps as Sternberg (2009) has pointed out are:

1. Recognize that there is an event to react to. No matter *who* is saying *what*, learners must be able to think whether or not the item of discussion is worth challenging or even questioning.
2. Define whether or not the event has an ethical dimension. It is important to teach the difference as well as making sure that the learners understand the significance of that dimension. If it is significant then it is worth pursuing, and expose the truth of the situation.
3. Take responsibility. There is nothing wrong with taking responsibility for an ethical solution to the problem. Learners at all levels must be taught and encouraged to speak up when they see injustices in society and even in the classroom with their own teachers without any form of retaliation.
4. Be careful to apply ethical rules. Sometimes knowing the rules is quite different from applying the rules. In many instances, understanding how to apply even a single ethical principle, forces one to grapple with deeply held values. Obviously an individual has to decide what he or she is willing to risk for the sake of doing what he or she believes is right. However, the driving force for any basis for ethical behavior must be the golden rule which states: *do unto others as you would have them do unto you.*
5. Learn to take action. One may be a great theorist of ethical behavior but eventually one has to deliver that ethical behavior through actions. If action is not taken, then the ethical issues will not be addressed.

Reform transfer credits from one college or university to another. All institutions of higher learning should be more open to accepting transfer students and should take a close look at increasing their efficiency in applying the appropriate credit hours. Currently a typical institution is like the famous Cookie Monster of the TV series *Sesame Street*. That is the institution has become a beast that gobbles up resources and grows without regard for efficiency. To be sure, in the past, there were no market pressures on tuition and families strove to buy the best education for their children that they could afford because they realized that an elite college might open more doors than one less esteemed. Today, that is changing and reform is expected.

De-emphasize frills as part of the educational process and focus on the mission of the school: There is no question that times are very tough. The great majority of all educational systems are looking for cost cuts for 2011 and beyond, in anticipation of the deepest budget cuts in more than a generation. But as bad as the financial situation may be, educational entities can survive if they take swift and strong emergency action. It is time for some straight talk, starting with the realization that organizations that can't or won't adapt will fail. This recession has caused many of the nation's largest retailers, banks, airlines, manufacturers, and brokerage houses to do so. Millions of Americans have lost jobs and homes. Why would we think any educational entity, and those employed by them, would be exempt from the same fate? The market sorts itself out at times like these.

If industries and services, of all types, realign their business, so must the educational institutions. The first message for education institutions has to be that competition is going to become fierce. For college leaders to believe that their main worries are the inwardly focused challenges and politics of maneuvering campus groups through an unpleasant budget realignment would be a major mistake. The institutions that will survive will be those that have built collaborations among internal groups in order to compete externally for students, faculty talent, and financial resources. Correspondingly, if the municipalities think that by passing millages it will solve their problems of the K-12 they will make an even greater mistake.

The second message is that higher education is part of the larger economic system. There will be casualties, just as commercial businesses will fail and other worthy nonprofit organizations will go broke. If a state's tax revenues fall by large percentages, given that the priorities of the states are usually public safety, unemployment support, transportation, basic services, and a balanced budget, then something will have to go. Often that something will be support for all types of education. We saw this with the latest situation in

California in the vote of May 2009. As the voters rejected tax increases the politicians threatened the public to cut education and safety programs.

Many policy makers regard education as both a public good and a private good. Insofar as it is the former, it is reasonable to support education as an economic engine and source of business, medical, legal, and technical progress. But much of that can wait, many people would say, until tax revenues rebound. Insofar as it is the latter, it is reasonable to reduce or defer support for colleges in bad times and to shift more of the cost onto students. So what can be done to reduce costs? The following are some examples:

When talking to people about the budget, be honest about it. Acknowledge the fiscal realities and anxieties that they feel. All economic problems have a human dimension. Students, administrators, and faculty members need to know that their leaders understand that. Do not underestimate or over estimate the problem. Transparency is the best policy.

Educate people about the realities of competition in education especially as it affects your territory or district.

Tell people the ground rules, the priorities and your strategies. Above all make sure and communicate your plans to assure students that they'll graduate on time, even though drastic changes may have to be taken. When making budget cuts, do it right the first time. Be decisive, candid, and quick. Nobody wants wave after wave of budget cuts. Avoid across-the-board cuts. It shows lack of understanding of the system and indecision. Be strategic in the cuts and then explain.

Consult with people throughout the district and institution. Use consensus for decision making, however, an ending point must be established. As part of the discussion establish strict deadlines by which decisions about budget reductions and revenue enhancements will be made. Do not fall in the trap of "we need more time." It is true that more time may indeed bring a better result but in the mean time a wait-and-see approach may position others to out-compete you for either students and or resources.

Work with your union. Everyone understands that unless the district or institution survives, nobody will have a job. Make periodic presentations about the district's or institution's financial situation to key groups. Inform administrators, trustees, faculty, and students of your decisions and teach them how the budget works. Let them know about gifts and endowments to the institution and how they are affected by the budget.

Protect your major revenue stream. For the vast majority of districts and institutions, that means faculty members teaching students, which translates directly into tuition revenue or state subsidies for instructional work. Because of that business reality, you must preserve students and the people who educate them.

Be realistic. For example, if you do not have a good track record, do not call on the faculty to dig you out of next year's budget problems with research or training grants from government agencies or philanthropic foundations. Competitive proposals presume months if not years of prior work.

What are the best ways to generate revenue, increase productivity, and cut expenditures? In a typical school district (K-12) the options are very limited as the revenues are based on taxes and grants from state or federal governments. However, productivity and expenditures are options that may be worked out within specific districts using innovation and quality techniques that we already have discussed.

On the other hand, in a typical institution of higher learning we can still use some of the initiatives of quality principles that we already have discussed but we can also use some innovative approaches. Here are just a

182

few examples, some of which may be familiar to you while others may run counter to your practices, cultural assumptions, policies, bylaws, or labor contracts. But given the circumstances, you may want to consider unusual alternatives:

- Create a "Work to Learn" program that fills office, buildings-and grounds, and custodial staff positions with student workers who will earn tuition credits. Students can be employed to perform a surprisingly wide variety of jobs.
- Require every administrator with a master's or doctoral degree to teach a course.
- Reduce office-staff expenses by pooling support-staff members in clusters of four and five departments. That will actually permit better services across the spectrum of needs.
- Increase productivity by increasing class size. For example, going from 40 to 46 students represents a 15-percent increase in productivity. In fact it has been reported that count of classes smaller than 50 does not have to change. If need be, suspend or close all undergraduate minors, and all graduate and undergraduate special-emphasis programs. Then suspend or close at least 25 percent of all undergraduate majors. Most colleges offer more programs than students demand and faculty members' energy justify. While closing programs reduces students' choices, it need not prevent them from graduating on time with a fine education.
- Suspend or close all nonprofessional master's programs and all doctoral programs that are not your signature programs or not ranked among the top 50 in the nation. Strategically it is important to preserve professional graduate programs that generate positive net revenues and to secure your signature master's and doctoral programs, provided they bring you genuine national recognition or international distinction. The professional and career advancement of faculty members is at best a secondary effect of, not a justification for, offering any program.
- To save jobs, reduce all salaries by a certain percentage. That amount should be higher for well-paid people and lower for people with midlevel salaries. If salary reductions are not possible, use furloughs for staff members and full-time faculty members. Two days of unpaid furloughs per month is roughly a 10-percent reduction in salary costs during the academic year.
- Offer employees temporary or partial leave without pay but with full benefits. Some may be able to afford and enjoy that. If your bylaws prevent offering it, then expand the number of sabbaticals and research leaves with partial pay and full benefits.
- Reduce debt-service payments by renegotiating long-term debt, seeking a lower interest rate, extending the term of the loan, or, if necessary, changing banks.
- Raise institutional revenue by improving student retention through excellent teaching and the best possible quality of service at every level in every program. Set numerical goals. Measure progress. Reward those programs and service providers that reach or exceed targets.
- Increase enrollments by providing tuition rebates or mini scholarships for graduate, professional, and adult students for a second course in the same term. Even a 15-percent discount can be a valuable and cost-effective recruiting tool.
- Provide cash incentives to schools, departments, and faculty members who exceed targets for enrolling and retaining students, and for graduating them on time.
- If tuition revenues exceed expectations, be sure to return a proportionate share to the student-aid budget to buy down the institutional discount rate and to have additional funds to support retention and further recruitment.
- Instead of inputs, focus on the quality of results. For example, create a one-stop service center with stand-up counters, like those at airports and hotels. Train the people who staff it to respond correctly and quickly to at least 80 percent of the questions that students ask, regardless of the topic. Just ending the time-wasting, buck-passing practice of referring students across campus to someone else's office will aid retention and improve student satisfaction.
- Offer students workshops and courses on financial management. Help them budget to stay in school.

- Lease prime ground-floor spaces in campus buildings to retailers, professional firms (legal, medical, and others), independent nonprofit organizations, and other revenue providers. Classrooms and offices can go on higher floors. Blending the campus with the community can have a beneficial impact on both town-gown relations and student retention.
- Close and lease remote campuses and unused buildings. Do not sell the land, unless the survival of the institution hangs in the balance. Instead find a developer, private or public, that has an interest in partnering with the institution to use the land or the buildings in clever and economically productive ways.
- Increase rental revenues by encouraging local governments, nongovernmental agencies, clubs, and cultural groups to use campus recreation fields, arenas, swimming pools, tennis courts, theaters, music venues, galleries, gardens, banquet halls, and meeting rooms.
- Collaborate in order to compete more successfully. Join with other institutions to share faculty members, facilities, registration and records functions, security, and parking.
- Halve the size of all committees and reduce the number of times any committee is allowed to meet by the same amount. Two essential committees are for assessment, to establish the educational effectiveness of the curriculum—crucial for financial support and accreditation—and for student success, to work on improving retention and graduation rates. The rest, even when they do useful jobs in ordinary times, can still perform with 75 percent fewer human-hours being consumed. Those hours can be put to better use in these tough times.

In the end, natural selection and market competition being the forces they are, some institutions will not survive financially, no matter what they do. But others can thrive, if they make all the right moves. In life, adaptation is everything.

Note 1: Outcome-based education (OBE) is a recurring education reform model. It is a student-centered learning philosophy that focuses on empirically measuring student performance, which is called *outcomes*. OBE became a popular term in the United States during the 1980s and early 1990s. It is also called standards-based education reform, mastery education, performance-based education, and other names. OBE contrasts with traditional education, which primarily focuses on the resources that are available to the student, which are called *inputs*. While OBE implementations often incorporate a host of many progressive pedagogical models and ideas, such as reform mathematics, block scheduling, project-based learning and whole language reading, OBE in itself does not specify or require any particular style of teaching or learning. Instead, it requires that students demonstrate that they have learned the required skills and content. However in practice, OBE generally promotes curricula and assessment based on constructivist methods and discourages traditional education approaches based on direct instruction of facts and standard methods. Though it is claimed the focus is not on "inputs," OBE generally is used to justify increased funding requirements, increased graduation and testing requirements, and additional preparation, homework, and continuing education time spent by students, parents and teachers in supporting learning.

Each independent education agency specifies its own outcomes and its own methods of measuring student achievement according to those outcomes. The results of these measurements can be used for different purposes. For example, one agency may use the information to determine how well the overall education system is performing, and another may use its assessments to determine whether an individual student has learned required material.

Considerations that may affect reform

In manufacturing we have long known that there are certain things that will stifle productivity, improvement and efficiency. In fact, Deming (1986) as part of his 14 points to management also identified those things that inhibit productivity as the *seven deadly diseases*.

For Deming, they were so critical pivotal ideas that unless management recognized them and planned for them they would not be successful in any improvement initiative undertaken. It is worth enumerating them here with a small editorial content. Whereas the Fourteen Points express Deming's philosophy of management, The Seven Deadly Diseases describe the most serious barriers that management faces in its current management actions. They are:

Lack of constancy of purpose to plan product and service that will have a market and keep the company in business, and provide jobs.

> As long as the focus is on short term thinking, management will fail to plan adequately. Without good long term planning, worker efforts will be irrelevant. More significantly this disease is warning that Total Quality Management (TQM) cannot be a fad. If management changes its philosophy by whatever was the latest book it read, then there will be no long term forward progress. Appropriate questions here are:
>
> - What are examples where planning was inadequate?
> - How do you plan for new products and services?

Emphasis on short-term profits: short-term thinking (just the opposite of constancy of purpose to stay in business), fed by fear of unfriendly takeover, and by push from bankers and owners for dividends.

> There is nothing easier to do than boost profits in the short term. All a manager has to do is cut any expense related to the long term: training, maintenance, purchase of new capital, etc. For non-profits like schools and hospitals, substitute "Emphasis on short term costs" instead of "Emphasis on short term profits." These institutions, especially when in budget crises, focus on cutting short term costs without regard to long term consequences. Appropriate questions here are:
>
> - What are examples of short term thinking that made things worse in the long run?
> - What pressures make it difficult to do long term thinking?

Personal review systems, or evaluation of performance, merit rating, annual review, or annual appraisal, by whatever name, for people in management, the effects of which are devastating. Management by objective, on a go, no-go basis, without a method for accomplishment of the objective, is the same thing by another name. Management by fear would still be better.

> The essential problem with merit systems is that they reward results rather than process improvement. Results will almost always have a lot of system luck mixed in. Some managers want to reward people who cooperate more or who seem to have better attitudes. These managers will insist that they can recognize the people who are most cooperative and have the highest work ethic. When managers reward these attitudes, however, they are setting up a system that will have two fundamental flaws: (a) it encourages "kissing up" to the boss and (b) psychological research indicates that the best way to develop cooperation is not through money rewards, but rather by focusing on the nature of work environment itself. Appropriate questions here are:

- Is merit pay being used?
- Is the annual evaluation focused on the past or the future?
- Does management rely on fear? If so, what are some concrete examples?

Mobility of management; job hopping.

This is perhaps the simplest and yet one of the most deadly of diseases. When top management changes organizations every three or four years, that means continuous improvement efforts will be broken and disjointed as the new "leaders" come on board. Moreover, with changes in leadership, there is frequently a change in management philosophy. How can there be constancy of purpose in such an environment? When management has no commitment to the long term, how will they ever start thinking long term? Managers who have an eye on the next promotion want results, now, to gain the next rung on the ladder. Appropriate questions here are:

- How long does the CEO typically last on the job?
- How many changes in management philosophy have there been in the last ten years?

Use of visible figures only for management, with little or no consideration of figures that are unknown or unknowable.

Many consultants in the quality field have been quoted to say, "If you can't measure it, you can't manage it." Certainly Deming would have been one of the first to argue that good data is essential and should be factored into all decisions whenever possible. Deming was in fact very critical of people who fail to use data when it is available. Furthermore, he pointed out that some facts are simply unknowable. In spite of that, Deming insisted that leaders must still make decisions and manage the situation. For instance, if a quality effort is truly justified, then it should cause operating costs to decline and overall sales to rise relative to what would have happened otherwise. This leads to a basic dilemma. How do you know what would have happened if you had kept on your prior course? How do you put a dollar value on the customer loyalty won through quality improvement efforts? You can't! These numbers are unknowable. If you decide that TQM can be justified only if the benefits are clearly measurable, then you might leave these factors out of your analysis and erroneously conclude that TQM is causing losses when in reality it is generating profits. Appropriate questions here are:

- What are some key unknowable numbers that have been ignored in the past?
- How do you manage in a systematic data based way when key numbers are unknowable?
- Do you agree that "If you can't measure it, you can't manage it."

Excessive medical/pension costs.

American organizations pay more for medical care and pension costs than they do for their salaries of their employees. This is even more prominent in the public sector including education. For the economy as a whole, health care as a percent of overall expenditures has steadily risen for decades gradually pushing numerous business and government budgets into a state of crisis. Deming would have approved of the political system attempting to reform health care. Appropriate questions here are:

- What percent of your labor costs is for medical care?
- How much has the percent grown over the last ten years?

- How do medical costs compare to other fixed costs such as advertising, investment in new capital, and interest payments on loans?

Excessive costs of liability.

Deming blamed America's lawyers in part for the problems of American business. The US has more lawyers per capita than any other country in the world. They make their livings to a considerable extent by finding people to sue. Like health care costs, Deming believed the solution to this disease will probably have to come from the government. Appropriate question here are:

- How much does your organization pay for liability insurance every year?

To avoid these diseases management must have its own belief system not only on paper but also to internalize its belief system, understand how these beliefs create dysfunctional behaviors and then embark on a journey to develop new beliefs and behaviors based on the quality body of knowledge. It cannot extract itself from its quandary of managing in the vacuum and things will work out for the best. For educational institutions, these diseases may be looked at as:

1. Placing budgetary considerations ahead of quality in education.
2. Placing schedule considerations ahead of quality education.
3. Placing political considerations ahead of quality in education.
4. Being arrogant.
5. Lacking fundamental knowledge, research or education.
6. Pervasively believing in entitlement and or tenure.
7. Practicing autocratic behaviors, resulting in "endullment."

In educational institutions we also have to worry about what the customers have to say. Much research has been done to identify what each customer cohort (remember there are several customers in education) needs, wants, expects and perceives as "quality education." So much research has been conducted to the point where in some cases there are contradictory results and or unattainable results because of a wrong measurement process.

It has been said that "one can only manage what they measure." In a sense then, we must make sure when we measure needs, wants and expectations from the voice of the customer that the measurement is correct and applicable to what we are trying to figure out. If not, for sure we are going to have wrong measurement that will lead to mismanagement. This of course, is the classic principle of garbage in, garbage out (GIGO) axiom: The wrong inputs or measures will produce erroneous results and lead to misguided conclusions. While most of us take this for granted with regards to computer codes, directions, formulas and numbers, it is amazing how little attention often is paid to this fundamental issue when it comes to capturing and analyzing voice-of-the-customer (VOC) data.

In the case of educational cultures, this wrong measurement has troubled me over the years, but a recent excerpt from *Faster, Cheaper, Better* (Hammer and Hershman, 2010) on the "seven (deadly) sins of corporate measurement" really hit me. I have seen all of these sins committed in various customer loyalty and customer experience programs conducted by major corporations as well as educational institutions. Wrong measurement in many VOC programs threatens to totally undermine the reputed efforts of those programs to strengthen customer loyalty and improve the customer experience. Furthermore when change in the name of "reform" is on the table of change, this wrong information will result in the wrong reform and certainly wrong or unwanted results.

Here are Hammer and Hershman's seven sins, with examples of how they have undercut VOC programs and hinder reform in the educational process.

Vanity: *Picking metrics that are easy to hit and which make managers (administrators) look good.* Not happy with the percentage of top scores they receive, I've seen institutions treat any nonnegative rating as a positive indication of loyalty or use scales that make anything short of the most egregious service failure look like success. This may make the dashboard results look better, but the illusion of excellence isn't excellence.

Provincialism: *Asking customers questions along organizational lines or using internal jargon that has no meaning to them.* Operational definitions may seem mundane, but they make more sense to readers than expecting them to appreciate nuanced differences between service management vs. service delivery or tellers vs. platform personnel. In the case of educational institutions provincialism is not only prevalent but also encouraged through the use of jargon to exclude the appropriate customers from understanding the issues.

Narcissism: *Measure from the institution's perspective, rather than from the customer's.*
On countless occasions I've had institutions of K-12 and post secondary insist that customers were wrong about timing and learning measures. The underlying issue is often different staring points. The firm would track the time to resolve a problem from the point when a service tech contacted the customer or opened a service order. OK, but customers begin marking time when they first call or log the issue (or even from the first moment they experience a problem). Of course, perceived time - even if inaccurate - is ultimately what matters to customers anyway (hence the Disney "magic" of turning wait time into part of the experience). Yet another concern in education is the fact that many educators at all levels think because they are more educated, therefore they "know" the best way to handle things not only in the learning environment but also issues that confront their customers.

Laziness: *Assuming that the institution knows what matters to customers better than customers do.* I battled with a superintendent of a local school district over a policy of expelling students with excessive absenteeism. He argued with me that that was the common general policy. He was viewing the issue as performance criteria for him since he was taking a specific action for a specific infraction. I was arguing that the act was not effective to the student because he was viewing the extra days off as a gift. That is what he was after – no school. Now the student not only does what he wants but more importantly is not learning anything about consequences. The punishment should be commeasurate with the offense and a learning experience to not repeat the offense. That of course would require more investigation and time spent to find exactly what the cause of absenteeism is based on.

Pettiness: *Taking too narrow a scope of a larger issue.* Asking customers about the geographic footprint of their cell service, for example, scarcely captures their sense of the quality and reliability of the service. Too many institutions spend tremendous amounts of time and money on insignificant things or items that are not related to education at all and yet they are the same ones who complain about inefficiencies and ineffectiveness. To be sure it is much easier to focus on petty things than serious and important things. However focusing on pettiness does not help productivity and or accountability.

Inanity: *Losing sight of the consequences of measurement.* If you measure and highlight the number of rooms housekeeping cleans in an hour or the call center turns in a shift, don't be surprised if the numbers you are tracking improve but the guest or customer experience deteriorates. Educational institutions are notorious for this. They measure many things but most of the measurements have nothing to do with learning. They are busy justifying money, time and effort in insignificant issues when the level of
188

educational learning in the United States as compared to the global market is steadily decreasing especially in science and mathematics.

Frivolity: *Failure to take measurement seriously.* This category is where I place many of my concerns about wrong measurement and poorly-designed VOC research, including social media and text analysis for the educational institutions. The *who* (sample or population), *what* (content), *when* (timing), *how* (mode of data collection) and *why* (type of analysis) of measurement need to be clearly understood and driven by business objectives. (Note: "We need to do a survey" is not a business objective. Yet, this is being repeated all the time by so many institutions). These aren't simply technical issues for the data wonks; these are the critical parameters that determine the application and utility of the results. In other words, these are the issues that guard against the garbage-in part of the GIGO problem and perhaps will provide a direction and or even results for reform.

Who, is not an existential question. Rather, it is the practical issue of the people (or parents, households, or organizations, etc.) that are included in the data and the underlying key question: What larger population is the data representative of or projectable to? Is it representative of all customers? Online users only? Those who post comments online only? Customers who came into the system and who participate for credit or not credit learning and who paid themselves or through a third party provider including the government? Or (gulp), do you have no idea how "the who" is defined?

Content may seem easy but how you ask what you ask is anything but. Are respondents answering the questions you intended to ask in a consistent, reliable manner? Do you have the right breadth and depth of inquiry? The *what* issues often bump up against practical concerns about survey real estate and the need to limit the length of the questionnaire.

When often is ignored but time of day, week, month or year can have significant impact on the customer experience, as well as the response rate. This becomes particularly important when it comes to trending.

While you might not have that many options with regards to the *how* of data collection, there is a mode effect (i.e., how you collect the data will affect the data). The mode of data collection also will affect how much you can ask, what you can ask and how you should ask.

Ultimately, the *why* is all about application. How do you plan to analyze and use the data? This is where the research meets the business objectives. In a well-conceptualized engagement, the why is specified up front and determines many of the who, what, when and how issues.

Failure to properly attend to these five measurement parameters will doom the results to the domain of the frivolous, in Hammer and Hershman's terms. In my words, lack of attention to these factors will lead to wrong measurement of VOC and mismanagement of your efforts to improve customer loyalty and the customer experience as well as redefined improvement and educational reform.

Summary

In this chapter we have addressed educational reform in a variety of ways. Our focus has been not only to introduce some changes in the system, but to make drastic changes for both efficiency and effectiveness. We started with some general changes and included the fundamental issues such as rules, resources, incentive programs and curricula. In addition we have discussed some shortcomings that may affect and effect all educational institutions.

References

Breneman, D. and W. Haarlow. (July 1998). *Remediation in Higher Education.* Thomas B. Fordham Foundation. Washington, DC.
Deming, W. E. (1986). *Out of crisis.* MIT. Cambridge, MA.
Gardner, H. (1983). *Frames of Mind: The Theory of Multiple Intelligences.* Basic. NY.
Gardner, H. (1993). *Multiple Intelligences: The Theory in Practice.* Basic. NY.
Gardner, H. (2000). *Intelligence Reframed: Multiple Intelligences for the 21st Century.* Basic. NY.
Greene, J. P. (September 2000). *The Cost of Remedial Education: How Much Michigan Pays When Students Fail to Learn Basic Skills.* Mackinac Center for Public Policy, September 2000). Midland, MI. p. 1.
Hammer, M. and L. Hershman. (2010). *Faster, cheaper, better.* Crown Publishing. NY.
Ladner, M. and M. J. Brouillette. (August 2000). *The Impact of Limited School Choice on School Districts.* The Mackinac Center for Public Policy. Midland, MI.
Petrilli, M. J., C. E. Finn Jr. And F. M. Hess. (January 2009). *Silver Cloud, Dark Lining: Why Obama's Stimulus may retard education reform, and what to do about it.* American Enterprise Institute. Washington, DC.
Phipps, R. (December 1998). *College Remediation: What it is, What it Costs, What's at Stake.* Institute for Higher Education Policy. Washington, DC.
Sternberg, R. J.(April 24, 2009). "A New Model for Teaching Ethical Behavior." The *Chronicle of Higher Education.* Pp. B14-B15.

Selected Bibliography

______ (July 2001). "A New Direction for Education Reform." *Imprimis.* Hillsdale College. Hillsdale, MI.
Armstrong, T. (November 1994). "Multiple Intelligences: Seven Ways to Approach Curriculum." *Educational Leadership.* Pp 43-52.
Brouillette, M. J. (January 2001). *The case for choice in schooling: Restoring parental control of education.* Mackinac Center for Public Policy. Mackinac City, MI.
Carnine, D. (2000). *Why Education Experts Resist Effective Practices (And What It Would Take to Make Education More Like Medicine).* Thomas B. Fordham Foundation. Washington, DC.
Darling-Hammond, L. (1997). *The Right to Learn: A Blueprint for Creating Schools that Work.* Jossey-Bass. San Francisco, CA.
Facione, P. A. (March 20, 2009). "20 Ways for Colleges to Cut Costs and Make Money." *The Chronicle of Higher Education.* Pp. A36-37.
Fain, P. (May 22, 2009). "Q & A: How Governing Boards Can Play a Bigger Role in Strategic Planning." *The Chronicle of Higher Education.* P. A15.
Farkas, S. and J. Johnson. (1997). *Different Drummers: How Teachers of Teachers View Public Education.* Public Agenda. NY.
Finn, C. E. Jr. and M. J. Petrilli. (Eds.). (2000). *The State of State Standards 2000.* Diane Publishing Company. Washington, DC.
Fukuyama, F. (1996). *Trust: The Social Virtues and the Creation of Prosperity.* Free Press. NY.
Hernandez, N. (February 25, 2008). "Some Teachers' Contracts Bind Reforms, Study Says: Agreements in D. C. Region Generally Praised." *The Washington Post.* P. B04.
Hess, F. M. and C. Loup. (February 2008). *The Leadership LIMBO: Teacher Labor Agreements in America's Fifty Largest School Districts.* Fordham Institute. Washington, D.C.
Hirsch, E. D. Jr. (1987). *Cultural Literacy: What Every American Needs to Know.* Vintage. Boston, MA.
Johnson, J. and S. Farkas. (1997). *Getting By: What American Teenagers Really Think About Their Schools.* Public Agenda. NY.
Kliebard, H. (1987). *The Struggle for the American Curriculum.* Routledge and Kegan Paul. NY.

Labi, A. (February 27, 2009). "Germany Provides Higher Education Without The Frills." *The Chronicle of Higher Education.* PP. A18-20.

Lax, H. L. (February 28, 2011). *The seven deadly sins of VOC research.* edition of Quirk's e-newsletter.

Mattimore, P. (February 6, 2009). "5 Fundamental Misconceptions About AP Courses." *The Chronicle of Higher Education.* P. A33.

Tyack, D. and L. Cuban. (1995). *Tinkering Toward Utopia: A century of public school reform.* Harvard University Press. Cambridge, MA.

EPILOGUE

A Greek ancient poet – Pindar – said: That which is silent, dies. However, it seems that everyone is complaining these days about something or other. No jobs, poor quality, no profitability, low salaries/wages, no qualified labor force, education is failing everyone, no specific tools (no silver bullet to universal problems) to solve problems and the litany of complaints goes on and on.

From my experience of over 30 years, as a quality practitioner, academic professional and consultant, I have come to a conclusion that the problems that we address are circumstantial and we really never put our minds to solve them, once and for all. Instead, we look at this and that, we propose this and that, and we forget some of the basic principles as to why we perpetuate these failures no matter what the tool or methodology used. In education we also have to contend with governmental laws and regulations which convolute the entire process. In effect, we keep silent in the hope that the "real" problem(s) will go away. In reality, they never do. Rather they keep on getting worse.

The first and perhaps the most common issue of "forgetting" is the notion of "**regression**." We keep forgetting that if things are left alone they will have a tendency over the long term to regress towards the average. This must happen because the long term average must be maintained unless there is a specific cause for a specific change. So, management knows this and even though nothing is done in any way shape or form things will indeed get better. Therefore, improvement will occur without changing anything.

This is what I have come to call the "**Casablanca principle**." If you remember in the last scenes of the movie *Casablanca*, Rick shot the Nazi officer in front of the French Chief of Police. At that point something remarkable happened. Whereas the audience may think that Rick is in definite trouble, when the police arrived at the scene of the crime, the Chief said "round up the usual suspects." This statement implies quite a lot. Perhaps the most important implication is that the police have done this before.

And so it is with many organizations, including education. Many teachers, staff and employees have seen decrees made by top administrators and the resulting programs that these decrees create. Employees have indeed been jaded and refer to the efforts as the "**flavor of the month**." They keep on watching administrators change programs with little or no real impact. What a waste of time!

The second principle that perpetuates failures is the "**Hawthorne effect**." Many of us are familiar with the famous studies of measuring the productivity of employees under controlling the light condition. However, we keep forgetting the results of the study. If you recall, the results showed that regardless of lumens the productivity increased as long as the employees felt that they were being watched.

And so it is with administrators today. Just because management decrees a specific improvement, to be sure, there is a temporary effect of "watching." After all the Hawthorne studies proved it long ago. When something is watched closely, individuals will have a temporary boost of both productivity and effort that appears to have a "true" performance improvement. That improvement, however, will be temporary.

The third principle that perpetuates failures is the **quotas** and **awards** – the propensity and eagerness to satisfy. The rationale goes something like this: As long as administrators tell me what to do, we will be OK. If management tells me that we need a reduction of scrap, no problem. We will not report as much. If management tells me to reduce safety incidents, no problem. We will report less incidents - the major ones will continue to happen but overall we will reduce the number by not reporting them (not eliminating) the incidents. If management wants less cost, no problem. We will reduce the work force. If management tells me to teach to the test so that grades may be improved, so be it. And so on.

In the case of quality we try to manipulate situations rather than FIX the problems to satisfy a quota and or a reward. We would rather spend millions of dollars in fixing things over and over again, rather than to use systematic approaches to design the right things, right the first time. We are always in a state of a race. There is no denying the fact that as a culture, we are preoccupied with rankings and awards. Rankings, lists, and awards, in that order. From Letterman's Top Ten, to the weekly football polls, through the annual listing of the world's 50 "most beautiful people," our capacity to receive material thus presented seems boundless. If the rankings, lists or awards are in some way certified, so much the better.

In the field of quality we do the same – no surprise, obviously. After all, people in quality are a sample of the total population. We do experience and have similar attitudes as our society. Just like in politics, just like in sports, so too in the quality field we are always looking for the silver bullet and when we find something "reasonable" we push it to the extreme until the next thing comes along. We fail to study and analyze the situation in a rational matter – even though we all claim to be rational.

Manufacturing as we know it in the United States is in major decline, thanks to the policies of the government and the price (not quality) oriented organizations such as Wal-Mart and Home Depot who lead the charge. What is the answer? Certainly not tariffs but well thought out policies and consumer training to recognize the pitfalls of this ever bleeding course. The politicians think that tariffs are the answer. However, the changes will benefit those with the deepest pockets who can afford to buy access to politicians. In any event, these actions will not solve the problem but rather redirect it and create more problems as severe or worse down the road. Case in point: The customer is not helped with a call center in India to respond to problems. However, it could help the customer if organizations would take the time to fix problems and therefore there is no need for the call center to begin with. Now that would be a novel approach to quality improvement.

By the same token education is also in decline. Why? This is so because we do not emphasize excellence. Rather we practice mediocrity. We focus on legalistic approaches to fairness of learning rather than individual excellence. We focus on making sure that no one is special rather than cultivating that individual who excels. We do not want to hurt anyone's feelings and as a consequence we see mediocrity everywhere. (Of course, there are some exceptions but very seldom). The result of this decline is that going from number one in educational excellence about 30 years ago, now we trail far behind the leaders from other countries. The funny part is that we pretend that the decline does not exist.

So who is responsible for these declines? We believe that the leadership of the organization not only sets the tone for behavior and execution of policies but also provides the vehicle of appropriate and applicable road map (as part of the vision of the organization) for that tone and execution. It is imperative to make a strong distinction between leaders and managers. Managers aim to shift balances of power toward solutions acceptable as compromises among conflicting values. Leaders on the other hand, develop fresh approaches to long standing problems and open issues to few options.

Therefore, to be an effective and responsible leader in any organization/institution the individual must project their ideas onto images that excite people. Leaders work from high risk positions and indeed they are often temperamentally disposed to seek out risk, and danger especially where the opportunity for high rewards appear promising. This is in total contrast to the managers who have a survival instinct that dominates the need for risk, and the ability to tolerate mundane, and practical work. (It must be emphasized here that when leaders lower their vision and react to mundane work they do it as part of an "affliction" rather than vision). So the question of "how do we fix problems correctly" has been around for a long time. Much has been written about it and to this date no one has found "the" right tool or methodology that solves every problem every time.

194

So the question of "how do we fix problems correctly" perhaps is the wrong question. What we should be asking is "how can we make real (measurable) improvement happen?" The two questions are drastically different and require different approaches to resolve them. The first is absolute and direct, the second is evolutionary and indirect. However, both depend on the scientific method which is: to identify the problem, to analyze the data, select solution and recommend a solution. [The reader should notice that there are many variations of this in the real world and all of them work pretty much the same. Typical examples of variations are the PDC(S)A which is the simplest and the six sigma approach which is more convoluted and technical].

To show this improvement one may use statistical and non-statistical methodologies. In this book we have tried to address both from an overview perspective. Specifically, we have tried to discuss some issues with the current education process from K-12 and post secondary education. We have indeed said that many problems exist and we do need to fix them in the short and long term. Certainly, we have not suggested or implied that education is a thing of the past. On the other hand, we have identified quite a few areas of improvement including the application of quality methodology in the educational system.

One of the key points that we have tried to emphasize is that education isn't just about where we get our resources. It's about our role in the world, about the communities we serve. And that role is something the public must continue to support. That support may be with participation in all avenues that the educational process offers (government regulations, taxation, parent involvement, employers and so on). We focused on sustainability and making good citizens as a result of a good education. In essence we recognized that today's students at any level will be the leaders of tomorrow. It is imperative then, that a good solid education is part of their lives and seen as an investment in their own future.

As any investment, so too education needs funding. We have explored that issue and we have offered several options recognizing that in the past, most of the budget in any institution came from a governmental entity (city, state or federal government). Today and in the future most of that burden (funding) is on the student or the student's family.

We also have recognized and addressed our changing world with its new technology. Today's students live in a different world than the one many of us grew up in. Fifty years ago, the public good of all education was widely understood, broadly proclaimed, and accepted. Today, we have a mind set of both educators and students that is quite different than the past not only in different States but also within states as well.

Educators claim that they do not have enough time to teach, students are not willing to work hard, they are underpaid and the litany of complaints is too long to record here. On the other hand, students claim that the curriculum is too boring, the information learned is irrelevant and the list is also too long to record here. Recognizing that something is obviously wrong, we have attempted to address these issues with a quality methodology in "fixing" these problems with alternatives, accountability and responsibility for each sector in the educational process.

Above all in this book we have emphasized the need for "quality thinking" in the educational process. We have introduced some key elements of education but we also have elaborated on several key methodologies such as total quality management, six sigma, lean and others and have provided templates, forms and implementation strategies as to how and where improvement may be introduced not only now but in the future as well.

Despite our scientific achievements, western society has allowed itself to be held hostage by doomsayers and politicians eager to gain advantage. We live in a country where citizens live longer, healthier lives than ever before, pollution levels continue to decline despite greater economic activity, and yet we have convinced ourselves the end is near. It probably is, but only because we have chosen to chase false presuppositions that will save us from an impending disaster that will never come.

While in most cases, we are able to be "traditional," there are alternatives if the situation warrants. Regardless, the analyst has a basic responsibility: validate, validate, validate, and then analyze and interpret with confidence.

Yes, indeed we have found the enemy. The enemy is us. And so it is with the tools and methodologies that both administrators and politicians introduce every so often. They think that the new law or regulation; tool or methodology will solve the problem, where in fact the only thing that they do, is buy time. All laws, tools, methodologies and the three just mentioned principles (regression, Hawthorne and quota/reward) will guarantee improvement. But that improvement is arbitrary and at best temporary. If you are lucky and move up the ladder of success you will not get in the whirlpool of deception, because the recorded improvement will surely disappear and you will be far removed from having to explain the failure again.

We all know that politics is the art of making the possible difficult, and the impossible law. However, as long as educational organizations - both profit and not for profit – exist, they will be looking for loopholes to entice you to buy their products and or services based on "some" quality. That quality we suggest must be based on legitimate improvement and must be validated over time. Nothing else will do. This depends on leadership.

Leadership is indeed a factor to the way of perceiving a situation and the way an organization is being administered. However, with so many things being devalued now days, it is no surprise that even leaders "talk" without "actions." Let us take the issue of the current fads on ethnicity and cultural diversity.

No one will deny the fact that a diverse make up in an industry and especially in education is better and healthier for everyone. Yet, year after year lack of diversity is observed and reported in many organizations. Where is the evolution that these "noble" thoughts preach? By the same token whereas diversity provides a "different" and perhaps a "unique" approach to problems, whatever happened to the notion of the "best" person for the job?

No one will deny that jobs are moving abroad, but what are the political leaders doing? They pour fuel into the debate with picking on organizations rather than fixing the laws that allow the organizations to bleed and eventually leave the country. No one will deny that the best students from all over the world are not coming to this country any more. No one will deny that graduates are not satisfied with what they have learned and how they can use their knowledge for a better life for themselves and their family.

No one will deny that "cheap" anything sells, but in order to have something "cheap" you must also produce it "cheap." In this country we are not willing to have lower cost of living at the expense of lower wages. However, we continually fail to recognize that by buying "cheap" from overseas eventually there is not going to be anyone who has a comfortable income to buy anything.

In the case of education we do the same thing. We emphasize budgets, cost rather than learning and excellence. We have created a class of graduates that for all intended purposes are less than what they should be. We have universities that offer remedial classes for classes that should have been taken in high school. And we have programs for degrees that are non functional in the real world. Yet, we have the local school board happy that they have a set number of graduates and a university happy for accommodating learning. Everyone is happy but the education itself is at risk, not to mention it costs much more if everyone is not doing what they are supposed to be doing – this is classic rework at its best! In addition, most of the professional degrees such as Law, Medicine, Teachers, Nurses and others have to be certified by other entities – usually the State – which implies that the institutions of higher learning are failing miserably to educate their students with a standardized education in the appropriate field of the student's choice.

196

No one will deny that quality problems exist in all organizations, including educational ones, but most organizations try to cover them up and pretend to solve them by using the latest fads in tools and methodologies. Furthermore, most of the organizations continue to focus on appraising methods rather than the planning for quality methodologies. They have become content to deal in warranty costs (in the case of education we deal with costs of remedial studies) rather than design for the customer. They have become complacent to customer complaints rather than delighting the customer. Quite often some of the problems in education are viewed as political and as a consequence laws are passed to close the gaps. However, the intent of the law may be acceptable but in most cases the law presents its own problems of interpretation and implementation.

No one will deny that quality is a major salient characteristic for any product or service, but most organizations do not really feel that way. How else can one interpret the amount of money that so many educational organizations spend on items that are not directly related to improving education itself? How can one explain the lack of quality, even though programs like TQM, Six Sigma, Lean, and so many others come in with such a great hope and gusto and then give away to something else? Major companies praise these programs and within a short period of time these same companies have the same problems as before? Is the reason perhaps one of the three principles that we discussed earlier? Or is it non-commitment of the leader? We suspect it is both! However, with a strong and visionary leader things can improve.

It is the leader's function then to make sure that the organization/institution has a vision that meets customer's needs and that a real partnership between all stakeholders of the organization/institution exist and are being followed. It is the leaders function to be aware of the three principles and try to identify real avenues of action that will improve "the" real process and profitability of the organization. When the leaders "walk the talk" they become the beacons, of what they are supposed to be. That is: Innovators, Motivators, Coaches and "true" Leaders. See Figure E.1. It is possible. It is doable. The only thing that prevents this from happening is commitment to "excellence." Are you on board? If you are, get ready for an exhilarating positive experience. Hopefully in this book we have given you something to think about.

We have echoed the proclamation of many that education in its current form is not sustainable and have attempted to give some basic solutions that may be used in all areas of education. We hope that we have been successful in at least making the reader aware of the need to change and how that change may be implemented given quality thinking a chance. We hope that by addressing these issues we will not fall victim of Pindar's line that we will die in silence.

Figure E.1. Leadership cycle

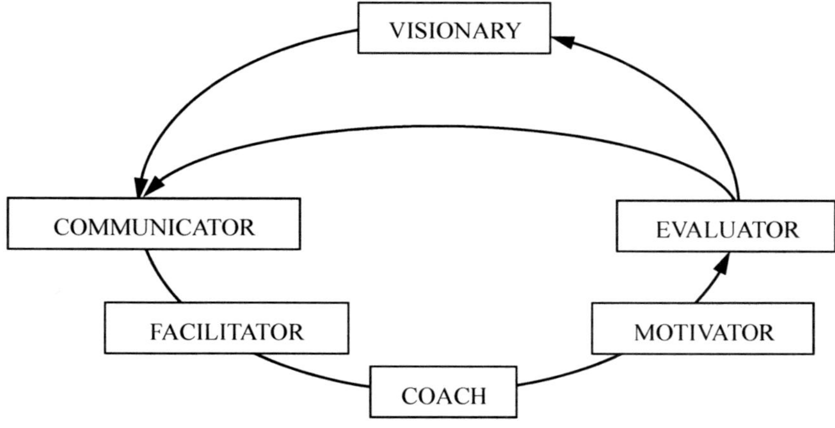

APPENDIX A

PLANNING GUIDE FOR DEVELOPING THE SCHOOL IMPROVEMENT PLAN

As we already mention in the text, a new format for School Improvement Plans reduces fragmentation by incorporating all school planning efforts into a single document. Successful school improvement planning is a collaborative process involving all school constituencies - administrators, teachers, support staff, parents, community and students (as appropriate). Active participation of all constituencies enhances creativity, personal ownership and commitment.

We believe that School improvement planning, program implementation and evaluation are essential to transforming our schools so that any School District, in any urban and non-urban environment to successfully educate all of its students. The School Improvement Plan provides the basic framework for all schools to improve student learning consistent with the District's Design for Excellence program. The *plan is a pledge* made between all school constituencies (administrators, teachers, support staff, parents, community and students) to engage in self-renewal through a continued search for improvement and excellence while fully implementing the contents of this (X-year) school improvement planning document.

Each school will develop a (Secific X-year) plan for implementation from September, XXXX through June, YYYY. The plan will clearly describe the school mission, objectives, improvement strategies, and other key attributes of the school that support the attainment of the District mission. For example: "The XYZ Public Schools will be the first large urban school district to successfully educate all of its students."

The School Improvement Plan incorporates all major school planning efforts into a single document. The plan includes Design for Excellence priorities, Public Act 25 requirements, Chapter 1 Schoolwide Plans, Chapter 1/Article 3 Program Improvement Plans, XYZ Compact objectives, student documentation portfolios, and state and federal compliance requirements including those for handicapped students (Section 504), special education and bilingual education. Plans will be reviewed and updated quarterly based on school needs assessment and evaluation data.

The key ingredient for successful development and implementation of a plan is the ongoing collaboration of all major school constituencies - students, staff (administrators, teachers, support staff), parents and community. Collectively, these constituencies can make a powerful difference in improving student learning. Further, the process of shared decision making builds personal ownership and commitment for those involved.

The school improvement planning process employs the same six steps that schools have used in the development of previous school plans.

- Collaborating - teaming and cooperation of all major school constituencies for both plan development and implementation;
- Assessing - determining needs based on an analysis of school data;
- Researching - reviewing literature and best practices, especially research on effective schools and effective teaching;
- Writing - completing the plan by including the mission, objectives, implementation plans, evaluation measures, professional development plan and other required components;
- Implementing - sharing the plan with the school community and carrying out the plan consistent with specified actions and responsibilities;

- Monitoring and evaluating - regularly checking plan implementation progress and collecting information for making ongoing decisions on what to keep, stop or revise (at least quarterly).

Upon completion of the plan, schools will be asked to publish a document which informs students and community about the school and includes, but is not limited to, the components of the plan and is consistent with Public Act 25 requirements. Therefore, in this appendix we provide the reader with a typical three-year cursory School Improvement Plan – based on Michigan's Public Act 25 – for a typical school district. The plan describes how a School District may pursue the mission, goals and objectives identified in a Design for Excellence program.

1. Mission

Guideline: Develop a school mission which clearly communicates the beliefs and expectations of the school relative to student learning and the learning environment and addresses excellence, equity and diversity. The school mission must support the attainment of the District Mission. For example: "The XYZ Public Schools will be the first large urban school district to successfully educate all of its students."

Guideline Development Activities
1. Discuss the three essential parts of a Mission:
   - *Beliefs* - Expressions of the school's fundamental values, its ethical code, its overriding convictions, its inviolate commitments (the ultimate "why" behind every action);
   - *Purpose* - The reason why the school exists; the determination or resoluteness of staff, parents and community;
   - *Promise* - The accountability piece, a declaration of assurance that specific results will occur.
2. Through a collaborative process of staff, parents and community, identify interests, strengths, and weaknesses of the overall school program and use this information as a basis for developing or refining the school mission.
3. Through discussion, be sure that all constituent groups see the role they serve in fulfilling the mission.

SAMPLE
The staff of School is dedicated to the belief that all students can learn in the positive and caring environment which we offer. Our purpose is to establish a ring of cooperation between the child, the home, and the school. We are committed to ensure that every child will develop their academic, social, creative and physical abilities. We will instill in our students an appreciation for learning as a lifelong process, and will increase their awareness of the world community and responsibility to it.

2. Objectives Based on Design for Excellence

Guideline: Select improvement areas and establish measurable three-year school objectives, based on school needs assessment data, which support the attainment of District objectives in all four goal areas of Design for Excellence: (1) Create Schools of the Future, (2) Ensure Management/Organizational Effectiveness, (3) Guarantee Student Success, and (4) Build Community Confidence. Number the objectives 1.1, 1.2, 2.1, 2.2, etc.

At least one objective must be established for each of District Goals 1, 2 and 4. Objectives must be established for all Goal 3 objectives. Other student outcome objectives may also be established based on school identified needs. XYZ Compact schools should include Compact objectives.

200

School objectives must support the attainment of (specific year) District targets listed below and annual targets set by the General Superintendent and area superintendents. Continuous improvement is expected of all schools. Because all school levels impact the dropout rate, all schools (elementary, middle, high, special education) must include an objective designed to reduce the four-year dropout rate. Example of 2011 District Targets may be as follows:

•	MEAP Reading (% Category 3)	50
•	MEAP Mathematics (% Satisfactory)	50
•	MEAP Science (% Category 4)	50
•	CAT Reading (% At or Above Grade Level)	50
•	CAT Mathematics (% At or Above Grade Level)	50
•	Four-Year Dropout Rate (%)	15
•	Student Daily Attendance Rate (%)	95
•	Staff Attendance (No. Schools at 96%+)	180

Guideline Development Activities
1. Collect and analyze data for determining school improvement needs.
   - Review Design for Excellence objectives for all four goal areas.
   - Examine School Progress Report data for the current school year and the previous two years.
   - Generate other school improvement needs through collaborative planning by staff, parents, community, and students (as applicable).
   - Conduct an in-depth analysis of school data for MEAP, CAT, student attendance, and other areas of school improvement focus for the next three years.
   - Disaggregate data to determine the extent to which subsets of students are attaining learning objectives, e.g., racial/ethnic groups, gender, and socioeconomic status (free and reduced lunch eligibility).
2. Select improvement areas and establish objectives for the next three years based on the school's needs assessment.
   - Identify improvement areas for all four goal areas of Design for Excellence: Examples: (1) XYZ District Compact, (2) reading, (3) staff development, (4) parent and community participation.
   - Write measurable three-year objectives which support the attainment of at least one objective each for Goals 1, 2 and 4 and all Goal 3 objectives. Area superintendents may establish school targets for Goal 3 Objectives.
   - Additional student outcome objectives may be written based on school identified needs.
   - Objectives should be written using the acronym SMART:
     - **S**pecific (states clearly what will be accomplished),
     - **M**easurable (states how well it will be accomplished),
     - **A**ttainable (can be accomplished by "stretching"),
     - **R**elevant (responds to district priorities),
     - **T**ime Frame (specifies when it will be accomplished).
3. Determine the evaluation measure(s) that will be used for verifying how well each objective is achieved, e.g., attendance data, test results.

SAMPLE
1. Improvement Area: Student Attendance
   - Objective: By June 2011, the student daily attendance rate will increase from 90 to 94 percent.
   - Evaluation Measure(s): Student Daily Attendance Rate results on School Progress Reports.
2. Improvement Area: Mathematics

- Objective: By June 2011, the percent of students who attain California Achievement Test scores in mathematics at or above grade level will increase from 40 to 48 percent.
  - Evaluation Measure(s): California Achievement Test results.
3. Improvement Area: Parent and Community Participation
   - Objective: By June 2011, parent/community participation in school support activities will increase by at least 30 percent in the following areas: parent-teacher conferences, school volunteers, School Improvement Team attendance, LSCO attendance, parent signing of school support contracts, and business/community human and financial support for the school.
   - Evaluation Measure(s): Pre- and post- school data for all specified improvement areas.

3. Curriculum to attain student learning outcomes

GUIDELINE
State the school theme or special curriculum focus that makes your school an attractive choice for students and parents.
Complete a curriculum assessment of subjects and courses for each grade level. Identify gaps in the curriculum which must be addressed to ensure equitable learning opportunities for all students.

Ensure that the curriculum is inclusive for diverse populations, aligned with District objectives, supports the attainment of District Goal 3 objectives, and fully implements District core curriculum outcomes as they are developed.

Guideline Development Activities
1. Indicate the theme or special focus of your school.
2. Examine the curriculum and complete a curriculum profile to determine if the subjects and courses being offered will enable the school to guarantee that students are receiving the instruction necessary to achieve academic success and that the core curriculum is being implemented.
3. List subjects and courses and the grades at which they are taught.
4. Identify gaps in the curriculum which must be addressed to ensure equitable learning opportunities for all students.

SAMPLE
The special curriculum focus of School X is ... .

CURRICULUM ASSESSMENT

Subjects/courses	Grades taught	Gaps
Language Arts		
Specific ones		
Mathematics		
Specific ones		
Science		
Specific ones		
World Studies		
Specific ones		
Arts		

Specific ones		
Health/Physical education		
Career and Employment		
Technology		
Life Management		
Cultural and Aesthetic Awareness		
Other		
Gaps in the school curriculum which must be addressed to ensure equitable learning opportunities for all students include …		

4. Special programs

GUIDELINE
List all special programs available in your school for improving student learning and indicate which school objective(s) each special program supports.

Guideline Development Activities
1. Conduct a survey among staff and the community to determine the number and kind of programs offered in the school.
2. Create a list, based on the survey, which is referenced to school objectives.
3. Identify which, if any, of your key objectives are not supported by special programs.

SAMPLE

Program	Objectives Supported
After School Tutoring	3.1 Reading Improvement
	3.2 Mathematics Improvement
Science Fair Club	1.1 Science Choice School
	3.3 Science Improvement
Parent Workshop	Parent Improvement

5. Student, Staff and Parent Responsibilities

GUIDELINE
Describe and/or list the responsibilities of students, staff and parents for guaranteeing student success. These responsibilities should relate to such areas as attendance, homework, student behavior, and classroom and home support. Include school policies, guidelines, and rules, if appropriate.

Guideline Development Activities
1. Convene a committee of staff, students and parents to generate a list of responsibilities.
2. Send a sample of the list to each constituency for input.

3. Incorporate items that generate agreement in handbooks and other communications distributed to staff, students and parents.

SAMPLE

Parent Responsibilities:
> Set aside a time and a quiet place for study daily and ensure that homework assignments are completed.

Staff Responsibilities:
> Communicate through word and action the expectation that all students can and will be successful learners.

Student Responsibilities:
> Attend school regularly, on time, and prepared to learn to the best of their ability.

6. Monitoring and Evaluation

GUIDELINE

Describe the school procedure for continuous monitoring and evaluation of school progress and the process for modifying the school plan and/or its implementation for ongoing school renewal. Regular monitoring of plan implementation is essential for school success. Checkpoints for reviewing school progress should occur at least quarterly.

Evaluation measures for school objectives are to be specified in each of the implementation plans within the School Improvement Plan.

A year-end Annual Educational Report of school progress will be prepared by each school consistent with applicable law. For example in the State of Michigan is Public Act 25 requirements.

Guideline Development Activities

1. Develop a monitoring schedule that indicates checkpoints at which internal observations will occur and when data will be collected to assess progress.
2. Identify clearly the persons who will monitor and the types of data required.
3. Develop a system for analysis and sharing of observation and progress data and making decisions on what to keep, stop or revise.
4. Consistent with applicable laws such as the P.A. 25 requirements, report school progress annually to the school community as part of the school's Annual Educational Report.

SAMPLE

1. Monitoring of the School Improvement Plan will be conducted by members of the School Improvement Team and the administration quarterly.
2. Classroom visitations will be made at random by administrators.
3. Data such as student attendance, performance indicators in reading, mathematics and science and program implementation status reports will be collected, analyzed and returned to teachers.
4. Evaluations will be conducted in May using data from standardized tests, observations and status reports.
5. A performance assessment process will be piloted in reading in 2010-11, mathematics in 2011-12 and science in 2012-13.

7. Accreditation Status

GUIDELINE
Specify the accreditation status of the school and timeline for implementation, consistent with applicable law e.g. Public Act 25 requirements. Include the type of accreditation as applicable and appropriate (e.g. Michigan Accreditation Program, North Central Association traditional or outcomes based).

Schools seeking accreditation for example through the Michigan Accreditation Program are required to have at least one cognitive, one affective and one school climate objective. Schools seeking outcomes based accreditation through the North Central Association are required to have at least three cognitive and two affective objectives.

Guideline Development Activities
1. Discuss with staff and parents the state requirements for accreditation and the school's current status and future plans regarding accreditation.
    a. Describe the state accreditation requirements.
    b. Discuss the links between state outcomes accreditation and applicable law such as P.A. 25 requirements.
    c. Review the school's 2010-11 XYZ P.A. 25 School Survey, Part II: School Accreditation.
    d. Review the accreditation section in the school's 2009-10 Annual Educational Report.
    e. Review the school's current status and future plans regarding accreditation.
2. Write a narrative to explain the school's current status in the accreditation process including the timeline for implementation.

SAMPLE
XYZ School is not currently involved in an accreditation program. We plan to begin participation in the Michigan Accreditation Program (MAP) process by the
________ school year.

8. Student enrollment procedures

GUIDELINE
This section is to be completed by schools designated as "specialized schools" for Public Act 25 Annual Educational Report purposes, e.g., public schools of choice, development centers, special education schools.

Describe the school's student enrollment procedures. Include information on student recruitment, application criteria, and student selection process.

Guideline Development Activities
Do this section if the school completes a "specialized schools" description for the school's Annual Educational Report as required under Public Act 25, e.g., public schools of choice, development centers, special education schools.

* Describe the school's student enrollment procedures by including information on student recruitment, application criteria, and student selection process.

SAMPLE
Students at ________ are recruited from throughout the school district by ________. Applications, obtained from ________, must be submitted to ________ by ________. Application criteria for admission include ________. Students are selected based on ________.

9. Building level integrated decision making

GUIDELINE
Describe the process used in your school to make decisions. Indicate constituencies represented and roles performed. Be sensitive to the fact that in integrated decision making the most effective decisions are made at the appropriate level of the organization (administrators, teachers, support staff, parents, community, students).

Empowered schools also complete the following information:

There are several decision making responsibilities which empowered schools may seek authority to carry out. Based on the readiness of the school, specify those responsibilities for which the school is requesting building level authority. Following are examples of responsibilities for school consideration.	
Staff hiring, rewards, assignments, evaluation, transfers, sanctions, salary, discipline Building security Teacher substitutes Staff development Selection of and contracting for texts, learning materials, equipment Teaching and student learning Budgeting Pupil transportation Attendance services Psychological services School volunteers, student mentors, school partners and compacts Management of grant funds	Building and grounds operation, maintenance, improvement Payroll services and benefits Curriculum development Assessment of student work, mastery performance Program evaluation Support services Data processing Social work Specialized aides Food Services Purchasing Audiovisual and computer equipment and services
Schools choosing to carry out any of the above authorities must continue to meet all state and federal compliance regulations.	

Guideline Development Activities
1. Identify how each major school constituency is involved in the school decision making process - administrators, teachers, support staff, parents, community, and students.
2. Indicate school organizational structures which involve school constituencies in making decisions, e.g., school cabinet, school improvement team, staff meetings, parent organization of record, student council, staff and community surveys and communications.
3. Discuss with staff, parents and community the decision making process used in the school and modify, as needed, based on their input.
4. Ensure that decisions are made at the appropriate level of the organization for maximizing their impact on improving student learning.

Empowered schools also complete the section relating to decision making responsibilities for which the school is requesting building level authority to carry out.

206

1. Review the *all* responsibilities for which the school might consider requesting building level decision making authority.
2. Involve all school constituencies in determining those responsibilities for which the school will request building level decision making authority including the anticipated role of each constituency in carrying them out.

SAMPLE
All major school constituencies - administrators, teachers, support staff, parents, community, students - are actively involved in school decision making processes through various forums.
- Administrators, teachers, support staff, parents, community, and students participate actively as members of the School Improvement Team which meets monthly as a full team, biweekly in subcommittees, and reports regularly to the full staff and the school's LSCO.
- Our Local School Community Organization (LSCO) meets monthly to receive updates on school progress and to provide input into school decisions impacting student learning and the school learning environment.
- Teachers and other staff wishing to make recommendations for school change do so by ...
- Student involvement and support for decisions in which they have interest and concern is attained by ...

Empowered schools only:
________ School is requesting building level authority for the following decision making responsibilities:
- Budgeting
- Purchasing

10. District policy and union contract waivers

GUIDELINE
State the District policies and contract provisions for which the school is seeking waivers.
All schools are entitled to request waivers of District policies and union contract provisions that are not in conflict with state and federal laws.

Guideline Development Activities
1. Determine District policies and contract provisions, which if changed, could result in improved learning of students.
2. Identify the relative advantages and disadvantages of requesting waivers for the identified policies and contract provisions including the ease or difficulty of school implementation of the changes.
3. Specify the District policies and contract provisions for which the school will request waivers.
4. Submit a written request to the area superintendent for waivers of specified District policies or contract provisions.

SAMPLE
________ School is requesting waivers of the following District policies and contract provisions:
- Student Report Card Marks - Change academic subject marks from A-F to A-C and I (Incomplete) for all except the final marking period. Students receiving an "I" will attend twice weekly tutorials after school until they receive A-C marks.
  or
- School is not requesting any waivers of District policies and contract provisions.

11. Budget

GUIDELINE
List the school's current year budget allocation and estimated three-year budget (multiply by 3). Include Board funding, Chapter 1, Article 3, grants, etc. Note: Beginning with the 2009-10 school year, Board monies for schools are based on a per pupil allocation.

Guideline Development Activities
1. List the amounts allocated to the school for the current school year in the following categories: Board funds, Chapter 1 funds, Article 3 funds, grants, other funding sources, and total school allocation. Also list the school's estimated three-year budget (multiply by 3).
2. Review the total budget to ensure that all funding is coordinated to directly impact the attainment of Design for Excellence objectives and objectives in the School Improvement Plan.
3. Ensure that funds are specifically allocated for carrying out improvement strategies in implementation plans of the School Improvement Plan.

SAMPLE

	Current year budget	Estimated three-year budget (Multiplied by 3)
Board Funds: Chapter 1 funds: Article 3 funds Grants: Other (specify)	$	$
TOTAL	$	$

12. Parent/Community involvement

GUIDELINE
Describe how parents and community are included in the development and implementation of school improvement efforts consistent with the District's Policy for the 20XX (be specific as to the year), Chapter 1 Parent Involvement Policies, and Individualized Educational Plan requirements for special education students.

Indicate the type of parent organization of record which is operational in the school - LSCO, PTSA or PTA. Consistent with the applicable law such as Public Act 25 requirements relating to parent -teacher conferences, state the number and percent of students during the school year who had a parent or guardian attend one or more face-to-face-meetings with a school educator for the purpose of improving learning for that student.

Improvement strategies for Goal 4 implementation plans must show how parents and community will be actively involved in supporting the attainment of school learning objectives.

Guideline Development Activities
1. Review and adhere to Policy for the specific year.
2. Review and adhere to Guidelines concerning Parent Involvement.
3. Review Public Act 25 School Survey "Parent-Teacher Conferences" definition and directions.

4. Appoint parents to the School Improvement Team and other committees that are convened to implement a strong viable program for students.
5. Distribute PA 25 Parent/Teacher Conferences form.
6. Develop method for logging Parent/Teacher Conference participants.
7. Review the Individualized Educational Planning Committee (IEPC) process with staff.
8. Distribute copies of Parent's Guidebook and other forms related to the IEPC process.

SAMPLE
The parent organization of record for XYZ School is the (LSCO, PTA or PTSA, select one). Consistent with the District's Policy for the 20XX, Chapter 1 Parent Involvement Policies, and Individualized Educational Plan requirements for special education students, parents and community are an integral part of all committees charged with school improvement and the attainment of school objectives. Thirty percent of our School Improvement Team is composed of parent and community members. Community representatives are welcomed to join the parent organization of record.

There are four parent-teacher conferences to discuss improving learning for students. During the 2009-10 school year, 695 of our 771 students had a parent or guardian attend one or more face-to-face meetings with a school educator for the purpose of improving learning, a participation rate of 90 percent. (A previous year may be used as a benchmark).

13. Collaborative partnerships

GUIDELINE
State how school volunteers function in the school including numbers, types, and roles.

List school community partnerships supporting school improvement efforts, e.g., compacts, health and social agencies, universities, businesses.

Guideline Development Activities
1. Determine the programs that would be enhanced by volunteers.
2. Contact available agencies, businesses and universities in the community to solicit human, material and/or financial resources to support school goals and objectives.
3. Match available resources in appropriate areas based on compatibility and need.

SAMPLE
There are twelve volunteers that assist the school in providing individualized assistance to students and maintaining a safe and orderly climate. Three volunteers are assigned on a rotating basis to classrooms, three are assigned to lunch duty, three are assigned (one each) to the reading laboratory, computer laboratory and library, and three are assigned to the halls and bathrooms.
We are pleased to have collaborative partnerships with A, B and C companies. These companies have committed financial and human resources to assist us in achieving our goals.

14. School progress reports

GUIDELINE
Attach a copy of at least two previous years final school progress reports and the most recent school progress report for this school year.

Guideline Development Activities
1. Gather baseline data including School Progress Reports.

2. Assess the data, e.g.:

MEAP	2008-9	2009-10	2010-11
Reading	25	19	18
Mathematics	NA	8	10
Science	20	32	26

3. Observations: Decreasing Reading scores, improving in Mathematics but stiff low, unstable Science score
4. Develop the School Improvement Plan based on the data reviewed.
5. Attach a copy of the final school progress reports for the previous two years and the most recent school progress report for this school year.

SAMPLE
School Progress Report – Final Report
2010-11 Total School   Principal: ______________

Objectives			Status Profile				School Grades Total Enrolment Spec. Ed.		
	2009-2010 results	2010-2011 targets	1ˢᵗ report	2ⁿᵈ report	3ʳᵈ report	Final report	Status	Profile	Standards
MEAP (%) Reading category (3) Mathematics (Satisfactory) Science (category 4) CAT (At/above Gr. Level % Reading Mathematics Grade point average (GPA) Student Code Violation (%) Student Daily Attendance Rate (%)									
Status									
Support Objectives									
Parent School of Choice (%) Approved Positions Budgeted (%) Perm. Personnel Fill Approved Position (%) Staff Daily Attendance Rate (%) On-time Del. Text, Sup. And Mat. (Gr. Avg.) Sch. Clean, Safe and Phys. Cond. (Gr. Avg.) Balanced Budget (% Diff. Rev./Expend.) Community Confidence (%)									
Overall Status									

15. Implementation plans

GUIDELINE
Develop a separate implementation plan for each school objective, except where a single plan might be applicable for two objectives, e.g., MEAP and CAT Reading; MEAP and CAT Mathematics. List improvement strategies for attaining the objectives, strategy rationales, responsibilities, resources to be used, a timeline of beginning and completion dates, and funding sources. Wherever possible, the improvement strategies should be research based.

Improvement strategies for attaining Goal 3 student outcome objectives must address how the academic learning of all students will be accelerated - low achieving, moderate achieving, high achieving - and including handicapped (Section 504), special education and bilingual students.

Improvement strategies should also support District implementation of the African Centered/Multicultural infusion plan, student pre-referral planning practices including school based intervention assistance teams, and student documentation portfolios.

Guideline Development Activities
1. List content Improvement Area.
2. Examine current achievement for the content area.
3. Establish the percent of projected growth by comparing current status with prior years and District's expectations.
4. Write a measurable Objective stating expected percentage of growth.
5. Indicate Evaluation Measure(s).
6. Review, discuss and brainstorm with staff, team members, parents, and others, current school practices, procedures, programs, resources and services to determine their measured effectiveness (related to low, moderate and high achievers).
7. Share current research/reform efforts related to instructional programs and practices.
8. Identify specific program strategies designed to address low, moderate and high achieving students.
9. List improvement strategies, strategy rationales, responsibilities, resources to be used, a timeline of beginning and completion dates, and funding sources.

SAMPLE

IMPROVEMENT AREA: 3 READING
OBJECTIVE:
      3.1 By June 2011, the percent of students attaining Category 3, (satisfactory) status on the MEAP reading test will increase from 40 to 65 percent.
      3.2 By June 2011, the percent of students who attain the California Achievement Test scores in reading at or above grade level will increase from 40 to 50 percent.
EVALUATION MEASURE(S): Michigan Educational Assessment Program Test
      California Achievement Test

Improvement Strategies	Strategy Rationale	Person(s) Responsible	Resources to be used	Time Line	Check Funding Sources		
					Bd.	Ch.1/Art. 3	Other
Identify reading categories tested on the MEAP test and the students' relative achievement in each category.	Identify clearly the proportion of the population at low, moderate and satisfactory levels.	Principal, teachers	MEAP test, test results	9/2008; 9/2009; 9/2010 9/2011	X	X	X
Identify reading skills tested on the California Achievement Test and the students' relative achievement in each skill area.	Identify clearly the proportion of the population at low, moderate and satisfactory levels.	Principal, teachers	CAT test, test results	9/2008; 9/2009; 9/2010 9/2011	X	X	X
Incorporate effective informational text strategies and other reading trategies (KWL, OAR, SQ3R) which address identified student learning needs.	Coordinate school efforts to incorporate effective informa-tional text and other reading strategies in all content areas.	Principal, teachers	MEAP test, CAT test, Textbooks and other instructional materials	9/2008; 9/2009; 9/2010 9/2011	X	X	X

16. Charter 1/Article 3

GUIDELINE

All Chapter 1/Article 3 services and activities, including Chapter 1 School wide Plans and Chapter 1/Article 3 Program Improvement Plans, are integral parts of the School Improvement Plan.

For any newly designated Chapter 1 School wide schools, the School Improvement Plan will be the school wide plan.

All schools, whose aggregate normal curve equivalent (NCE) gain for Chapter 1/Article 3 students in reading and/or mathematics is 2.0 or less, are required to develop a one-year Chapter 1/Article 3 Program Improvement Plan. The plan is to be included in this section of the School Improvement Plan. In compliance with state requirements, the school will prepare a duplicate copy of the school's Chapter 1/Article 3 Program Improvement Plan and Professional Development Plan for forwarding to the state.

Guideline Development Activities
1. All Chapter 1/Article 3 Schools.
   - Secure school's Chapter 1 and Article 3 budgets and program descriptions.
   - List all Chapter 1 and Article 3 funded academic and support services being provided.
   - Include these services among the strategies of the Implementation Plan, (#15)
2. New Chapter 1 School wide Schools.
   - Check the school's Implementation Plans (#15) for strategies that address students achieving below grade level in reading and mathematics.

- Complete the Chapter 1 school wide budget page.
- Send a copy of the School Improvement Plan with the Chapter 1 budget page to the Area Special Projects Administrator.

3. Schools required to complete a Chapter 1/Article 3 Program Improvement Plan.
    - Secure the NCE gains data for subjects requiring a Chapter 1 /Article 3 Program Improvement Plan.
    - Check your school's California Achievement Test data and MEAP data for subjects requiring improvement to determine the grade level(s) which most likely contributed to the failure of Chapter 1/Article 3 students.
    - Review the Chapter 1/Article 3 services that are being provided to Chapter 1/Article 3 students in the grades and subjects determined in the previous two actions.
    - Plan new strategies to bolster the achievement gain of Chapter 1/Article 3 students in the subject areas and grades affected.
    - Include those strategies on the Implementation Plan form(s) in the Chapter 1/Article 3 Program Improvement Plan (same forms as #15) and/or Professional Development Plan (#17).
    - Complete all required sections of the Chapter 1/Article 3 Program Improvement Plan.
    - Send a copy of the Chapter 1/Article 3 Program Improvement Plan (#16) including the Professional Development Plan (#17) to the Area Special Projects Administrator.

SAMPLE

1. NCE gains for Basic Reading were +0.95
    NCE gains for Advanced Math were -3.03
2. CAT aggregate gains in NCE's for Basic Reading were as follows:

Grade	Value
Grade 1	12.60
Grade 2	8.29
Grade 3	1.08
Grade 4	-12.34
Grade 5	-4.87

3. CAT aggregate gains in NCE's for Advanced Math were as follows:

Grade	Value
Grade 1	8.97
Grade 2	-3.50
Grade 3	11.12
Grade 4	0.15
Grade 5	-9.67

4. MEAP results in percents per category were as follows:

	Reading				Mathematics			
	3	2A	2B	1	4	3	2	1
Grade 4	13.4	23.4	0.0	63.2	13.4	37.5	11.9	37.2

5. Based on the above test results, a change in instructional strategies seems to be necessary in basic reading for grades 4 and 5 and in advanced mathematics for grades 3 and 5.
6. Review of Chapter 1/Article 3 services shows that the Chapter 1/Article 3 Reading Lab enrolled only 2nd and 3rd grade students, and that mathematics tutoring was provided by paraprofessionals on an individual student basis to all grades.

7. New strategies to be incorporated into Implementation Plan form(s) in the Chapter 1/Article 3 Program Improvement Plan (same form as #15) include:

- *Basic Reading*: The Chapter 1 funded Reading Lab teacher will be assigned to a Board funded homeroom. A Board funded teacher, specially trained in Strategic Reading, will be assigned to the Reading Lab. Enrollment to the lab will be limited to 4th and 5th grade students.
- *Advanced Math*: Three teachers with special college preparation in methods and materials in elementary school mathematics instruction will participate in several workshops entitled: "Mathematical concepts used to solve story problems." Beginning with the second semester, a platoon system will be operational for at least three hours per week. These classes will be taught by the three teachers who participated in the workshops. Paraprofessionals will assist Article 3 students inside these mathematics rooms under the guidance of the teachers.

17. Professional development plan

GUIDELINE
Design a professional development plan for both staff and parents which supports the attainment of the school's objectives. Specify professional development activities, school objectives which the plan supports, responsibilities, resources, a timeline, and budget.

Incorporate Accelerating Change in Education (ACE) and Drug Free Schools and Communities staff development activities, as appropriate.

Each Chapter 1 school must, in collaboration with parents, plan and implement parent workshops in methods for helping their children at home and in helping parents improve their own skills.

Guideline Development Activities
1. The professional development plan must:
    - o Include both parents and staff,
    - o Support the attainment of the school's objectives,
    - o Include realistic activities that show a direct correlation to the school's objectives,
    - o Include a timeline, budget and person's responsibility.
2. Each Chapter 1 school must, in collaboration with parents, plan and implement parent workshops in methods for helping their children at home and in helping parents improve their own skills.
3. Include federal and state funded programs such as Drug Free Schools and District initiatives such as ACE.

SAMPLE

Professional Development Plan					
Estimated Three Year Professional Development Plan					
Professional Development Activities	Supports Objective #s	Person(s) Responsible	Resources to be used	Timeline	Estimated Budget
Dimensions of Learning (Staff)	1, 2, and 4	School Improvement Team; Ad hock Committee for Professional Development	Management Academy, In-house Professional Development Coordinators	9/2009 2/2010	Chapter 1 $8,500
STEP: Systematic Training for	3	LSCO Chair; Assistant Principal	STEP consultant and Manual	2/2010 6/2010	Article 3 $7,000

Effective Parenting (Parents)					
Eliminating Substance Abuse through Parent Education (Staff and Parents)	1	Assistant Principal	Drug Free Schools and Communities Staff Development	2/2010 2/2011	Drug Free Schools
Comprehension and Cognition (Staff)	1, 2, 3, and 4	Professional Development Ad hoc Committee	ACE facilitator Division of Educational Quality	2/2011 2/2012	ACE $16,000

18. School improvement team approach

GUIDELINE

School Improvement Team members representing all school constituencies must sign the School Improvement Plan indicating their approval. Team membership must include representation from administrators, teachers, support staff, parents/community, and students (as appropriate).

Consistent with Design for Excellence, each school improvement team must include a minimum of 25 percent parent and community membership.

Guideline Development Activities
1. Team members must represent all constituencies and include a minimum of 25 percent parent and community participation. A high performing School Improvement Team operates with an understanding of:
    a. *A self-generated commitment* - Each member feels a sense of ownership and control with regard to the team. That feeling comes from being involved as a valued participant.
    b. *Agreement through consensus* - Consensus taking, a team decision making process, in which conflicts can be resolved without rancor, produces decisions and actions that represent the interests, needs, wishes, and abilities of each member.
    c. *A healthy degree of conflict and creativity* - Conflict is healthy when it produces creativity and high quality results. Conflict matched with consensus encourages new ways of solving old problems or new directions or new outcomes.
    d. *Communication* - A high level of communication runs through and connects the first three traits; they are impossible without effective communication. All the members, not just the leader, encourage good solid communication for ownership to occur.
    e. *Empowerment* - The larger organization's mandate empowers and supports the team, thereby creating a basis for influencing the whole organization. The team then empowers and supports its members in the same way.
3. School Improvement Team members, representing all school constituencies, sign the School Improvement Plan indicating their approval.

School Improvement Team Approval			
Type	Number		Number
1. Administrators	2	4. Parents	3
2. Teachers	7	5. Community	1
3. Support Staff	1	6. Students	1
Name	Position	Signature Approval	
-------- (Chair) --			
--			
Principal's Signature:		Date:	

19. Public ACT 25 Requirements

1. *Process For Change*
   a. School Improvement Plan: Each school shall adopt and implement a 3-5 year school improvement plan. It should include:
      i. Mission statement
      ii. Goals
      iii. Curriculum development
      iv. Evaluation
      v. Staff development
      vi. Building level decision making
2. *Content Of Change*
   a. Core Curriculum: Make available to all students in the district a core curriculum.
      i. Outcomes for all Students
      ii. District developed and controlled
      iii. Local core curriculum
      iv. State model outcomes provided as a guide in:
      v. Arts
      vi. Career and employability
      vii. Cultural and aesthetic awareness
      viii. Language arts
      ix. Life and personal management
      x. Mathematics and science
      xi. Physical education and health
      xii. Technology
      xiii. World studies
3. *Verification Of Change*
   a. Accreditation: Ensure that each public school within the school district is accredited.
      i. Levels
         1. Candidacy
         2. Conditional
         3. Fully accredited
      ii. Programs
         1. North central association
         2. Michigan accreditation program
      iii. Process
         1. School data collection

2. Self-Study
3. Visitation and validation
4. Determination of outcomes data to be used
5. Development of a school
6. Improvement plan

4. Communication Of Change

a. Annual educational report: Each school in the district distributes to the public at an open meeting an annual educational report. A typical report may include:

i. School improvement plans
ii. Student achievement
iii. Retention and dropout
iv. Specialized schools
v. Parent participation
vi. Accreditation status
vii. Core curriculum

20. Guidelines to comply with handicapped and special educational requirements

Overview of special education state and federal compliance school checklist

DIRECTIONS: The thirteen items listed below include descriptive statements of expected compliance standards for special education. Retain this document as a resource for future reference. The rule numbers refer to the Revised Michigan Special Education rules. The state requirements reflect the federal regulations from the Individuals with Disabilities Education Act (IDEA).

Audit items

1. *Pre-Referral Assistance* - Pre-referral consultation with special education support staff is made available to teachers prior to the initiation of a referral for evaluation. The Intervention Assistance Team Model should be utilized.
2. *Initial Referrals* - A building referral coordinator having responsibilities for all initial special education referrals has been designated and has necessary information and referral forms R. 340.1721.
3. *IEP committee process* - IEP Committees are conducted in compliance with federal and state law. R 340.1733 (e).
4. *Related Services* - Special education students are being serviced by related service personnel as identified on the IEP (SSW/Speech/FC and others). R. 340.1721(e)(3)(f).
5. *Mainstreaming* - There is an established mainstreaming procedure in effect for providing access to academic or elective classes. Mainstreaming is implemented so that the mandated class sizes are maintained at all times. The additional teacher service is adequate to implement effective mainstreaming. R 340.1722(1)(2)(3)
6. *Lesson Plans/Curriculum* - IEP development, lesson plans and instruction are monitored regularly.
7. *Supplies And Equipment* - Supplies and equipment are comparable to those provided in general education program. Supplies and equipment are necessary to meet the defined IEP objectives. R. 340.1733(h). Supplies and equipment are inventoried and maintained.
8. *Equal Access To Services* - Special education students have equal access to:
   a. Extracurricular activities
   b. Counseling services
   c. Lunch and recess

    d. Physical education program
    e. Department/unit head services
    f. School-community partnership
    g. School volunteer R. 340.1722(3)(a)

9. *School Hours* - The length of the school day for special education students is not less than the general education students. R. 340.1733(g)
10. *Classroom Space* - Special education classrooms are of adequate size for all type and number of students being served. R. 340.1733(a)(b)(c)(d). Related services personnel also have adequate working space. R. 340.1733(a)(b)(c)(d)
11. *Three Year Evaluation* - Federal and state legislation mandates that special education students receive a comprehensive evaluation every three years. The school principal and special education teachers are aware of the special education students that are due for re-evaluation during each school year. R 340.1722(d)
12. *Discipline of Handicapped Students* - An IEPC must be convened when a student may be subject to a suspension exceeding a total of ten school days within a school year. R. 340.1721d(2)(b). Honig vs. Doe R 340. 1701(f)
13. *Out-of-District* - Students from out-of-district, currently residing in the city of (name) with evidence of eligibility for special education programs and services are receiving the necessary services. R. 340.1722(e)

Overview of Section 504

Section 504 of the Rehabilitation Act of 1973 is civil rights legislation. School districts are required to identify and evaluate students who may be handicapped. A free appropriate public education (FAPE) is ensured for all handicapped students. School districts must develop and implement a system of procedural safeguards for this identification/evaluation/placement process. This applies to all programs and activities of the school district, whether or not the specific program or activity is a direct recipient of federal monies.

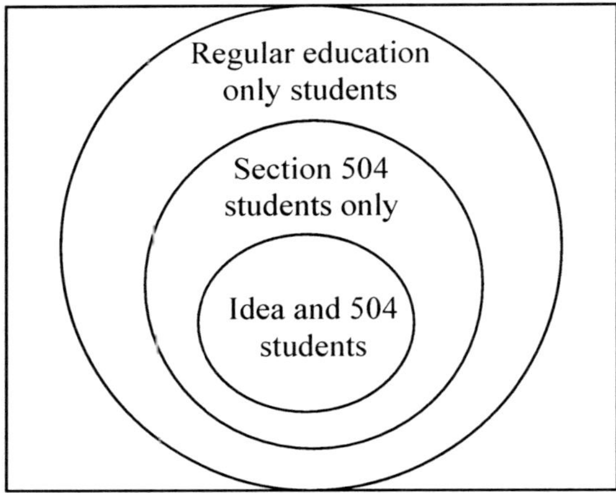

Idea/504 Students: Students are qualified under one or more of thirteen (13) IDEA disabling conditions. Specially designed individual education programs are planned for each student by IEPC Teams.

Section 504 Students Only: Due to mental or physical impairments that substantially limit one or more of the student's major life activities, special accommodations to the student's program are required. A 504 accommodation plan is designed for each student according to individual need. Examples of potential 504 handicapping conditions that may not be covered under IDEA are:

- Communicable diseases - HIV, Tuberculosis

- Medical conditions - asthma, allergies, diabetes, heart disease
- Temporary medical conditions due to illness or accident
- Attention deficit disorder (ADD, ADHD)
- Behavioral difficulties
- Drug/alcohol addiction
- Other conditions

Specific guidelines and procedures may also be included in a document entitled "Section 504 of the Rehabilitation Act: Support D -Preschool, Elementary and Secondary Education," of each School District.

Pre-referral Practices: Intervention assistance team model
It is expected for school-aged students that local building level administrators and teaching staff will explore alternative learning strategies, classroom management techniques, and other pertinent interventions in the regular education classroom before referring students to more restrictive options such as special education placement. A vehicle for accomplishing this expectation is the Intervention Assistance Team (IAT).

The IAT is a school based problem solving group whose purpose is to provide a vehicle for the discussion of issues related to specific needs of students and to offer collaborative consultation and follow-up assistance to teachers. The team uses an ecological-interactive approach to identify, analyze and find solutions to students' problems. Special education support staff can collaborate with regular education in the IAT process. This will create a more balanced responsibility between special and regular education to provide support to teachers in meeting the unique needs of all students. This approach involves parental and community support, and considers the student's classroom, the instructional strategies, the curriculum, and the opportunities to learn.

The intervention Assistance Team (IAT) is a collaborative effort between parents, regular education, special education, and support personnel with its emphasis on using problem solving for intervention development. The IAT model is designed to provide support to teachers. Teachers refer their student/classroom concerns to the team within the building. The team and the teacher requesting assistance jointly engage in a structural process of conceptualizing the problems, brainstorming solutions and planning interventions. The IAT model focuses on the following goals:

1. To structure a school based intervention plan that responds to the immediate needs of the student using collaboration and consultation with the classroom teacher.
2. To implement systematic intervention strategies in the regular education classroom and to evaluate the effectiveness of these strategies before a student is formally referred for consideration for special education placement.
3. To aid in developing a shared problem solving process that is more instructionally relevant by using data on the effectiveness of interventions as a major component of the process.
4. To increase the availability of specialized support services to teachers, students and their families.

This concept can be supported by any of the following persons:

Administrators	Counselors
Classroom teachers	School psychologists
Resource teachers	School social workers
Teacher consultants	Teachers of speech/language impaired
Chapter one /article three teachers	Community
Parents	Remedial or instructional specialists
Mentors	Agencies

Specific guidelines and procedures maybe included in the document entitled "Intervention Assistance Team (IAT) Model: A School Problem-Solving Model To Assist Teachers In Addressing Students' Individualized Needs," of each School District.

Procedures for implementation of the state endorsed 7 diploma requirements for students with disabilities

Test accommodations for students with disabilities: Any student with a disability, whether or not he/she is receiving special education is entitled to an appropriate accommodation as long as the accommodation does not subvert the purpose of the test. The selection of accommodations should be based on their appropriateness to the nature of the student's disability and its impact on the individual. A student should not be expected to use a different accommodation in testing than used in instruction (OCR 1987). Provided below is a list of examples. This list should not be considered exhaustive.

Extended time**	Reader/Audio Tape
Alternate date	Signer/Interpreter
Divided exam over more days	Computer adaptations (input and output)
More frequent breaks	Home-Hospital location
Separate room	Calculator

**The current MEAP is untimed; it is recommended that this option be fully utilized.

Prior to exercising the special education exemption under 104a (6), the appropriateness of providing accommodations should be exhausted. Staff will prepare suggested procedures for determining the need for accommodations and/or reasonableness of any specific accommodation requested.

Exemption from proficiency testing for special education students: It is the role of the IEPC to determine if an exemption from the general proficiency testing is warranted and if it is so determined, what assessment criteria will be used as the basis for awarding a state endorsed diploma. Any assessment for determining a state endorsement must measure areas in which the student has received instruction.

To determine if a student should be exempted, the IEPC must consider the following:

- The student's unique needs and career/life goals;
- The alignment of the curriculum to the skills, attitudes, and knowledge required by those unique needs and career/life goals; and
- The effectiveness of the assessment procedures to measure student proficiency in the skills, attitudes, and knowledge taught in the curriculum.

If it is determined that the assessment requirements of Section 104a are not effective options to measure student proficiency in the skills, attitudes, and knowledge appropriate to his/her unique needs, career/life goals, and related instruction, the IEPC may exempt the student from all or part of those requirements. No other group or individual may determine an exemption from the requirements of Section 104a.

Excerpt from: *Michigan Department of Education memorandum of September 24, 1992 on Special Populations and the MEAP.*

21. Guidelines to comply with bilingual education requirements

1. *Michigan Bilingual Education Public Act 294 (1974)*: "A school district shall perform a home language survey for the purpose of identifying enrolled students whose native language is a language other than English or whose primary language spoken in the home or environment is a language other than English."

   ".. . the Board of a school district having an enrollment of 20 or more children of limited English-speaking ability in a language classification in Grades K-12 shall establish and operate a bilingual instruction program for those children .. "

   "Bilingual instruction means the use of two languages, one of which is English, as the media of instruction for speaking, reading, writing or comprehension."
2. *Federal Bilingual Education Act Of 1968*: "No state shall deny an equal educational opportunity to any individual on account of his or her national origin by failing to take appropriate action to overcome language barriers that impede equal participation by its students in its instructional programs."
3. *Office for Civil Rights, Department of Health, Education And Welfare, 1970*: "Where inability to speak and understand the English language excludes national origin-minority group children from effective participation in the educational program offered by a school district, the district must take affirmative steps to rectify the language deficiencies in order to open its instructional program to these students."

22. School improvement plan checklist

School___________   **Area**________________

Directions: **Each statement maybe answered with a YES or a NO. Comments of course are encouraged to be noted.**

Mission
- Clearly communicates beliefs and expectations of the school
- Addresses excellence, equity and diversity
- Supports attainment of the District mission

Objectives Based on Design for Excellence
- Improvement areas and measurable three-year objectives
- One or more objectives supporting Goal 1: Create schools of the future
- One or more objectives supporting Goal 2: Ensure management/organizational effectiveness
- One or more objectives supporting Goal 4: Build community confidence
- Objectives established to support all objectives in Goal 3: Guarantee student success
  - MEAP Reading (% Category 3)
  - MEAP Mathematics (% Satisfactory)
  - MEAP Science (% Category 4)
  - CAT Reading (% At/Above Grade Level) CAT Mathematics (% At/Above Grade Level) four-year dropout rate (%)
  - Student daily attendance rate (%)
  - Staff attendance (No. Schools at 96%+)
- Other student outcome objectives (Optional)

Curriculum to attain student learning outcomes
- School theme or special curriculum focus
- Curriculum assessment completed for each grade level and curriculum gaps identified
- Curriculum inclusive for diverse populations, aligned with District objectives, supports District Goal 3 objectives, and implements District core curriculum

Special programs
- Special programs and school objectives they support

Student, staff and parent responsibilities
- Student, staff and parent responsibilities

Monitoring and evaluation
- Monitoring and evaluation procedures

Accreditation status
- Accreditation status of school and implementation timeline
- Schools seeking state accreditation have at least one cognitive, one affective and one school climate objective
- Schools seeking North Central outcomes accreditation have at least three cognitive and two affective objectives

Student enrollment procedures
- Student enrollment procedures including information on student recruitment, application criteria, and student selection process (Required for schools designated as "specialized schools" for Public Act 25 Annual Educational Report purposes)

Building level integrated decision making
- Building level decision making process
- Responsibilities for which the school is requesting building level authority (Required for empowered schools)

District policy and union contract waivers
- Policies and contract provisions for which the school is seeking waivers

Budget
- School budget allocation for current year and estimate for three years

Parent/Community involvement
- Description of parent and community involvement in development and implementation of school improvement efforts
- Type of parent organization of record
- Number and percent of students who had a parent or guardian attend one or more face-to-face meetings during the school year for the purpose of improving learning for that student
- Improvement strategies in implementation plans for Goal 4 show how parents and community are actively involved in supporting attainment of school objectives

Collaborative Partnerships
- School volunteers
- School community partnerships

School Progress Reports
- 2009-10 and 2010-11 final school progress reports
- Most recent school progress report

Implementation plans
- Implementation plan for each objective (except where a single plan might be applicable for two objectives, e.g., MEAP and CAT Reading; MEAP and CAT Mathematics)
- Evaluation measures
- Improvement strategies for attaining objectives
- Strategy rationales
- Persons responsible
- Resources to be used
- Timelines of beginning and completion dates
- Funding sources
- Improvement strategies address how the academic learning of all students will be accelerated
- Improvement strategies support African Centered/ Multicultural infusion plan, student pre-referral planning practices, and student documentation portfolios

Chapter 1/Article 3
- School Improvement Plan serves as Chapter 1 School wide Plan (Ch. 1 school wide schools)
- Program improvement plan included as integral part of school improvement plan (Chapter 1/Article 3 schools required to develop a one-year program improvement plan in reading and/or mathematics)

Professional Development Plan
- Professional development planned for both staff and parents
- Professional development activities
- School objectives the activities support
- Persons responsible
- Resources to be used
- Timelines of beginning and completion dates
- Budget

School Improvement Team Approval
- Representative mix of school constituencies
- Minimum of 25 percent parent and community membership
- Names and positions
- Signature approvals

General Comments

23. Charter 1 Article 3 Program Improvement Plant

XYZ Public School District Chapter One/Article 3 Program Improvement Plan 2009-12

School:________ Area Office Signature: _______ Principal:__________

Standardized Test Score Measures

Please list the normal curve equivalence (NCE) loss for Chapter 1/Article 3 students at this school between Spring, 2009 and Spring, 2011 in:

Basic Reading _____   Advanced Reading ________
Basic Mathematics ______   Advanced Mathematics ___

As you look at the above data consider the following factors which must be improved in order to raise Chapter 1/Artide 3 student's achievement in the identified area(s).

Contributing Factors	Check Item Appropriately
Daily attendance	
Parental involvement	
Student behavior patterns	
Instructional strategies	
Testing strategies	
Other (specify)	

Your plan must reflect the areas of academic needs and contributing factors. A typical example of capturing this may take the form of:

List Chapter 1/Article 3services at your school in two categories

School funded services   District funded services

Program improvement strategies

Consider the following points as you design your program improvement strategies:

1. Direct the efforts of your Chapter 1/Article 3 staff DIRECTLY toward support of the regular class reading and/or mathematics programs *e.g.*, the Chapter 1/Article 3 staff should pre-teach, tutor, provide additional practice and explanations of the language arts and mathematics materials being used in the regular classrooms.
2. Include strategies for the regular board-funded teachers to use which change their instructional strategies in ways which offer promise of raising the achievement levels of Chapter 1/Article 3 students in their classroom *e.g.*, participate in in-service training designed to raise the expectations of performance of these students so that their rate of mastery of daily lessons increases.
3. Direct the school's efforts toward improving those contributing factors which your review of data has shown to be less than satisfactory *e.g.*, increase and improve parental involvement.
4. Direct the school's efforts toward the implementation of those aspects of the "Design for Excellence" which offer promise of improving the achievement of Chapter 1/Article 3 students in your grade levels

Chapter 1/Article 3 Program improvement plan (form)

Improvement area: ______________ Objective: __________
Evaluation Measure(s): ______________

Improvement Strategies	Strategy Rationale	Person(s) Responsible	Resources to Be Used	Time line	Check Funding Source		
					Bd.	Ch.1/ Art. 3	Other

Documentation of parent and staff involvement in the planning of the school's Chapter One/Article Three Program

The involvement of parents and staff in the planning of Chapter One/Article Three programs is required by law. Individuals implementing the program must also be involved in the planning process. Consider the assistance of parents, PAC members, regular teachers, Chapter One/Article Three teachers, librarians, paraprofessionals, pupil service personnel, administrators and secondary students when planning the school's Chapter One and Article Three programs:

1. The following parents of participating students assisted in the planning:

2. The following staff members assisted in the planning:

3. The following Parent Advisory Council members assisted in the planning:

4. The following secondary students assisted in the planning:

5. The above named individuals met to plan the Chapter One/Article Three Program Improvement Plan on the following dates:

Copies of sign-in sheets for each of the meetings should be attached attached.

APPENDIX B

SIX SIGMA HELPS: TOOLS AND FORMS

In constructing these forms I want to thank Cary D. Stamatis and Stephen D. Stamatis for their contribution in both designing and drawing the forms. In addition their help with the computer was very valuable especially with very short notice. Thanks guys!

General requirements of understanding the six sigma
    A typical calculation for a six sigma capability
    Brainstorming thought starters – general
    Brainstorming thought starters – what if
    Verb- noun listing: products
    Verb- noun listing: process
    Function identification example for a product
    Function identification example for a process
    Cascading the $Y = f(X)$

Forms

Define
Maslow's Theory of needs
1. Translating the voice of the customer (VOC) to requirements (CTQs)
2. Understanding inputs and outputs
3. Cause and effect matrix
4. Project charter
5. Project plan milestone chart
6. Process and boundary development
7. Input, process and output measures
8. Computing the cost of quality (COQ)
9. Six key areas to address when improving the cost of quality

Measure
10. Check sheet development
11. Data collection plan
12. FMEA form
13. Gage R&R – long form
14. Gage R&R – short form
15. Attribute gage study
16. 5S observation summary
17. Control plan
18. Simplified control plan
19. Sources of data

Analyze
20. Main effect and interaction set up

Improve
21. Criteria matrix (evaluating improvements)
22. A form that may be used to direct effect and resources
23. Pay-off matrix

24. Understanding systems and structures for the 6 sigma methodology
Control
  Some of the previous forms are used here: Such as: # 8, 12, 13, 15, 17, 21, 23

Miscellaneous forms
25. Problem statement
26. Understanding the operational definition of the problem
27. Gage control plan
28. Work breakdown structures
29. Who does what in the project
30. How the work gets done
31. Exploring the values of the organization

Typical forms – in addition to the above – used in design for six sigma
32. Risk identification and mitigation
33. Competition matrix
34. CTQ matrix and assessment of design risk
35. Design score card
36. Pugh matrix
37. Score card: Critical to satisfaction (CTS) items
38. P-diagram
39. Translating language data to numeric data
40. Brand profiler
41. Status of items critical to satisfaction and relationship to customer satisfaction
42. Customer dimensions
43. Reliability and Robustness checklist
44. Design verification (DV) test plan
45. Triple 5-why analysis worksheet
46. Project proposal worksheet
47. Action Plan
48. Cost function
49. Process sequence flow chart
50. Cost index worksheet
51. Manufacturing information gathering worksheet
52. QFD block diagram
53. Function identification worksheet
54. Function diagram
55. Alternative action plan
56. Competitive evaluation
57. Reliability and robustness demonstration matrix
58. Assessment of six sigma status

A Typical calculation for a sigma capability

Step	Action	Equations	Your calculations
1	What process do you want to consider	N/A	Billing
2	How many units were put through the process?	N/A	2167
3	Of the units that went into the process, how many came out OK?	N/A	2059
4	Compute the yield for the process defined in Step 1	Step 3/step 2	2059/2167 = .9502
5	Compute the defect rate based on Step 4	1-step 4	1-.9502 = .0498
6	Determine the number of potential things that could create a defect	Number of CTQ characteristics	18
7	Compute the defect rate per CTO characteristic	Step 5/step 6	.00498/18 = .0028
8	Compute the defects per million opportunities (DPMO)	Step 7 x 1,000,000	.0028 x 1,000,000 = 2,800
9	Convert the DPMO (Step 8) into a sigma value. You may use a conversion chart or calculate the number	N/A	4.3
10	Draw conclusions	N/A	Little better than average performance

Brainstorming Thought Starters

ADAPT	What else is like this?
	Does the past offer similarities?
	What could we copy?
	What other ideas does this suggest?
COMBINE	Use a blend, alloy, assortment?
	Can we combine units?
	Combine purposes, functions?
	Combine ideas?
MAGNIFY	What can we add?
	Thicker?
	More frequent?
	Stronger?
	Duplicate?
MINIMIZE	What can we subtract?
	Smaller?
	Lighter?
	Condensed?
	Omit?
	Streamline?
REARRANGE	Can we interchange components?
	Different layout?
	Different sequence?
	Change pace?
	Different pattern?
	Different schedule?
REVERSE	What's the opposite?
	Can we turn it around, upside down, backward?
	Can we reverse roles?
MODIFY	Could we change the color, sound, motion, form, shape, meaning, odor?
	What new twist?
SUBSTITUTE	What can we use instead?
	Who else can?
	Another approach?
	Another material?
	Another ingredient?

WHAT IF You were spending your money?
Money was no object?
You combined two functions?
You were a man from mars - what questions would you ask about this?

You were 8 years old - what questions would you have?

You knew your managers would buy an idea you came up with - what would it be?
You were from 1000 years in the future?
You didn't perform the function at all?

You had the perfect material - what would you expect?
You performed the function backward?

Gravity did not exist - what would you do then?
You were trying to prevent the function from being performed?
You had an unlimited amount of time?
Nothing was sacred?

Verb -Noun Listing: Products

* Try to avoid use of these verbs.

VERBS		NOUNS	
*ABSORB	GENERATE	ACCESS	FRICTION
ACCESS	GUIDE	AIR	HEAT
ACTUATE	IMPROVE	APPEARANCE	IMPACT
*ALLOW	INCREASE	BENDING	LIGHT
APPLY	ISOLATE	CIRCUIT	MASS
ATTACH	LIMIT	CLIMATE	MATERIAL
ATTRACT	MAINTAIN	COLD	MOISTURE
CIRCULATE	PIVOT	COMFORT	MOTION
CONDUCT	POSITION	COMPONENT	NOISE
CONNECT	PREVENT	CORROSION	OCCUPANT
CONTAIN	PROTECT	CURRENT	PARTS
CONTROL	*PROVIDE	DEFLECTION	PATH
CONVERT	REDUCE	DIRT	PERFORMANCE
CREATE	REGULATE	DRAG	PRESSURE
DECREASE	RESIST	ENERGY	STABILITY
DIRECT	ROTATE	ENTRY	SURFACE
ENCLOSE	SEAL	ENVIRONMENT	TORQUE
ENHANCE	SENSE	FLOW	TRAVEL
EXTEND	SUPPORT	FLUID	VIBRATION
*FACILITATE	TRANSMIT	FORCE	WEIGHT

* Try to avoid use of these verbs.

VERBS		NOUNS	
*ALLOW	JOIN	ALIGNMENT	FLASH
APPLY	LOAD	ASSEMBLY	GAGE
ASSEMBLE	MAINTAIN	BURR	GAS
ASSURE	MAKE	CASTING	HEAT
BLEND	MOVE	CAUSE	HOLE
CLEAN	POSITION	CLEANLINESS	INVENTORY
CONTROL	PREVENT	COLD	LENGTH
CONVERT	PROTECT	COMPONENT	LOCATOR
CREATE	*PROVIDE	CONTAINER	MACHINE
DECREASE	RECEIVE	CORRECTION	MATERIAL
DELIVER	RELEASE	DAMAGE	MOLD
*FACILITATE	REMOVE	DEFECT	OPERATION
FASTEN	REPAIR	DEVICE	PART
FILL	ROTATE	DIE	PRIORITY
FINISH	SEAL	DIMENSION	SCHEDULE
FORM	STORE	DIRT	SHAPE
IDENTIFY	SUPPLY	ENVIRONMENT	SURFACE
IMPROVE	THREAD	EQUIPMENT	TOOL
INCREASE	TRANSPORT	FINISH	UNIFORMITY
INSPECT	VERIFY	FIXTURE	WASTE

TEAM MEMBERS: DATE:
PROJECT:

LISTING OF FUNCTIONS PERFORMED	
ACTIVE VERB	**MEASURABLE NOUN**
Improve	Appearance
Position	Parts
Enhance	Stability
Prevent	Vibration
Improve	Assembly
Assure	Location
Reduce	Margin Variation
Enhance	Cooling
Control	Location
Support	Part
Limit	Deflection
Fasten	Parts

Function Identification Example for a Process

TEAM MEMBERS: DATE:
PROJECT:

Listing of functions performed	
ACTIVE VERB	**MEASURABLE NOUN**
Transfer	Material (parts)
Move	Material
Position	Material (parts)
Apply	Material (sealer)
Actuate	Circuit
Weld	Assembly
Remove	Assembly
Position	Assembly
Store	Assembly
Produce	Assembly
Ship	Assembly
Supply	Material
Repair	Assembly

Cascading the Y = f(X)

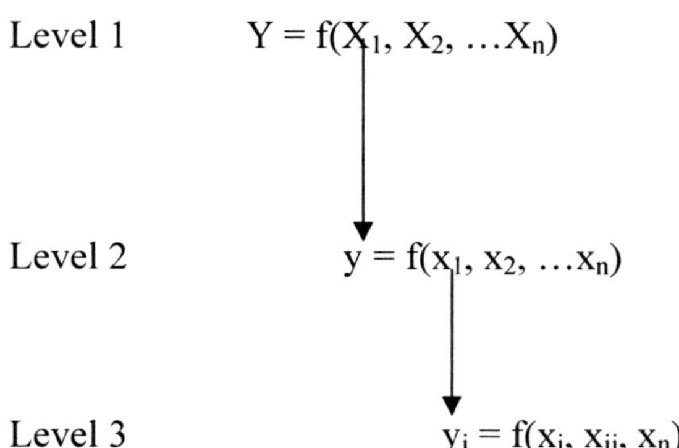

Level 1 $Y = f(X_1, X_2, \ldots X_n)$

Level 2 $y = f(x_1, x_2, \ldots x_n)$

Level 3 $y_i = f(x_i, x_{ii}, x_n)$

Where:

Y is influenced by a number of potential Xs

The y is the new requirement based on X_1's and so on. The X_1 is further examined for more potential xs

The y_i is yet another requirement of the customer based on x_1's and so on. The x_i is further examined for more potential xs

Example: High level application of a "meal in the restaurant":

Level 1   Y = a good meal in the restaurant is depended on X1 = price, X2 = service, X3 = satisfaction

Level 2   y = the result in satisfaction (which is the X3) is depended upon x1 = service and x2 = food selection

Level 3   yi = the result in satisfaction (X3) with service (which is the x2) is depended upon xi = availability of food, xii = management

Level 4   and so on

DEFINE

To know who and what the customer needs or wants one must understand him through Maslow's theory of motivation and human needs. Furthermore, to extend that understanding into the concept of "customer service" we must be cognizant of the PACT principle. PACT is essential in this understanding because customer service" is very perishable and it depends so much at the moment of service. PACT is the acronym for (P = prompt, professional, personable); A = (accurate, attentive, acknowledging); C = (courteous, caring, concise); and T = (tailored, timely and thoughtful). Maslow's theory is based on a hierarchical pyramid of needs shown as:

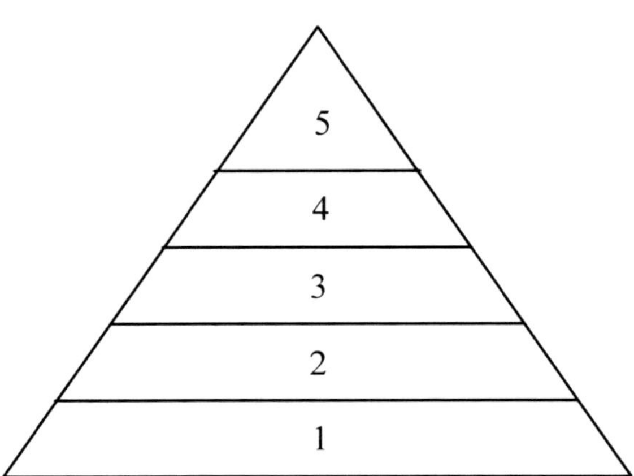

LEVELS OF NEEDS	MOTIVATION & BEHAVIOR
Level 1 = Your Body: PHYSICAL SAFETY & SECURITY Need to stay alive! Biological and cultural imperatives to live. Includes having enough healthy food, air, and water to survive.	**Level 1** = Your Body: SURVIVAL SKILLS Eat, sleep, and take care of your bodily needs, provide for clothing, shelter, comfort, be free from pain.
Level 2 = Your Family & Work: SOCIAL SAFETY & SECURITY Need to be safe from physical and psychological harm in the present and future, and trust in a predictable future.	**Level 2** = Your Family & Work: SURVIVAL SKILLS Work, save for future, improve skills and talents, be responsible, and want an organized predictable world.
Level 3 = Love & Relationships: COMMUNICATION & RESPONSE Need to be loved and to love. Includes the desire for affection and belonging.	**Level 3** = Love & Relationships: VALIDATION Join and be active in clubs and groups, be able to talk to others, contribute to society, marry and have a family.

Level 4 = Self-Esteem: SELF RESPECT & ACCEPTANCE Need for reputation, prestige, and recognition from others. Contains the desire to feel important, strong and significant.	**Level 4** = Self-Esteem: BRAINPOWER Display your talents and skills, have self-confidence, appreciate attention and recognition from others.
Level 5 = Self-Actualization: FULFILLMENT OF GOALS & DREAMS Need for self-fulfillment. Desire to realize your full potential and become the best you are capable of becoming.	**Level 5** = Self-Actualization: CREATIVITY Be a self-starter, have enthusiasm, be creative, be dedicated, enjoy challenges, love to accomplish results!

1. Translating the voice of the customer (VOC) to requirements (Critical to Quality - CTQs)

Level	VOC	Key Issues	Requirements	
			Good	**Bad**

2. Understanding inputs and outputs

Process input variables	Process output variables

3. Cause and effect matrix

Rating of importance to customer								
	1	2	3	4	5	6	7	
Process inputs (X's) CTP's	Process outputs (Y's), CTC, CTD, CTQ							Total

4. Project Charter

Project Charter			
Project Title:		Key Roles: Name: Title: Task:	
Problem Statement:		Timing: Start: End:	
Company's Impact:		ROI: Expected benefit	
Project scope Statement:		Team Members:	
Project Goal:			
Project Location			

5. Project plan milestone chart

Cycle of project	Time line in weeks or months				
Project start					
Define					
Measure					
Analyze					
Improve					
Control					
Project finish					

6. Process and Boundary development

Process name	Starting point	Ending point
1		
2		
3		
4		

7. Input, process and output measures

Input measures	Process measures	Output measures

8. Computing the Cost of Quality (COQ)

COMPUTING THE COST OF QUALITY	
Currently measured	**Not measured – at this time**
Scrap:	Increased maintenance:
	Lost sales:
Warranty expense:	Customer dissatisfaction:
	Downtime:
Inspection costs:	Engineering and product:
	Development errors:
Overtime:	Bill of material inaccuracy:
	Rejected raw materials:
INTERNAL FAILURE	**APPRAISAL**
Scrap:	Inspection:
Rework:	Testing:
Supplier scrap:	Quality audit:
Supplier rework:	Initial cost and maintenance of test equipment:
EXTERNAL FAILURE	**PREVENTION**
Cost to customer:	Quality planning:
Warranty cost:	Process planning:
Complaint adjustments:	Process control:
Returned material:	Training:

9. Six key areas to address when improving the cost of quality

KEY DRIVERS	BASIC ISSUE
1. Basic organizational capabilities:	Skills and tools required to implement improvements in business processes are lacking:
2. Industrial process variations:	Poor industrial process capabilities result in high cost of poor operations (rework, scrap, field failure): Customer demands are frequently not passed on to engineering: Inefficient front-end engineering:
3. Business process variations:	Product cost estimation is often widely off the mark, resulting in poor financial performance and incorrect manufacturing decisions:
4. Engineering/design process and documentation:	Engineering systems and design processes and documentation are often inadequate and flawed:
5. Quality of specifications:	Specifications sent to suppliers/ subcontractors vary considerably in their quality, resulting in poor-quality parts:
6. Supplier capabilities:	Lack of quality suppliers, resulting in poor-quality parts/services, late deliveries, higher parts/service costs, etc.:

Measure

10. Check sheet development

Name:		Date:	
Defect type	**Frequency**	**Comments**	

11. Data collection plan

What			Why	Who	How	When	Where
Needed measures	Operational definition	Formula or formulae	Purpose of data	Individual responsible for the collection	Method of selection	Date, time or frequency	Source

12. FMEA Form

Process or product name:	FMEA TEAM:	Prepared By:	Original date:	Revised date:	Page _ of _	FMEA Number:
Responsible:						

Process Step	Potential Failure Mode	Effect	SEV	Class	Causes	OCC	Controls	DET	RPN	Actions Rec.	Actions Taken	SEV	OCC	DET	RPN

13. Repeatability and Reproducibility study (Gauge R&R) – long form

Part No. and Name: Gage Name: Date:
Characteristics: Gage No.:   Performed by:
Specification: Gage Type: _______________

From data sheet: $\overline{\overline{R}} =$ $\overline{X}_{Diff} =$ $R_p =$

Measurement Unit Analysis	% Total Variation (TV)
Repeatability- Equipment Variation (EV) $EV = \overline{\overline{R}} \times K_1$ $= \underline{\quad} \times \underline{\quad}$ $= \underline{\quad}$ Trials / K_1: 2 → 0.8862; 3 → 0.5908	$\%EV = 100 \times [\, EV / TV \,]$ $= 100 \times [\, \underline{\quad} / \underline{\quad} \,]$ $= \underline{\quad\quad} \%$
Reproducibility- Appraiser Variation (AV) $AV = \sqrt{\left(\overline{X}_{Diff} \times K_2\right)^2 - \left(EV^2 /(n \times r)\right)}$ $= \sqrt{\left(\underline{\ } \times \underline{\ }\right)^2 - \left(\underline{\ }^2 /(\underline{\ } \times \underline{\ })\right)}$ $= \underline{\quad\quad}$ n = number of parts r = number of trials Appraisers: 2, 3 K_2: 0.7071, 0.5231	$\%AV = 100 \times [\, AV / TV \,]$ $= 100 \times [\, \underline{\quad} / \underline{\quad} \,]$ $= \underline{\quad\quad} \%$
Repeatability and Reproducibility (GRR) $GRR = \sqrt{\left(EV^2 \times AV^2\right)}$ $= \sqrt{\left(\underline{\ }^2 \times \underline{\ }^2\right)}$ $= \underline{\quad\quad}$	$\%GRR = 100 \times [GRR / TV]$ $= 100 \times [\, \underline{\quad} / \underline{\quad} \,]$ $= \underline{\quad\quad} \%$
Part Variation (PV) $PV = R_p \times K_3$ $= \underline{\ } \times \underline{\ }$ $= \underline{\quad\quad}$	$\%PV = 100 \times [\, PV / TV \,]$ $= 100 \times [\, \underline{\quad} / \underline{\quad} \,]$ $= \underline{\quad\quad} \%$
Total Variation (TV) $TV = \sqrt{\left(GRR^2 \times PV^2\right)}$ $= \sqrt{\left(\underline{\ }^2 \times \underline{\ }^2\right)}$ $= \underline{\quad\quad}$	$ndc = 1.41 \times \left(PV \big/ GRR\right)$ $= 1.41 \times (\underline{\ } / \underline{\ })$ $= \underline{\quad\quad}$

Parts / K_3:

Parts	K_3
2	0.7071
3	0.5231
4	0.4467
5	0.4030
6	0.3742
7	0.3534
8	0.3375
9	0.3249
10	0.3146

For information on the theory and constants used in the form see *MSA Reference Manual*, Third edition. AIAG.

14. Repeatability and reproducibility study (Gauge R&R) – short form

Parts	Operator A	Operator B	Range
1			
2			
3			
4			
5			
		Sum of Percentage	
D$_2$ values for distribution of R			
Parts	2 operators	3 operators	
1	1.41	1.91	
2	1.28	1.81	
3	1.23	1.77	
4	1.21	1.75	
5	1.19	1.74	

$$\text{R-bar} = \frac{\sum R}{n}; \quad \text{RR error} = (\frac{\overline{R}}{d_2})x5.15; \quad \text{R\&R} = \frac{RRError}{Tolerance}x100\%$$

15. Attribute gage study

Operation title:		Gage name:		Attribute	Legend	
Characteristics:		Gage number:		A	Accept	
	Name:		Data:	B	Bad	
Operator A				D	Defect	
Operator B				G	Go	
Operator C				G	Good	
				NG	No Go	

Known attribute		Operator A		Operator B		Operator C		Score
Sample ID	Attribute	Trial 1	Trial 2	Trial 1	Trial 2	Trial 1	Trial 2	
1								
2								
3								
…								
…								
30								
Must have at least 30 items								
Score via Trial via operator								
Score via operator								
		Operator A		Operator B		Operator C		
		Trial 1	Trial 2	Trial 1	Trial 2	Trial 1	Trial 2	

Result Summary:

	% Appraiser effectiveness	
	Operator A	
	Operator B	
	Operator C	
% effectiveness		
	Total	

16. 5S Observation summary

5S Summary Report:		Score results: (X /100)
Shift:	**Area/Department:**	

5S target objective:
Historical 5S success(es):

Priority Items that need attention	Existing situation: Score	Future situation: Score
1		
2		
3		
4		
5		

17. Control plan

Department:		Prepared By:	Page ___ of ___	Document Number:
Process:		Approved By:	Revision Date:	Other:
Location:			Supersedes:	

Employee Check	CHARACTERISTIC	CTQ or Critical level (CL)	REQUIREMENT	MEASUREMENT METHOD	SAMPLE SIZE	FREQUENCY	Who MEASURES	Where RECORDEd	Decision Rule or CORRECTIVE Action	Reference Number

18. Simplified control plan

Project Title:				Date:		
Task/Action to be accomplished	Specific steps to be taken	Responsible person for task	Starting data	Finish date		Deliverable(s)

19. Sources of data

	Y (CTQ)	X_1	X_2	X_n
Existing Data				
Needed Data				

Analyze

20. Main effect and interaction set up

	Orthogonal array (Set up of experiment with appropriate levels)	Individual factors and or interactions				Response (It may be a single or a multiple response)
Level Effect +						
Level Effect -						
Main Effect difference						

246

Improve

21. Criteria matrix (evaluating improvements)

Desirable criteria	Weights	Alternatives			
		Alternative 1		Alternative 2	
		Score	Weighted score	Score	Weighted score
	Totals				

22. A form that may be used to direct effort and resources

Part name:			
Functional area	Present cost	Hi	Low
X			
Y			
Total cost			

23. Payoff matrix

		Effort	
		Low	High
Benefit	High		
	Low		

24. Understanding systems and structures for the six sigma methodology

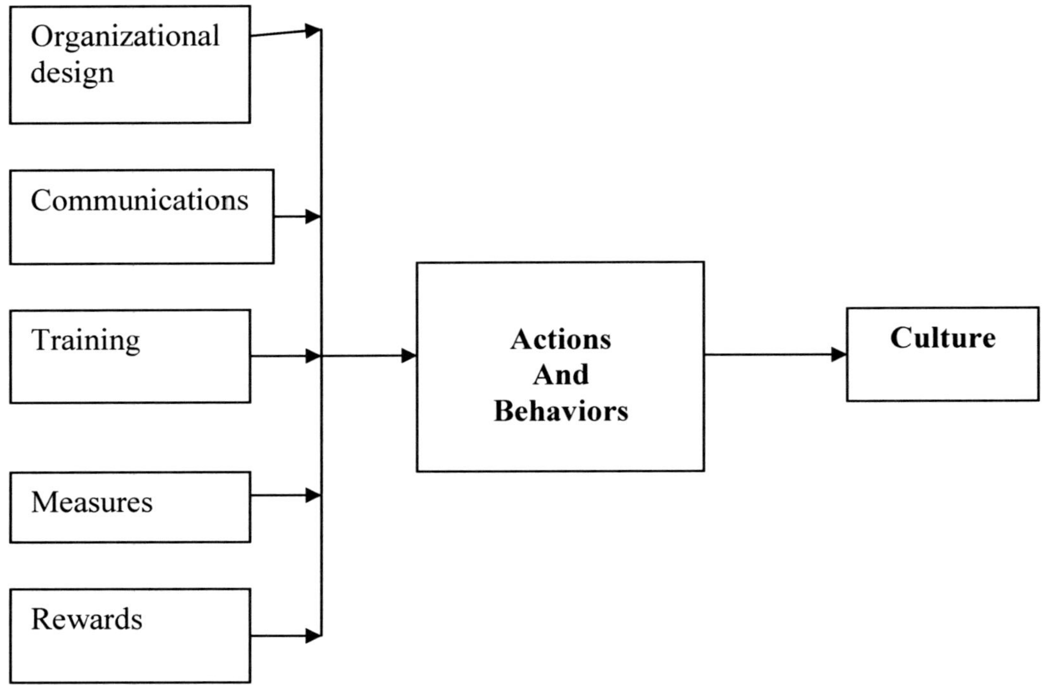

Miscellaneous forms

25. Problem statement

According to…	Definition of the problem	Unit of measure	Source of data. Data type

26. Understanding the operational definition of the problem

Problem statement and project definition (original)	
Customer	CTQs
Nonconformance or variation (I will reduce…)	Data needed and units of measurement (relating to the non conformance)
Current performance and reduction Goal	
Potential benefits (COPQ)	
Project scope, limits and boundaries	Potential team members
Problem statement and project definition (Final)	

27. Gage control plan

Gage ID:		Department:		MSA reference:		Page __ Of ___
Gage name:		Gage location:		Calibration procedure:		Document number:
Gage Type:		Storage:		Date:		Revision number:

Baseline	Date	Resolution	Bias	Linearity	Calibration		GR&R		Remarks
					Date	By	%R&R	P/T	

28. Work break down structures (WBS)

Task #	Task name	Predecessor	Duration

29. Who does what in the project

Stakeholder	Wants, Needs And concerns	Relationship to the project					
		Impacted	Authority	Expertise	Influence	Resources	OTHER

30. How the work gets done

Who needs information	Message forum	Message frequency	Message goal	Best way to present message	Who delivers the message

31. Exploring the values of the organization

Priority	Description of what is valued

Typical forms - in addition to the above - used in Design for six sigma

32. Risk identification & mitigation

Risk Element	Risk Management	Risk Score	Mitigation plan

33. Competition matrix

Customer needs	Priority	Competitor A	Competitor B	Best in Class	Best in Class performance
Total Impact					

34. CTQ matrix and assessment of Design Risk

Customer needs	IMPORTANCE	PERFORMANCE	MEASUREMENT	TARGET	USL	LSL	DATA TYPE	DEFECT RATE	MAP TO CRITICAL X	IMPACT ON CUSTOMER	IMPACT ON COMPANY	TAKE AWAY

35. Design score card

CTQ	Measurement	Data type	Target	USL	LSL	Sigma	DPMO

36. Pugh Matrix

CTQs & Business needs	Pugh priority	Concept A	Concept B	Concept n
Sum of positives				
Sum of negatives				
Sum of sames				
Weighted positives				
Weighted negatives				
Next score				

37. Scorecard: Critical to satisfaction (CTS) items

Project Description:								Date:				
CTSs	Units	Range		Contribution to variability		Specs		Sample statistics			z-score	
		min	max	capability	%	LSL	USL	μ	σ	conf	σ shift	D P M

38. P-diagram

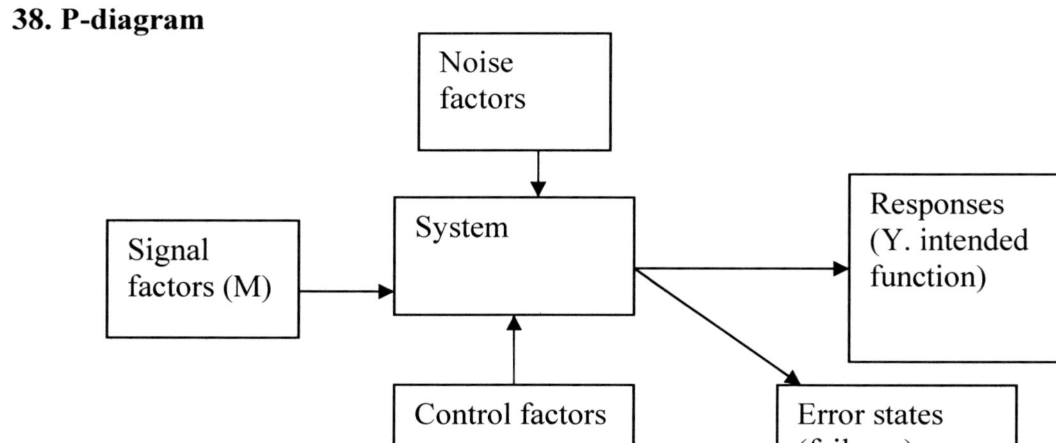

39. Translating language data to numeric data

Steps	Language data	Numeric data
Convert information to data		
Find the underline message		
Identify the structure		
Evaluate importance plan appropriate actions		

40. Brand profiler

Attribute	Attribute class	Priority	Primary brand positioning	Nameplate brand positioning	Program specifics		Present nameplate entry
					Target objectives	S T A T U S	
Usage experience							
Attribute Differentiation:				Product attribute leadership strategy:			

41. Status of items critical to satisfaction and relationship to customer satisfaction (May be used at each stage of the DCOV model)

CTS Or S U R R O G A T E	UNITS	T.F.? Y/N	STATUS		C O M P E T I T O R (BIC)		TARGET: INITIAL			TARGET: AGED			C U S T. S A T. I M P R O V.
			μ	σ	μ	σ	μ	LSL	USL	μ	LSL	USL	

42. Customer dimensions

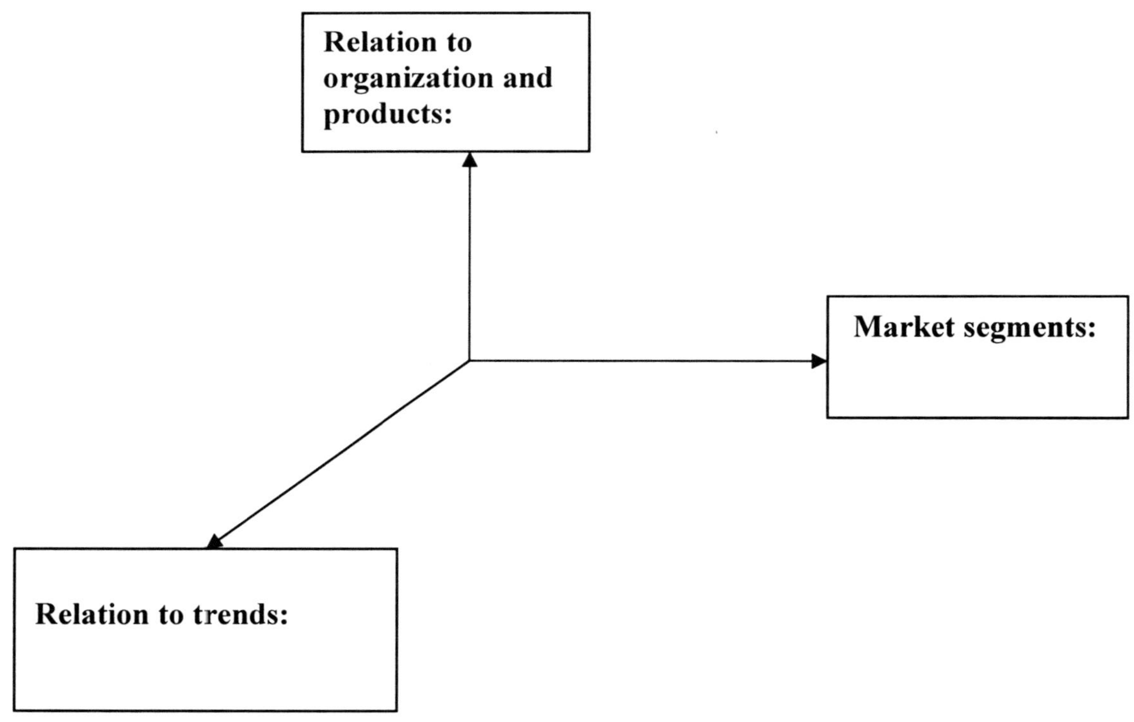

43. Reliability and Robustness checklist

Functional requirement Life target (CTSs)	Design parameters (number and name)	Tests (number, name and strategy)	Error states and their management

44. Design verification (DV) test plan

Test (name, type and frequency)	Objective	Expected results	Real outcome of test

45. Triple 5-Why Analysis Worksheet

For each root cause selected in Step 5, use this table to determine technical, detection, and systematic root causes.

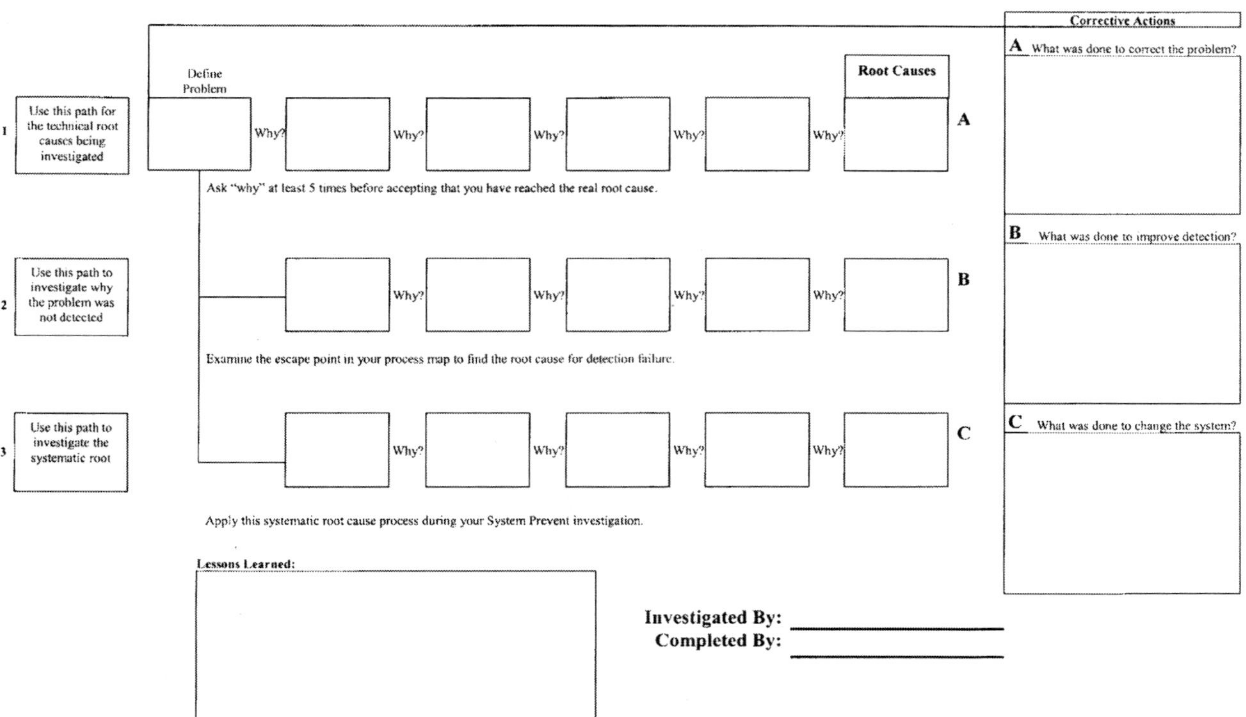

46. PROJECT PROPOSAL WORKSHEET

PROPOSAL NAME:

PROPOSAL #:

BLACK BELT:

DATE:

PART NAME:	CARL LINES AFFECTED:		CURRENT FUNCTION RATING	PROPOSED FUNCTION RATING
PART NUMBER:	VOLUMES:		CURRENT VALUE RATIO	PROPOSED VALUE RATING
PRESENT CONDITION (PLEASE DESCRIBE).	PROPOSAL DESCRIPTION:		ADVANTAGES:	
			DISADVANTAGES:	

(1) COST SAVINGS PER PART - MATERIAL	(2) COST SAVINGS - LABOR	(3) NUMBER OF PARTS PER VEHICLE	(4) ANNUAL VOLUME	(5) LIFETIME VOLUME	WEIGHT REDUCTION	SAVINGS AS % OF PIECE COST		IF ALL ACTIONS COMPLETED, IMPLEMENTATION DATE
(6) TOOLING COST	(7) ENGINEERING COST	(8) ANNUAL SAVINGS $[(1+2)*3*4]$	FIRST YEAR SAVINGS $[8-(6+7)]$	LIFETIME SAVINGS $[(1+2)*3*5-(6+7)]$	PAYBACK PERIOD (mos.): $[(6+7)/8]*12$	EVALUATION RANK	IMMEDIATELY OK	NOT ACCEPTED
						(CIRCLE SELECTION)	NEEDS EXAMIN-ATION / TESTING	NEXT ITERATION

47. ACTION PLAN WORKSHEET

Workshop Subject: ____

Date: ___________

Proposal #: ___________

	WHAT NEEDS TO BE DONE (Be Specific)	WHO DOES IT (Name of Person Responsible)	POSSIBLE ROADBLOCKS (Names of people most likely to get in the way)	HOW TO OVERCOME	COMPLETION DATE	COST TO COMPLETE
DESIGN						
SAMPLES						
EVALUATION & ENGRG. JUDGEMENT						
TOOLING						
OTHER						

BLACKBELTS: PROJECT: CUSTOMER REQUIREMENTS: WORKSHOP DATES:

48. COST / FUNCTION WORKSHEET

#	PART / OPERATION	COST	FUNCTION (ACTIVE VERB / MEASURABLE NOUN)									
			1	2	3	4	5	6	7	8	9	10

BLACKBELTS: PROJECT: CUSTOMER REQUIREMENTS: WORKSHOP DATES:

49. PROCESS SEQUENCE FLOW CHART

#	WHO DOES IT / WHAT HAPPENS								COST PER EVENT	TIME PER EVENT	LABOR RATE

TEAM MEMBERS: PROJECT: CUSTOMER NEEDS: WORKSHOP DATE:

50. COST INDEX WORKSHEET

COMPONENT / MODEL	OURS	COMPETITOR 1	COMPETITOR 2	COMPETITOR 3	COMPETITOR 4	COMMENTS
SKETCH →						
PART						
MATERIAL						
SIZE						
WEIGHT						

51. INFORMATION GATHERING WORKSHEET

INFORMATION REQUIRED	PERSON RESPONSIBLE		COMMENT
	MANUFACTURER	O.E.M.	
Bill of Materials (Complete Parts List)			
Material cost			
Labor cost			
Freight & Packaging costs			
Material flow / Inventory costs			
Inspection costs			
Scrap & Rework costs			
Any other cost components			
Original tooling costs			
Tooling capacity			
Standard Volume			
Process description with detailed costs			
Video of Process			
Process Flow Charts			
Plant Layout Drawings			
Detail Part Drawing			
Material Specifications			
Assembly Drawing			
Photos of parts and / or processes			
Competitive parts			
Test / govt. requirements			
Warranty Information			
List of Suppliers' suppliers' phone #'s			
Invitation to Employees & Supervisors			
Conference Room & Equipment			

52. QFD Block Diagram

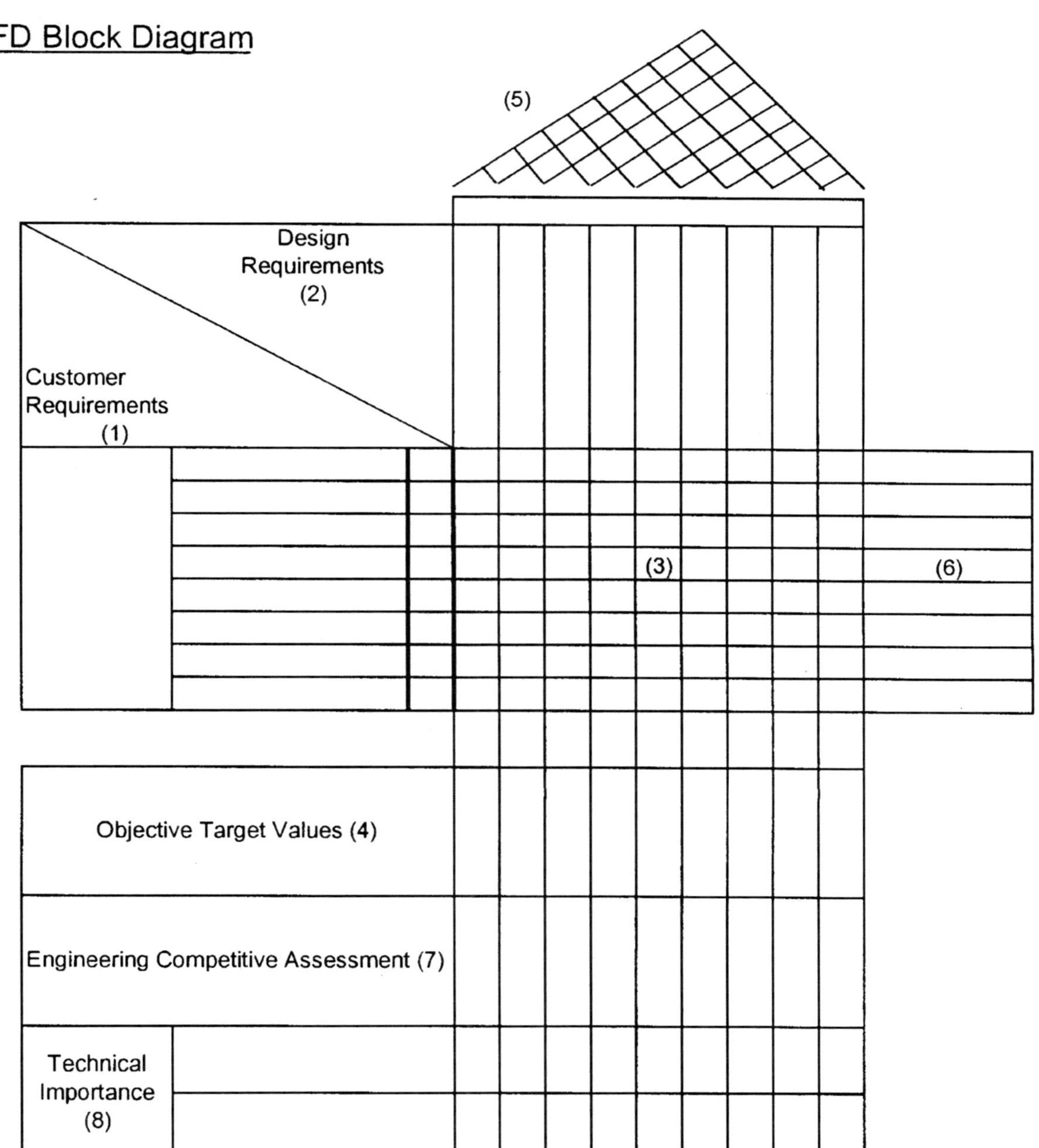

1. Customer requirements (focus on functionality) 2. Engineering Requirements (based on customer's functionality) 3. Weighted relationshipof customer functionalities. 4. Realistic target goals 5. Relationship of engineering requirements 6. Competitive cost relationship 7. Engineering competitive evaluation 8. Technical priority

53. FUNCTION IDENTIFICATION WORKSHEET

TEAM MEMBERS: _________________________________ WORKSHOP DATES: _________

PROJECT: _________________________________

LISTING OF FUNCTIONS PERFORMED	
ACTIVE VERB	**MEASURABLE NOUN**

BLACKBELT(S): _________________________   COMPANY: _________________________

54. FUNCTION DIAGRAM

WHY? ⟶   ⟵ HOW?

PROJECT: _________________________   DATE: _________________________

55. Alternative Action Plan

Legend

I	Initiate action and monitor performance
W	Perform work
C	Consultation required
R	Review/comment/ summarize/ recommend
A	Approve action or make decision
D	Make final decision if "A's" do not agree
N	Must be notified of decision

Title: _______________

Number: _______________

Objective: _______________

Prepared by: _______________

Date: _______________

Number	Steps to be taken	Characteristic of Step Taken													Dates		Resources Required or Anticipated Obstacles
		A	B	C	D	E	F	G	H	I	J	K	L		Start	Stop	

56. Competitive Evaluation

Product/Market: _______________

Please Rank Each Company. 10 is Best, 1 is Worst

Key Reasons to Buy	Weight	Company	Competitors		
			1	2	3

57. Reliability and robustness demonstration matrix

Reliability and Robustness demonstration matrix													
Program:			Project:						System:				
Date:			Team Lead:						Supplier Lead:				
Define Requirements						Design for Robustness				Verify Design			
Quality history analysis				SDS And Or DVP		VM Conditions [here we ID the high impact noise factors]		CRITICAL METRIC	RANGE	Reliability demonstration			
CRITERIA	COMPONENT	HIGH IMPACT ERROR STATE	VM NUMBER	VM DESCRIPTION	VM TARGET	NUMBER	NAME			DEMONSTRATED RESULT	RISK ASSESSMENT	ISSUES	FINISH DATE

262

58. Assessment of six sigma status
(The desired direction is always at the higher level.
For your organization you may modify this to reflect your own needs)

	6 sigma category	Man. Commit.	Obsession With excellence	Org. Is Customer driven	Customer Satisfaction	Training	Employee involvement	Use of incentives	USE OF TOOLS	
D E S I R E D	5	Is continual improvement a natural behavior even for the routine tasks?	Is there a constant improvement in quality, cost, and productivity?	Is the primary goal to satisfy the customer?	Are customers maintaining a long term relationship?	Is appropriate and applicable training available among employees?	Are employees proud to participate? Are employees self directed? Are effective teams utilized in appraising and preventing of problems	Are incentives appropriate and applicable for the entire team?	Is Statistics used as a common language throughout the organization?	**B E N C H M**
D I R E C T I O N	4	Is focus on improving the system?	Are cross functional teams used?	Is customer feedback used in decision making?	Is improvement for value to the customer inherent in all routine behaviors of management?	Is top management aware of the six sigma methodology and apply it appropriately?	Is manager the key decision with employees following his lead?	Are incentives appropriate and applicable for individuals in the team?	Is it at least some statistics and SPC used?	**A R K I N G**
	3	Is appropriate resources applied to training?	Is six sigma supported by executives and managers?	Are appropriate and applicable tools and methodologies identified and used for identifying the wants, needs in the design?	Is there a verification of using the customer's feedback to improve processes and or complaints?	Are there ongoing training proposals?	Is the manager asking for input before a decision is made?	Is there a quality related selection and promotion criteria for employees?	Is it at least some SPC used to reduce variation?	**M A T R I X**
	2	Is there a policy of balancing long term goals with short term objectives?	Is there an executive steering committee set up? Is there a Champion for specific areas designated?	Are you sure that the customer's wants and needs are known?	Do you know how the customer is rating you?	Is there a big picture training plan developed?	Is the manager the key person for decision making? Is the manager the person who decides and then asks his employees for ideas?	Is there an effective employee suggestion program in place?	Is it at least some SPC used in key processes?	
	1	Traditional approach to quality control -- very ineffective Emphasis is on inspection Quality is found only in manufacturing facilities								

APPENDIX C

LEAN TOOLS AND FORMS

Lean is a methodology that focuses on eliminating or reducing waste. Fundamentally lean is based on the following concepts:

- **Work flows continuously** with minimal inventory and or difficulties
- **Production is synchronized** to shipping schedules, not based on machine utilization
- **Defects are prevented**
- **Organizations are team-based** with multi-skilled operators
- **Measurables are used to solve problems.**
- **Operators are empowered** to make decisions and improve operations with few indirect staff
- **Top management and workers are actively involved together** in trouble-shooting and problem solving to improve quality and eliminate waste
- **Value stream is closely integrated** from raw material through finished goods with the support of suppliers and customers
- **Order-to-Delivery (OTD)** lead-time is the time required to deliver an item to the customer from the time that the item was ordered. The Order-to-Delivery process is a set of business practices that reduce this lead-time.
- Lean is based on identifying and eliminating waste
- Not all waste can be eliminated immediately
- Identification of waste makes the opportunity for improvement visible
- Process creates results—use results to define areas for improvement
- Average leads to complacency
  - Average companies say "we're better than the status quo", and lose their motivation to get better
  - Great organizations say "How can we be the best in the world" and strive to be the best across all industries
- Make decision at the value added task
  - Develop systems to encourage change to occur where the value is added
    - Don't develop a suggestion system
    - Do develop an implementation system
  - Have a bias for action: A plan for improvement is worth nothing until it is implemented
- Implement ideas, this is the true measure of Lean Deployment success

Therefore, everything that is being done in the name of lean is value and waste.

VALUE: *An activity that transforms or shapes raw materials or information to meet customer needs*
WASTE: *Activities that consume time, resources and/or space, but do not contribute to satisfying customer needs, such as:*

- Over-production
- Inventory
- Transportation
- Waiting
- Motion
- Over-processing

- Correction
- Not utilizing the talent and knowledge of human resources

Causes of waste
- Layout (Distance)
- Long setup time
- Incapable processes
- Poor maintenance
- Poor work methods
- Inadequate training
- Product design
- Performance measures
- Ineffective production planning & scheduling
- Equipment design and selection
- Poor workplace organization
- Supplier quality / reliability
- More . . .

Perhaps one of the most important concepts of all lean is based on the notion of the 5S philosophy. What is 5S?
- More than housekeeping
- The beginning of waste reduction
- Built on the foundation of discipline

Why implement 5S?
- Set a standard
- Develop discipline
- Eliminate waste
- And more

A place for everything...
- Separate--sort and eliminate unnecessary items
- Straighten--put necessary items in order for easy access
- Scrub--clean everything; tools and workplace

And everything in its place
- Sustain/Standardize--make cleaning and checking (previous 3 steps) routine
- Systematize--spread the previous 4 steps throughout the organization and continually improve

Starting the 5s campaign
- Red Tag = Unneeded or rarely used items that need to be moved or thrown away
- Yellow Tag = Items that need to be repaired or adjusted

By far the second important principle in lean is the simplicity of the visual factory (VF) implementation. VF is an operational philosophy based on fast absorption of information to make effective decisions. Fundamentally it captures with pictures the essence of the process based on the following three items:
- Organize, Standardize, Communicate
- A picture is worth a thousand words
- Act like an aircraft controller

Tools

- Work Cells
- Production control boards
- Shadow boards–Tools, Tables
- Color keyed bins–Scrap, Rework
- Horns, Whistles, and Lights
- Inventory control cards

Visual layout

- Can see everything from one point
- Highlights abnormalities
- Designed for visual control

Process standards

- Standardize
- Improve
    - improvement comes before innovation
    - Normally no-cost or low-cost
    - Every improvement, no matter how small is worthwhile, small improvements over time add up to a large total improvement
- Innovate
- Best, easiest, safest way you know today
- Only one standard at a time
- Documentation of know-how
- Objective, simple, conspicuous
- Consistent with quality, cost, and delivery requirements
- Show relationship between cause and effect

Benefits of standards

- Result in balanced production with minimum inventory and labor
- Focus management
    - Maintenance and improvement
- Basis for training
- Basis for audit and diagnosis
- Control variability
- Ensure sharing of "Best Practices"

3 Elements of standardized work

- Takt time
- Standard work-in-process inventory
- Work sequence (Order of operations)

Takt

- Overproduction = Worst waste
    - How do you know if you are overproducing?

- Takt Time = $\dfrac{Available\ Time}{Customer\ Requirements}$

    German word "To Pace", "Rhythm"
    - Available time: run time if everything was perfect

Lean Functions for the Lean Enterprise

To understand the fundamentals just mentioned this section will address some specific functions for a typical organization. First and foremost *all* activities fall into one of these three categories:

- Value Added
- Type I Waste - adds no value but necessary "Non-value added work"
- Type II Waste - adds no value and avoidable

Categories of Action	Action	Examples
Value Added	Work that is worth something to the customer	Instruction; Weld flange onto part Bolt muffler to vehicle
Type I Waste	Non Value added work	Hanging posters on the wall; Pull down impact ranch Clamp and unclamp
Type II Waste	Inspection Inventory	Sorting Waiting

Lean deployment sheet

Do you see this	Do you see this?	Do you see this	Do you see this
Visual factory		**Pull systems**	
Non-Lean	**Lean**	**Non-Lean**	**Lean**
No notification information-(Andon) Boards No/little evidence of Lean metrics used Variations in work performance Standard procedures not being followed Dirty, cluttered, messy work areas Messy bathrooms Materials piled everywhere Unmarked gauges & tools No min/max levels at line side Empty shadow boards, tools missing, disorganized dirty floors, overflowing drawers, cabinets and desks	Used notification/information (Andon) Boards Demonstrate use of key Lean metrics Standardized Work forms prominently displayed/workers knowledgeable Workers do the job the same way every time Sparkling, clean equipment, tools, work areas and bathrooms Designated area for empty/full containers Marked gauges & key equipment Min/Max levels clearly marked Shadow boards for tools that are used and maintained Shiny clean floor-painted	High level of inventory on lines & in plant-receiving & shipping Materials waiting & stacked at line side Delivery timing of materials unregulated Centralized schedules w/out Takt times Products "pushed" to the next area	Low level of inventory on lines & in plant Real Kanban system in use Material delivered frequently to line side Use of small supermarket areas Localized/Customer demand with Takt times Use of Load Leveling
Evidence of teams		**Returnable container/dunnage**	
No production data visible (or outdated) Lack of conference room for teams to use Suggestion campaign old, suggestion box not active, little implementation of suggestions accepted No problem solving involvement at operator level 8D done in quality department Team not actively involved in Standardized Work activity or work flow	Available team meetings areas Team data prominently displayed - Quality data - Production real time data - Problem solving evidence Training depth chart Teams implemented many of their own suggestions Proof of problem solving activities many places in plant (Fishbone diagrams filled out and displayed, PDCA cycle being followed, 5 Why's) Aggressive team Standardized Work input Six Sigma used to reduce variation	Cardboard containers Wooden pallets Large number of parts/containers	Re-usable containers (plastic, metal) recycled between organization and suppliers Small number of parts/containers
		Equipment stability	
		Little visible evidence of preventive maintenance process Frequent breakdowns & no tracking No Overall Equipment Effectiveness (OEE) data No study/analysis into major losses	Maintenance schedule posted and carried out - employees involved Breakdowns fixed quickly and prevented OEE at 85% or better (posted and tracked by teams)
Changeover		**Layout and good material flow**	
Usually done by one person No tracking of changeover time Most work done when machine is down Lack of standardized methods - no specific work task/procedures identified	Changeover done by team Clear internal/external task identification Changeover chart tracks times, improvements, goals, ideas Use of changeover chart, visual organization used, standard methods	Insufficient, poorly spaced docks Cluttered staging areas Warehouse/Storage poorly placed for continuous flow Designated scrap areas that are full Long conveyors, full of WIP	Point of use shipping & receiving docks Visually clear and simple staging areas Well placed small market area Little scrap/use of mistake proofing Short conveyors, min/max levels marked
		Cell design	
		Inefficient, assembly configurations Assembly long way from point of use Storage of completed materials (more than 1 Day's supply)	U-shaped cells/no wasted motion Cells adjacent to point of use Sub-assembly and raw materials storage of 4 hours to support production

		Lean process flow	
		Operation running much faster than customer requirements Large buffers/production push product Large off-line repair bays	Operation tied to customer requirements Small buffers used sparingly to de-couple major processes Production pulled from prior operation

First Time Through (FTT)

Definition: First Time Through is the percentage of units that complete a process and meet quality guidelines the first time without being scraped, rerun, retested, diverted for off-line repair, or returned. It is a measure of the quality of the process.

$$\frac{\text{Units entering process - (scrap + reruns + retests + repaired off-line + returns)}}{\text{Units entering process}}$$

Stretch Objective: One hundred percent (100%) FTT capability = Zero defects made or passed on

Why:
Improvements in First Time Through will result in:
- Increased capacity
- Improved product quality to internal and external customers
- Reduced need for excess production inventory resulting in improved Dock to Dock time
- Improved ability to maintain sequence throughout the process resulting in improved Build to Schedule performance
- Increased quality input to constraint operations resulting in improved Overall Equipment Effectiveness
- Elimination of wastes due to scrap, repair, and excess inventory resulting in improved Total Cost

Where:
FIT data should be collected at the end of processes.

When:
First Time Through data should be collected and used, at minimum, by shift. FTT data must drive business practices behavior. In the educational process it may be considered to be used as a graduate measure of the students.

First Time Through Calculation

Units entering process - (scrap + returns + repaired off-line + retests) Units entering process	
Units entering (students)	1000
Scrap (failing; not passed)	10
Returns (repeating grade)	15
Retest (taking test over)	5
Repair off line (counseling and or tutoring)	0
FTT%	1000-(10+15+5+0)/1000
FTT%	970/1000
FTT%	97.0%
FTT Multiple Operations Calculation Examples	
FTT – Operation 1	92.87%
FTT – Operation 2	87.65%
FTT –Operation 3	82.34%
Final Inspection – Operation 4	82.34%
Total FTT%	(.9287x.8765x.6598x.8234)
Total FTT%	44.22%

Dock to Dock (DTD)

Definition: Dock to Dock is the elapsed time between the unloading of raw materials and the release of finished goods for shipment. DTD measures how fast raw materials are converted to finished goods and shipped. It is a measure (in hours) of the speed of material through the plant, not the speed of the processes. In the education process we can evaluate DTD based on cohorts of students. Of course we can still use it in the classical sense as well.

Why:

- Organizations and or facilities must eliminate waste and move towards customer "Pull" systems.
- By building large buffers you produce more parts (increase the speed of your process) but slow down the speed of materials.
- Decreasing inventories leads to less material handling and storage, which results in fewer opportunities to damage parts.

Where:

- Raw Material -- Purchased Part (control part) - Begin counting when it is received in the plant, even on consignment, because it is already in its product form
- Raw material that is changed to its product form.
- Work-in-Process (WIP), including material in repair/rework areas, and all buffers
- Finished Goods End Item Products - All finished goods containing the control part are included in the DTD calculation until they are physically shipped from the dock.

When:

Data should be collected at the same time which best represents the operating pattern of a product line.

Total Dock To Dock Calculation

DTD (Single Operation)   = $\underline{\text{Total Units of Control Part}}$
                                       End of Line Rate

DTD (Multiple Operation) = $\underline{\text{DTD (Operation 1) + DTD (Operation 2) + DTD (Operation 3)...}}$
                                                            End of Line Rate

The End of Line Rate is calculated off the last operation in the service line for a product:

Total Unit Produced	730 (from last operation)	
Production Hours	12 hours (10 scheduled production hrs = 2 unplanned overtime hrs)	
End of Line Rate	730/12 = 60.83	
Units in Area	Raw Material + Work-in-Process (by Operation) + Finished Goods	
Raw Material	300	
Operation 1	181	
Operation 2	3	
Operation 3	3	
Finished Goods	200	
DTD (Raw Material)	300/60.83	4.93 hrs
DTD (Operation 1)	181/60.83	2.98.hrs
DTD (Operation 2)	3/60.83	0.05 hrs
DTD (Operation 3)	3/60.83	0.05 hrs
DTD (Finished Goods)	200/60.83	3.29 hrs
Total DTD = 4.93 hr + 2.98 hr + .05 hr + .05 hr + 3.29 hr		
Total Dock to Dock time = 11.3 Hours		

Overall Equipment Effectiveness (OEE)

Definition: OEE is a combination of three different calculations. It is a measure of the availability, performance efficiency, and quality rate of a given piece of equipment. OEE data will help identify several wastes caused by machine/process inefficiencies.

Stretch Objective: World class standard, 85% OEE.

Why:
- Higher throughput (increases capacity) decreasing Total Dock to Dock times.
- More stable processes improve production predictability, therefore improving Build to Schedule.
- Higher throughput and lower rework/scrap leads to improved First Time Through and Total Cost.

Where:
OEE should be measured on machines in your constraint operations.

When:
Data should be collected by shift and by product or job if applicable. OEE data should be reviewed daily, and trended over time to identify improvement opportunities and verify the effectiveness of process changes.

Special consideration: OEE data must not be used to compare facility-to-facility performance. Too many variables exist in physical environments, facility layout, and machine/process uniqueness, to compare on a valid basis.

OEE	Availability x Performance Efficiency x Quality
Availability	$\dfrac{Operating\ Time}{Net\ Available\ Time}$
Performance Efficiency	$\dfrac{Ideal\ Cycle\ Time - Total\ Parts\ Run}{Operating\ Time}$
Quality	$\dfrac{Total\ Parts\ Run - Total\ Defects}{Total\ Parts\ Run}$

OEE Calculation Example

Availability	
Total schedule time (including overtime)	720 min
Required downtime (e.g. 30 min. lunch; 30 min breaks, etc.)	30 + 30 = 60 min
Net available time All other downtime (e.g. machine downtime and die changes)	720 − 60 = 660 min 45 + 45 = 90 min
Operating time	660 − 90 = 570 min
Availability	$\dfrac{570}{660} = 86.3\%$
Performance Efficiency	
Ideal cycle time	0.33 min/part
Total parts run	1440
Operating time	570 min
Performance	(.33 x 1440) = 83.4%
Efficiency	570
Quality Rate	
Total items run	1440
Rework	50
Scrap	40
Quality Rate	$\dfrac{1440 - (50 + 40)}{1440} = 93.8\%$
Overall Equipment Effectiveness	
Availability	86.3%
Performance efficiency	83.4%
Quality rate	93.8%
OEE	.863 x .834 x .938
OEE	67.5%

Quick Changeover

Definition: A method for people to analyze and significantly reduce setup and changeover time.
Changeover Time: The time between the last good piece off one activity run and the first good piece off the next activity run after the changeover.
Internal: Activities performed while the machine is shut down.
External: Activities performed while the machine is safely running.

		Changeover Time				
1	Run A	External	Internal	External	Run B	
		Start: Document current changeover elements				
2	Run A	Internal		Run B		50% reduction
		Separate internal/external activities				
3	Run A	Internal		Run B		75% reduction
		Shift internal activity to external				
4	Run A	Internal	Run B			90% reduction
		Streamline internal and or external activities				

Quick Changeover Process

1. Document Current Changeover Process
   - Document each element (Consider Photo's/Video)
   - Time the process and the elements
   - Establish baseline
2. Separate Internal and External Activities
   - Internal activities must be performed while the machine is down
   - External activities can be performed while the machine is running
3. Shift Internal Activities to External
   - Analyze each element
   - Ask five (5) whys
   - Resolve if the element can be made external
4. Locate Parallel Activities
   - Tasks that are independent of each other can be performed simultaneously
   - Changeover time can be reduced significantly by doing jobs in parallel (simultaneously)
5. Streamline Internal/External Activities
   - Adjustment elimination
   - Fixtures and jigs
   - Functional standards
   - Quick die change hardware
6. Implement the Revised Plan
   - Examine feasibility of all ideas
7. Validate the Method/Verify the Results
   - Develop draft procedures
   - Test procedures

276

- Verify results with data
8. Document the New Method on a Standard Worksheet
   - One Standard Worksheet for External
   - One for each set of parallel internal activities
9. Notify Other Areas

Visual Factory

Definition: A facility in which anyone can know in 5 minutes or less the who, what, where, when, how, and why of any work area, without talking to anyone, opening a book, or turning on a computer.

Visual Factory Levels
Visual display
Level 1: Share information. Sharing all information about activities lets everyone see how closely performance conforms to expectations.

Level 2: Share standards at the site. Sharing information about standard specifications and methods lets everyone identify non-conformance as it occurs and helps to correct it.

Visual controls
Level 3: Build standards into the workplace. Make the work environment (space limits, standard containers, equipment barriers) communicate established standards.

Level 4: Warn about abnormalities. Incorporate lights, alarms, bells, buzzers and other devices that alert workers when an abnormality is detected, such as a defect generated or a shortage of parts.

Level 5: Stop abnormalities. Prevent defects from moving on after detection by stopping the process or rejecting the part. Devices are installed at the source of abnormalities.

Level 6: Prevent abnormalities. Level 6 means 100% prevention of abnormalities. Once the exact cause of a defect is known, an error proofing device is installed to prevent the defect from occurring at all.

5 Steps to Workplace Organization (Known as the 5S system)

Step 1: Sort (Organization)
- Distinguish between what is needed and what is not needed.

Step 2: Stabilize (Orderliness)
- "A place for everything and everything in its place."
- Determine the best location for all necessary items.

Step 3: Shine (Cleanliness)
- Eliminating dirt, dust, fluids, and other debris to make the work area clean.
- Adopting cleaning as a form of inspection

Step 4: Standardize (Adherence)
- Maintain and monitor the first three "S's".
- Check/Standardize/Maintain/Monitor/Improve

Step 5: Sustain (Self-discipline)
- Correct procedures have become habit.
- The workplace is well ordered according to agreed upon procedures.
- Manager, operator, and engineers are deeply committed to 5S.

Error Proofing

Definition: Error Proofing is a process improvement to prevent a specific defect from occurring.

Three Sides of Error Proofing
      Physical   - Install hardware
      Operational   - Enforce procedure, sequence and/or execution
      Philosophical - Empowerment of workforce

Approaches to Error Proofing
      Prevention   - Prevents errors from creating defects
      Detection   - Detects defects and immediately initiates corrective action to prevent multiple defects from forming

Definition of a Defect: A defect is the result of any deviation from product specifications that may lead to customer dissatisfaction. To classify as a defect:

- The product has deviated from operating or design specifications.
- The product does not meet internal and/or external customer expectations.

Definition of an Error: An error is any deviation from a specified operating process. There can be an error without a defect. There cannot be a defect without an error first. The result of an error is demonstrated in a defect.

Error Proofing Approach

Error Proofing Teams: Error Proofing Teams may be composed of teachers, Department Heads, administrators, and support personnel. The observations, abilities and creativity of each individual are combined to:
- Make changes to the work environment
- Increase instruction efficiency
- Take ownership in the educational process
- Support continual improvement in the workplace

Error Proofing Method
1. Identify the problem
2. List possible errors
3. Determine the most likely error
4. Propose multiple solutions
5. Evaluate effectiveness, cost, complexity of solutions
6. Determine the best solution (include data analysis)
7. Develop implementation plan
8. Analyze preliminary benefits
9. Develop plan for long-term measure of benefits
10. Congratulate the team

Benefits of Error Proofing
- Business Costs - cost of additional energy and equipment required to manage a poor quality educational environment

- Liability Costs - cost of losing business due to poor product quality
- Cultural Costs - reduction of worker moral

Just in time

Just-In-Time (JIT) establishes a system to supply work (data, information, etc.) or services at precisely the right time, in the correct amount, and without error. Just-In-Time is the heart of a Lean system and is an overriding theme for Lean education. JIT is attained through the understanding and application of continuous flow, the pull system, and kanbans.

Continuous flow

Continuous Flow is characterized by the ability of a process to replenish a single unit of work (or service capacity) when the customer has pulled it. The concept of continuous flow is used to move work, students or provide a service between processes with minimal or no wait (queue) time. It is further used to ensure that the process is performing the work required, no sooner or no later than requested, as well as in the correct quantity, with no defects (non conformances). The goal is to not do any work or service that is not requested by the downstream process (or customer). It is synonymous with Just-In-Time. By focusing on continuous flow the team will be able to:

- Reduce or eliminate transport, delay, and motion waste
- Decrease lead times
- Reduce queue times
- Allow staff to identify and fix problems earlier
- Provide the needed flexibility in meeting demand changes
- Improve patient and staff satisfaction levels

True (100%) continuous flow in an educational facility will most likely not be achieved because of the staff and departmental interdependencies required in the various educational pathways. Therefore, the tools of in-process supermarkets, FIFO Lanes, and Kanbans can be used at certain times when cycle lime differences between processes exist and flow needs to be improved.

In-process supermarket

The In-process supermarket is a physical device between two processes that stores a certain quantity of work or service capacity that, when needed, is pulled by the downstream process. Its origination came from the grocery stores and how the clerks replenish food items. Supermarkets do not typically have large storage areas for many of their goods. Every item is received and transferred straight to the shelves (especially the perishable items), where it is made available to the customer. No costly storage. No large storage areas. No waiting. Minimum inventory.

The In-process supermarket (i.e., the grocery store shelf between the supplier of the goods and the consumer) exists due to the variations in customer demand. The customer's lead time is minimal (the time it takes to remove something off the shelf), therefore, it would not be feasible to have just one item there. In order to establish the In-process supermarket, an ordering pattern, establishing minimum and maximum levels needs to be determined to create a balance between what the customer demand is and the frequency of delivery to the store (and shelf). In-process supermarkets can also be explained in terms of cycle time. A supermarket exists between two processes to accommodate the differences in the cycle times of those processes. This is called the pull system. Only the amount that has been used by the customer for that day, week, or month (depending on the ordering pattern), or "pulled" from the shelf, is reordered. The maximum level is never exceeded. For In-process supermarkets to be successful, the following will need to be in place:

- A quantitative understanding of the downstream requirements
- Known cycle times for the downstream and upstream processes
- Communication system between the upstream and downstream processes
- Minimum and maximum number of work units or service capacity assigned to the supermarket
- Standard work created explaining the operation of the supermarket
- Training of all process workers on the supermarket operation
- Adequate documentation and visual controls communicating to the downstream process when there is a disruption in the flow
- A signal or "kanban" triggers a "pull" from the downstream process to the upstream process to replenish with what was removed

Kanban

Kanban is a card or visual indicator that serves as a means of communicating to an upstream process precisely what is required at the specified time. In Japanese, kanban means "card," "billboard," or "sign." Kanban refers to the inventory control card used in a pull system. It is used to regulate the flow or work in and out of supermarkets as a visual control to trigger action.

Kanban is a form of visual control (information that allows a process to be controlled). This information states when, who, what, and how many work units are needed for movement. A kanban can be anything from an actual index card, a file folder, or some type of electronic signal. There needs to be a mailbox or some repository for the kanban to be deposited in, as well as the signal system identifying it is there.

The most common use for the In-process supermarket is the ordering of supplies. Kanbans for supplies will ensure that the dollars allocated for supplies will be at the minimum required. The kanban system is used to create a "pull" of material, in this case a supply item, from the downstream process to the upstream process. The formal application to kanban is an eight step approach:

1. *Conduct the supply survey*: The team will need to create a standard list of supplies from which to draw upon. Distribute the list to all staff in the area requesting them to determine their usage level for a period of time (day/shift, week or month). Examples are: lab supplies, exam gloves, blue pads, books, general use office items and so on. A typical form will look like Table C.1.

Table C.1. A typical Supply survey form

Supply survey form		
Select from the list below the frequency of the items you will most likely use within a specific time (shift, week, month and so on). If not on the list, please add the item at the bottom of the list. This info will be used in the Lean initiative to reduce or eliminate excess waste.		
Item Description	Quantity used/time period	Comments

2. *Establish minimum/maximum levels*: Once the list and special requests have been collected, gain a consensus on usage and establish minimum/maximum levels. Include the following:
   a. Type of standard supply (there are numerous glove sizes, so agreement must be made on a certain quantity for each size – small, medium, large or one size fits all.)
   b. Weekly or monthly usage for the items
   c. Establish a minimum quantity to have on hand
   d. Establish a maximum quantity to have on hand
3. *Create the Supply Order Form*: The Supply Order Form will list all the supplies represented by information obtained from the Supply Survey Form – see Table C.2. The minimum quantity to have on hand is the quantity of items expected to be used during the time it takes to re-supply that item (plus some X factor or buffer). The X factor or buffer is to ensure no stock-out occurs at any time. The X factor is typically determined by the team and their experience (historical data) with the supplies. It may be one day's worth of a particular supply; it may be a week's worth, again depending on the experience of the team. The maximum quantity to have on hand will be the minimum quantity plus the number of items that would be used during the supply or replenishment time.

Table C.2. A typical order form

Supply Order Form				
Fax this form to the Central supply at extension XXXX by 16:00 hours. Your supplies will be delivered by 06:30 hours the next day				
Number	**Item description**	**Item #**	**Quantity ordered (Maximum – Minimum)**	**Unit price**
1				
2				
3				

4. Create the kanban cards: There should be one kanban card identified as the *Supply Re-order Kanban* for each supply item. It should be laminated and color coded, differentiating more than one supply ordering location (i.e. Lab, Central Supply Office, Janitorial/ Maintenance Service, etc.). Kanban cards should be affixed to the minimum re-order quantity item. For example, attach the kanban card to the last box of working gloves size (X) on the shelf, or the last bottle of a reagent in the lab shelf. The card should be appropriate size to visually convey the need. It is important here to note that in order to ensure that special items are identified a Special Order Kanban Card is created and is filled in by the staff for each of the special order items (e.g., latex-free gloves). Monitor the Special Order Kanbans to determine if they should be included on the standard Supply Order Form. This will be the case if the special items are used quite frequent and are part of the normal process. A typical card is shown in Table C.3

Table C.3. A typical re-order Kanban card

Supply Re-order Kanban Card
Item Name:
Maximum Quantity:
Minimum Quantity:
Re-order Quantity:
Supplier Name:
Catalog Page Number:
Return this card to the Kanban envelop

5. *Create standard work*: Once the system has been designed and the reordering process has been determined now the team is ready to begin creating the standard work chart. This should be posted in a place where it can be seen and used by the appropriate staff. It can also be used as a training vehicle for the new staff. A typical standard work may be a procedure and or instruction. It can be in a prose form or a process flow diagram.

6. *Conduct the training*: The training for the department should be done prior to implementation to ensure integrity of the system. The training should include the following:
   a. A brief explanation on the purpose of kanbans
   b. Explanation on how the minimum/maximum levels were established and convey appreciation for everyone's input when the Supply Survey was conducted
   c. Explanation of how the system will work (distribute process flowcharts)
   d. Explanation of the two types of kanbans: Supply Re-order and Special Order Kanban A demonstration at the supply cabinet on how the kanban system will work
   e. Acknowledgement of the key individuals within the team that contributed to this system
   f. Communication that this is a work-in-progress trial and improvement ideas from all staff members will be welcomed

7. *Implement the kanban system*: Training and implementation should occur simultaneously. Once the training has been completed, the kanban for supplies will be ready to use.

8. *Maintain the standards*: After a month or two of usage, review the appropriate budget supply line item, determine the cost savings, congratulate the team, and convey the success of the initiative to management. At all times during the kanban implementation, take suggestions on how the process can be improved. The responsibility to maintain the system should be rotated among the staff on a regular basis. This will help to ensure, as they take care of the system, that they will have an appreciation for how it works, and therefore, be more supportive of using the system as it was intended to be used. The benefits of implementing a kanban system for supplies are:

   a. Ensures minimum inventory
   b. Creates staff awareness of the cost of supplies
   c. Easy tool to implement and train
   d. Encourages teamwork
   e. Minimizes transactions on ordering supplies
   f. Reduces stress
   g. Reduces excess inventory waste
   h. Allows staff to understand the concepts of flow and supermarkets
   i. Reduce costs
   j. Eliminates the waste of motion of searching through excess supplies

First-In First-Out (FIFO)

FIFO is a work-controlled method to ensure the oldest work upstream (first-in) is the first to be processed downstream (first-out). For example, in central supply areas, certain chemicals are kept for the ground maintenance and sport fields. However, because some of these chemical have a defined life they are continuously rotated, replacing them with the up-and-coming expiration dates to the front of the shelf. This can also apply to work requests in other areas such as laboratories, and so on. The FIFO lane has the following attributes:

- Located between two processes (supply and demand)
- A maximum number of work units (written orders, lab requests, etc.) are placed in the FIFO lane and are visible
- Is sequentially loaded and labeled
- Has a signal system to notify the upstream process when the lane is full
- Has visual rules and standards posted to ensure FIFO lane integrity
- Has a process in place for assisting the downstream process when the lane is full and assistance is required

The team can be creative in establishing the signal method, within the FIFO system, to indicate when the system is full. This could be a raised flag, a light, a pager code, an alert email, or text message to the upstream process. The important point is to ensure the signal established will work effectively. When the signal is released, the upstream worker lends support to the downstream worker until the work is caught up. There is no point in continuing to produce upstream when the downstream process is overloaded. When this happens, it becomes an overproduction waste, which is considered the greatest waste of all. A typical example of this is processing clerical forms and delivering them correctly to the appropriate person and or department. Often this does not happen due to incorrect or missing information. However, the clerk keeps on producing these forms. The result is that the clerk ends up with a pile of incomplete forms and frustrated.

FIFO lanes help to ensure smooth work flow between processes with little or no interruption. Keep in mind that In-process supermarkets and FIFO Lanes are compromises to true continual flow. They should be viewed as part of a continual improvement system and efforts should be made to find ways to reduce or eliminate them in the quest for continual flow.

Pitch

Pitch is the time frame that represents the most efficient and practical work flow throughout the value stream. It can be a multiple of Takt time. Since Takt time, for many educational practices typically will be too small of a unit of time to move the work or information to the next process immediately, pitch is a solution that can be used. Pitch is the *optimal flow* of work at specific times through the value stream. Pitch is the adjusted Takt time (or multiple of) when Takt time is too short of a time to realistically move something. Typically, each value stream (or process-to-process timed movement) will have its own pitch. Pitch will:

- Assist to determine the optimal work flow
- Set the frequency for movement of the work to the next process
- Assist in reducing transport and motion waste
- Allow for immediate attention when interruptions to work flow arise
- Reduce wait (or queue) times
  Very important note: Each value stream may require a separate pitch.

Pitch is used to reduce wait time and other wastes that exist within and between processes. The steps for calculating Pitch are:

1. Calculate Takt time.
2. Determine the optimal number of work units to move through the value stream.
3. Multiply Takt time by the optimal number of work units. Pitch = Takt time (x) optimal number of work units

Pitch increments must be monitored to ensure they are being met. If an interruption of work arises, a system should be in place to address why the work is behind schedule. There are different ways this can occur:

- The group leader communicates the need for assistance when pitch cannot be met
- The employee who cannot meet the next pitch work increment communicates the need for assistance
- The runner (see next section) communicates the need for assistance

The communication signal required for assistance can include:

- A pager code or text message to the supervisor or departmental manager
- An alert email, text message, etc. can be sent to all employees for a pre-defined round-robin type of support
- A phone call to the supervisor
- A physical meeting with the departmental leader or supervisor

Creating a visible pitch board will allow employees to think and work differently about the process that is being improved. A visible pitch board is a bulletin board, whiteboard, etc. displaying the pitch increments and/or associated work that is required to be done for that day or week. The simple fact of having a visual board at a location where the work is being done will be a motivating factor for employees to meet the goal (or pitch increment) that has been determined. This will create a sense of satisfaction each time the work (or pitch increment) is completed. The benefits of a visible pitch board are it:

- Begins to remove the work from desks and to make it known
- Allows managers/supervisors to monitor hourly/daily progress and be aware of situations when work is getting behind
- Provides a foundation to advance to a more sophisticated scheduling system (i.e., Leveling system) at a later date

If an employee gets behind (say more than 1 pitch increment) of what is required there should be a standard procedure to follow (i.e., notify supervisor, request assistance from another staff member, etc.). The important point regarding pitch is to group work that can be aligned around a specified value stream, thereby reducing the queue time and other wastes that exist between two processes. Making the pitch increments as a visual cue is a great way to get everyone involved to a work rhythm (i.e., Takt time). It places emphasis on completing a certain quantity of work in an allotted time to meet customer demand and further provides the team a common purpose of maintaining this "demand." After a specific period of time usually a month or two of using visible pitch for a value stream, and as other value streams use the visible pitch board tool, then they all can be incorporated into a Heijunka or Leveling system.

Work load balancing
Work load balancing is the optimal distribution of work units throughout the value stream to maintain Takt time or pitch. Also known as employee/staff balancing or line balancing, work load balancing assures that now one worker is doing too much or too little work. Work load balancing begins with analyzing the current state of how work relative to the value stream is allocated and ends with an even and fair distribution of

work, ensuring that customer demand is met with a continuous flow mentality. Work load balancing will accomplish the following:

- Determine the number of staff needed for a given demand (or value stream)
- Evenly distribute work units
- Ensure cycle times for each process are accurate
- Assist to standardize the process
- Assist in creating the future state value stream (or process) map
- Improve productivity
- Encourage teamwork through cross-training

The best tool to perform the work load balancing is an Employee Balance Chart. The Employee Balance Chart is a visual display, in the form of a bar chart, that represents the work elements, times, and workers for each process relative to the total value stream cycle time and Takt time (or pitch). The seven steps to work load balancing are:

1. *Visually display the list of processes from the current state value stream map*: Be very clear about identifying each process, its beginning and end as well as the process's parameters. The team should have a good understanding of the processes from previously creating the current state value stream map.
2. *Obtain individual cycle times for the various process activities*: Cycle times should be derived from the current state value stream map and the Document Tagging Worksheet and/or observation data. Revisit these times to ensure accuracy. Members of the team may want to use a stopwatch to time any process activities that may be questionable, evaluating the processes as they check the times. Take time to analyze the processes.
3. *Add the individual cycle times to obtain the total cycle time for each process*: Each process's total cycle time should match the process times located on the step graph at the bottom of the current state value stream map.
4. *Create the Employee Balance Chart of the current state*: The Employee Balance Chart is a bar chart identifying each process and staff, along with the various individual cycle times as derived from the current state value stream map. This may be the entire current state value stream map or sections of it where it is known that duties can be shared or consolidated to improve the overall flow. It is recommended that you visually display the chart on an easel with a flip chart so the team can review it as a group and comment. Use Post-it Notes to represent the tasks associated with the processes. Make the Post-it Notes proportional to the time element for each individual task. Draw a horizontal line to represent Takt time.
5. *Determine the ideal number of staff for a value stream*. When determining the ideal number of workers needed to operate the process or processes for the value stream, keep in mind that staff will most likely have multiple value streams they are responsible for throughout the day. The ideal number of staff is determined by dividing the total process cycle time by the Takt time (or pitch). For example, in the lab, if an average blood draw took 5 minutes (total cycle time) and the demand (Takt time) was determined to be 5 minutes (12 patient draws per hour), then the ideal number of staff needed would be 1 person (5 minutes total cycle time / 5 minute Takt time). However, it rarely comes out that evenly. Use this to assist in determining staffing levels. However, if the decimal number from the calculation is less than X.5 workers required, balance the value stream to the lesser whole number. Ensure each worker is balanced to Takt time and allocate any excess time to one worker. Utilize the excess time to improve standard work procedures and conduct kaizen activities, attempting to reduce additional wastes within the processes. Once the employee's efforts are no longer needed on the original project, that person can be placed in another continuous improvement

capacity or position in the organization. Lean is not about reducing the number of people, it is about eliminating waste. Without this understanding, Lean will never be accepted. If the decimal number from the calculation is equal to or greater than X.5, then balance to the larger whole number.

6. *Create the Employee Balance Chart of the future state*: Work with team members to move the Post-it Notes around to balance the various work elements with each employee balanced to Takt (or pitch) time, while maintaining the flow of work.
7. *Create standard work procedures and train staff*: Once a consensus has been obtained on balancing, redistributing, and/or modifying the process activities, update all necessary standards and then train staff to those standards.

Standard Work

Standard work (Standard Operating Procedures) establishes and controls the best way to complete a task without variation from the original intent. These tasks are then executed consistently, without variation from the original intent. Standard work offers a basis for providing consistent levels of healthcare productivity, quality, and safety, while promoting a positive work attitude based on well-documented work standards. Standard work, done properly, reduces all process variation. It is the basis for all continual improvement activities. Creating the standard work procedures is comprised of using two main tools: the Standard Work Combination Table and the Standard Work Chart.

The Standard Work Combination Table is the visual representation displaying the sequential flow of all the activities related to a specific process. The Standard Work Combination Table will:

- Document the exact time requirement (i.e., cycle times) for each work element or task in the process
- Indicate the flow (or sequence) of all the work in the process
- Display the work design sequence based on Takt time (ideally)
- Demonstrate the time relationship between physical work (patient care, dispersing meds, charting, etc.) to the movement of the patient or work (transporting patients, retrieving equipment, checking doctors' orders, etc.), queue times, and computer access time

The Standard Work Combination Table is an important tool for allocating work within the value stream when total cycle times are greater than Takt time. Capturing the motion of the process that is being reviewed is a good method to accurately document the times of each work element. The 7 steps for creating the Standard Work Combination Table are:

1. Break the process into separate work elements (record motion to obtain accuracy).
2. Time each work element from step (1) by observation or EMR/EMS database retrieval.
3. Complete the Standard Work Combination Table.
4. Review each work element (task). Question whether it should be eliminated or if the time can be improved.
5. Gain a consensus on any changes.
6. Create a new Standard Work Combination Table. Update the standard work procedures.
7. Train everyone on new standard work procedures and audit.

The Standard Work Combination Table is a powerful tool and should be used as the basis for all improvement activities. It does require time to thoroughly complete, but will be well worth the effort in the long run. It illustrates the sequence of the work performed and it provides a visual training aid for employees. Specifically, it a) Displays the work sequence, process layout, and work-in-process in relationship to each other b) Displays the worker movement for each activity, task, or operation and c)

286

Identifies quality standards, safety concerns, and/or critical opportunities for errors. The process of creating the standard work chart is:

- Draw the area layout or process flow on the chart. Label all items.
- Designate work element locations by number to correspond to items listed in (1).
- Use arrows to show movement of patients, information, staff, and any special instructions or safety concerns
- Post the chart in the work area and use as basis for continual improvement.

It will do little good to improve a process if it is not from an existing standard. If you do not work from some type of standard, you will be attempting to improve to a moving target, one of process variation.

Column Chart: Traditional approach to process balancing (Tenth grade metal shop)

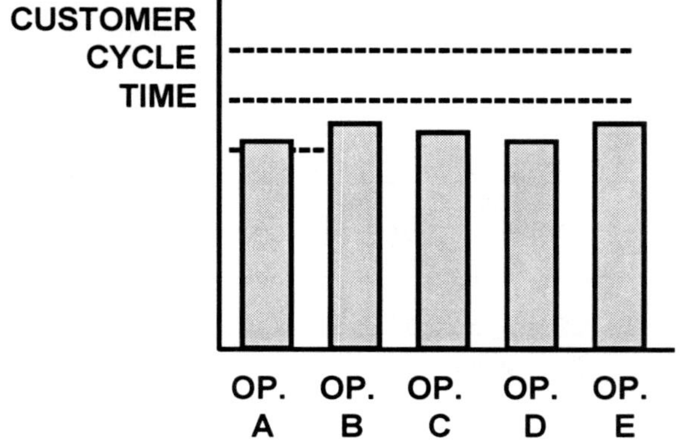

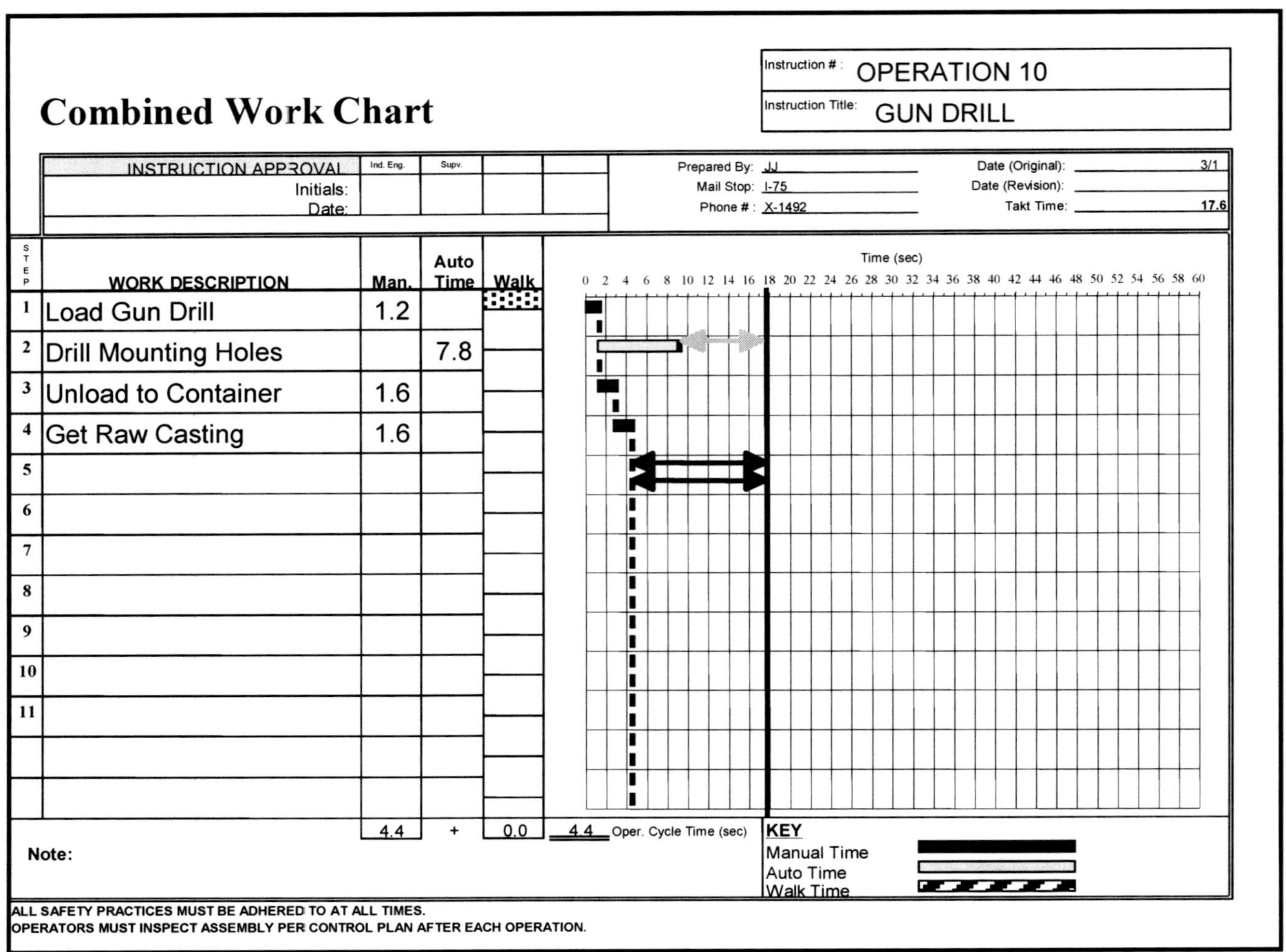

Yokoten

Yokoten means "best practice sharing" or "taking from one place to another." It encompasses the methods of communicating, documenting, and distributing knowledge horizontally within an organization (peer-to-peer) about what works and what doesn't work from an improvement project (i.e., PDCA Kaizen Event). Yokoten is a form of knowledge management. At its most basic level, Yokoten can be the notebook that a team keeps as a history of the group and problems/solutions encountered. Yokoten can be the library of A3 problem reports (Storyboards) that a team or work group maintains for all to access. As a knowledge management device, the Yokoten process ensures information becomes part of the organizational knowledge base. At Toyota there is an expectation that copying a good idea will be followed by some added "kaizen" to that idea (copy + kaizen = yokoten). Yokoten standardizes a solution and shares it. Sharing of standard procedures across an organization is ideal.

Approach Yokotens as follows:
1. Create a standard improvement methodology that problem solving, Lean, or Six Sigma teams will follow. Ensure adequate training is conducted.
2. Create standard forms and worksheets to be used. Inform employees where these forms are located on the Local Area Network.
3. Assign a certain date and time each month (or quarter) for groups and/or departments to share their PDCA Kaizen Event failures and successes. Allocate 10-15 minutes per group (or representatives) to share their improvement projects.
4. Document all completed PDCA Kaizen Events on the network (LAN) or company intranet.

288

5. Ensure each team completes a Yokoten Worksheet

Basic flowchart (macro level)

Approach creating this flowchart as follows:

1. Define the process boundaries with the beginning and ending points of the process.
2. Create no more than six boxes denoting what is occurring between the start and end points.
3. Review the flowchart with management to ensure everyone is on the same page with this macro view of the process or work flow.
4. Continue with more detailed flowcharting or value stream mapping (if appropriate) and follow the PDCA Kaizen Event methodology.

Deployment flowchart

Approach creating this flowchart as follows:

1. Identify the right people needed to develop the flowchart.
2. Define the process boundaries with the beginning and ending points of the process.
3. List the major steps (or time element) of the process vertically on the left sheet of paper.
4. List the responsible department (or process worker) across the top, each in a separate column.
5. List all the steps in their appropriate column and ensure they are connected by arrows.
6. Circulate the flowchart to other people within the process for input and/or clarification (if appropriate).
7. Identify areas for improvement.
8. Create the new flowchart and continue with the PDCA Kaizen Event methodology.

Opportunity flowchart

Approach creating this flowchart as follows:

1. Create a process flowchart (micro level).
2. Create separate columns on a flip chart or whitebeard. Label one Value-Added and the other one Non Value-Added (or Cost-Added Only).
3. List each step from the process flowchart in either column and ensure they are connected by arrows. Expand the steps to show specific areas of concern, if needed.
4. Identify areas for improvement.
5. Create the new flowchart and continue with the PDCA Kaizen Event methodology.

Spaghetti diagram

Approach creating this flowchart as follows:

1. Define the beginning and ending of the process.
2. Obtain an engineering drawing or create a scale representation of the physical layout of the process.
3. List each step of the process on the flowchart (or on a separate piece of paper).
4. Label and draw each of the steps (3) sequentially as how the process flows. Connect each step with an arrow line denoting the flow.
5. Gain a consensus if the process is inefficient (i.e., too many touches, too many hand-offs, too much travel, etc.).
6. Identify areas for improvement.
7. Create the new flowchart and continue with the PDCA Kaizen Event methodology.

Process flowchart (micro level) Approach creating this flowchart as follows:

1. Identify the right people needed to develop the flowchart. This may require people from outside the PDCA Kaizen Team for their expertise and knowledge.
2. Define the process boundaries with the beginning and ending points of the process.

3. Define the level of detail required.
4. Determine conditions and boundaries for the process flow.
5. List all the steps contained within the process flow. The Kaizen Event team may need to walk the process.
6. Circulate the flowchart to other people within the process for input and/or clarification.
7. Identify areas for improvement.
8. Create the new flowchart and continue with the PDCA Kaizen Event methodology.

Physical layout

A Lean physical layout work area is a self-contained, well-ordered space that optimizes the flow of patients and work. Typically, many facilities have areas or departments separated by physical walls that may impede the efficiency of work flow. Eliminating walls may be difficult to achieve, but once people understand some of the efficiencies that can be gained, they become engaged in tackling the challenges. Many different methods can be used, such as the computer and visual controls simulating these walls coming down. It is important to realize that there are delays in many processes due to the physical separations. Figure C.1 shows the comparison between the current physical arrangement with walls and a future Lean state designed without walls. Lean designs without walls remove any and all barriers that impact work flow, improving all types of communication and movement; no design should ever compromise patient safety or confidentiality.

Figure C.1. A typical physical layout

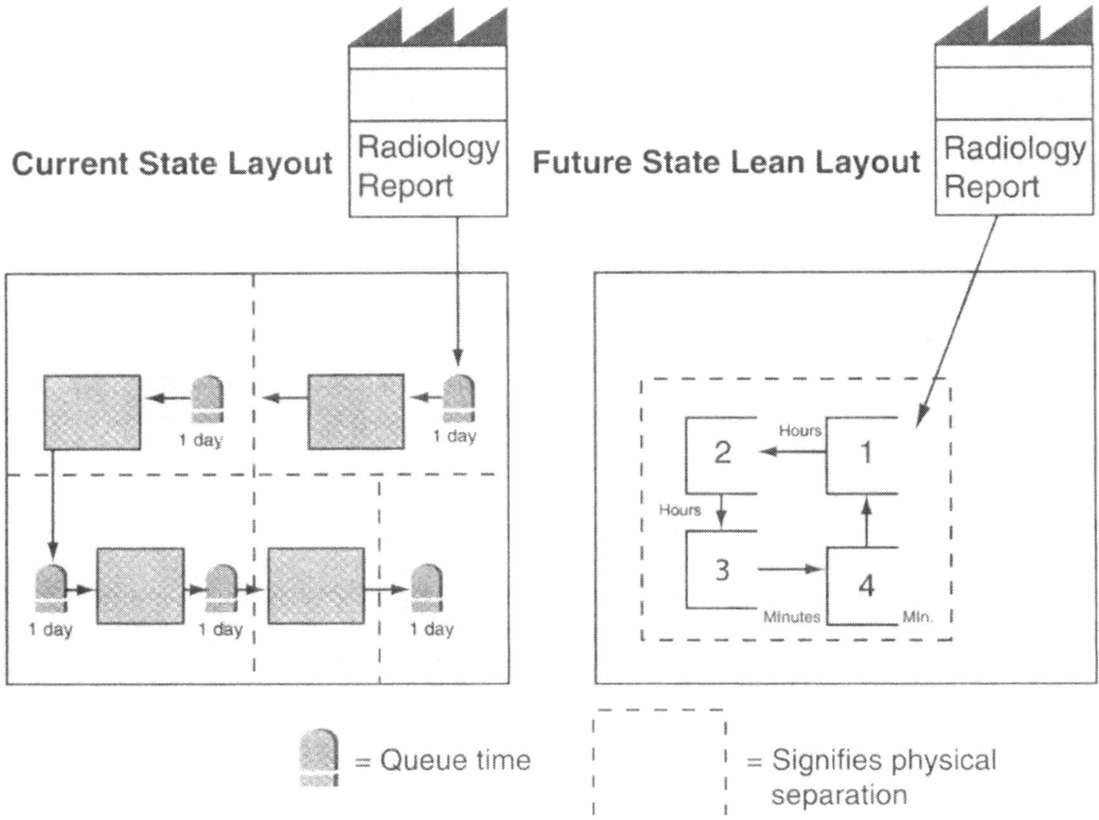

In education there are at least four possibilities in utilizing physical layout principles. They are:
1. Product focused
   a. Equipment laid out in process order
   b. Straight stream flow

2. Machine closer – see Figure C.2
    a. Facilitates one piece flow
    b. Reduces non value added walking
3. U shape configuration – see Figure C.3
    a. Allows volume flexibility with staffing
    b. Reduces non value added walking
    c. Improves communication and visual management
4. Customer focus
    a. Modules of capacity matched to major customer sites
    b. Allows operation to match customer needs
    c. Facilitates learning in the classroom environment

Figure C.2. A typical Layout configuration

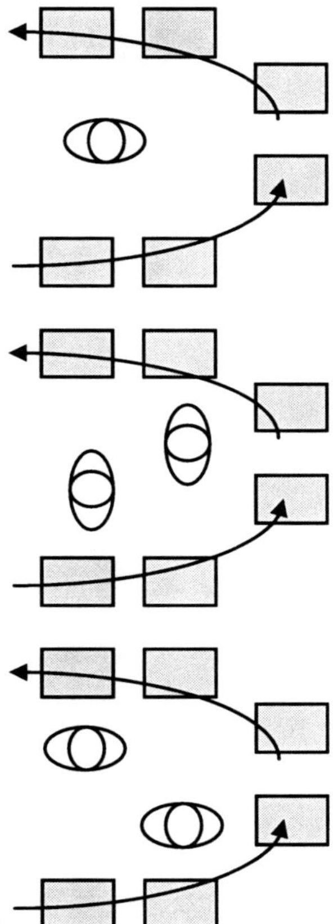

Figure C.3. A typical combination Layout to take advantage of both equipment and students or operators

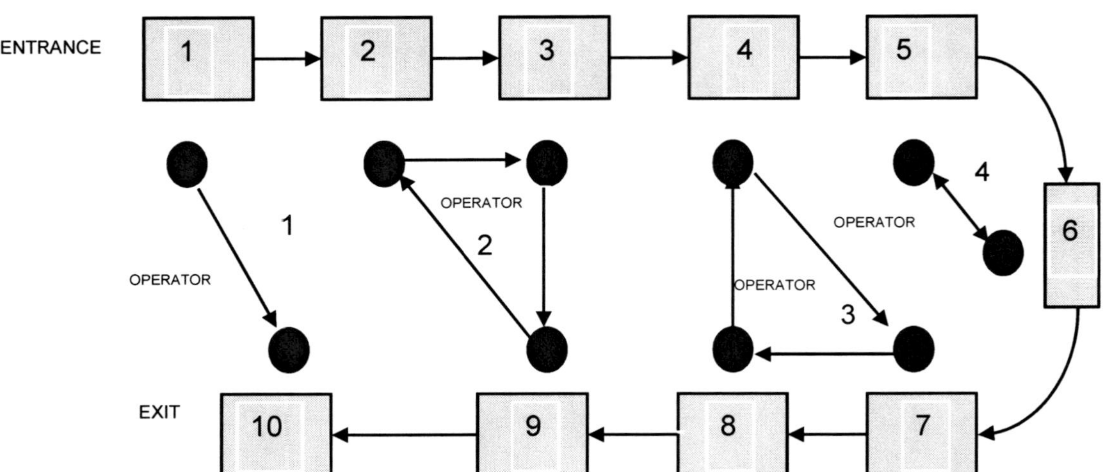

The benefits for selecting a physical layout are:

- Process knowledge can be better shared among the staff to allow everyone to be better trained
- Improved communications will occur between processes
- Wastes of delay, motion, and transport will be reduced or eliminated
- Most efficient use of equipment, people, and materials will be ensured
- Greater job flexibility will occur if someone is absent
- Less floor space will be required
- Work throughput will be increased as well as overall productivity

The following guidelines can be used when determining a new physical layout.
1. Review the current physical layout and associated process tasks to determine which wastes occur due to the current layout in terms of travel, motion, and delays.
2. Brainstorm to consolidate where to reduce or eliminate the wastes identified in (1). Processes may need to be modified or standardized and may require additional cross-training.
3. Determine if an In-process supermarket or FIFO lane is required.
4. Prepare a plan, including result expectations, to implement proposed changes.
5. Obtain management approval.
6. Implement new layout at a time when minimal disruption to the area would occur. Post any new standards when new layout has been completed.
7. Balance workloads amongst teachers and train accordingly.
8. Consider new technologies and software enhancements as you continue to improve.
9. Many educational facilities (especially universities) are building or expanding their facilities to accommodate the Baby Boomers and their expected demand for services. As these new facilities are being built, keep a Lean focus in mind to ensure many of the concepts contained in this book are incorporated in the design phase of the project.

APPENDIX D

SELECTED STATISTICAL FORMULAE

Parameters

- Population mean = $\mu = (\Sigma X_i) / N$
- Population standard deviation = $\sigma = \text{sqrt} [\Sigma (X_i - \mu)^2 / N]$
- Population variance = $\sigma^2 = \Sigma (X_i - \mu)^2 / N$
- Variance of population proportion = $\sigma_P^2 = PQ / n$
- Standardized score = $Z = (X - \mu) / \sigma$
- Population correlation coefficient = $\rho = [1 / N]*\Sigma\{[(X_i - \mu_X)/\sigma_x] * [(Y_i - \mu_Y)/\sigma_y]\}$

Statistics: [Unless otherwise noted, these formulas assume simple random sampling].

- Sample mean = $x = (\Sigma x_i) / n$
- Sample standard deviation = $s = \text{sqrt} [\Sigma (x_i - x)^2 / (n - 1)]$
- Sample variance = $s^2 = \Sigma (x_i - x)^2 / (n - 1)$
- Variance of sample proportion = $s_p^2 = pq / (n - 1)$
- Pooled sample proportion = $p = (p_1 * n_1 + p_2 * n_2) / (n_1 + n_2)$
- Pooled sample standard deviation = $s_p = \text{sqrt}[(n_1 -1)*s_1^2+(n_2 -1)* s_2^2]/(n_1 + n_2 - 2)]$
- Sample correlation coefficient = $r = [1 / (n - 1)]*\Sigma \{[(x_i - x)/ s_x] * [(y_i - y) / s_y]\}$

Correlation

- Pearson product-moment correlation = $r = \Sigma (xy) / \text{sqrt} [(\Sigma x^2) * (\Sigma y^2)]$
- Linear correlation (sample data) = $r =[1/(n - 1)]*\Sigma\{[(x_i - x) / s_x] * [(y_i - y) / s_y]\}$
- Linear correlation (population data) = $\rho = [1 / N] * \Sigma \{[(X_i - \mu_X) / \sigma_x] * [(Y_i - \mu_Y) / \sigma_y]\}$

Simple Linear Regression

- Simple linear regression line: $\hat{y} = b_0 + b_1 x$
- Regression coefficient = $b_1 = \Sigma [(x_i - x) (y_i - y)] / \Sigma [(x_i - x)^2]$
- Regression slope intercept = $b_0 = y - b_1 * x$
- Regression coefficient = $b_1 = r * (s_y / s_x)$
- Standard error of regression slope = $s_{b1} = \text{sqrt}[\Sigma(y_i - \hat{y}_i)^2 /(n - 2)]/\text{sqrt}[\Sigma(x_i - x)^2]$

Counting

- n factorial: $n! = n * (n-1) * (n - 2) * \ldots * 3 * 2 * 1$. By convention, $0! = 1$.
- Permutations of *n* things, taken *r* at a time: $_nC_r = n! / (n - r)!$
- Combinations of *n* things, taken *r* at a time: $_nC_r = n! / r!(n - r)! = {}_nP_r / r!$

Probability

- Rule of addition: $P(A \cup B) = P(A) + P(B) - P(A \cap B)$
- Rule of multiplication: $P(A \cap B) = P(A) P(B|A)$
- Rule of subtraction: $P(A') = 1 - P(A)$

Random Variables

In the following formulas, *X* and *Y* are random variables, and *a* and *b* are constants.

- Expected value of $X = E(X) = \mu_x = \Sigma [x_i * P(x_i)]$

- Variance of X = Var(X) = $\sigma^2 = \Sigma\,[\,x_i - E(x)\,]^2 * P(x_i) = \Sigma\,[\,x_i - \mu_x\,]^2 * P(x_i)$
- Normal random variable = z-score = $z = (X - \mu)/\sigma$
- Chi-square statistic = $X^2 = [\,(n - 1)\,*\,s^2\,]\,/\,\sigma^2$
- F statistic = $f = [\,s_1^2/\sigma_1^2\,]\,/\,[\,s_2^2/\sigma_2^2\,]$
- Expected value of sum of random variables = $E(X + Y) = E(X) + E(Y)$
- Expected value of difference between random variables = $E(X - Y) = E(X) - E(Y)$
- Variance of the sum of *independent* random variables = $Var(X + Y) = Var(X) + Var(Y)$
- Variance of the difference between *independent* random variables = $Var(X - Y) = E(X) + E(Y)$

Sampling Distributions

- Mean of sampling distribution of the mean = $\mu_x = \mu$
- Mean of sampling distribution of the proportion = $\mu_p = P$
- Standard deviation of proportion = $\sigma_p = \mathrm{sqrt}[\,P * (1 - P)/n\,] = \mathrm{sqrt}(\,PQ\,/\,n\,)$
- Standard deviation of the mean = $\sigma_x = \sigma/\mathrm{sqrt}(n)$
- Standard deviation of difference of sample means = $\sigma_d = \mathrm{sqrt}[\,(\sigma_1^2/n_1) + (\sigma_2^2\,/\,n_2)]$
- Standard deviation of difference of sample proportions = $\sigma_d = \mathrm{sqrt}\{\,[P_1(1 - P_1)\,/\,n_1] + [P_2(1 - P_2)\,/\,n_2]\,\}$

Standard Error

- Standard error of proportion = $SE_p = s_p = \mathrm{sqrt}[\,p * (1 - p)/n\,] = \mathrm{sqrt}(\,pq\,/\,n\,)$
- Standard error of difference for proportions = $SE_p = s_p = \mathrm{sqrt}\{\,p * (1 - p) * [\,(1/n_1) + (1/n_2)\,]\,\}$
- Standard error of the mean = $SE_x = s_x = s/\mathrm{sqrt}(n)$
- Standard error of difference of sample means = $SE_d = s_d = \mathrm{sqrt}[\,(s_1^2\,/\,n_1) + (s_2^2\,/\,n_2)\,]$
- Standard error of difference of paired sample means = $SE_d = s_d = \{\,\mathrm{sqrt}\,[\,(\Sigma(d_i - d)^2\,/\,(n - 1)\,]\,\}\,/\,\mathrm{sqrt}(n)$
- Pooled sample standard error = $s_{pooled} = \mathrm{sqrt}\,[\,(n_1 - 1) * s_1^2 + (n_2 - 1) * s_2^2\,]\,/\,(n_1 + n_2 - 2)\,]$
- Standard error of difference of sample proportions = $s_d = \mathrm{sqrt}\{\,[p_1(1 - p_1)\,/\,n_1] + [p_2(1 - p_2)\,/\,n_2]\,\}$

Discrete Probability Distributions

- Binomial formula: $P(X = x) = b(x;\,n,\,P) = {}_nC_x * P^x * (1 - P)^{n-x} = {}_nC_x * P^x * Q^{n-x}$
- Mean of binomial distribution = $\mu_x = n * P$
- Variance of binomial distribution = $\sigma_x^2 = n * P * (1 - P)$
- Negative Binomial formula: $P(X = x) = b*(x;\,r,\,P) = {}_{x-1}C_{r-1} * P^r * (1 - P)^{x-r}$
- Mean of negative binomial distribution = $\mu_x = rQ\,/\,P$
- Variance of negative binomial distribution = $\sigma_x^2 = r * Q\,/\,P^2$
- Geometric formula: $P(X = x) = g(x;\,P) = P * Q^{x-1}$
- Mean of geometric distribution = $\mu_x = Q\,/\,P$
- Variance of geometric distribution = $\sigma_x^2 = Q\,/\,P^2$
- Hypergeometric formula: $P(X = x) = h(x;\,N,\,n,\,k) = [\,{}_kC_x\,]\,[\,{}_{N-k}C_{n-x}\,]\,/\,[\,{}_NC_n\,]$
- Mean of hypergeometric distribution = $\mu_x = n * k\,/\,N$
- Variance of hypergeometric distribution = $\sigma_x^2 = n * k * (N - k) * (N - n)\,/\,[N^2 * (N - 1)]$
- Poisson formula: $P(x;\,\mu) = (e^{-\mu})\,(\mu^x)\,/\,x!$
- Mean of Poisson distribution = $\mu_x = \mu$

- Variance of Poisson distribution = $\sigma_x^2 = \mu$
- Multinomial formula: $P = [\, n! / (\, n_1! * n_2! * \ldots n_k! \,) \,] * (\, p_1^{n_1} * p_2^{n_2} * \ldots * p_k^{n_k} \,)$

Linear Transformations

For the following formulas, assume that Y is a linear transformation of the random variable X, defined by the equation: $Y = aX + b$.

- Mean of a linear transformation = $E(Y) = Y = aX + b$.
- Variance of a linear transformation = $Var(Y) = a^2 * Var(X)$.
- Standardized score = $z = (x - \mu_x) / \sigma_x$.
- t-score = $t = (x - \mu_x) / [\, s/sqrt(n) \,]$.

Estimation

- Confidence interval: Sample statistic $\pm$ Critical value * Standard error of statistic
- Margin of error = (Critical value) * (Standard deviation of statistic)
- Margin of error = (Critical value) * (Standard error of statistic)

Hypothesis Testing

- Standardized test statistic = (Statistic - Parameter) / (Standard deviation of statistic)
- One-sample z-test for proportions: z-score = $z = (p - P_0) / sqrt(\, p * q / n \,)$
- Two-sample z-test for proportions: z-score = $z = z = [\, (p_1 - p_2) - d \,] / SE$
- One-sample t-test for means: t-score = $t = (x - \mu) / SE$
- Two-sample t-test for means: t-score = $t = [\, (x_1 - x_2) - d \,] / SE$
- Matched-sample t-test for means: t-score = $t = [\, (x_1 - x_2) - D \,] / SE = (d - D) / SE$
- Chi-square test statistic = $X^2 = \Sigma[\, (\text{Observed} - \text{Expected})^2 / \text{Expected} \,]$

Degrees of Freedom

The correct formula for degrees of freedom (DF) depends on the situation (the nature of the test statistic, the number of samples, underlying assumptions, etc.).

- One-sample t-test: $DF = n - 1$
- Two-sample t-test: $DF = (s_1^2/n_1 + s_2^2/n_2)^2 / \{[(s_1^2 / n_1)^2 / (n_1 - 1)] + [(s_2^2 / n_2)^2 / (n_2 - 1)]\}$
- Two-sample t-test, pooled standard error: $DF = n_1 + n_2 - 2$
- Simple linear regression, test slope: $DF = n - 2$
- Chi-square goodness of fit test: $DF = k - 1$
- Chi-square test for homogeneity: $DF = (r - 1) * (c - 1)$
- Chi-square test for independence: $DF = (r - 1) * (c - 1)$

Sample Size

Below, the first two formulas find the smallest sample sizes required to achieve a fixed margin of error, using simple random sampling. The third formula assigns sample to strata, based on a proportionate design. The fourth formula, Neyman allocation, uses stratified sampling to minimize variance, given a fixed sample size. And the last formula, optimum allocation, uses stratified sampling to minimize variance, given a fixed budget.

- Mean (simple random sampling): $n = \{z^2 * \sigma^2 * [N/(N - 1)]\} / \{ME^2 + [z^2 * \sigma^2 / (N - 1)]\}$
- Proportion (simple random sampling): $n = [(z^2*p*q)+ME^2]/[\, ME^2 + z^2 * p * q/N]$
- Proportionate stratified sampling: $n_h = (\, N_h / N \,) * n$
- Neyman allocation (stratified sampling): $n_h = n * (\, N_h * \sigma_h \,) / [\, \Sigma (\, N_i * \sigma_i \,) \,]$

WHEN TO USE QUALITY TOOLS: A SELECTED LIST

Activity network: The Activity Network is generally used to schedule dependent activities within a plan. It can be used for describing and understanding the activities within a standard work process. The resulting diagram is useful for communicating the plan and risks to other people.

When to use it:
- Use it when planning any project or activity which is composed of a set of interdependent actions.
- Use it to calculate the earliest date the project can be completed, and to find ways of changing this.
- Use it to identify and address risk to completing a project on time.

Affinity diagram: The Affinity Diagram provides a visual method of structuring a large number of discrete pieces of information.

When to use it:
- Use it to bring order to fragmented and uncertain information and where there is no clear structure.
- Use it when information is subjective and emotive, to gain consensus whilst avoiding verbal argument.
- Use it when current opinions, typically about an existing system, obscure potential new solutions.
- Use it, rather than a Relations Diagram, when the situation calls more for creative organization than for logical organization.

Bar chart: Bar Charts are used to show the differences between related groups of measurements.

When to use it:
- Use it when a set of measurements can be split into discrete and comparable groups, to show the relative change between these groups.
- Use it when there are multiple sets of measurement groups, to show the relationship and change within and between groups.
- Use it, rather than a Line Graph, to display discrete quantities rather than continuing change.
- Use it, rather than a Pareto Chart, when a consistent ordering of bars is wanted. This can ease recognition and comparison of current and previous charts.

Brainstorming: Brainstorming is used to creatively generate new ideas. The creative synergy of a Brainstorming session is also useful in helping a team bind together.

When to use it:
- Use it when new ideas are required, to generate a large list of possibilities.
- Use it when a solution to a problem cannot be logically deduced.
- Use it when information about a problem is confused and spread across several people, to gather the information in one place.

Cause and effect: The Cause-Effect Diagram is used to identify and structure the causes of a given effect. Use it in preference to a Relations Diagram where there is one problem and causes are mostly hierarchical (this will be most cases).

When to use it:
- Use it when investigating a problem, to identify and select key problem causes to investigate or address.
- Use it when the primary symptom (or effect) of a problem is known, but possible causes are not all clear.
- Use it when working in a group, to gain a common understanding of problem causes and their relationship.
- Use it to find other causal relationships, such as potential risks or causes of desired effects.

Check sheet: The Check Sheet is used to manually collect data in a reliable, organized way.

When to use it:
- Use it when data is to be recorded manually, to ensure the data is accurately recorded and is easy to use later, either for direct interpretation or for transcription, for example into a computer.
- Use it when the recording involves counting, classifying, checking or locating.
- Use it when it is useful to check each measurement as it is recorded, for example that it is within normal bounds.
- Use it when it is useful to see the distribution of measures as they are built up.

Control chart: The Control Chart is used to identify dynamic and special causes of variation in a repeating process. It is only practical to use it when regular measurements of a process can be made.

When to use it:
- Use when investigating a process, to determine whether it is in a state of statistical control and thus whether actions are required to bring the process under control.
- Use it to differentiate between special and common causes of variation, identifying the special causes which need to be addressed first.
- Use it to detect statistically significant trends in measurements; for example, to identify when and by how much a change to the process has improved it.
- Use it as an ongoing 'health' measure of a process, to help spot problems before they become significant.

Decision tree: The Decision Tree is used to select from a number of possible courses of action.

When to use it:
- Use it when making important or complex decisions, to identify the course of action that will give the best value according to a selected set of rules
- Use it when decision-making, to identify the effects of risks.
- Use it when making plans, to identify the effects of actions and possible alternative courses of action.
- Use it when there are chains of decisions, to determine the best decision at each point.
- Use it only when data is available, or can reasonably be determined, on costs and probabilities of different outcomes.

DOE: 'Design of Experiments' is use to understand the effects of different factors in a given situation.

When to use it:
- Use it when investigating a situation where there are many variable factors, one or more of which may be causing problems.
- Use it when variable factors may be interacting to cause problems.
- Use it when testing a solution, to ensure that there are no unexpected side-effects.
- Use it when there is not the time or money to try every combination of variables.

FMEA: FMEA is used to identify and prioritize how items fail, and the effects of failure.

When to use it:
- Use it when designing products or processes, to identify and avoid failure-prone designs.
- Use it when investigating why existing systems have failed, to help identify possible causes and remedies.
- Use it when investigating possible solutions, to help select one with an acceptable risk for the known benefit of implementing it.
- Use it when planning actions, in order to identify risks in the plan and hence identify countermeasures.

Fault tree: Fault Tree Analysis is used to show combinations of failures that can cause overall system failure.

When to use it:
- Use it when the effect of a failure is known, to find how this might be caused by combinations of other failures.
- Use it when designing a solution, to identify ways it may fail and consequently find ways of making the solution more robust.
- Use to identify risks in a system, and consequently identify risk reduction measures.
- Use it to find failures which can cause the failure of all parts of a 'fault-tolerant' system.

Flow chart: The Flowchart is used to show the sequential steps within a process.

When to use it:
- Use it when analyzing or defining a process, to detail the actions and decisions within it.
- Use it when looking for potential problem points in a process.
- Use it when investigating the performance of a process, to help identify where and how it is best measured.
- Use it as a communication or training aid, to explain or agree the detail of the process.

Flow process chart: The Flow Process Chart is used to record and illustrate the sequence of actions within a process.

When to use it:
- Use it when observing a physical process, to record actions as they happen and thus get an accurate description of the process.
- Use it when analyzing the steps in a process, to help identify and eliminate waste.
- Use it, rather than a Flowchart, when the process is mostly sequential, containing few decisions.

Force field analysis: The Force Field Diagram is used to weigh up the points for and against a potential action.

When to use it:
- Use it when decision making is hindered by a number of significant points for and against a decision.
- Use it when there is a lot of argument and indecision over a point, to clarify and agree the balance of disagreement.
- Use it to help identify risks to a planned action and to develop a strategy for counteracting them.
- Use it to help identify the key causes of successful or unsuccessful actions.

Gant chart: Gantt Charts are used to show the actual time to spend in tasks.

When to use it:
- Use it when doing any form of planning, to show the actual calendar time spent in each task.
- Use it when scheduling work for individuals, to control the balance between time spent during normal work hours and overtime work.
- Use it when planning work for several people, to ensure that those people who must work together are available at the same time.
- Use it for tracking progress of work against the scheduled activities.
- Use it when describing a regular process, to show who does what, and when.
- Use it to communicate the plan to other people.

Histogram: The Histogram is used to show the frequency distribution of a set of measurements.

When to use it:
- Use it to investigate the distribution of a set of measurements.
- Use it when it is suspected that there are multiple factors affecting a process, to see if this shows up in the distribution.
- Use it to help define reasonable specification limits for a process by investigating the actual distribution.
- Use it when you want to see the actual shape of the distribution, as opposed to calculating single figures like the mean or standard deviation.

IDEFO: Integration Definition for Function Modeling (IDEF0) is used to make a detailed and clear description of a process or system. It is generally used in conjunction with the inputs, controls, outputs and mechanisms (ICOM) model. It is very similar to the supplier, input, process, output, customer (SIPOC) model used in the Six Sigma methodology.

When to use it:
- Use it when formally describing a process, to ensure a detailed, clear and accurate result.
- Use it when the process is complex, and other methods would result in more complex diagrams.
- Use it when mapping a wide variety of processes, as a consistent and scalable Process Description Language (or PDL).
- Use it when there is time available to work on understanding and producing a complete and correct description of the process.

Kano model: Kano analysis is a quality measurement tool used to prioritize customer requirements based on their impact to customer satisfaction.

When to use:
- Kano analysis is a tool which can be used to classify and prioritize customer needs. This is useful because customer needs are not all of the same kind, not all have the same importance, and are different for different populations. The results can be used to prioritize your effort in satisfying different customers.

Kappa statistic: The Kappa is the ratio of the proportion of times the appraisers (see Gage R&R) did agree to the proportion of times the appraisers could agree. If you have a known standard for each rating, you can assess the correctness of all appraisers' ratings compared to the known standard. If Kappa = 1, then there is perfect agreement. If Kappa = 0, then there is no agreement. The higher the value of Kappa, the stronger the agreement. Negative values occur when agreement is weaker than expected by chance, but this rarely happens. Depending on the application, Kappa less than 0.7 indicates that your measurement system needs improvement. Kappa values greater than 0.9 are considered excellent.

When to use it:
- Use it when there is a need for comparison

Line graph: The Line Graph is used to show patterns of change in a sequence of measurements.

When to use it:
- Use it when an item is repeatedly measured, to show changes across time.
- Use it when measuring several different items which can be shown on the same scale, to show how they change relative to one another.
- Use it when measuring progress towards a goal, to show the relative improvement.
- Use it, rather than a Bar Chart, to show continuous change, rather than discrete measurements. It is also better when there are many measurements.
- Use it, rather than a Control Chart, when not measuring the degree of control of a process.

Matrix data analysis chart: The Matrix Data Analysis Chart (MDAC) is used to identify clusters of related items within a larger group.

When to use it:
- Use it when investigating factors which affect a number of different items, to determine common relationships.
- Use it to determine whether or not logically similar items also have similar factor effects.
- Use it to find groups of logically different items which have similar factor effects.

Matrix diagram: The Matrix Diagram is used to identify the relationship between pairs of lists.

When to use it:
- Use it when comparing two lists to understand the many-to-many relationship between them (it is not useful if there is a simple one-to-one relationship).
- Use it to determine the strength of the relationship between either single pairs of items or a single item and another complete list.
- Use it when the second list is generated as a result of the first list, to determine the success of that generation process. For example, customer requirements versus design specifications.

Nominal group technique: The Nominal Group Technique (NGT) is used to collect and prioritize the thoughts of a group on a given topic.

When to use it:
- Use it when a problem is well understood, but knowledge about it is dispersed amongst several people.
- Use it when a rapid consensus is required from a team, rather than a more detailed consideration.
- Use it when the team is stuck on an issue, for example when they disagree about something.
- Use it when the group prefers a structured style of working together.
- Use it, rather than Brainstorming, when a limited list of considered opinions is preferred to a long list of wild ideas, or when the group is not sufficiently comfortable together to be open and creative.

Pareto chart: The Pareto Chart is used to show the relative importance of a set of measurements.

When to use it:
- Use it when selecting the most important things on which to focus, thus differentiating between the 'vital few' and the 'trivial many'.
- Use it after improving a process, to show the relative change in a measured item.
- Use it when sorting a set of measurements, to visually emphasize their relative sizes.
- Use it, rather than a Bar Chart or Pie Chart to show the relative priority of a set of numeric measurements.

Prioritization matrix: The Prioritization Matrix is used to sort a list of items into an order of importance.

When to use it:
- Use it to prioritize complex or unclear issues, where there are multiple criteria for deciding importance.
- Use it when there is data available to help score criteria and issues.
- Use it to help select priority items from a larger list of possible items.
- When used with a group, it will help to gain agreement on priorities and key issues.
- Use it, rather than simple voting, when the extra effort that is required to find a more confident selection is considered to be worthwhile.

Process Capability: Process Capability calculations indicate the ability of a process to meet specification limits.

When to use it:
- Use it when setting up a process, to ensure it can meet its specification limits.
- Use it when setting specification limits, to ensure they are neither too wide nor too narrow.
- Use it when investigating a process that is not meeting its specification limits.
- Use it only when the process is stable and has a Normal distribution.

Process Decision Program Chart (PDPC): The process decision program chart (commonly just referred to as PDPC) is used to identify potential problems and countermeasures in a plan.

When to use it:
- Use it when making plans, to help identify potential risks to their successful completion.
- When risks are identified, use it to help identify and select from a set of possible countermeasures.
- Also use it to help plan for ways of avoiding and eliminating identified risks.
- It is of best value when risks are non-obvious, such as in unfamiliar situations or in complex plans, and when the consequences of failure are serious.

Relationship Diagram: The relations diagram is used to clarify and understand complex relationships.

When to use it:
- Use it when analyzing complex situations where there are multiple interrelated issues.
- Use it where the current problem is perceived as being a symptom of a more important underlying problem.
- It is also useful in building consensus within groups.
- It is commonly used to map cause-effect relationships, but also can be used to map any other type of relationship.
- Use it, rather than an Affinity Diagram, when there are logical, rather than subjective, relationships.
- Use it, rather than a Cause-Effect Diagram, when causes are non-hierarchic or when there are complex issues.

Scatter diagram: The scatter diagram is used to show the type and degree of any causal relationship between two factors.

When to use it:
- Use it when it is suspected that the variation of two items is connected in some way, to show any actual correlation between the two.
- Use it when it is suspected that one item may be causing another, to build evidence for the connection between the two.
- Use it only when both items being measured can be measured together, in pairs.

Simulation in Lean: Simulation is a practical tool that changes complex parameters into mathematical, logical models which are possible to analyze under different scenarios. Models can be classified from various aspects. They can be categorized as being mathematical or physical, static (Monte Carlo) or dynamic (Shows a system that always changes), deterministic (Includes no random variables) or stochastic (Contain at least one random variable) and also discrete or continuous models. But the simulation beside its benefits has also some disadvantages.

When to use:
- Assessing hospital operations in different wards.
- Estimating the number of needed doctors and nurses in emergency ward.
- Reducing the length of time that patient has to stay in emergency ward.
- Predicating the required number of beds according to the patient interval.

Advantages:
1- The most important benefit of simulation is to get results at less cost.
2- Assumptions about specific phenomena can be checked for feasibility.
3- The simulation answers "what if" questions.
4- Analysis of bottlenecks and finding the roots is easier.
5- The system can be tested without allocating any resources.

Disadvantages:
1- Working with simulation modeling requires experience and specific training.
2- Understanding the simulation results is difficult because they are based on random inputs.

String diagram: The string diagram is used to investigate the physical movement in a process.

When to use it:
- Use it when analyzing a manual or physical process that involves significant physical movement, in order to make movements easier and quicker. Movements may be of people, materials or machines.
- Use it when designing the layout of a work area, to identify the optimum positioning of machines and furniture

Surveys: Surveys are used to gather information from people.

When to use it:
- Use it when information that is required is held by an identifiable and dispersed group of people.
- Use it to help decision-making, by turning disparate qualitative data into useful quantitative information.
- Use it only when the time and effort are available to complete the survey.
- Use it, rather than Brainstorming or Nominal Group Technique to gather real data about what a diverse group of people think (rather than an opinion of what they think).

Tables: Tables are used to organize and relate multiple pieces of information.

When to use it:
- Use it when gathering information, to help prompt for a complete set of data.
- Use it when information is disorganized, to help collate and understand it.
- Use it for summarizing information to make it easier to present and understand.
- Use specific table tools as frameworks for particular tasks, either to organize existing information or to prompt for specific categories of information.

Tree diagrams: The tree diagram is used to break down a topic into successive levels of detail.

When to use it:
- Use it when planning, to break down a task into manageable and assignable units.
- Use it when investigating a problem, to discover the detailed component parts of any complex topic.
- Use it only when the problem can be broken down in a hierarchical manner.
- Use it, rather than a Relations Diagram, to break down a problem when the problem is hierarchical in nature.

Value analysis: Value analysis is used to determine and improve the value of a product or process.

When to use it:
- Use it when analyzing a product or process, to determine the real value of each component.
- Use it when looking for cost savings, to determine components that may be optimized.
- Use it only when the item to be analyzed can be broken down into sub-components and realistic costs and values allocated to these.

Voting: Voting is used to prioritize and select from a list of items.

When to use it:
- Use it as a quick tool when a group must select one or more items from a list, for example as generated by a Brainstorming session.
- Use it when it is important that the group accept the result as fair.

- Use it when the knowledge to enable selection is spread within the group.
- Use it when the opinion of all group members is equally valued.
- It can also be used to 'test the water', to determine opinions without committing to a final selection.
- Use it, rather than a Prioritization Matrix, when the added accuracy of the Prioritization Matrix is not worth the extra effort.

APPENDIX F

TRAINING AND DEVELOPMENT GUIDE FOR SUBJECT MATTER EXPERTS (SMEs)

This appendix is a short introduction to: analyze the need for training; set training objectives; determine the most effective method(s) of delivering training; and the role of editing

Creating training and or lesson plan requires a unique set of skills. The trainer and or teacher needs to know the subject matter to be trained or taught, must know how to write the training or lesson, and, of course, deliver it successfully so that the students have a good learning experience. During the creation process, there are many considerations that go into making effective training and or lesson plans.

For many years, Schools of many different types have worked with trainers to help them develop classroom and recorded training and materials. This appendix is the culmination of some of the critical issues in training and development from the author's experience. It will help novices and experts alike design, develop, and deliver quality training in the classroom.

This appendix specifically will cover how to:

- Analyze the need for training.
- Set training objectives...
- Determine the most effective method(s) of delivering training.
- Work with Educational teachers and staff for production of materials and training.

Using this appendix as a guide, the trainer and or instructor will avoid many pitfalls common to developing courses. *As always, educational consultants will be glad to assist trainers with questions or concerns about developing training.*

Needs Assessment Planning

This section contains information about:
- Why training is needed or desired.
- Analyzing the performance gap.
- Determining the audience and its needs.
- At the end of this section you will be able to:
- Identify the need for training based on your investigation of your own topic.
- Analyze the gap between existing and desired performance.
- Identify the learner characteristics for your audience and determine their impact on training.

Why Training is Needed or Desired

Sometimes the need for training is obvious. When a new piece of equipment is developed, the people who will work with that equipment must learn to use it. When a new safety procedure is put in place, the people who will be affected by that procedure must learn how it works.

However, at other times, the need for training is not as obvious. For instance, when only a few people know how to do something, an administrator, a supervisor or manager may determine that there is a need to train more people so that replacements are available as people move on to other jobs. In other cases, job performance may fall short and training may be the best way to improve performance.

At this point, you (or someone else) have determined that there is a problem or a gap between the way things are and the way they ought to be. This is the beginning step of your analysis to find solutions.

Analyzing the Performance Gap

Identify the problem or gap in many cases, is completed by the time Subject Matter Experts (SMEs) have been assigned a project. However, even if you know what the problem is, you may not have enough information to begin working on a solution. Good problem identification may very well be the most important step in the entire process, so here are some recommendations to make problem identification complete.

The Problem Statement

Write a complete statement of the problem as you currently understand it. A complete statement includes:

- Indicators of the problem (identify and state what the gap is).
- Who has the problem.
- The issues that the problem causes.
- What steps have been taken to repair the damage caused by the problem.
- What factors could contribute directly and indirectly to the problem.

An incomplete problem statement characterizes the problem at a very high level:

✓ Students and staff (customers) have been complaining about out-of-date dairy products

being sold to them in the school cafeteria. A complete problem statement consists of a more detailed

breakdown:

✓ Store returns indicate that we are averaging returns of 10 gallons of milk and 4 cartons of cottage cheese per day, all because they were left on the shelves past their use date and customers purchased them. Customers are angry at having to return to the store.

✓ The dairy manager has identified the midnight stock shift as the cause of the problem. They have placed new stock in front of old stock and do not remove the old stock.

✓ To satisfy customers, they have been given free milk and cottage cheese to replace their out-of-date purchases. Cost to the store is approximately $150.00 per week.

✓ Factors that contribute to the problem may include lack of supervision on the midnight shift, three new employees who restock the dairy shelves, mixing of old and new stock by customers who are checking dates on the cartons and lack of quality control inspections by store management. There may also be problems with the way product is stored and rotated in the back room coolers of the school cafeteria.

308

You should note that, even if you can't describe your training need as a "problem," the methods for gap investigation stay the same. The overall purpose stays the same. That is: determine the way things are and then determine the way they ought to be. A process flow diagram may be of help here.

With a more complete statement, the trainer can begin to narrow the focus as to what can be done with training and non-training methods. Now for the next steps.

Identify Causes

A Gap Analysis Chart (Table F.1) will help you organize the information you collect. An example of a completed Gap Analysis Chart is shown here.

Table F.1. A Gap Analysis Chart

Learning & Development		**Gap Analysis Chart**	
Performed by: Date performed:			
The gap and what causes it?	Who has it?	Who can fix it?	How can it be fixed?

Use a separate line for each component of the gap. Work to deconstruct the gap into its relevant parts. For instance, if the problem is a new laboratory procedure, you could have a gap in basic skills, a gap in knowledge about equipment or other materials, a gap in time to do training, and so on.

Who has it? This is the audience you will teach, inform, or otherwise address. Following the problem identification process, you may have people with different entry level skills so their gaps may differ. Be sure to list each different group on a separate line. It may take many different interventions to fix the gap for each group. [Using the out-of-date dairy problem, under "Who has it?", you would need lines for the stock people, customers, dairy manager, and store manager].

What causes it? This helps you identify the reasons for the gap. Reasons can include a faulty process, poor equipment, lack of knowledge of a new procedure, and so on. Again, use a separate line for each cause.

Identify Potential Solutions

Who can fix it? These are the people with expertise who can supply you with the necessary information to fix the gap. You may not be able to fill this in without additional investigation. It is imperative to remember that solutions to educational problems don't always involve training. Be aware of other factors that can cause a gap in performance such as attitude, the environment, poor procedures, and lack of communication.

How can it be fixed? Finally, you will have to decide how the gaps can be bridged. This section will be completed later, but it serves as a reminder to be thinking about solutions and methods for training and non-training interventions. At this point, you will turn your focus to the learners who are the subjects of the gap. You will need information about them before you begin proposing solutions.

Gap Analysis Chart Example

This chart (Table F.2) will help define the needs of the audience (the student). The main focus is to identify the type of job they perform, how many years they were doing it, and how they will use this information.

Table F.2. Gap Analysis Chart Example

The gap and what causes it?	Who has it?	Who can fix it?	How can it be fixed?
New technicians do not know how to connect and use an oscilloscope for a test.	New service technicians	School training staff	Training methods include a video on the oscilloscope, hands-on exercises that require the same performance as used on the job, and a test of skills upon completion of the training.
Supervisors do not have the time to teach new technicians how to use the oscilloscope, nor to correct their mistakes after training.	Supervisors and their managers	Managers and supervisors	Request training. Free up some supervisor time to inspect the use of the oscilloscope by former students
New technicians do not have reference materials showing them how to connect an oscilloscope.	New service technicians	Check with oscilloscope manufacturer. If not available, training will have to create the materials	Create a job aid or get one from the manufacturer.

Determining the Audience and Its Needs

You may know many of your potential students personally, and in that case, understanding their learner characteristics should be relatively easy. However, if you do *not* know your audience, you should take the time to find out about their learning characteristics. For example, you would not design the same training for experienced people as you would for those with little exposure to the topic. Nor would you design the same training or materials for managers who monitor the work as you would for technicians who will be performing the task.

Learner Characteristics Chart

The Learner Characteristics Chart (Table F.3) helps you organize your information. Consider the following guidelines as you complete this chart:

Table F.3. Learner Characteristics Chart

Learning & development		Learner Characteristics chart	
Performed by:		Category	
Date Completed:			
List learners by their function	Experience with subject matter	How will they use this information	Characteristics and or impact on training or lesson

List Learners by Their Job Functions

Identify all your students including supervisors, managers, engineers, technicians, and others by their specific work functions, not their titles. For example, a person may be titled a medical doctor, but if his job is to perform autopsies, his job function would not be the same as a surgeon who is also a medical doctor. Group the learners that will have the same or similar use of this information, but be careful to allow for differences in how they will apply the training.

Experience with Subject Matter

Estimate the amount of information students already have about the topic. Use the number of years on the job, amount of schooling, or any other criteria that will identify experience levels.

How They Will Use This Information

Describe how students will apply the training on the job. For example, they may be making hands-on application of the information or they may be supervising others who will do the work. Will they use only a part of the information or do they need to know everything to do their jobs?

You may want to gather other information about your students at this time. For example, students may have downtime when they are available for training. You can never gather too much data. Here are some additional learner characteristics categories that may affect your training or reference materials:

- Age of student or reader.
- Previous training taken on related topics.
- Best time and date for training.
- Level of education.
- Previous job positions.
- Interest in the topic.

- Training methods preferred by the learner.
- Attitudes toward training, content, supervision, company.
- Existing knowledge on the topic.
- What logistics need to be considered for training.

If you have difficulty identifying how the information will be used, you may want to spend some time with your prospective students doing a *task analysis.* A task analysis is a step-by-step listing of how an expert performer does a job. It includes information about the difficulty of each step in the performance, and estimates the frequency of the step.

Characteristics/Impact on Training

To understand how learner characteristics affect training, consider the materials' content, the depth of the training, and the profiles of the learner – see Table F.4. Using the same topic as before — training people to use an oscilloscope, the table below shows learner characteristics and how the learner is affected by the training.

Table F.4. Characteristics/Impact on Training

Characteristics	Impact on Training
All learners are new to their field.	Begin training with a complete coverage of basics.
Learners prefer to learn by doing things not by seeing them done and not by listening.	Make all explanations brief. Use demonstrations that lead to hands-on activities. Use drawings or photos of the performance required. Limit text.
All learners are new.	Explain all acronyms and limit their use. Provide a glossary of terms.
All learners are under the age of 30.	Has no impact on this training.
All learners are high school graduates.	Set vocabulary choices to 10th grade level.

In addition to management, internal and or external consultants can help you correlate learner characteristics with possible impacts on training and reference materials.

Bridging the Gap

Now is the time to begin finalizing solutions for bridging the gap you have identified. The first thing to do is to go back to your gap analysis chart, shown in Tables F.1 and F.2, and begin filling in the last column — "How can it be fixed?" These answers will shape your training and allow you to build an outline of the training. This is a most critical point in your process, so you will want to be as thorough as possible during this analysis portion of the assessment you are doing.

Specifically, this section contains information about:

- Writing learning objectives.
- Determining the best delivery mode.
- Developing a training outline.
- Planning exercises.

At the end of this section you will be able to:

- Write effective performance objectives that align with the level of learning required for mastery.
- Select appropriate methods to help students learn from the materials.
- Select an instructional sequence that helps students organize learning, and building on previous knowledge.

- Write an outline.

- Determine what types of exercises are required to ensure learning.

Writing Learning Objectives

The next step in course development is to write instructional objectives. Instructional objectives tell students what they will be able to do when they complete the training. In general, objectives should be *performance based.* That means the student must complete a performance to prove mastery of the information. You can also create knowledge-based objectives that say the student will not have to prove any mastery (be aware), or will prove mastery by taking a test (must know, but will not have to perform).

There are many different names for types of objectives, but we will concern ourselves with the two most common types, terminal and enabling objectives.

Terminal objectives are the broad ones that usually cover a whole training program. For example:

- Upon completion of this course, the student will be able to diagnose six common electrical malfunctions and repair all six of them to restore equipment performance to normal.

The second type of objective is called an *enabling objective.* This type of objective is subordinate to the terminal objective. Enabling objectives help the learner reach the mastery required by the terminal objective. For example:

- Given a tester, the student will test six electrical connections and identify which are operational and which are not.

- Given wire, caps, and tape, the student will make a secure electrical connection that meets city code requirements.

Note: You should write objectives for each piece of instruction that requires mastery by the student. Key characteristics are: a) performance b) measurability c) condition and d) criteria. [In some cases performance and condition may be the same].

Use the Writing Objectives Chart (Table F.5) as a guide to writing valid objectives: The questions you must answer are:

- What does the student need to do the performance (equipment)?

- Who will be doing the performance?

- What is the performance?

- What degree of completion is good enough to meet the level of mastery?

- Who will judge mastery or how will we know that the performance is good enough? (Optional)

Table F.5. An example of a completed writing objective chart

Question	Answer
What does the student need to do the performance (equipment)?	Students will require wires, wire cutters, twist cap, and electrician's tape.
Who will be doing the performance?	The student will complete the electrical procedure (performance).
What is the performance?	The student will make a sample electrical connection using wires and twist cap.
What degree of completion is good enough to meet the level of mastery?	The performance must meet city code requirements.
Who will judge mastery or how will we know that the performance is good enough? (Optional)	Mastery will be determined by the instructor.

Sample Learning Objective based on above writing objectives chart: Given wires, wire cutters, twist cap and electrician's tape, you will be able to make a sample electrical connection that meets city code requirements as determined by the instructor.

Short version of learning objective: You will be able to make a sample electrical connection that meets city code requirements.

Determining the Best Delivery Mode

At this point, we must discuss the intent of the materials you are about to write. If you combine the information from the Gap Analysis and Learning Objectives charts, you should have a good picture of what kinds of material you will develop. Consider all the uses for your materials before you decide what format they should take. Check with your students to see what they will or will not use at their jobs. You have three basic choices of types of materials:

- Training materials (web-based or instructor-led)
- Reference materials (text books, manuals, job aids, single point lessons, etc.)
- Combined training and reference materials

Training materials

Training materials are used in conjunction with some form of training such as self-study or computer tutorials. They support training but may not need to contain the same detail of information as reference materials, since they could be supplemented with classroom (virtual or regular) or on-the-job instruction. Training materials often contain job aids to help performance back at work. Training materials can contain exercises or tests, training objectives, and goals.

Reference materials

Reference materials can back up training and or instruction that will be done, or can be used on the job. Reference materials can be highly organized and include an index, a glossary of terms, background information and history, step-by-step information, necessary charts, graphs, and other detailed information. Reference materials can also be single point lessons (SPLs) that are used when needed (see below). Reference materials can stand alone without instruction. They may be organized in many different ways such as topically, alphabetically, or in some form of linear organization. An operations manual is a good example of reference material. A textbook is also a good example of a reference.

- *Single Point Lessons (SPL)* are short, 1-topic lessons that can be used as job aids and as training. Generally, they reflect a process or step in a process and give information on how to do something. You can also use single point lessons to cover material that has a short shelf life or whenever the performer will not be doing something frequently enough to learn to do it.

- *Job aids* are a specific form of reference material intended for use on the job. They generally are small, easy to use, contain pertinent information, and give the reader just enough information to get a task done. Job aids are often laminated cards that are pocket size.

- *Electronic Performance Support Systems (EPSS)* are computer-based reference materials that improve worker productivity by providing on-the-job access to integrated information, advice, and learning experiences. EPSS support Knowledge on Demand, empowering individuals to effectively communicate their knowledge, tap each others' expertise, and collaborate to solve existing problems and develop new innovations. They take on a number of forms, including:

  ✓ Wikis — Wikis are used to create collaborative websites and to power community websites. They are designed to enable anyone who accesses it to contribute or modify content.

  ✓ Blogs — Compared to centralized traditional centralized content publishing and sharing, proliferation of individual weblogs (blogs) allows effective sharing of niche knowledge that was usually difficult to find in the past.

  ✓ RSS — RSS (Really Simple Syndication) readers allow you to subscribe to blogs or news feeds from the sites that are important to you so the new content is sent to your computer whenever it's available.

It is important to note that if you are creating web-based training (WBT), there are some steps that you *must* take in designing your training, and these steps can have a big impact on how you gather your information. We have included some information on WBT, but because it involves more complex methods, you will want to work directly with the person programming your training for each step in this process.

Combined training and reference materials

Combined training and reference materials are the most common types of materials used in training. These materials are used online or in the classroom with accompanying instruction, but will also be used as reference materials back at the job. Reference and training materials often contain job aids to **help** students do tasks or remember data they would not normally memorize. Combination materials take a little more time to write, but are economical because you will not have to produce separate reference materials to supplement instruction.

Note that there are some programs that will allow you to build web-based training quickly. For example, you can use PowerPoint ™ or Camtasia™ to develop a presentation and have it ready for the web in a short period of time. The opportunity also exists to create a DVD or a CD with additional references and information for the learner.

Instructional and Non-Instructional Delivery Modes

Simply stated, the delivery mode you choose should assist the learner in learning. You will have to take into account the logistics of training, cost, time factors, and skills when you make your choices. Table F.6 lists the advantages and disadvantages of each major delivery mode.

Table F.6. Advantages and disadvantages of major delivery modes

Delivery Mode	Used For	Advantages	Disadvantages
Lecture (classroom, webinar, podcast)	Conveying information to a group.	1. Can address large groups. 2. Economical method for training. 3. Primarily effective for people who learn by listening. 4. Usually takes the least amount of time to develop.	1. Passive activity for the audience. 2. Audience attention span is six minutes without new stimulus. 3. Does not give time to the students to process and learn information. 4. May not be consistent, depending on the instructor. 5. Requires that other methods be used with it to be effective.
Demo	Showing students how to do something.	1. Allows students to see the performance that they are learning. 2. Helps model equipment that will be used on the job. 3. Reduces the amount of talking that the instructor has to do. 4. Addresses people who learn by seeing, hearing, touching, or doing.	1. Equipment used in the demonstration must be available. 2. Is most effective when everyone can see and hear what is happening. 3. Should be combined with students having hands-on experience to make sure that learning takes place.
SPLs, Job Aids	Self-paced study either in a classroom or on the job.	1. Is cost effective. 2. Allows students to progress at their own rates. 3. Benefits the visual learner. 4. Easy to distribute. 5. Allows the instructor to track answers and grade students easily.	1. Inhibits the students from asking questions. 2. Provides no external stimulation for the student. 3. CAUTION: Must be delivered in a manner that allows students to absorb materials into long-term memory.

Delivery Mode	Used For	Advantages	Disadvantages
Web-based Training	Training needs across a decentralized population.	1. Can be accessed at any time making it useful to cover multiple time zones. 2. Can contain audio and video. 3. Can be available on the job or in a computer lab.	1. Can be expensive to develop. 2. May require special applications and programming skills
Simulations	Training on equipment or computer programs. Also used to build skills.	1. Allows practice in a safe environment—no penalty for failure 2. Allows sufficient time to master something before having to do it on the job.	1. May be expensive to program or create.
Webinars / Podcasts	Teaching students at remote locations.	1. Promotes global training. 2. Learning levels are typically high. 3. Students are not usually inhibited by the equipment or format. 4. Can be cost effective.	2. Equipment must be installed and available. 3. Student input may be limited. 4. Initial startup cost can be high. 5. Students cannot ask questions in recorded sessions. 6. May need licenses for software.
Coaching	On-the-job training where the student uses the actual equipment and performs real work.	1. Allows the learner to learn and to use the learning immediately, avoiding the loss of retention with normal training. 2. Students are more familiar with the setting than in a remote classroom. 3. Students are able to get one-on-one attention. 4. Cost is reasonable and productivity continues, perhaps at a slower pace.	1. Not always practical to train on the job. 2. Equipment and materials must be available for training which can be a problem when a new process or piece of equipment is being set up. 3. Coaches must be trained before they can coach.

Delivery Mode	Used For	Advantages	Disadvantages
Just-In-Time Training	Short classroom (virtual or live) or web-based training to learn essentials prior to on-the-job use. Balance of learning is done on-the-job using coaching and job aids.	1. Quickly makes the learners productive. 2. Learners work on live information and can be done at a reasonable cost. Less possibility of forgetting when there is no time gap between learning and application.	1. Initial on-the-job performance may be slow or inadequate. 2. Someone has to monitor performance at the work site. 3. Less chance for exchange of ideas among students. 4. May need performance support tools.

Delivery Strategies

You should choose more than one delivery strategy to use within your program because all learners benefit from variety. Some examples of selected delivery strategies are shown in Table F.7.

Table F.7. Delivery strategies

Strategy	Provides
Case Study Use a case study throughout the training.	Practical experience in working with the information given throughout the course. Students will be able to apply their learning to a case study that should imitate situations they would be facing on the job.
Guided Discussion Students read material and then discuss it. Instructor prepares discussion questions prior to class, but allows the discussion to follow its own course as long as it stays on the topic.	An opportunity for students who learn by reading a chance to excel. It also reduces the amount of talking that the instructor does and allows for some quiet time. It provides good variety in a lecture-heavy course.
Individual Activity Use written questions for students to answer as an option to reading and discussing.	An opportunity to write down answers which reinforce their learning. It also provides for quiet time.
Group Activity Group activities or workshops help learners teach each other. Students will discuss a problem, case study, or the actual work, and cooperate in getting the work done.	An effective way to have students work together without a strong pressure to perform. There is security in giving a group answer. Be aware that it may take a little longer for this to be done, but the level or learning makes it worth it.
Research Research activities where students are responsible for finding and presenting information to the class is another alternative.	An experience in which participants expend effort to produce materials and learning in the process. Requires more time and access to research facilities.

Presentations Presentations can be group or single student activities. Students present material to the whole group and can use visual or other creative means for getting the information across.	A clear demonstration of learning. (One problem associated with this is that students may not concentrate on other presentations when they have not yet done their own. Then too, single presentations are inhibiting unless the classroom atmosphere is very friendly.)
Games Build games to either teach or to reinforce learning.	Immediate feedback. If the games are done well, they can be extremely effective. Sometimes competition is beneficial, but at other times can be threatening. Games should never involve any activity that could be embarrassing to a segment of the class. For example, avoid any games where quick physical activity is required.
Brainstorming Organize discussion groups to brainstorm a topic, to work out a problem, or to help each other understand a concept.	Cooperative learning, i.e., students teaching each other. Set ground rules so everyone has a chance to participate. The instructor must monitor each group to make sure that the basics are accomplished.
Role Plays Each student takes the role of a person affected by an issue or faced with a new task.	An emphasis on "real-world" application of subject matter. In particular, role-playing presents the student a valuable opportunity to learn not just the course content, but other perspectives on it.

Comparisons

Table F.8 provides additional criteria to use when selecting the best delivery mode for your program.

Table F.8. Criteria for selecting the best delivery mode

	ILT	**WBT**	**Webinar**
Experience	✓ Event-based	✓ Learner initiated	✓ Event-based
Time	✓ Occurs at a specific time and place	ᵛ Available 24/7 ✓ Can be integrated into work schedule	✓ Provisions for re-broadcast
Cost	✓ Travel increases cost	✓ Incremental costs mitigated by widely distributed audience	✓ Incremental costs mitigated by widely distributed audience
Activities	✓ Characteristically linear and time-bound ✓ Learner support/ feedback is immediate	✓ Occur over time ✓ Encourages analytical participation, self-assessment ✓ Learner support/ feedback may be delayed	✓ Interactivity similar to classroom instruction Participants are not required to demonstrate physical skills during training ✓

Best Uses	✓ Critical need for interaction, support, or physical props Easier to view participant performance	✓ Maximizes access (24/7) Best deployment for standardized content, ✓ with ongoing performance support, collaboration, and dialog	✓ Training with durations of no longer than one hour (delivery of longer training to take place in sessions or modules)
Ease of Use	Instructional materials ✓ generally include text, graphics, and physical props Easy to use ✓	✓ Instructional materials can be challenging to use Technical support for learner critical ✓	✓ Need for only one facilitator to communicate information over a large geographical area and to a large audience ✓ Logistics can be challenging ✓ Technical support for instructor is important

Training vs. Non-Training Materials

You may have decided that training is necessary and that some training decisions are obvious. If people do not know how to do something that they *should* know how to do, then they will have to be taught to do it. However, there are non-training interventions that can work as well as, or better than training. Here are some examples of non-training interventions that can also bridge the gap.

Job Aids: Job aids are cards, charts, computer programs, Wikis, and many other helpful reference materials that lead the performer through the steps of a process. The help screens in a computer program are job aids. The quick reference charts on a copier are job aids. The signs you see in restaurants to administer first aid for choking victims are job aids.

Coaching: Coaching (tutoring) is often used in conjunction with training and is a form of training. A coach works with performers on the job to help them learn tasks or to validate and improve performance after training. [Coaching is especially effective one-on-one teaching, allowing the coach to give all his/her attention to one student].

Remediation: Instruction should not be used to correct behavior problems, unless a lack of knowledge causes flawed behavior. By knowing your learners, you can decide if a few people need guidance, or if training is the appropriate remedy. Remediation usually includes discussing problems and solutions with only those who need it, and changing performance by using coaching, performance monitoring, and other methods.

Procedures: If the gap you identify can be closed with a change in procedures to improve performance, training will only be necessary to update people on the new procedure.

320

Ergonomics: In your investigation, you may find that a part of the problem is ergonomics. Workers may be doing their best, but the location of materials, the shape of the test instruments, the laboratory, or other flaws in the workplace environment are causing problems. Training is not a remedy for solving these problems. Correction of the gap comes when materials are located conveniently to the worker, when test instruments do not cause physical distress, when the laboratory has better lighting, and so on.

Motivation and Incentives: Employees may show a lack of motivation to do the job right or even to do it at all. Correcting this behavior usually involves human resources people who have the skills necessary to close this gap.

In general, be aware that more than one factor can affect the gap you find in your investigation, and you may have to make other changes in addition to training to have a successful outcome. Work with us to find total solutions for your gap. The best time to find a total solution is during the investigative stages of your planning.

Summary

WBT delivery makes more sense when...

- ✓ Online delivery clearly supports business goals

- ✓ Employees are comfortable using technology for learning and information

- ✓ Learners have access to the technology and the skills to use it

- ✓ They have enough time to use the instruction

- ✓ They perceive the instruction as valuable and necessary

ILT delivery makes more sense when...

- Learners require hands-on interaction and/or demonstrations

- Online delivery doesn't fit into the organizational culture or process

- Resources or support are insufficient

- Learners aren't comfortable with technology

- ✓ They don't have access or time

Webinar delivery makes more sense when...

- ✓ Business drivers require frequent delivery to a small number of participants, or an aggressive deployment requires simultaneous delivery to a very large target audience

- ✓ Learners have access to the technology and the skills to use it

- ✓ They have enough time to use the instruction

- ✓ They perceive the instruction as valuable and necessary

- ✓ Consistent content delivery is key

Developing a Training Outline

Sequencing

Why is instructional sequence so important? Why is it necessary to do a flowchart or outline before you begin to write the instructional or reference materials? Simply stated, this is what students expect to receive—organized, sensible instruction because this is how students remember best. When we learn new information, we first try to attach it to something we already know. Then, we put it into a sequence that helps us memorize and retrieve it when we need it. To help you understand the importance of instructional sequence, read the following tale:

- Once upon a time, a little girl found one bed was too big. She ate the porridge that was just right and broke into the three bears' house. She got very sleepy.

- The papa bear said "Who's been sleeping in my bed?" The mama bear said, "Someone has been eating my porridge." The little girl sat in the rocking chair and rocked. She tasted the porridge in the big bowl, but it was too hot.

Without organization, students do not have a clue as to how things fit together!

Proper sequencing also helps to avoid inconsistencies in the content of the instruction. When material is carefully sequenced, duplication is far less likely. Some of the techniques and considerations used in sequencing are:

- *Job Performance Order:* The learning sequence is the same as the job sequence.

- *From Simple to Complex:* Objectives may be sequenced in terms of increasing complexity.

- *Critical Sequence:* Objectives are ordered in terms of their relative importance.

- *Known to Unknown:* Familiar topics are considered before unfamiliar ones.

- *Dependent Relationship:* Mastery of one objective requires prior mastery of another.

Whatever you choose, students should be well aware of the organization, and you can be sure of that if you use an outline or flowchart.

A proper sequence provides the learners with a pattern of relationship so that each lesson and/or activity has a definite purpose. The more meaningful the content, the easier it is to learn and, consequently, the more effective the instruction.

Developing the Outline

Once you begin to determine course objectives and sequence, it's time to start to outline the content you will use to support the learning solution. Perhaps the easiest way to begin is to get all the top levels-written down and then drill down to the lower levels.

Every time you drill down to a lower level, you should verify that previous levels are as complete as possible. You will probably move information around several times before the sequence seems correct. You may even move information after you begin to write the training, and don't be surprised if you discover omissions or unnecessary topics as well. The outline content should be flexible until training is completely developed.

Align Content to Objectives

- Organize the topics and key learning points required for each objective in the module/lesson format

- Ensure that topics contain the content required to achieve the enabling objective(s)

- Use key learning points to highlight the importance of the content presented and its impact on the job

- Include as many lessons as needed to logically organize the content. Consider the following when presenting specific topics and learning points:

  - Transition into each content element from the previous content element
  - Relate content to the objective being addressed
  - Explain how the content aligns with the overall goal of the course
  - Emphasize how job performance is influenced by the learning point
  - Promote retention through activities, exercises, or practice
  - Transition into the next content element

Structuring the Outline

The preferred methodology for integrating objectives in the course design is to apply terminal objectives at the course level and support them with enabling objectives at the module level. *Content should be "chunked" into lessons that are conducive to learning.* The sequencing performed earlier is the basis for organizing the content around the enabling objectives based on the class relationship between them. A high-level example would be:

Terminal Objective *(Course Level)*: **HOW TO CHANGE A TIRE**

    Upon completion of this course, participants will be able to change a flat tire *(behavior/task)*, given proper equipment and conditions *(condition)*, free from injury or defect *(criteria standard)*.

- Enabling Objectives *(Module Level)*
  - Module 1 ✓ Survey environmental conditions and dangers
  - Module 2 ✓ Locate required vehicle resources
  - Module 3 ✓ Operate a mechanical or hydraulic jack
    - ✓ Remove and replace wheel assembly

The fundamental structure of all learning solutions should include the following:

Course Introduction

- Course introduction
- Purpose statement
- Terminal objective(s)
- Course outline
  - Instructions for participation

Modules

Module description

Learning objectives (module level)

Lesson(s)

✓ Lesson (content) pages

✓ Interaction/Activities

Module summary

Knowledge assessment (as required)

Course Summary

Glossary (The glossary should contain content-specific terms and all acronyms used within the course.)

Formatting the Outline

Use one of the following two methods for outlining. The first is alpha-numeric. This format is preferred because it is easier for students to locate materials when there are many subheadings.

I.

    A.

    B.

       1.

       2.

          a.

          b.

The second is numeric. This format is typically used for flowcharts, technical manuals and legal papers such as contracts.

1.0
1.1
1.2
2.0
2.1
2.1.1
and so on.

If you do a flowchart for your writing, keep it simple. Flowcharts are especially valuable for complex reference material that branches off in many directions. They will ensure that you complete each topic fully before going on to another one. Flowcharts are also essential for web-based training (WBT).

Why do you need to spend so much time on a flowchart or outline? You will be using this outline to guide you in writing or presenting training, so it must be as thorough as possible. You will also use this outline or flowchart to write the training or reference materials. The better the preparation, the easier it is to do the work.

Reference Materials

If you are writing reference materials, produce a flowchart first and then an outline.

- Set a starting point.

- Select an outline format for organizing your material.

- Determine the appropriate depth for each topic.

- Mark words and terms for inclusion in a glossary, acronym list, table of contents or index.

- Note what your illustrations are and where they will be placed.

- Identify any areas where you need more information.

Training Materials

In addition to following the above steps, you will also:

- Write your objectives to match each module/lesson of the training.

- Identify methods to be used in the training.

- Include outlines of exercises, labs, and tests.

- Estimate the amount of time each lesson will take to teach and the total time for the course.

- Identify visuals that will be used.
- List the location, supplies, and other materials (i.e., props) needed for the training.

Web-Based Training Considerations

You will also need to:

- Determine how the training will be delivered. Will you be doing WBT, webinar, recorded webinar? Each medium makes a difference in how you prepare training and training materials.

- Decide how much material you want to cover in each lesson based on learner needs, time constraints, programming constraints, and your objectives. Consider breaking up the training into short modules that can be taken as needed.

- Flowchart your information before you begin to write. Be aware that you may have parallel topics that are neither hierarchical nor related.

- Identify content that needs to be hyperlinked to other content. For example, you will want to link definitions to the actual use of the words in the text. You may want to link words to examples, drawings, or more information.

- Determine how you will retain information such as students' answers, numbers of attempts, and whether students have completed a portion of the program.

- Decide if you need to create supporting materials such as workbooks or job aids for the web-based training.

As you can see, your training outline contains significant details that will shape the training to be done. Be sure to refer to the lists you have made in the needs assessment phase because they will keep you focused on the solutions for bridging the gaps.

Planning Exercises

A critical portion of the training that you will be doing is having the students complete some exercises. This application of information is what makes a student learn. How can you be certain that the exercises you create will help your students learn? Let us go back to your instructional objectives. If you have written objectives, the exercises will match them. Here is an example.

- *Objective:* Given a wire, twist cap, and electrician's tape, the student will make a sample electrical connection that meets city code requirements as determined by the instructor.
- *Instructional Procedure:* The instructor will provide each student with a copy of the city code electrical requirements. They will be told about stripping the wire, what size twist caps to use, and how to find the section of the code that applies to what they are doing.

Next, the instructor will demonstrate making the connection. Finally, the instructor will give each student wire, a twist cap, and electrician's tape and have them make the connection. The instructor will then inspect the students' work and correct anything that is wrong. [Note: In-class exercises allow the students to practice in a safe environment. Be sure to make the exercises as close to on-the-job performance requirements as you can possibly do].

You can see how simple it is to match an exercise to an objective when the objective exists! In the above example, the students are exposed to the performance three times. They hear it, they see it, and they do it.

Essential Reinforcement

Reinforcement also has to be accounted for. Not only the rate at which people learn must be accounted for, but also the rate of decay that takes place after an objective is mastered. To address this decay factor, reinforcement loops must be built into the instructional process. Effective content transitions greatly help to accomplish this.

Transitions provide flow and connection by clarifying the relationship between then end of one section and the beginning of the next. For example: a course supporting policy incentives for fuel cell vehicles that is intended for a business (but not expert) audience might conclude a lesson on funding technology with this sentence:

"The technical challenges of fuel cell vehicles pale in comparison to the market obstacles that such a major switch in vehicle fuels would face." *(example adapted from Amy Gahran's blog continuous.com).*

Information Processing

When something new is taught, there are many steps that the learner must go through before the new skill becomes "natural." Figure F.1 Shows the generic approach.

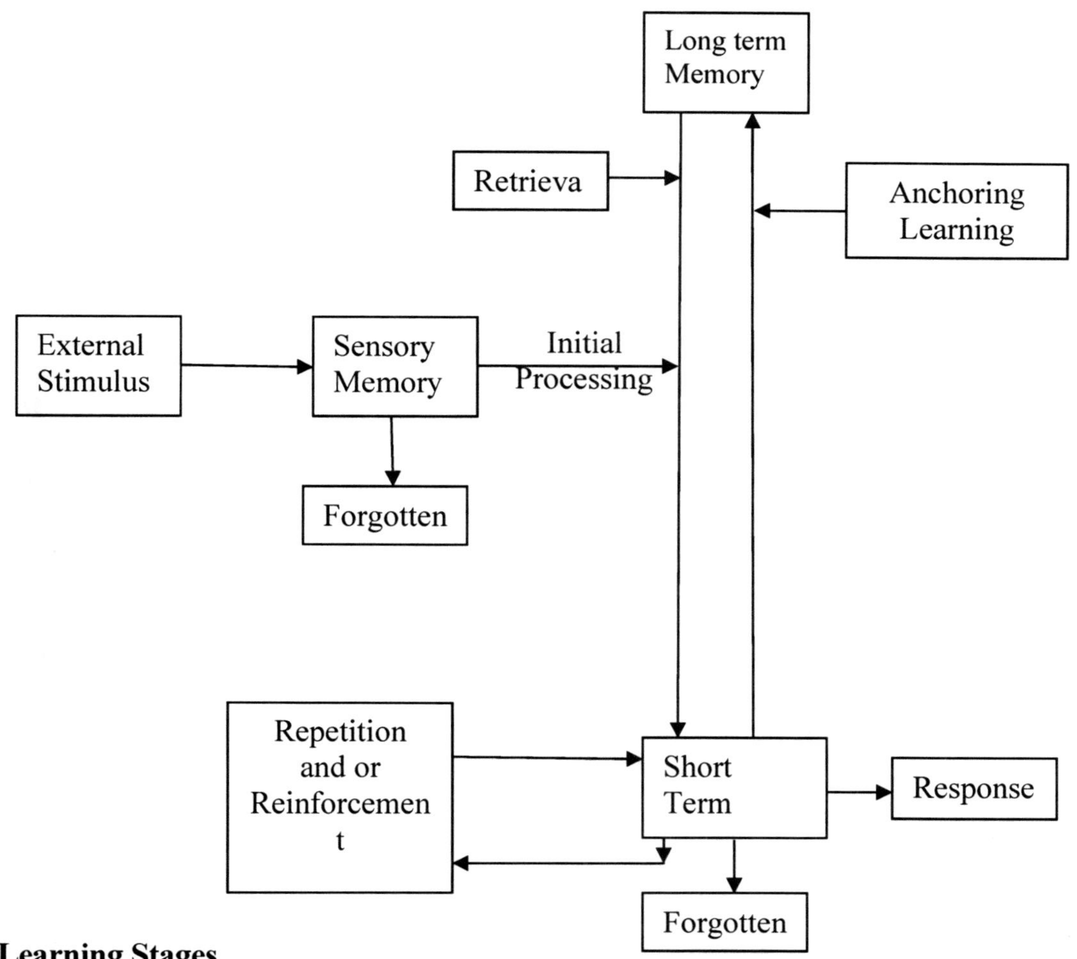

Learning Stages

When planning exercises and other types of reinforcement, it is critical to take the learning level of your target audience into account. Learning levels (see Table F.9) may be characterized by using the following five "stages to expertise"

Table F.9. Stages of expertise

Stage	Characterized By
Novice	Learning "the basics", i.e., facts and rules about the area they are beginning to study
Advanced Beginner	Learning with increased practical experience and a larger sense of context
Competence	Learning accompanied by effective decision-making
Proficiency	Quick, effective, often unconscious decision-making
Expertise	Complete fusion of decision-making and action

Testing

Let's look at some instructional theory regarding testing before we discuss creating tests.

What is a test? It is an instrument an instructor uses to measure the learning that the student has done. Please notice that we did not mention testing to grade someone. That is an entirely different issue. We are also not talking about qualifying for certification or licensing. Again, that is a different issue. Testing in training is an instructional tool that lets both the student and the instructor know what the student has learned and understands and *what still needs to be learned.* This makes testing a valuable instrument. Here are some characteristics of tests.

Testing is a duplication of the performance required in the objectives. If the objective states that the student must demonstrate replacing a fuse in a fuse box, then the test is that the student must physically replace the fuse, not just tell you how to replace it. If the objective says that the student must *explain* how a fuse is replaced, then the student will tell the instructor, verbally or in writing, how to replace a fuse. The test matches the performance.

Testing should be done while the student still has a chance to learn what has not been learned. Testing at the end of a course defeats one of the benefits of testing — the ability to know what still has to be learned. When the testing is done intermittently during training, the student still has a chance to learn. Here we must also emphasize the notion of variety. Variety is important to the student, even with testing. Using a variety of testing methods helps the student who has problems with one method who is able to perform better when tested a different way. For example, oral tests may be easier for some who have problems writing—perhaps because of a language issue.

Special consideration should be given to situations where if the teaching material is dependent, meaning that one item must be learned before a second and third one can be taught and understood, a student missing the initial instruction will not be able to understand the second or third bit of instruction. You, as the instructor, must recognize this and test for learning at appropriate times before a student gets too far behind to be able to catch up.

Pre-tests are a valuable way of knowing what your students already know and what they need to learn. A pre-test is a test given before class starts and covers the content of the course. Students are told the purpose of the test. They are also told that they will be given the same test again at the end of the course, so you can assess your teaching and their learning. We are sure that this is a concept that most students will have difficulty with as most people perceive tests as something to fear, or a sign of failure or success. Pre-tests are not that at all. They are assessment tools that let the instructor know where the students are when they enter the class. Tests are tools.

Finally, on this topic you may be asking yourself if you should test at all. Discuss this with the instructional designer and, based on the performance required, you may be able to gather other feedback to assess the amount of learning that took place instead of using tests.

Table F.10 shows some common tests and their characteristics. We have also included a chart of sample types of questions (Table F.11) that can be used for oral and written tests.

Table F.10. Common tests and their characteristics

Method	Applications
Paper Test Web-based test	Used to measure knowledge and comprehension. Effective for grading purposes. Effective for testing large groups of students. Most useful when followed by an opportunity to correct the student, or for them to have time to learn the material they could not answer correctly. Drawbacks include poor performance by students who have test anxiety or who are poor writers, readers, spellers.
Oral Test	Used to measure knowledge and comprehension. Generally effective for small groups. As with paper tests, students should have an opportunity to learn what they did not know on the test. Drawbacks include poor performance by students who are not good speakers or who cannot think quickly. Issues of anxiety, as with a paper test, can also cause poor performance.
Performance Test	Students are required to do the actual performance being taught. Benefits include an ability to coach during performance to perfect it. Deeper learning takes place when the students do the performance and everyone has visible proof that the student has mastered the objective. Drawbacks include longer preparation time for demonstration tests and for gathering equipment. Students may require many opportunities to exhibit proficiency.
Project, Paper, Report	This type of testing requires that the students gather information and present it in some manner: a written report or oral report to the instructor and class. Benefits include saving class time for other purposes, allowing students to work in groups (if possible), and letting students teach each other. Drawbacks include the possibility of asking students to spend their own time out of class to work on the project paper or report. There is a concern that the material that the student collects is not accurate or that the student misinterprets the information. This type of assignment is most effective for good writers, good speakers, and when there is time to correct any flaws.
On-the-Job Performance	While not an actual test, on-the-job performance can directly reflect the learning that took place in the classroom. Evaluation is usually done by a supervisor or a manager. Drawbacks include a lack of feedback to the instructor and fear by the student of working in a live situation. Another important drawback is that when correction takes place, only one person is corrected, not an entire classroom.

Table F.11. Question types

Question Type	Example	Benefits	Drawbacks
Open Ended or Essay (cannot be answered by yes or no)	Why is the internal combustion engine not efficient?	Should gain a lot of information from the student to cover a topic completely. Can elicit opinions, feelings, as well as facts.	Bad choice for students who are not good writers. Difficult to correct. Easy for a student to miss a portion of an answer.
Closed Ended (must be answered by a yes or no)	Can an X vehicle run on regular gasoline? [ ] yes [ ] no	Easy to grade and easy to answer.	Students have 50% chance of being right. Does not guarantee proof that student has mastered the topic.
Multiple Choice	Select the correct answer: 1. XYZ can run on: [ ] a. Regular gasoline [ ] b. Waste byproduct from landfills [ ] c. Dry gas	Allow a choice of one of 3-5 possible answers. Easy to grade and easy to answer. Students have to differentiate between answers and think about their selection.	Sometimes answers can be distorted or tricky which angers the students. May be difficult to come up with 5 plausible answers. Again, student can guess at an answer. Does not prove comprehension.
Fill-in-the-Blank	Fill in the blank. 1. On modern vehicles, fuel ______ spray fuel into the combustion chamber.	Easy to grade. Shows the student's knowledge of terms. Can be completed quickly. Easy to write.	Does not prove comprehension, just knowledge of a term or phrase.

Question Type	Example	Benefits	Drawbacks
Matching	Match the color to the object. Sun white grass yellow sky brown milk green chocolate blue	Easy to grade. Forces the student to use all the answers and perhaps learn the ones he/she does not know.	Most times, this type of question offers no challenge to the student. Does not Prove comprehension.
Ordering	Place these directions in the order you would use them to repair a tire. Loosen lug nuts. 2. Be sure you place the jack on solid grass. 3. Remove the jack and handle from the frame in the trunk.	Easy to grade. Good for performance-based learning. Makes the student think about the entire process.	If steps are simple or logical, there is no challenge to this. If one part of the answer is wrong, the whole answer is wrong

Gathering More Data

You may have been asked to write your materials based on your expertise of the topic. If this is the case, you do not have to go far to get your information, but you may face other problems that affect the outcome of your work. If you are developing the materials but are not the expert, you will have to find contacts who will supply you with the information you need.

This section contains information about:

- How to work with subject matter experts.
- The importance of sources for training and reference materials.
- How to log and catalog all materials.
- How to verify materials to preserve the integrity of your content.
- Information about training and non-training materials.

At the end of this section you will be able to:

- Work with subject matter experts to gain needed information.
- Identify all information sources and refer to them.
- Validate content included in the solution.
- Select training or non-training interventions.

How to Work With Subject Matter Experts

Let's work with this generalization: *Most subject matter experts (SMEs) do not have time to help you write your training materials.* If this is the case, and it most often is, you will have to find ways to save time spent with the experts and still gain exact, verified information to work with. Here are the Ways that help you do that.

Locate the Experts

The Technical experts may be outside or internal to your organization. It is up to you to request them from your supervisors and find them.

Existing Training (Internal)

Another method is to find out if anyone else has developed training on your topic or a related topic. You will then want to talk to the person who developed that training to find additional sources for materials.

Existing Training (External)

You may also consult suppliers of equipment, raw materials, and processes, who should have data concerning the material they are supplying. Contact them for this information. Collect drawings, models, and parts from them as well. Quite often even publishers will provide additional support for development of material – if they do not already have it.

Research

The internet, public and university libraries, and of course your local or personal library can provide you with current information on your topic. These will help you gather data before talking with the subject matter expert. Journals, professional papers, and other relative publications can provide information to help you as well. You will be surprised to find many journals with the information that you are looking for on line.

These are methods you can use to get more information. When looking for contacts, don't forget to check with people who are "visionaries;" able to tell you where things are going, not just where they are now. You can choose among the following methods to gain more information:

One-on-One Interview: Prepare your questions in advance, and learn as much about the topic as possible before you begin to interview. Set both an interview time and a time for the subject matter expert to review the materials generated from the interview. If possible try to arrange a conversation with a visionary who can save you considerable heartache when you know about change before it happens.

Focus Groups: Prepare open-ended questions and then gather people who can answer them including potential students, subject matter experts, management, and visionaries. *Be sure to select participants who adequately represent the group from which you need information.* A benefit of focus groups is that you will get many opinions and answers as participants feed off of each others' information. As with interviews, you should schedule some time for the members of the focus group to review your materials after you write them. Because many people may be talking at the same time, ask if you can record the session. You will also want to enforce staying on topic if the group tends to wander. Two techniques you can use to enhance the effectiveness of the focus groups include:

- Distribute the questions ahead of time so that participants can prepare answers.

- Ask participants to write notes about the questions and collect those notes to review after the focus group is held.

Surveys, Questionnaires: These formats are most effective when you are trying to gather general data about training. You can survey your experts for information the same way you would in a focus group, but get answers in writing. You can collect information from potential students using this method. You can also gather information from supervisors and managers that can impact your training.

There are a few problems with this method. You will not get the benefit of many people thinking together about your topic as with a focus group. Nor will you be able to ask spontaneous questions as you could with a focus group or interview. Finally, the number of responses may vary or come in from one group but not another. Be sure that your respondents are representative of the whole group to make your information valid.

There are a few more things to consider in working with subject matter experts. First, is the problem of unresolved issues between experts, where you receive more than one set of opinions or facts? Solutions for these problems often involve forcing a decision between experts as to what is correct information. The second problem is that your SME may just be wrong. This emphasizes the need to verify all the information you receive.

The Importance of Sources for Training and Reference

Materials

As you gather information, start collecting materials you will use in class such as parts, documentation, instructions or specifications for equipment and tools, photographs, schematics, screen captures, and data. Collect everything you possibly can, and then sort it out later. You can always dispose of materials, but it wastes time to have to go back for them.

Please remember that to publish, you need to know the sources of your information. Copyright laws require that you have permission to reproduce anything in print that is copyrighted.

- At a minimum, secure:
  - ✓ Authors' names.
  - ✓ Exact title of the publication.
  - ✓ Who published it and when (include city and state of publisher).
  - ✓ Page numbers of materials you want to use.
  - ✓ Copyright date.

In general, you must submit a request to the publisher of the document for permission to quote, citing the exact text that you intend to use. Be sure to include drawings and charts you will be using with your request. If you are not using direct quotes or exact copies of charts and graphs, you may not need permission to use the information.

Any trade names must be trademarked when used in print, and copyrights must be identified. Note whether the symbol that follows is ™ for trademark, © for copyright, or ® for registered.

334

How to Log and Catalog All Materials

The *Materials Log* (Table F.12) will become critical during the development process. A materials log records the item, source, and use of materials for your training text.

Table F.12. Material Log

<table>
<tr><td colspan="4" align="center">Material log</td></tr>
<tr><td colspan="4">Prepared By:</td></tr>
<tr><td colspan="4">Date:</td></tr>
<tr><td>Item</td><td>Source</td><td>Use in Material Training</td><td>Other information</td></tr>
<tr><td></td><td></td><td></td><td></td></tr>
<tr><td></td><td></td><td></td><td></td></tr>
</table>

Item

List the item in the first column. It could be information, a piece of equipment, a chart, diagram, or drawing.

Source

The second column is the most important column of this log. In it, you will list where you obtained the material. For example:

- *Book or publication (external source):* Author, title, publisher, address, copyright date, page(s) used, and permission to use.

- *Book or publication (internal source):* Author, title, print date, who received copies, who collaborated on the information, page(s) used, and permission to use. Verify with the author that the materials are up-to-date. ISO-controlled documents should be taken from their permanent source, *e.g.,* the Intranet, and instructions to the students must cover verifying content based on the permanent source each time they are used.

- *Equipment:* List the type of equipment, make and model number, date of production, source materials such as service manuals, condition of equipment, and transfer of ownership, if necessary.

- *Data from existing training or job materials:* Identify source(s) including page numbers, computer filenames, who has the files, what format they are in (Word™, Excel™, *etc.*). State whether you have an electronic copy or hard copy of the file, or if it is on the web. Every attempt should be made to get electronic copies of all of the documents. You can import computerized data into your file and save considerable time by not having to re-enter it.

- *Special Materials:* Finally, identify any materials that are confidential or require special handling.

Use in Materials/Training

In this column of the log, you may want to identify the segment of training that requires these materials. You may not be able to complete this section until you outline your training, but that is fine since you may end up with materials you cannot use.

Other Information

If you are collecting samples like parts or specific physical items, be sure to label and log the parts.

- The minimum you should include in the log and have on the tag includes:

✓   Part name

✓   Source

✓   Features of the part

✓   Model year

✓   Used as an example of _____

How to Verify Materials to Preserve the Integrity of Your Content

As discussed before, a subject matter expert's time is often limited. It is important, therefore, to maximize the time you do have. If *you* are the SME, you *must* validate your own material with another expert at some point. To verify the information you have gathered from SMEs, it is better if you write out the information and return it to them for review. Ideally, you can have them review it both after data collection *and* after the training material has been written.

Ask them to verify the following:

- Completeness of content.
- Accuracy of steps in procedures.
- Correctness of content organization.
- Correctness of any formulas and equations.
- Validity of drawings, charts, and graphs.
- Accuracy of any quotations you will be using.
- Acronyms and their definitions.

If *you* are the subject matter expert, you should record your own information and subject it to a peer review so that another person who knows your topic can verify it. After you write the training or materials, you should plan another review by peers of other experts.

Reviews

CAUTION: Why are we recommending review of the materials more than once and by more than one person? In our experience, SMEs tend to make assumptions about information that may not be valid or skip steps that seem intuitive. Here is an example of some instructions to help you understand the problem:

Printing from a Word Processing Program

- Select print from the File Menu.

  - Determine the number of copies you will be making and enter that number at the cursor.

- Decide what pages you will print and enter that range of pages. If you are printing all the pages, click that item.

- Select "OK" and the material will print.

Good procedure? Sure, it is acceptable if you are an experienced word processing program user. If not, you may not know how to use the pull-down menu to get to the print command. You may not be able to identify the page numbers you want to print if you do not know where those numbers are located.

Finally, the expert has assumed that the printer was already selected and that you knew about additional options that you should consider before printing. By having another subject matter expert review your materials, gaps like these can be identified and filled.

After the materials have been written, you should test their validity by using the *piloting method.* During a pilot, the students or readers will use the instructions, read the materials, take the training, and evaluate the course and the materials. This evaluation helps you refine your materials so they can be released for general use.

The Editing Process

The Editor will review your material to look for:

- Punctuation and spelling errors.

- Content accuracy including:

✓   Sentence construction.

✓   Continuity of thought.

✓   Clarity.

If you need additional help with editing there are professional editing guides available that detail all the above items and more. We highly encourage you to purchase one and use this resource while developing your program.

Your document should be edited by the instructional designer (ID) to be sure it is instructionally sound. When you have your document returned to you, it will contain both sets of comments and the writers will be identified by ink color and name.

Now, let's talk about the edit itself. We know that receiving a document that has red ink on it can be upsetting. For some of us, it conjures up thoughts of school where it signified a failure to perform. Well, in this editing process, it does not work that way. With the exception of punctuation and spelling errors, we review your material as a student would see it and use it. This means that, if the material can be understood by your readers, it does what it is supposed to do. If on the other hand the ID believes that the material would benefit from a change, he or she will let you know his or her suggestions for that change, and you will decide whether or not to make the change.

You may ask: "What if I disagree with the edit?" The simplest answer is to talk to the editor and come to an agreement about the edit. We will not change any of your text without your agreement to do so.

All editing will be done online in the original file you submitted. You may accept or reject edits right in the file and save as a new version.

Final Review

Now, we are down to the wire. We have all had a chance to review your material, and now we are ready to publish it or put it up on the web. It may sound like a complex process, but it is really very simple.

Piloting

The Instructional Designer (ID) will pilot, with your help, all training materials with a real audience. The audience will supply us with comments and corrections that we will incorporate into the training and materials.

This critical step ensures that all of us will be proud of the final product. In some instances, we may choose to pilot materials more than once, especially if significant changes are needed during the first pilot. In the case of global training, we may choose to host a few pilots to get the entire audience's reactions.

Final Version—Written Materials

The instructional designer assembles all your training materials into one document. Text will be integrated with illustrations and you will receive it for final review.

After the document is assembled, you will have a chance to see it and make minor adjustments to it.

Changes

At this point, only minor changes should be made. Because the editing process is so thorough, we should not make extensive changes.

Final Version—Web-based Materials

The instructional designer/developer will finish programming all of your materials. At this time, you will review the actual training for any minor changes you may need to make. Please remember that some of the last-minute changes may delay the launch of your course when web-based training is the medium. Every attempt should be made to get the content accurate before the course is programmed.

Evaluation

The ID will evaluate all courses over time. This is done to:
- Get student reactions and make sure the course is appropriately taught
- Find out if the students learned from the training
- Discover if what was learned in training is being used on the job
- Find out if the training had impact on the organization
- Make sure the content is still relevant

Instructional Domains

So far we have summarized the issues of identifying a need, writing objectives to close that need (gap), and all the mechanics that will make the teaching/training environment effective and productive. In this section we will address some key points about the 12 instructional domains that affect and effect learning. They are:

1. **Objectives**: There are two principles here a) Learning activities/experiences and assignments align with objectives and b) Objectives are not changed by the instructor once they have been issued.
    a. *Things to consider*
        i. State objectives and method of assessment as clearly as possible.
        ii. Explain the difference between learning activity/experience and results (objectives).
        iii. Plan around assessment.
        iv. Return often to objectives.
        v. Evaluate results against objectives.
        vi. Match any new activities not in the lesson (module) to lesson (module) objectives.
        vii. Frequently restate/summarize results of learning activities/experiences in terms of objectives
    b. *Things not to consider*
        i. Assume that student understands objectives because they're included in the syllabus or module.
        ii. Ignore or undermine objectives by focusing attention on a technique or activity.
2. **VARIETY OF METHODS AND ACTIVITIES**: There are two principles here they are: a) A variety of teaching methods focus on all learning styles and b) Activities are well paced, engaged, organized, and are used consistently to maximize learning throughout the course.
    a. *Things to consider*
        i. List objectives.
        ii. Elicit active involvement (participation) from all students.
        iii. Be clear, concise.
        iv. Use an activity each hour.
        v. Be prepared, organized.
        vi. Summarize and make connections.
    b. *Things not to consider*
        i. Use variety for variety's sake-no gimmicks.
        ii. Stray from predetermined objectives.
        iii. Trivialize specific topics.
        iv. Lecture for the entire session.
3. **STUDENT INVOLVEMENT**: There are two principles here: a) Students learn by teaching and can contribute to the learning process of others and b) Discussion and activities are designed to provide equal opportunities for interaction.
    a. *Things to consider*
        i. Ask open-ended questions.
        ii. Give and ask for examples.
        iii. Ask questions related to or from text.
        iv. Have lots of group activities.
        v. Have student teach a principle.
        vi. Keep students focused.
        vii. Give positive feedback.

viii. Value expertise.
   b. *Things not to consider*
      i. Lecture too much.
     ii. Cut students off (redirect as needed).
    iii. Let students dominate.

4. **CLASSROOM MANAGEMENT**: There are two principles here they are: a) Materials, activities, transitions, off-task behavior and paperwork are managed smoothly and b) Time during class session is used appropriately.

   a. *Things to consider*
      i. Establish expectations in the first session (attendance, grading, breaks, rules of behavior, etc).
     ii. Keep students on track through having clear agenda for each session.
    iii. Monitor in class small group activities to ensure progress, timing, and effective results.
    iv. Allow for humor and fun; but use judgment to keep student focus on learning.
     v. Involve all students, including the "quiet thinkers."
    vi. Discuss distracting behaviors and set classroom rules.

   b. *Things not to consider*
      i. Allow students to attack one another.
     ii. Give in to claims that other instructors have allowed lower standards.
    iii. Allow students to stray too far and too long from your learning agenda.
    iv. Just lecture.
     v. Let the class get lost on tangents.
    vi. Negotiate assignments and grades.
   vii. Make exceptions to objectives and expectations.

5. **LEARNING ATMOSPHERE**: There are three principles here they are: a) Professional, respectful, and collaborative learning environments are supported and maintained b) Students experience fairness, high expectations, and a safe place to take risks and c) Respect for academic rigor and an excitement for learning is conveyed.

   a. *Things to consider*
      i. Come to class early and make sure equipment is in working order.
     ii. Make sure the logistics (tables/chairs) are set up to facilitate the session's activities.
    iii. Create opportunities for the class to work with all members of the class.
    iv. Set the example, the model.
     v. Work to draw out all personality types.
    vi. Be flexible.

   b. *Things not to consider*
      i. Tolerate or participate in putdowns.
     ii. Let one individual dominate.
    iii. Stifle creativity.
    iv. Over-use passive learning tools.

6. **PROCEDURAL REQUIREMENTS**: There are two principles here they are: a) Instructors adhere to requirements and procedures and b) Instructors are responsible.

   a. *Things to consider*
      i. Read confidential disclaimer at start – if necessary or needed.
     ii. Follow syllabus requirements.
    iii. Start and stop on time
    iv. Follow objectives.
     v. Sign roles.
    vi. Assign study groups.

vii. Use module and books as needed.

viii. Be positive.

ix. Identify resources and ask for help.

x. Be in class early, check equipment in advance – especially computer and overhead equipment.

xi. Attend faculty training – if available.

b. *Things not to consider*

i. Let them out in prolonged and frequent breaks.

ii. Let them out early.

iii. Be negative about school or books or module.

iv. Don't compromise standards.

v. Dismiss early.

vi. Assume other faculties are non-compliant with procedures.

vii. Make your own rules.

7. **PREPARATION AND ORGANIZATION**: There are three principles here they are: a) Instructors are prepared to utilize the entire session time b) Instructors have read the text and assignment lesson(s) and c) Activities and examples that support learning have been developed.

a. *Things to consider*

i. Read text.

ii. Be familiar with module.

iii. Address assignments at the beginning.

iv. Prepare syllabus.

v. Plan ahead for speakers/resources.

vi. Evaluate and adjust activities.

vii. Personalize activities.

viii. Put yourself in the place of the student.

ix. Communicate expectations.

x. Review activities, resources, and Web sites.

b. *Things not to consider*

i. Try to wing it.

ii. Be too locked into your plan.

8. **EVALUATION**: There are three principles here they are: a) Instructors are fair, objective, timely, valid, growth-oriented not punitive, consistent, and positive. Grades reflect student achievement. After all the grade is earned by the student it is never given by the instructor b) Instructors monitor application, process, products, and progress in order to be responsive to student needs and c) Instructors use quizzes and tests as learning tools. Feedback enhances learning.

a. *Things to consider*

i. Give constant feedback on application, process, and product.

ii. "Read" the class—constant assessment of student understanding.

iii. Ask for student self-reflection.

iv. Let students use assessment process on themselves.

v. Explain why you did what you did.

vi. Use multiple forms of assessment.

vii. Give models of criteria.

viii. Be able to justify grade.

ix. Be constructive.

x. Keep supporting documentation of grades.

xi. Formulate/communicate expectations.

  b. Things not to consider
    i. Don't assume they know.
    ii. Don't keep criteria a secret.
    iii. Don't give true/false tests.
    iv. Don't be defensive when students ask questions.
    v. Don't be disrespectful of any student.
    vi. Don't give "destructive" feedback; keep all feedback constructive.
    vii. Be judgmental.
    viii. Don't negotiate grades.
    ix. Do not grade based on your personal ideology or point of view.

9. **INTERPERSONAL SKILLS**: There are two principles here they are: a) Mutual respect, synergism and teamwork enhance learning and b) Difficult situations are diffused.
  a. Things to consider
    i. Respect contribution of each student.
    ii. Encourage positive relationships.
  b. Things not to consider
    i. Criticize students in class (no put downs.)

10. **TEXT AND MATERIAL ISSUED BY SCHOOL**: There are two principles here they are: a) The designated text and materials are used and b) Student learning is enhanced when the text and materials are valued.
  a. Things to consider
    i. Read the text, refer to it each week.
    ii. Use activities/questions in the text.
    iii. Expect students to read the text and hold them accountable for reading it.
  b. Things not to consider
    i. Substitute another text.
    ii. Tell students their text is worthless.

11. **FACILITATE LEARNING**: There are four principles here they are: a) The instructor is the content expert and provides supplementary materials and activities b) The instructor utilizes a variety of learning supports to help students make connections—visuals, examples, activities, feedback, modeling, lecture and discussion c) The instructor stimulates critical thinking d) The instructor is flexible and responsive to student needs.
  a. Things to consider
    i. Pay attention to various learning styles.
    ii. Capitalize on student strengths.
    iii. Listen.
    iv. Be consistently flexible.
    v. Expand on objectives
  b. Things not to consider
    i. Be too authoritarian / controlling.
    ii. Lecture/talk too much.
    iii. Assume level of student's knowledge.
    iv. Be consistently flexible.
    v. Stifle participation.
    vi. Get attached only to your viewpoint

12. **GROUP ACTIVITIES**: There are two principles here they are: a) Activities promote positive interdependence and individual accountability and b) Activities align with objectives and connect theory with practice.

    a. Things to consider
- i. Use group activities in every class session.
- ii. Use differentiated grading.
- iii. Explain purposes clearly.

    b. Things not to consider
- i. Lecture for the entire session.

SELECTED BIBLIOGRAPHY

_____ (1990). "Costing the factory of the future." *The Economist*. Pp. 61-62.

Aft, L. (October 2002). "Evaluating Higher Education Program in Quality." *Quality Progress*. Pp. 30-32.

American National Standard Institute (1983). *Dimensioning and tolerancing ANSI YI4.5M-1982*. The American Society of Mechanical Engineers. New York.

Anderson, N. (May 21, 2007). "You Cannot Build an Education System on Eloquence and Righteous Indignation." *USA Today*. P. 29.

Benjamin, S. Warda, R. (April 2009). "Keeping Score." *Quality Progress*. Pp. 38-45.

Beveridge, D. (December 9, 1985). Cost of quality. *Sales and Marketing Management*. P.12.

Bogardy, A. E. (March 1987). When should management think about cost. *California Management Review*. P.67.

Bollag, B. (October 27, 2006). "Making an Art Form of Assessment." *The Chronicle of Higher Education*. Pp. A5-A50.

Burbules, N. C. (August – September 2004). "Ways of Thinking About Educational Quality." *Educational Researcher*. Pp. 4-18.

Campanella, J. (Ed.) (1990). *Principles of quality costs: Principles, implementation, and use.* 2nd ed. American Society for Quality Control. Quality Costs Committee. Milwaukee, WI.

Carey, K. (April 3, 2009). "What Colleges Should Learn From Newspapers' Decline." *The Chronicle of Higher Education*. P. A21.

Chadderdon, R. A. (September 1992). *GD&T training programs*. Quality. Pp. 55-56.

Chase, J. P. (May 1986). "Yanks borrow Japanese keys to quality cost." *Electronics*. P. 95.

Chrysler, Ford, and General Motors. (1995). *Potential failure mode and effect analysis.*

Chrysler, Ford, and General Motors. Distributed by Automotive Industry Action Group (AIAG). Southfield, MI.

Cochran, C. (October 2004). "Improving the Quality of Leadership." *Quality Digest*. Pp. 34-37.

Cooper, R. (September 1990). "ABC: A need, not an option." *Accountancy*. Pp. 86-88.

Cooper, R. (January 1991). "ABC: The right approach for you." *Accountancy*. Pp. 70-72.

Cronin, J. M. (May 22, 2009). " Will Higher Education Be the Next Bubble to Burst?" *The Chronicle of Higher Education*. P. A56.

Cullota, P. and H. Gonzales. (September 1997). "Quality Pioneers in Education Provide Immeasurable Value to Students." *Quality Progress*. Pp.67-72.

Daniels, S. (May 2006). "Oklahoma School District Goes Over the Top." *Quality Progress*. Pp. 51-59.

Denson, D. (Spring 1992). "The use of failure mode distributions in reliability analysis." *RAC Newsletter*. Pp. 1-3.

Detert, J. R. and R. Jenni. (2000). An Instrument for measuring Quality Practices in Education. *Quality Management Journal*. ASQ. Vol. 7. Issue 3. pp. 20-38.

Emanuel, E. J. (October 20, 2006). "How to Redefine a Medical Education." *The Chronicle of Higher Education*. Pp. B12-B13.

Escriba-Moreno, M. A., M. T. Canet-Giner and M. Moreno-Luzon. (2008). "TQM and Teamwork Effectiveness: The Intermediate Role of Organizational Design. *Quality Management Journal*. Volume 15. Issue 3. pp. 41-59.

Evans, J. R. (August 1996). "What Should Higher Education Be Teaching About Quality?" *Quality Progress*. Pp. 83-89.

Fallace, T. (June 2009). "John Dewey's influence on the origins of the social studies: An analysis of the historiography and new interpretation." *Review of Educational Research*. Pp. 601-624.

Fant, G. C. (February 6, 2009). " Real Tenure Is Portable." *The Chronicle of Higher Education*. Pp. a34, 36.

Feng, L. (2010). Reading abilities and strategies: A short introduction. *International Education Studies*, 3(3), 153-157.

Fieckens, T., B. G. Dale, D. A. Littler and W. Wob. (2000). "Benchmarking for Postgraduate Admission Process". *Quality Management Journal*. ASQ Vol. 7. Issue 4. pp 45-58.

Ford Motor Co. (1988). *Potential failure mode and effect analysis*. Ford Motor Co. Dearborn, MI.

Ford Motor Co. (1989). *Potential failure mode and effect analysis*. Ford Motor Co. Dearborn, MI.

Ford Motor Co. (November 2002). *Potential failure mode and effect analysis*. Ford Motor Co. Dearborn, MI.

Ford Motor Co. (1987). *Team oriented problem solving*. Power Train Operations. Ford Motor Co. Dearborn, MI.

Foster, L. (1982). *Modern geometric dimensioning and tolerancing*. NTMA. Ft. Washington, PA.

Gagne, M. L. and Discenza, R. (October 1992). "Accurate product costing in a JIT environment." *International Journal of Purchasing and Materials*. Pp. 28-31.

Garcia, C. J. and St. Charles, D. P. (June 1988). "Automating GD&T." *Quality*. Pp. 56-58.

Glen, D. (May 29, 2009). "Colleges seek new ways to give students a general education." *The Chronicle of Higher Education*. P. A8.

Goldberg, J. S. and B. R. Cole. (2002). Quality Management in Education: Building Excellence and Equity in Student Performance. *Quality Management Journal*. ASQ Volume 9.. Issue 4. pp 8-23.

Goldratt, E. M. (1994). *It's not luck*. North River Press. Great Barrington, MA.

Goldrick-Rab, S. (May 22, 2009). "America Must Put Community Colleges First." *The Chronicle of Higher Education*. P. A27.

Grimm, A. F. (Ed.) (1987). *Quality costs: Ideas and applications*. Vol. 1. 2nd ed. American Society for Quality Control. Quality Costs Committee. Milwaukee, WI.

Hagen, J. (Ed.). (1986). *Principles of quality cost*. American Society for Quality Control. Quality Cost Technical Committee. Milwaukee, WI.

Harris, M. C. (September 1997). "Leadership Will Prevail." *Quality Progress*. Pp. 83-88.

Harry, B., K. M. Sturges and J. K. Klingner. (March 2005). "Mapping the process: An Exanplar of Process and Challenge in Grounded Theory Analysis." *Educational Researcher*. Pp. 3-13.

Haynes, C. C. and M. W. Berkowitz. (February 20, 2007). "What Can Schools Do?" *USA Today*. P. 13A.

Hovell, J. F. Jr., B. M. Krauss and A. A. Malinchak. (March 2009). "Leading by Example." *T&D*. pp. 44-49.

Jones, A. (March 27, 2009). "Washington Has Failed the Workhorses of American Higher Education. *The Chronicle of Higher Education*. Pp. B16-B17.

Josephs, F. (1987). *Production management: Concepts and analysis for operation and control*. The Ronald Press. New York.

Juran, J. M. (1988). *Quality control handbook*. 4th ed. McGraw-Hill. New York.

Juran, J. M. and Gryna, F. M. (1980). *Quality planning and analysis*. McGraw-Hill Book Co. New York.

Juran, J. M. (September 1997). "Early SQC: A Historical Supplement." *Quality Progress*. Pp. 73-82.

Karl, D. P., Morisette, J., and Taam, W. (1994). "Some applications of a multivariate capability index in geometric dimensioning and tolerancing." *Quality Engineering*. 6(4): 649-665.

Ketter, P. (March 2009). "Leadership Development: One Size Does Not Fit All." *T&D*. pp. 50-61.

Krulikowski, A. (1994). *Geometric dimensioning and tolerancing: A self study workbook*. Quality Press. Milwaukee, WI.

Labi, A. (February 27, 2009). "Germany provides higher education without the frills." *The Chronicle of Higher Education*. Pp. A18-A19.

Landrum, H., V. R. Prybutok, L. A. Kappelman and X. Zhang. (2008). "Services: A Parsimonious Instrument to Measure Service Quality and Information System Success." *Quality Management Journal*. Volume 15. Issue 3. pp. 17-25.

Lewis, C. (2005). Speed strategies. *The British Journal of Administrative Management*, 1.

Liebesman, S. (May 2006). "Bridge Between Classroom and Real World." *Quality Progress*. Pp. 60-64.

346

Mangan, K. (May 29, 2009). "In Texas, transfer students get an extra pat on the back." *The Chronicle of Higher Education*. P. A30.

Mariotti, A.P. (2010). Sustaining students' reading comprehension. *Kappa Delta Pi Record, 46*(2), 87-89.

Maurana, C. A., A. E. Langley, K. Goldberg and J. A. Engle. (September 1997). Applying TQM to an Academic Partnership." *Quality Digest*. 50-71.

McNamara, D.S. (2007). *Reading comprehension strategies: Theories, interventions, and technologies*. Retrieved from http://www.netlibrary.com

Moos, D. C. and R. Azevedo. (June 2009). "Learning with computer based learning environments: A literature review of computer self-efficacy." *Review of Educational Research*. Pp. 576-600.

Nation, P. (2009). Reading faster. *International Journal of English Studies, 9*(2), 131-144, 168-169.

Paradise, A. (June 2008). "Learning and Globally Dispersed Workforces." *T+D*. pp. 60-67.

Parry, M. (May 29, 2009). "On line education: Growing, but painfully." *The Chronicle of Higher Education*. P. A4.

Potashnik, M. *and J. Capper. (March 1998). "Distance Education: Growth and Diversity." Finance & Development*. Pp. 41-45.

Pauly, D. (September 8, 1986). *The cost of doing things better*. Society of Manufacturing Engineers. Dearborn, MI. P. 196.

Rust, R. T., Zahorik, A. J., and Keiningham, T. L. (1994). *Return on quality: Measuring the financial impact of your company's quest for quality*. Quality Press. Milwaukee, WI.

Salegna, Gary, J. and J. H. Bantham. (March 2002). "Curriculum Assessment – A Systems Approach." *Quality Progress*. Pp. 54-59.

Sarava, P. M., M. J. Rosa and J. L. D'Orey. (November 2003). "Applying an Excellence Model to Schools." *Quality Progress*. Pp. 46-51.

Selingo, J. (February 27, 2009). "Do Frills Have a Future?" *The Chronicle of Higher Education*. Pp. A17-A18.

Sharman, P. (February 1990). A practical look at activity based costing. *CMA Magazine*. P. 8-12.

Sinn, J. W. (July 2002). "Education and the Future of Quality." *Quality Progress*. Pp. 69-73.

Smith, W. (June 1980). Let's take a closer look at quality cost. *Industrial Research*. P. 154.

Soyars, M and J. Brusino. (March 2009). "ZEssentials of Engagement." *T&D*. pp. 62-67.

Stamatis, D. H. (August 1992). ISO 9000 standards: Are they real? *Technology*. Pp.13-17.

Straub, E. T. (June 2009). Understanding technology adoption: Theory and future directions for informal learning. *Review of Educational Research*. Pp. 625-649.

Tersine, T. (1972). *Engineering economics*. Viking Press. New York.

Tischler. L. (July 2006). "Bringing Lean to the Office." *Quality Progress*. Pp. 32-38.

Turner, D. (April 3, 2009). "The Global Campus Meets a World of Competition." *The Chronicle of Higher Education*. P. A10

Warda, R. (April 2009). "Know Thyself." *Quality Progress*. Pp. 30-37.

Wearing, C. and Karl, D. P. (February 1995). The importance of following GD&T specifications. *Quality Progress*. Pp. 95-98.

West, J. E. (October 2004). "Why Quality Principles Matter: Long-term success depends on stakeholder convictions." *Quality Digest*. Pp. 23.

Westfall, J. E.., J. W. Peltier, J. Sheehan and H. Weber. (November 2006). "Extending School Improvement Beyond Curriculum." *Quality Progress*. Pp. 43-49.

Whitmire, G. (March 1991). Why use GD&T. *Quality*. Pp. 41-42.

Willis, J. (2008). *Teaching the brain to read: strategies for improving fluency, vocabulary, and comprehension*. Retrieved from http://www.netlibrary.com

Wilson, R. (February 6, 2009). Downturn Threatens the Faculty's Role in Running Colleges." *The Chronicle of Higher Education*. Pp. A1, A7-A8.

CPSIA information can be obtained at www.ICGtesting.com
Printed in the USA
LVOW022143271011

252456LV00004B/1/P